Complete Coverage of Cubase VST Score and

Cubase
POWER!

Robert Guérin

Cubase Power!

Copyright ©2001 Muska & Lipman Publishing

All rights reserved. No part of this book may be reproduced by any means without written permission from the publisher, except for brief passages for review purposes. Address all permission requests to the publisher.

All copyrights and trademarks used as examples or references in this book are retained by their individual owners.

Credits: Cover and interior design, Stephanie Japs, Michelle Frey, Cathie Tibbetts, and John Windhorst, *DOV Graphics*; technical editors, Mike Uwins, Laurence Payne, and Jay Ts; copy editor, Martin Sterpka; index, Kevin Broccoli, *Broccoli Information Management.*

Publisher: Andy Shafran

Technology and the Internet are constantly changing, and by necessity of the lapse of time between the writing and distribution of this book, some aspects might be out of date. Accordingly, the author and publisher assume no responsibility for actions taken by readers based upon the contents of this book.

Library of Congress Catalog Number: 2001089637

ISBN 1-929685-45-9

5 4 3 2 1

Educational facilities, companies, and organizations interested in multiple copies or licensing of this book should contact the publisher for quantity discount information. Training manuals, CD-ROMs, and portions of this book are also available individually or can be tailored for specific needs.

MUSKA & LIPMAN

Muska & Lipman Publishing
2645 Erie Avenue, Suite 41
Cincinnati, Ohio 45208
www.muskalipman.com
publisher@muskalipman.com

About the Author

Robert Guérin
zerodb.ca or www.wavedesigners.com
rguerin@zerodb.ca

A composer for the past fourteen years and a music enthusiast since 1976, Robert has worked on various personal and commercial projects, including feature and short films, television themes, and educational and corporate videos. Composing, arranging, playing, recording, and mixing most of his material, he has developed working habits that allow him to be creative without losing the sense of efficiency.

As a professor, Robert has put together five courses covering a wide range of topics, such as computer software for musicians, digital audio technologies, sound on the Web, sound in multimedia productions, how musicians can get job interviews, hard disk recording, and many more. He has been program coordinator at Trebas Institute in Montreal, Canada, and a part-time professor at Vanier College, also in Montreal. Robert has developed an online course on sound integration in Web pages for eHandsOn (available at **www.ehandson.com**.)

As an entrepreneur, Robert has expanded his knowledge and expertise to ensure his business survival by adopting new multimedia and Web-related technologies.

Technical Editors

Mike Uwins
Senior product specialist and support engineer for Steinberg UK by day, Mike Uwins is a singer/songwriter/wannabe goth-popstar by night (**www.manuskript.co.uk**).

Laurence Payne
Laurence Payne is a London-based piano/keyboards player working mainly in theatre and variety/cabaret. He has been using Steinberg software since the Atari Pro 24.

Jay Ts
A musician as well as a computer systems and network specialist, Jay Ts has many years of experience working with computer hardware, software, and electronic and audio engineering.

Dedication

I dedicate this book to my parents, who have always supported my decision to make a living out of music, and to Jean-Claude Lamy, who through his dedication and passion for music and teaching has made a difference in the lives of many students.

Acknowledgments

I would like to thank to the following people for their help, encouragement, and support throughout the writing process: Andy Shafran and his team at Muska & Lipman; Benoit Lortie from Cubase Canada; Kathy Kennedy and the technical support team at Rocket Network and Inwire Studio; Scott Garrigus for his inside view; and to friends at home (you know who you are) who have understood that it takes time to write a book.

Contents

Introduction 1

1—Introducing Cubase 5
What Is Cubase? 5
    Key Equivalencies on Macintosh Computers 6
A Brief Overview of MIDI 7
    What Does MIDI Really Transmit? 7
    MIDI Connectors 8
A Brief Overview of Digital Audio 9
    What Is Analog Sound? 9
    What Is Digital Sound? 11
    How Sampling Works 13
How Does Cubase Handle MIDI and Audio? 14
    MIDI Port 15
    MIDI Channel 16
    MIDI Track 17
    Audio Channel 17
    Audio Track 18
    Audio Output 20
About 32-bit Recording 20
    Do I Have the Right Hardware? 22

2—Setting Up Your Environment 23
Software Setup 23
    MIDI Drivers and Setup 23
    Audio System Settings 26
    ASIO Drivers 28
    Running Other Audio Applications Simultaneously 32
Hardware Setup 33
    Hard Drive Configuration 33
    Video Display Adapters 37
    Hooking Up Your Equipment 38
Backing Up and Folder Management 42

3—Navigating the Arrange Window ... 43

Configuring the Arrange Window Options ... 45
- Snap ... 46
- Quantize ... 47
- Part Colors ... 48
- Markers ... 49
- Link Editors ... 51
- Record Mode ... 52

The Transport Bar ... 53
- Cycle Recording ... 53
- Recording Mode ... 56
- Start and End Play Locators ... 57
- Transport Controls ... 58
- Tempo Settings ... 59
- Signature Settings ... 61
- MIDI Activity ... 62

The Toolboxes ... 64
Now You Try It ... 71

4—Setting Up Your MIDI Recording ... 73

Track View ... 74
Track List ... 75
- Track Classes ... 79
- Programming Mutes and Solos ... 83
- Recording Mutes and Solo ... 83

Track Info ... 84
- Setting Up Instruments ... 85
- Play Parameters ... 88
- Adding a Shadow MIDI Track ... 90
- Program Changes ... 91
- MIDI Volume and Pan Control ... 92

What Is a VST Instrument (VSTi)? ... 94
- VSTi included with Cubase ... 96
- VSTi and Latency ... 97

Step Recording ... 97
Realtime Recording ... 99
MIDI Filtering and Mapping ... 100
Now You Try It ... 101

5—MIDI Editing Windows ...103
The Editors ...103
Toolbox Options ...105
Toolbar Options ...110
The Info Line ...115
Editing Multiple Tracks ...117
Editing MIDI Controller Events ...118
Drum Edit Window ...120
The List Window ...126
Understanding the Information ...127
The Event Display ...129
About Masks ...129
Controller Editor ...130
Event Types ...130
Editing Controls ...132
Now You Try It ...135

6—Making Sense of Track Editing ...137
Folder Tracks ...138
Group Tracks ...139
Logical Editing ...141
Logical Editor Parameters ...143
Easy vs. Expert Mode ...146
Setting Values ...147
Quantize and Grooves ...148
Groove Control ...151
Locator Functions ...154
Cut ...155
Insert ...156
Split ...157
Copy ...158
Explode ...159
Merge ...160
The Arrange Window Toolbox ...161
Now You Try It ...167

7—Score Editing 169

- About Score Editing 170
- Score Edit Window 171
  - Score Preferences 173
  - Page and Edit Mode 175
  - Status Bar 177
  - Score Toolbar 182
- Symbol Palettes 184
- Working with Chords 185
- Adding Text 188
- Drums and Percussion 192
- Layouts 195
- Printing and Page Setup 197
- Now You Try It 198

8—Setting Up Audio Recording 199

- VST Channel Mixer 199
  - Channel EQ 207
  - Audio Channel Dynamics Control 210
  - Channel Effect Routing 215
- VST Master Mixer 219
  - VST Audio Bus System 221
  - Master Effect Routing 224
  - Rewire 224

9—Working with Audio Files 227

- Audio Recording 228
  - Selecting a Recording Resolution 233
  - Controlling Your Input Levels 234
- The Audio Pool Window 234
  - Files, Segments, and Audio Events 235
  - Headings and Columns 236
  - Customizing the View 238
- How to Use the Audio Pool 239
  - File and Segment Usage 239
  - Audio File Operations 240
  - Segment Operations 241
  - Importing and Exporting Audio from the Pool 243

Dragging Segments into Other Windows	.243
Archiving Files	.244
Saving Your Audio Pool for Later Use	.245
Importing Audio Files	.245
Recycling Files with Recycle	.245
About Mixman	.246
Now You Try It	.247

10—Audio Editing 249

The Audio Editor	.250
Events, Lanes, and Segments	.251
Customizing Your View	.254
Importing Audio	.255
Auditioning Audio	.256
Editing Audio Events	.257
About Q-Points	.260
About M-Points	.261
Quantizing Audio	.265
Audio Envelope Controls	.269
About Audio Functions	.272
Wave Editors	.275
Built-In Wave Editors	.276
External Wave Editors	.278
Now You Try It	.279

11—Mixing 281

VST Channel Mixer Automation	.282
Recording and Playing Your Mix	.283
Editing Your Mix	.285
MIDI Track Mixer	.287
The Controls	.288
MIDI Automation	.289
Working with Effects	.291
Earlier Effects	.294
Available in Cubase 5.0	.298
DirectX Effects	.307
Now You Try It	.308

12—Working In Sync 309

About Word Clock, SMPTE, and MIDI Clock 309
    Timecode 310
    MIDI Clock 312
    Digital Clock 312
Resolving Differences 314
    Internal and External References 315
    Setting Up Synchronizations 316
Hitpoints 325
    About the Master Track Editor 326
    Working with Hitpoints 329
About Time-Locked Tracks 335
    Tempo Mapping Locked Tracks 336
Working with Online Video Files 337

13—Distributing Your Work 339

Including Your MIDI in the Mixdown 340
    Converting Your MIDI Tracks 341
    About VSTi and Rewire Channels 342
    About Dithering 343
    Exporting Your Final Mix 345
    Exporting Formats 347
    Real Networks 348
    MP3 350
About Mastering 352
Creating an Audio Compact Disc 353
Backing Up Your Work 357
Distributing Your Work on the Web 358

Appendix A—Optimizing Your Experience 361

Changing the Def.All File 361
Key Commands 363
Creating a Toolbar 364
Working with Window Sets 364
Turning off the Wave Image Creation 365

Appendix B—Interactive Phrase Synthesizer 367

Appendix C—Making the Most of Modules 377
MIDI Processor 379
Arpeggio to the Rescue 382
Style Tracks 385
Studio Modules 389

Appendix D—Interacting with Others over the Web 391
It's Not Just for Rocket Scientists 391
How Rocket Network Integrates into Cubase 394
Connecting with Rocket Control 396
Additional Tips 397

Appendix E—Cubase Resources on the Web 399
Finding Help 399
Plug-in Resources and VST Instruments 400

Index 403

Introduction

Cubase has been around for a while now. I remember using its ancestor, the Pro 24 software on my Atari ST, in 1987 to create musical arrangements for composition assignments during my university training years. Since then, many things have changed, and Cubase has made the transition from a MIDI sequencer to a Virtual Studio Technology (VST) software. Since I have been mostly involved with music for film and television, I also thought it would be interesting to provide some information in this book on how to use Cubase to synchronize music with images.

Like any software, as it allows you to do more things and do them in a more intuitive way, the learning curve becomes more and more abrupt. You will find very extensive documentation on all available features found in Cubase on the CD-ROM provided with the software, but you will have to sift through more than 1,400 pages of electronic documentation. For most users, this might seem like an overwhelming task. But this book will provide you with the most important features as well as some lesser-known features in step-by-step examples and online tutorial files to practice what you have learned in many of the chapters.

Beyond describing the features of the program and how they work, I address *why* to use certain features and *when* they can become useful to you. All of the Cubasis features are included in Cubase, so for those of you who have this version of the software, the book should address your questions as well. Since Cubase is available in both Macintosh and PC versions in quite similar environments, it doesn't really matter which platform you are using: The way to use the features and functions will be the same.

I offer you my fifteen years of experience working with the software as well as my insight into some tips and tricks that have been very useful in getting the job done throughout these years. As a professor and program coordinator in sound design vocational schools in Canada, I have answered questions from many students who have wanted to work with this tool to create music. I have drawn from their most-frequently-asked questions and answered them in a way that I hope you will find enlightening.

Enjoy.

How This Book is Organized

This book is separated into thirteen chapters that roughly form four parts.

The first part is an introduction and offers clues on how to set up your hardware and software environment. This is covered in Chapter 1, "Introduction to Cubase," and Chapter 2, "Setting Up Your Environment." These two chapters will give you an overview of MIDI and digital audio and how Cubase handles both of them. They will also help you set up your software to receive and transmit both MIDI and audio using your system's virtual and hardware MIDI ports as well as your computer's sound card.

The second part discusses the MIDI sequencer portion of Cubase. In Chapter 3, "Navigating the Arrange Window," you will find out about the main interface, how it works, and how to use the Transport bar and Cubase's many toolboxes. In Chapter 4, "Setting Up Your MIDI Recording," you will learn how to understand the information displayed onscreen and how to assign the many parameters to record MIDI events. Once you've recorded MIDI events, Chapter 5, "MIDI Editing Windows," talks about the different MIDI editing windows, as the title suggests, and how to use them to fine tune your MIDI recording. Chapter 6, "Making Sense Of Track Editing," discusses ways to organize what you have edited in the MIDI editing windows in Cubase's main Arrange window, as well as how to navigate in an arrangement (or project). If you are using Cubase as a music creation laboratory and would like to print out music sheets for musicians, Chapter 7, "Score Editing," will show you the basic step of transforming your MIDI events into musical notation.

The third part discusses the audio multitrack recording and editing portions of Cubase. Chapter 8, "Setting Up Audio Recording," focuses on the Cubase audio routing system within the Mixer windows. Chapter 9, "Working With Audio Files," discusses how to record audio, import audio, and manage audio files found inside a Cubase project, as well as how audio files are organized and referenced by Cubase. Chapter 10, "Audio Editing," like Chapter 5, discusses editing windows available in Cubase, but in this case, it's audio editing windows rather than MIDI editing windows. Chapter 11, "Mixing," focuses on the mixing automation process within Cubase from a MIDI and audio point of view as well as providing a how-to guide to using and automating effects. If you have ever wanted to know about or have been in the position where you had to synchronize Cubase to a video to create a score, Chapter 12, "Working In Sync," will provide you with information on how Cubase handles all types of synchronizations, including time code, word clock, and MIDI clock.

The fourth part discusses the final steps of your production in Chapter 13, "Distributing Your Work." You will learn how to export the MIDI and audio files found in your project to a stereo master copy and, even better, understand the steps involved in the mastering. Since music is intended to be heard, knowing how to prepare a copy of your work for distribution is essential. This chapter will give you hints on how to save your files in Web-ready formats.

As you can see, this book will bring you every step of the way from setting up your computer to recording your MIDI and audio, editing these events, synchronizing with other devices and mixing them, to finally distributing your work using all the tools available in Cubase. I hope that by the end of this book you will have conquered Cubase and can allow the creative juices to flow without feeling the restraints of a misunderstood tool.

Music is a communication vehicle, Cubase is a tool that allows you to create this musical communication, and this book—I hope—will allow you to master this tool and let you ride the music as you always imagined it.

Conventions Used in This Book

As you begin to read, you'll see that most of the information in this book is solid and useful. At the end of some chapters, you will find a section called "Now You Try It," which refers to online tutorial files. If you wish to use these tutorial files to test your comprehension of the content provided in that chapter, you can log on and visit the site indicated in that section of the chapter. Once you have downloaded the necessary work files, you may proceed to complete the exercises. To avoid unnecessary wordiness, all commands and keyboard shortcuts in the books are given in reference to the PC platform. For Macintosh users, please read the relevant section in Chapter 1, which will give you the Macintosh equivalencies. To help guide you through all this material, I use several different conventions that highlight specific types of information that you should keep an eye out for.

TIP

Tips are extra information that you should know related to the current topic being discussed and, in some cases, personal experiences and/or specific techniques not covered elsewhere.

NOTE

Of course, sometimes you might like to know, but don't necessarily need to know, certain points to learn about the current topic. Notes provide additional material to help you avoid problems, and they also offer related advice.

1

Introducing Cubase

Before starting your work in Cubase, it is important to understand what Cubase is all about, what it can do, and how different MIDI and digital audio really are. So, in this chapter, you will learn about these and gain a better understanding of some basic MIDI and digital audio principals. Furthermore, you will learn about a new feature for Cubase VST/32 and above: 32-bit recording.

What Is Cubase?

Cubase is a toolbox for musicians. In that toolbox, you will find tools to record and edit MIDI information, tools to record and edit audio information, and, finally, tools to print your music sheets. In 1984, Steinberg created its first MIDI sequencer, which became known in 1989 as Cubase. This tool was designed to help musicians capture their performances in a MIDI sequencer. With the advent of MIDI, the computer could talk to musical instruments and vice versa. At that time, the processing power of computers was insufficient to properly record digital audio. Therefore, musicians had to wait almost ten years before they could record audio digitally using a computer. Steinberg was one of the first companies to develop an integrated system that could record to both MIDI and digital audio.

In 1996, Cubase became not only a MIDI sequencer but a full audio production tool, contributing in many ways to the development and democratization of the creative process that lies inside every musician. Cubase VST (Virtual Studio Technology) allows you to do this by providing you with the necessary software tools, replacing many hardware components with its software equivalent. Here is an overview of these tools:

- ▶ **MIDI recording environment**—Cubase allows you to record and play back MIDI information.
- ▶ **MIDI editing environment**—Once your MIDI information is recorded, you can edit it using one of many views available in Cubase.
- ▶ **Virtual Instruments**—If you do not own external sound modules, Cubase provides you with a way to generate sounds using a format called VST Instruments. A Virtual Instrument is the software version of a synthesizer, residing inside your computer and using your sound card to generate the sounds it produces. You no longer need to purchase expensive synthesizer modules, since they are part of your Virtual Studio environment.

- **Audio recording environment**—Cubase is a very powerful multitrack recorder that uses a sophisticated 32-bit recording system. Combined with a good sound card, microphone, and preamplifier, this can only lead to high-quality recordings. Obviously, the result depends on your creativity and musical "chops" as well, but at least the tools are within your reach.
- **Audio editing environment**—Once your sound is captured on disk, Cubase offers you all the tools necessary to cut, copy, paste, punch in, punch out, enhance, and manipulate your audio signals in an intuitive working environment.
- **Mixing environment**—Once you have recorded, edited, and manipulated your MIDI and audio information, you can mix every track using a virtual mixing board not unlike its hardware counterpart. This virtual mixer can accommodate multiple buses, multiple effects, MIDI tracks, Virtual Instrument tracks, and audio tracks. Finally, you can automate your mix easily and create complex mixes without leaving your computer.
- **Effects galore**—Using the built-in effects, adding third-party effects, or using effects already present on your system (like the DirectX effects protocol available in Windows 98), you can color your sound in a wide variety of ways. Your imagination is your only barrier here.
- **Multimedia production environment**—Along with audio production, Cubase offers many synchronization tools useful in multimedia productions and video productions, making it a great postproduction environment for today's producers. You can even interact with other musicians around the world using Cubase and the Internet.

Key Equivalencies on Macintosh Computers

As you will see throughout this book, Cubase often uses both mouse buttons on a PC mouse and several keyboard shortcuts to access commonly used functions, as in any other software. Beyond this, Cubase often offers different ways of using a function by holding down a key while doing the operation. To make this text easier to read, only the PC versions of these keystrokes have been included in the book. However, you may refer to Table 1.1 to get the Macintosh equivalent of these PC keystroke/mouse combinations.

Table 1.1
PC to Macintosh keyboard and mouse equivalencies.

PC	Macintosh
Right-click on a mouse	Control or Ctrl+Click (If you have a two-button mouse it stays the same)
Ctrl+Click	Command+Click
Alt+Click	Option+Click

A Brief Overview of MIDI

The acronym MIDI stands for "Musical Instrument Digital Interface." It represents two things: First, MIDI is a coding system used to transmit information from one MIDI-compatible device to another. These devices include musical instruments (samplers, synthesizers, sound modules, drum machines) and computers (this could be managed by software inside your computer or could be hardware-based like a synchronization device). Secondly, it represents the hardware—the ports and jacks found on all MIDI instruments and the MIDI cables connecting them to allow the transmission of musical data. Every time a key is pressed or a wheel is moved, one or more bytes are sent out from a device's MIDI Out port. Other devices connected to that sending device are looking for those bytes to come over the wire, which are then interpreted back into commands for the device to obey.

MIDI sends information at a rate of 31,250 bps (or bits per second). This speed is called baud rate. Since MIDI is transferred through a serial port, it sends information one bit at a time. Every MIDI message uses 10 bits of data (8 for the information and 2 for error correction). This means that MIDI sends about 3,906 bytes of data every second (31,250 bps divided by 8 bits to convert into bytes). If you compare this with the 176,400 byte (or 172.3 kilobytes) transfer rate that digital audio requires when recording or playing back CD-quality sound without compression, MIDI may seem very slow. But in reality, it's fast enough for what it needs to transfer. At this speed, you could play approximately 500 MIDI notes per second.

What Does MIDI Really Transmit?

MIDI sends or receives the following information:

- ▶ The pressing or releasing of a key.
- ▶ What channel notes play from or on. Each MIDI cable or port can support up to sixteen channels of information, much like having up to sixteen separate instruments playing at once.
- ▶ Wheels and pedal controls (pitch bend wheels, modulation wheels, sustain pedals, and switch pedals).
- ▶ Key pressures of pressed keys, also known as *Aftertouch* information sent by the controller keyboard or by the sequencer to a sound module. Note that not all keyboards support this function, but when they do, the information is sent as MIDI data.
- ▶ Program changes (or patch changes).
- ▶ Synchronization (for MIDI devices that have built-in timing clocks that let you set them to a desired tempo, like a drum machine, then follow or trigger another sequencer or drum machine to play in beat-to-beat synchronization).
- ▶ Special information, also called System Exclusive messages, used to alter synthesizer parameters and control the transport of System Exclusive-compatible multitrack recorders.

▶ MIDI Time Code or MTC (this is a way for MIDI-compatible devices to lock to a SMPTE device—a translation of SMPTE into something MIDI devices can understand).

You can think of MIDI as an old mechanical piano using a paper roll. The holes in the paper roll contained the moments where the musician played the notes but not the sound of the piano itself. MIDI information is transmitted in much the same way, capturing the performance of the musician but not the sound of the instrument he or she played on. You will always need some kind of sound module that can reproduce the sounds recorded in MIDI. This sound module could be an external synthesizer module, a sampler, a virtual synthesizer inside your VST environment, or even the synthesizer chip on your sound card. This is precisely what Cubase allows you to do: record a musical performance from a MIDI instrument into your computer, thus creating a virtual paper roll

MIDI Connectors

There are two or three plugs on MIDI devices: In and Out, or In, Out, and Thru. These are located on the backs of every hardware-based MIDI instrument or device. Usually, two-port configurations are reserved for computer-related hardware. As you will see with virtual synthesizers, you still have MIDI Ins and MIDI Outs, but you won't have physical sockets in which to plug cables.

NOTE
Since most software can control what goes to the MIDI Out port and can switch between Out and Thru inside the application, there is no need for a third port. This is the case in Cubase.

MIDI Out

The most important concept to understand is that MIDI does not transmit sound over wires the way audio components in a sound system do. Instead, it sends a digital code that represents what and how an event is being played on the instrument. As you play on a MIDI keyboard, the computer in the instrument examines your performance. The instrument's computer then converts it into a stream of MIDI codes that translates your actions. That information is sent out over an instrument's MIDI output to other synthesizers that reproduce the performance, but they use their own sounds to reproduce this performance.

MIDI In

MIDI keyboards can be viewed as being two machines in one: the computer processor that monitors the keyboard, program memory, front panel displays, and MIDI ports; and the part under the control of the onboard computer, the electronics that actually make the sounds.

The MIDI input receives incoming MIDI information and sends it to the instrument's computer. The computer analyzes and acts upon the information in much the same way as a performance on the original instrument, such as pressing a key to play notes. There is no difference to the soundmaking parts of a synthesizer, whether the command to play notes comes from a key press on the instrument itself or as a command from other MIDI devices.

MIDI Thru

In order to send MIDI data on to other instruments in a chain, a third MIDI connector called Thru duplicates any MIDI messages that come through the MIDI input of an instrument. This repeats the MIDI information, sending it to another device. An important concept to understand when putting together a MIDI-based music system is that anything played on a keyboard goes only to the MIDI Out and not to the MIDI Thru. This third port is very useful when you want to avoid MIDI loops when hooking your MIDI devices together.

A MIDI loop occurs when MIDI information is sent from one instrument to another and then back to the initial instrument. This will cause the instrument to play each note twice and, in some cases, will cause a feedback of MIDI data that could potentially cause your sequencer to crash.

If you have a MIDI patch bay—a MIDI device with multiple MIDI inputs and outputs—you are better off using a separate MIDI output for each connected device, thus reducing the amount of information flowing in a single MIDI wire. But if you do not own such a device, using the MIDI Thru socket is your best bet.

A Brief Overview of Digital Audio

Digital audio is quite different from analog audio. Let us take a moment to see what the differences are and how this can affect your result. Digital audio recordings, like analog audio recordings, are not all created equal. Recording with higher digital resolutions and superior equipment (analog-to-digital converters) in conjunction with the technology available in Cubase VST Score or VST/32 will allow you to create a better-sounding result. How this works and why digital recordings are different from analog recordings is important to understand.

What Is Analog Sound?

We hear sound when our eardrums vibrate, moving back and forth anywhere between twenty and 20,000 times every second. This is called *frequency* and is measured in Hertz, which in this case would be between 20 Hz and 20 kHz. When a musical instrument is played, it vibrates. Examples of this include the string of a violin, the skin of a drum, and even the cone of a loudspeaker. This vibration is transferred to the molecules of the air, which carry the sound to our ears. If the frequency of the vibration is slow, we hear a low note; if the frequency is fast, we hear a high note. If the vibration is gentle, making the air move back and forth only a little, we hear a soft sound. This movement is known as *amplitude*. If the amplitude is high, making the windows rattle, we hear a loud sound!

If you were to graph air movement against time, you could draw a picture of the sound. This is called a *waveform*. You can see a very simple waveform at low amplitude on the left in Figure 1.1. The middle waveform is the same sound, but much louder (higher amplitude). Finally, the waveform on the right is a musical instrument, which contains harmonics—a wider range of simultaneous frequencies. In all of these waveforms, there is one constant: The horizontal axis always represents time and the vertical axis always represents amplitude.

Figure 1.1
The amplitude of a waveform is represented by the vertical axis and the time is represented by the horizontal axis.

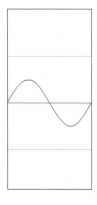
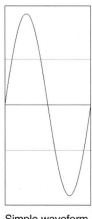

Simple waveform with low amplitude

Simple waveform with high amplitude

Complex waveform of a musical instrument

Real life sounds don't consist of just one frequency but of many frequencies mixed together at different levels of amplitude (loudness). This is what makes a musical sound interesting. Despite its complexity, a waveform can be represented by a graph. At any given time, the waveform has a measurable amplitude. If we can capture this "picture" and then reproduce it, we've succeeded in our goal of recording sound.

A gramophone record does this in an easily visible way. Set up a mechanism that transfers air vibration (sound) into the mechanical vibration of a steel needle. Let the needle draw the waveform onto a groove in tinfoil or wax. "Read" the wiggles in this groove with a similar needle. Amplify the vibration as best you can. Well done, Mr. Edison!

Instead of wiggles in a groove, you might decide to store the waveform as patterns of magnetism on recording tape. But either way, you're trying to draw an exact picture of the waveform. You're making an analog recording using a continuous stream of information. This is different from digital audio recordings, as you will see later in this chapter.

The second dimension of sound is amplitude, or the intensity of molecule displacement. When many molecules are moved, the sound will be louder. Inversely, if few molecules are moved in space, the sound is softer. Amplitude is measured in volts, because this displacement of molecules creates energy. When the energy is positive, it pushes molecules forward, making the line in Figure 1.1 move upward. When the energy is negative, it pushes the molecules backwards, making the line go downward. When the line is near the center, it means that fewer molecules are being moved around. That's why the sound appears to be softer in volume.

There is a third dimension to sound, which is space. This dimension does not have its own axis, because it is usually the result of amplitude variations through time, but the space will affect the waveform itself. In other words, the space will affect the amplitude of a sound through time. This will be important when we talk about effects and microphone placement when recording or mixing digital audio. But suffice it to say now that the environment in which sound occurs has a great influence on how we will perceive the sound.

What Is Digital Sound?

To understand digital audio, we have to compare it to its analog counterpart.

Analog sound is represented in time by a continuous wave of energy. It is the variation of this energy that moves a speaker forward and backward in its place, creating the air molecule displacement once again. As we mentioned earlier, sound is the continuous change of amplitude (or energy) through time. In digital audio, there is no such thing as continuous—only the illusion of continuum.

In 1928, mathematician Harry Nyquist developed a theory based on his finding that he could reproduce a waveform if he could sample the variation of sound at least twice in every period of that waveform. A period is a full cycle of the sound, measured in Hertz (this name was given in honor of Heinrich Hertz, who developed another theory regarding the relation between sound cycles and their frequency in 1888). So, if you have a sound that has 20 Hz, you need at least 40 samples to reproduce it. The value that he kept in the sample is the voltage of that sound at a specific point in time. Obviously, in the '20s, computers were not around to keep the large number of values needed to reproduce this theory adequately, but as you probably guessed, we do have this technology available now.

Figure 1.2
The bits in a digital recording will store a discreet amplitude value, and the frequency at which these amplitude values are stored in memory as they fluctuate through time is called the sampling frequency.

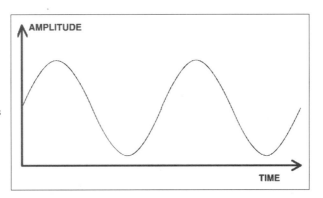

In computer terms, the amplitude (or voltage) is measured and its value is stored as a number. The size or precision of this number is determined by the number of bits used to store it. Every bit keeps the value of the amplitude (or voltage) as a binary number. The more bits you have, the more values you have. You may compare this with color depth. When you have 8 bits of color, you have a 256-color palette. A 16-bit resolution yields 65,000 colors, and so on. In sound, colors are replaced by voltage values. The higher the resolution in bit depth, the smaller the increments are between these voltage values. This also means that the more increments you have, the less noise your amplifier will create as it moves from one value to another.

Because the computer cannot make the in-between values, it jumps from one value to the next, creating noise-like artifacts, also called digital distortion. Need we say that this is not something you want in your sound? So, the more values you have to represent different amplitudes, the closer your sound will resemble the original analog signal in terms of amplitude variation. Time (measured in Hertz) is the frequency at which you capture and store these voltage values, or bits. Like amplitude (bits), the frequency greatly affects the quality of your sound. As mentioned earlier, Nyquist said that you needed two samples per period of the waveform to be able to reproduce it. This means that if you want to reproduce a sound of 100 Hz, or 100 vibrations per second, you need 200 samples. This is called your sampling frequency, and like the frequency of your sound, it is also measured in Hertz. Since, in reality, you will have complex sounds and high frequencies, you will need much higher sampling frequencies than the one mentioned above. Since most audio components such as amplifiers and speakers can reproduce sounds ranging from 20 Hz to 20 kHz, the sampling frequency standard for compact disc digital audio was fixed at 44.1 kHz—a little bit more than twice the highest frequency produced by your monitoring system.

The first thing you notice when you change the sampling rate of a sound is that the more samples you have, the sharper and crisper the sound. The fewer samples you have, the duller and mushier it gets. Why is this? Well, since you need twice as many samples as there are frequencies in your sound, the more samples you have in your recording, the more high harmonics you will capture in a sound. When you lose high harmonics, you will notice that the sound will appear duller to your ears. It is those harmonics that add definition to the sound. So, the more samples you have, the sharper the sound will be. If your sampling rate is too low, you not only lose harmonics but fundamentals as well. And this would change the tonal quality of the sound altogether.

How Sampling Works

Figure 1.3 shows two sampling formats. The one on the left will use less memory because it samples the sound less often than the one on the right and has fewer bits representing amplitude values. As a result, there will be fewer samples to store, and each sample will take up less space in memory. But consequently, it will not represent the original file very well and will probably create artifacts that will render it unrecognizable. In the first set of two images on the top, you can see the analog sound displayed as a single line.

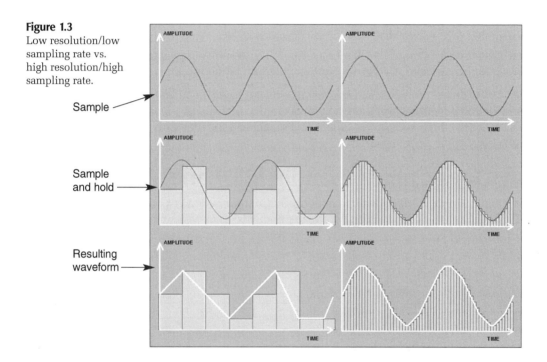

Figure 1.3
Low resolution/low sampling rate vs. high resolution/high sampling rate.

Sample

Sample and hold

Resulting waveform

The center set of images demonstrates how the amplitude value of the sample is kept and held until the next sampled amplitude value is taken. As you can see in the right column, a more frequent sampling of amplitude values will render a much more accurate reproduction of the original waveform. If you look at the resulting waveform in the lower set of images, this becomes even more obvious when you look at the yellow line representing the outline of the resulting waveform. The waveform on the right is closer to the original analog signal than the one on the left.

http://www.muskalipman.com

Sampling is simply the process of taking a snapshot of your sound through time. Every snapshot of your sound is kept and held until the next snapshot is taken. This process is called "Sample and Hold." As mentioned earlier, the snapshot keeps the voltage value of the sound at a particular point in time. When playing back digital audio, an amplifier keeps the level of the recorded voltage value until the next sample. Before the sound is finally sent to the output, a certain amount of low-level noise is sometimes added to the process to hide the large gaps that may occur between voltage values, especially if you are using a low bit-rate and low sampling rate for digital recording. This process is called dithering. Usually, this makes your sound smoother, but in low-resolution recordings (such as an 8-bit recording), it will add a certain amount of audible noise to your sound. Again, if this dithering wasn't there, you might not hear noise, but your sound might be a little distorted.

So how does this tie into Cubase? Well, Cubase is, in many ways, a gigantic multitrack sampler, as it samples digital audio at various sampling rates and bit depths or resolutions.

Whenever you are recording an audio signal in a digital format, you are sampling this sound. Cubase will allow you to sample sound at rates of up to 96 kHz per second and at bit depths of up to 32 bits. How high you can go will, of course, depend on your audio hardware.

How Does Cubase Handle MIDI and Audio?

Unlike a tape recorder, Cubase records not only audio information but MIDI as well. The way it handles the information depends on two basic principals: track assignment and channel assignment.

Figure 1.5
How the MIDI data flows from inputs to outputs in Cubase.

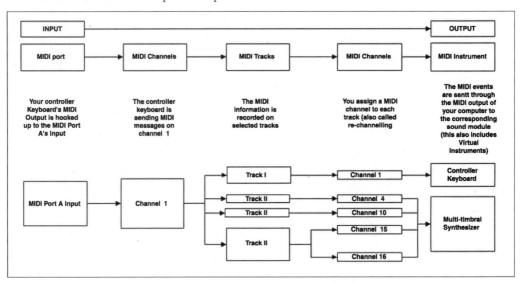

Figure 1.6
How the audio signal flows from inputs to outputs in Cubase.

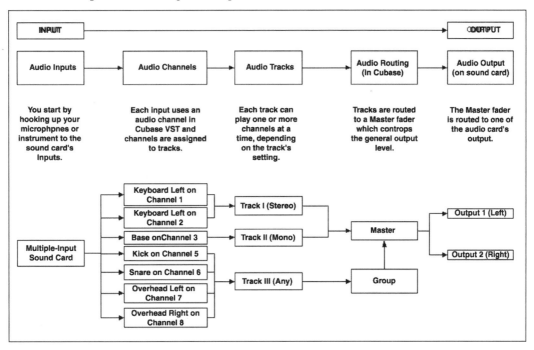

Figure 1.5 shows how Cubase handles MIDI, and Figure 1.6 shows how Cubase handles audio. The flow of information goes from left to right. In Figure 1.5, there is only one MIDI port, but you can have as many MIDI ports as you have available in your studio. If you have only one MIDI port, you will have only sixteen channels of MIDI available using that port. Fortunately, every time you use a Virtual Instrument, you add an additional MIDI port, which means an additional sixteen channels of MIDI. In Figure 1.6, you have an example showing a multiple input sound card. The number of inputs and outputs on a sound card are independent from the number of audio channels you can use inside Cubase.

MIDI Port

A MIDI port is a physical or virtual point of entry or point of exit for your MIDI data. The number of physical MIDI ports is determined by your computer's hardware. If you have a sound card that has four MIDI inputs and four MIDI outputs, you will have four MIDI ports available in Cubase. On the other hand, if you are using Cubase to send or receive MIDI information to and from another application inside your computer, chances are you are using virtual MIDI ports. Why virtual? Because they do not require additional hardware. This is the case when you are using a VST Virtual Instrument (this will be discussed in Chapter 4) or when working with third-party software such as Reason, Nemesys' Gigasampler, and others. Whenever you load these Virtual Instruments, they create virtual ports that are available in Cubase for you to use as if they were plugged in to your computer through an actual MIDI port.

The MIDI port determines which physical or virtual MIDI socket information is coming from and going to. Each MIDI port can carry up to sixteen MIDI channels. A MIDI channel is assigned to a track (see Figure 1.5).

One nice feature of Cubase is that you don't have to select the MIDI input port from which you record. As long as your MIDI input port has been activated in the MIDI System Setup, Cubase records all MIDI coming from all MIDI inputs at once. Which MIDI input port appears in your System Setup window depends on the ports you activate in the MME Setup Window. This will be discussed later in this chapter.

MIDI Channel

You have to select a MIDI channel in order to send information to a particular patch or preset in your MIDI instrument. Once your MIDI channel is selected, you can assign a patch to it, like a bass, for example. A MIDI channel can play only the assigned patch for the instrument you wish to play or record MIDI with. You can change the patch or preset along the way, but you can have only one patch or preset assigned to that channel at a time. Imagine that a track or a part is like a television set and that you can watch only one show at a time. Now, imagine that your arrangement is your house, where you have many television sets playing different shows at the same time. You can switch channels in a part or a track, but once you select one, there is only one show playing at a time. Once the show ends, you can watch the next one. And the same is true for every TV set in your house.

If you run out of MIDI channels for one MIDI port, you will need to use another MIDI port to play the MIDI data. If you are out of MIDI ports, you will need to convert some of your MIDI data into audio data. This is where it becomes a little tricky. That's why you will see this later on in this book. Figure 1.7 shows the Arrange window. In this window, the MIDI track can be identified by its symbol in the C column. The Midi Channel can be identified by the Chn column and the MIDI Out port can be identified by the Out column. To view the active MIDI In port, select Options > MIDI Setup > System in the menu bar.

Figure 1.7
This Arrange window shows thirteen different tracks, nine of them MIDI and four of them audio.

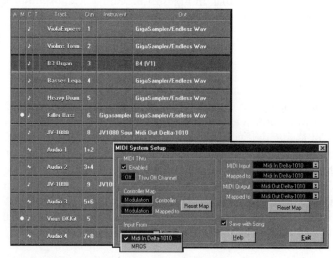

MIDI Track

A MIDI track usually contains MIDI information for one channel at a time. You play on your keyboard, and it's sending out MIDI data on a MIDI channel that is recorded on a MIDI track. You then assign a MIDI channel to that track to get the appropriate sound at the output.

Sometimes, you may also have more than one channel on a track at the same time. It is like a highway with many lanes. Each vehicle is a MIDI event on this highway. Cars in one lane of this highway can be playing one channel of MIDI and cars on another lane would play another channel. If you decide to assign a MIDI channel to all the events on a MIDI track, it will play only that channel. Here's an example:

Let's say you have two separate keyboard controllers sending MIDI data to Cubase on the same MIDI port. Keyboard 1, playing the bass line, is sending on MIDI Channel 1, and Keyboard 2, playing the melody, is sending on MIDI Channel 2. Both signals will be recorded on the selected MIDI track. Once recorded, if you set this track to play through MIDI Channel 1, both recorded lines (bass and melody) on this track will play on the Channel 1 instrument—in this case, the bass sound. This technique is called re-channelizing. If, on the other hand, you set your MIDI track to the "Any" setting, both lines will play their respective channel from this track.

You see, Cubase doesn't replace the original MIDI data that you record. It simply puts a filter at the output of the track.

Audio Channel

An audio channel is an audio voice. It is similar to a singing voice in the sense that if you are singing a note, you can't sing another note unless you stop singing the first one. Before you start recording or playing back a track, you must select a channel for your audio to be played back on or recorded onto. The number of channels your arrangement can handle is limited by your RAM (memory), hard disk speed, and other hardware and operating system factors. Once you have created a number of voices in your audio system, you can assign these voices to tracks. As shown in Figure 1.8, double-click in the Number of Channels field to enter the desired number of channels you wish to use or left-click on the number in the field to decrease the value and right-click to increase it.

Figure 1.8
In this example, Cubase is set to have sixteen channels.

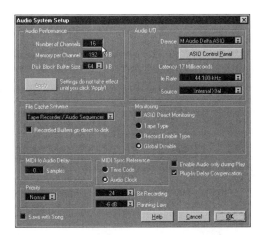

Audio Track

You can have up to seventy-two audio channels with Cubase VST and up to 128 audio channels with Cubase VST/32. Then again, you might also be limited by your hardware capabilities as well. Unlike analog audio tape recorders, a track can be mono, stereo, or multichanneled. The channel setting for your track determines this. You will find this setting in the "Chn" column of the track view in your Arrange window.

When you decide that you want to record a stereo instrument, simply set your track properties to Stereo in the Track Info section of the selected track. Note that this applies only to audio tracks, not to MIDI tracks. You would also do the same thing if you wanted to insert an audio segment that you imported from the audio pool. Once a track is designated mono or stereo, you can import or record other material of the same nature in this track. If you try to insert or record a mono segment into a stereo track, Cubase will tell you it can't do so because the track's property is not set up correctly for the material you are trying to import.

To be able to set your track to Stereo, you must first select an odd-numbered channel (1, 3, 5, 7, and so on) for which the even-numbered channel is not used by any other track in your arrangement. For example, if you are trying to use Track 3 to record a stereo file using channels 3 and 4, but your Track 4 is already using Channel 4, you would be better off using channels 5 and 6 on Track 3.

Any Channel setting

This option allows you to record from more than one input source at a time. This might be useful if you meet certain conditions:

1. Your sound card must have more than one stereo input.
2. If you do have more than one pair of inputs available, you are not using them to record on other tracks.
3. You need to record these sources simultaneously onto one track, such as a drum kit, using a channel for the snare, a channel for the kick, and a stereo pair for the toms and cymbals.

Once you've determined that this is what you want to do and that your hardware supports multichannel recording, you need to activate your inputs in the VST Input window found in the Panels menu.

Figure 1.9
The VST Input window allows you to activate or deactivate inputs on your sound card.

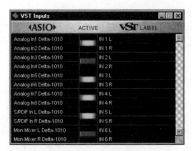

You will need more than one stereo pair of inputs activated if you want to use the "Any" setting when recording, especially if you wish to record from more than two sources at once. In Figure 1.9, the Analog In1 of the Delta card will be labeled as 1INL for the left input and 1INR for the right input, and so on for the other inputs. You may change these labels, but this will be discussed further in Chapter 9.

Following this, you will need to assign these inputs to each channel in the Channel Mixer panel found in the Panels menu. Here, you will see one fader for each channel or voice you've set up in Cubase. If your configuration is set up for eight channels of audio, you should have an eight-channel mixer; a sixteen-channel setup would display a sixteen-channel mixer, and so on.

Figure 1.10
The VST Channel Mixer 1 window.

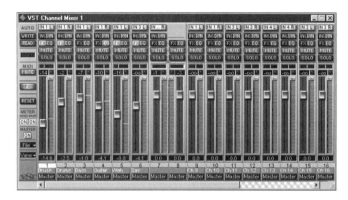

In Figure 1.10, you can set the inputs for each channel by pressing Ctrl+Left Click at the top of the desired channel for which you wish to record in a multichannel recording. In this figure, channels 11 and 12 would receive their signal from inputs 3 left and right, and channels 13 and 14 would receive their signal from inputs 4 left and right, respectively. The name of the input that appears in this field can be modified in the VST Input window. To bring this window up, select it from the Panels menu. This will also be discussed in further detail in Chapter 8.

Finally, when you've enabled the inputs in the channel mixer, you can arm or enable the Record Info button for the channels you wish to record on in the Track Info view for the selected track. This Track Info panel will appear automatically when you select "Any" from the audio track type.

Figure 1.11
The track titled "Track 12" will record on channels 11 through 14 when you press the Record button in the transport bar.

Audio Output

As you can see by looking back at Figure 1.6, audio tracks are routed to either a Group or the Master VST output under the Audio Routing section of the drawing. In reality, Cubase allows you to send your signal virtually to any output on your sound card using different routing schemes. This can appear complicated at first if you are not familiar with the concept of a mixing console, but the basics are the same. For now, you should understand that most of the time, your signal will come out of the Master output. When you bring up the VST Mixer Master Output Panel from the Panel menu (see Figure 1.12), you can click on the button at the bottom, below the Master Output faders, to select which sound card output to use to send the signal through.

Figure 1.12
The Master Output will be routed to Analog output 1 and 2 of this sound card.

About 32-bit Recording

Most audio hardware available out there today supports 16-bit resolution. Some better quality sound cards also support 20- and 24-bit resolutions. Table 1.2 illustrates the different values that can be stored in their respective resolutions:

Table 1.2
Minimum and Maximum values for 16-, 24- and 32-bit resolution audio signal

Resolution	Minimum Value	Maximum Value	Dynamic Range	Hard Disk Space (min/mono)
16-bit	−12,768	32,767	96 dBFS	5,168 Kb
24-bit	−18,388,608	8,388,607	144 dBFS	7,752 Kb
32-bit	−12,147,483,648	2,147,483,647	193 dBFS	10,336 Kb

But what do these numbers mean? Look at Figure 1.13. With 16-bit resolution, the steps corresponding to voltage values are few and far between. In the 24-bit resolution, there are many more steps (also called Quantum) than in 16-bit recordings. In the 32-bit, the binary word is twice as long, but as you have seen in the table above, instead of having 65,535 steps, you have more than four billion steps. Finally, in 32-bit floating point resolution, you still have more than four billion steps; however, they are not fixed but variable points that adjust themselves according to the needs of the audio waveform.

Figure 1.13
Understanding the importance of bit resolution in digital audio recording.

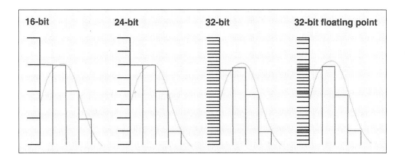

NOTE

The 32-bit and 32-bit TrueTape recording capabilities of Cubase are available only in the VST/32 version of the software. If you own the VST Score or VST version of the software, you will be able to record in either 16- or 24-bit formats.

Recording audio up until now was limited to fixed integer values, as mentioned above. With floating point, the computer adds a decimal value and can move that decimal point wherever it needs it in order to get greater precision. Here's an example: Let's say you have an analog signal coming in at 1.2245 volts. If you have a system that provides only two decimal points, your resulting value would be 1.23 or 1.22. In both cases, this would not be very precise, but it's as precise as the recording system could be. Floating point technology simply adds a decimal value (up to seven) as needed, making the recorded value exactly 1.2245. This kind of technology yields a dynamic range of almost 200 dB! This dynamic range means that you can drive your guitar without ever worrying about digital clipping. You should still be careful, though, because while there might not be digital clipping in your signal, you might still have digital distortion, which sounds like analog distortion. And any way you look at it, unwanted distortion is never a good thing.

Remember that the bit depth of the mixdown does not have to be the same as the recorded tracks. Cubase allows you to select a different format to mix down your tracks when you are finished working on them. This is because Cubase allows you to record in a format that is superior to the quality available on regular CD players. So, a good rule of thumb to follow is always work with the best quality you can, saving the downgrading for the last step before burning to CD. If your hardware and software can handle it, go for it. But remember this: Audio CD format supports only 44.1 kHz, 16-bit stereo files. So, if you don't convert your audio beforehand, you won't be able to write it in audio CD format, since this format requires that your audio be in 44.1KHz, 16-bit, stereo channel.

http://www.muskalipman.com

Do I Have the Right Hardware?

To use 24-bit or 32-bit recording, you need to have a 24-bit compatible sound card to actually have better quality sound. Recording in 24-bit or 32-bit with a 16-bit sound card will only make your file larger; it will not give you better results. Not to mention that your 16-bit sound card might not even be able to play back the audio recorded at 24-bit. This said, you have to understand that 24-bit recordings take up 1.5 times as much space as a 16-bit recording, and that 32-bit recordings take up twice the space of a 16-bit recording and make more demands on the CPU and hard disk performance of your computer. The kind of hard disk and RAM you have in your computer will greatly influence the performance of your system when using 24- or 32-bit recording.

On the other hand, if you have a 16-bit sound card but would like to get the feeling of analog tape, you can use the TrueTape 32-bit recording technology provided in Cubase VST/32 or above versions. The TrueTape 32-bit technology encodes the signal in 16-bit using a dithering system. This is different than the 32-bit recording, because it uses software-enabled 32-bit recording rather than true 32-bit recording. The result is similar, but TrueTape allows you to use an interface to control the amount of overdrive you want to add to the sound. This is like putting your volume knob at 11 on a scale from 1 to 10, but unlike Spinal Tap (for all you fans out there), this really makes a difference in sound volume! How to use this and what it does to your audio signal will be discussed in Chapter 9.

2
Setting Up Your Environment

In this chapter, you will learn how to configure both your software and hardware for optimal performance. You will also have a glimpse of ASIO drivers and how to use the configuration panels provided with both Cubase and by hardware manufacturers.

Software Setup

Before you can do anything in Cubase, you must make sure that your software is properly installed on your system. This implies that you have a stable operation system and that the latest drivers for all your peripherals are installed, including peripherals you think are not related, like video card and network card drivers. If you find that your operating system crashes often for no apparent reason, reinstalling it might be a good idea. This may save you from experiencing problems later on. In a perfect world, this would be done automatically. But because there are probably as many systems out there as there are Cubase users, you will need to run some little tests to allow the software to establish what is the best configuration for its optimal performance. You must then tweak this a bit further before you can establish what is the best configuration for your optimal performance.

The first thing you will want to set up is how Cubase communicates with the operating system, the MIDI device, and the sound card's driver. Because Cubase uses both MIDI and digital audio, you will need to set up both drivers properly.

MIDI Drivers and Setup

Installing a MIDI card requires you to use the driver that comes with the hardware. This is usually quite simple and is explained in your hardware documentation. Hardware specifics will not be discussed here, because there are too many MIDI and audio interfaces out there to cover them thoroughly. But to make sure everything is set up properly, one good starting point is to verify that your MIDI port appears in your system configuration. To check this, click on Start > Settings > Control Panel > Multimedia, then select the MIDI tab in the Multimedia Properties window (see Figure 2.1). You should see the driver for your MIDI device listed in this panel. If you don't, you will need to make sure your MIDI interface and device driver are properly installed before using Cubase. Note that Mac users need to configure through OMS (Open Music System) as there is no MME Setup utility for Macintosh computers.

http://www.muskalipman.com

You might want to consult your manufacturer's Web site for specific settings related to your MIDI or audio device. This Web site will probably provide you with driver updates and tips on configuring your device with Cubase and other software.

Figure 2.1
The Multimedia Properties window allows you to see if your MIDI device is properly installed on your computer.

The next step is to configure which MIDI port will be active in Cubase. To do this, you will use the Setup MME application provided with Cubase (you should find this in the program group where you installed Cubase > Setup MME). This application (see Figure 2.2) allows you to activate or deactivate inputs and outputs to be used in Cubase.

Figure 2.2
In this Setup window, the LBI through LB4 input ports have been deactivated. They will therefore not appear in my available MIDI input ports in the Cubase MIDI System Setup window.

To rename a port, you simply select it and press the Rename button. This will affect how the name is displayed in the MIDI System Setup dialog box, available through the Options menu in Cubase (Options > MIDI Setup > System).

You can also deactivate a MIDI port to clean up the selection of MIDI Out ports in the Arrange window. When creating a new MIDI track, VST will default to the first MIDI Out port whether or not it's actually in use.

To set a MIDI port inactive, select it and press the Set Inactive button.

Setting Up Your Environment – Chapter 2

If you wish to see certain inputs or outputs before others—for example, you know that you will be using your MIDI port C the most—you can move it to the top of the list by selecting the port in the list and then clicking Move Up or Move Down. This will change the order in which the ports appear once you restart Cubase.

NOTE

Changing the order of your ports will have no effect on the MIDI signal or priority of data inside your system. It affects only the layout in the list that appears when you want to select a MIDI port.

Once you are done configuring the MIDI ports, click OK.

The Setup MME program is only for setting preferences that need to be defined before Cubase is started. While running Cubase, the other MIDI settings are accessed through Cubase's MIDI System Setup dialog box (Options > MIDI Setup > System).

Figure 2.3
Configure your MIDI ports here.

The MIDI Thru option allows you to echo any MIDI information coming from your MIDI input port through your MIDI output port for your selected track. This should always be on, and you should set your controller keyboard from which you are sending MIDI data to "Local Off." When your controller keyboard is set to Local Off, the sound part of the keyboard is turned off for the notes you play on the keyboard part. It will, however, play the notes it receives when MIDI information is sent to the controller's MIDI input. Since you are sending MIDI events to Cubase, Cubase will then echo these events to the MIDI input port of your keyboard, therefore playing the sounds anyway.

So why set your keyboard to Local Off? We do this simply to avoid having the sound play twice—once when you press the keys and another time when Cubase sends the MIDI events back to the keyboard. If you are unsure about how to use this function or an equivalent function on your controller keyboard, please read the manufacturer's documentation or visit its Web site. This way, you let Cubase determine which MIDI channel is being sent to a MIDI output. As mentioned in the section about MIDI earlier in this book, computer MIDI interfaces do not have a physical MIDI Thru. This is where you tell the computer to use the MIDI Out as a MIDI Thru. Remember that the MIDI Out port does not echo information coming from the MIDI In port.

If, for some reason, you need to disable the MIDI Thru from Cubase, try setting the Thru Off Channel option first. This will allow all other MIDI information coming in the MIDI port to flow through its output, with the exception of the specific channel you select. For example, if you can't set your controller keyboard to Local Off and this keyboard is sending MIDI messages on Channel 1, set the Thru Off Channel to 1. This will echo all MIDI information except for Channel 1.

NOTE
Here's an example of when you would need to disable the MIDI Thru from Cubase: A Yamaha CS6X has an arpeggiator, which its MIDI output can be recorded to in order to reuse the arp for another sound. However, with Local Off in the synth and Thru on in VST, the input to VST—which includes the arp output—is fed back out, and Thru again effectively chokes the notes of the keyboard. In order to record the arp's output, you must turn Local On and Thru off in VST, then record the track.

The Controller Map setting allows you to convert a type of MIDI controller into another type of MIDI controller. In most cases, this option may be left alone. But if you wish to convert a Modulation Wheel control into a Breath controller, for example, this would be how you would do this. After passing through the converter, each Modulation Wheel message received would be translated into a Breath controller message.

The Input From field allows you to activate or deactivate, inside Cubase, your MIDI input ports. Remember that Cubase receives from all input ports selected at recording time, so if you have only one MIDI keyboard controller, you need only one active input port. But if one of your devices is set to transmit System Exclusive messages during your performance, you should activate its port. Here's another example for this: Let's say you are using a digital mixer with MIDI controls. You could send MIDI messages, such as volume or pan controls, to Cubase, recording them as you are playing on your keyboard at the same time.

The MIDI Input and Output mapping options are global settings for MIDI filtering. Therefore, they can be used any time you want to remap information coming in from one MIDI port to another MIDI port or when you want to send out MIDI information from one port to another. Since this is a global setting, you will not be able to select what you want to be remapped in the MIDI data. To control or remap only certain MIDI information, you can use the Track Info later and determine exactly what MIDI information should be going where. This topic will be covered later in this book. The MIDI filter is active when a checkmark appears in the checkbox.

Audio System Settings

Like MIDI, your audio sound card should be properly installed in your computer before you try to run Cubase. To make sure it is running smoothly and is properly installed, select Start > Settings > Control Panel > System > Device Manager. Scroll down in the window and click on the plus sign next to Sound, Video, and Game controllers. If a question mark or an exclamation mark appears in front of your device, this could mean one of several things: Your device driver might be installed improperly; there is a resource conflict, such as two peripherals trying to share the same IRQ setting; or it could be a hardware problem. You should troubleshoot your system in order to run your sound card properly without the question mark or exclamation point. To do this, consult the documentation provided by your sound card manufacturer or its FAQ section on the Web and then download the latest drivers for the sound card, also available on the manufacturer's Web site.

Figure 2.4
The System Properties dialog box in Windows 95, 98, NT, Me, and 2000 will display a list of devices installed on your system.

TIP

Many of the conflicts on Windows-based systems are due to conflicting IRQ settings. Make sure that your sound card is not sharing an IRQ with another device, such as the video card or a modem. If this is the case, consult your manufacturer's documentation to find the IRQ setting that is best suited for your device and then find an IRQ that is not being used on your system to see if a match can be made between the two. If this doesn't work, try downloading new drivers for your sound card. When installing new drivers, it is always a good idea to uninstall all old drivers before installing new ones. This will help you to establish a clean setup without mixing old driver files with new ones, avoiding possible conflicts or corruptions in your system.

You should also make sure your sound system is compatible with Cubase before purchasing either the sound card or Cubase. This will prevent you from making unnecessary purchases. A list of compatible cards for Cubase is available at the following address:

http://service.steinberg.de/knowledge.nsf/show/list_audiocards

ASIO Drivers

ASIO is the acronym for Audio Stream Input/Output, which is a technology developed by Steinberg to allow a sound card to efficiently process and synchronize inputs and introduce the least amount of latency, or delay, between the inputs and the outputs of the sound card. What is latency? It is the time difference between the input and output. The smaller the latency, the shorter the time will be between what you record and what you hear recorded once the signal has been processed by the computer. High latencies are often troublesome when recording live material because there is always a delay when monitoring the audio. ASIO drivers have a short latency because they do not send the signal into the operating system before sending it to its outputs. Therefore, you can record music while playing back tracks without any noticeable differences. A typical latency for a sound card using a dedicated ASIO driver should be below 10 milliseconds. The greater the latency time, the more noticeable the delay will be. Note also that latency also affects the VST Instruments, the LEDs on the VST Channel Mixer, and the faders' and knobs' response time inside Cubase.

To select the ASIO driver you wish to use, you will need to access the following option in Cubase: Options > Audio Setup > System. Then, click the drop-down menu for the ASIO device.

TIP
If you find that lowering your latency makes your system unstable, try lowering it only when you are recording VST Instruments. Once your VST Instruments are recorded, bring the latency back up to a point where you feel your system is more stable. To lower the latency, lower the number of audio channels and audio buffer size in the ASIO Control Panel. Note that not all ASIO cards have latency (buffer) adjustments. The Korg 1212 I/O, for example, on the PC has a fixed latency of 46ms within Windows. You can improve this with a faster CPU, but only by a few milliseconds.

The Audio I/O section of the Audio System Setup dialog box allows you to select the ASIO device, bring the ASIO control panel up for that device, and set the global sampling rate and the clock source. You can also see the Latency indicator for this selected device, as shown in Figure 2.5.

Figure 2.5
The Audio I/O section of the Audio System Setup dialog box.

ASIO Dedicated Drivers

It goes without saying that if you have a dedicated ASIO driver for your sound card, this is your best bet at having the lowest latency available. When using your dedicated ASIO driver, you will be able to control how the sound card handles the audio information through a dedicated control panel designed by the hardware manufacturer. You can access this control panel by clicking on the ASIO Control Panel button in the Audio I/O section of the Audio System Setup dialog box, as shown in Figure 2.5. Figure 2.6 shows the control panel for the Delta 1010 sound card, but every manufacturer has its own control panel, so don't expect to see the exact same thing on your computer if you don't have the same sound card.

Figure 2.6
This is the control panel for the M-Audio Delta 1010 card.

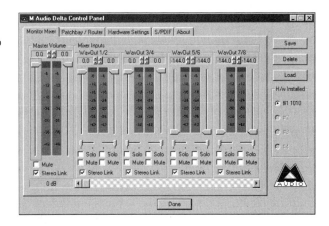

If possible, use the Direct ASIO monitoring when using a dedicated driver, as shown in Figure 2.7. Most hardware using dedicated drivers will allow this. By doing so, you send whatever is coming from the inputs of the sound card directly to the outputs, bypassing Cubase all together, thus reducing your latency once again. If you don't have ASIO direct monitoring, then the Global Disable option (as shown in Figure 2.7) will need to be selected. Otherwise, a ping-pong echo will occur. As you might have guessed by now, latency is not something you want to have to deal with. It does not affect how the sound is recorded or processed once it's recorded, but it does play an important role when playing VST Instruments through your sound card or playing back tracks when recording a live performance. If your sound card does not support Direct ASIO monitoring, this option will be grayed out. In conjunction with the Tape Type option, it will allow you to monitor directly any incoming signal when a track has been set to "record enable" in both Stop or Record mode. The other option is to set the Direct ASIO monitoring to Record Enable Type. This will allow you to monitor a signal coming in for a track that has been enabled for recording as well.

Figure 2.7
Settings for ASIO direct monitoring.

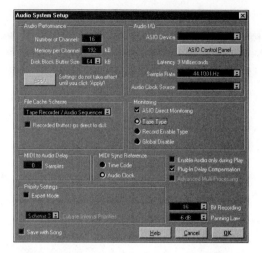

To access the Audio System Setup dialog box, as shown in Figure 2.7, choose Options > Audio Setup > System. Once in this dialog box, you will be able to make changes to your ASIO Direct Monitoring options.

ASIO Multimedia Drivers

If your sound card does not have a dedicated ASIO driver, Figure 2.8 shows the default window used to set up for your card. An ASIO Multimedia Driver is a standard (generic) ASIO driver provided by Steinberg, allowing you to record and play audio through your sound card when using Cubase. You should use this driver only if you don't have dedicated ASIO drivers. Before running Cubase for the first time, you will be asked to profile your ASIO Multimedia driver. If you've never done this, now is a good time to start. You can find the ASIO Multimedia Driver Setup application in the Cubase Program folder in Start > Programs or by accessing the Options > Audio Setup > System window and selecting ASIO Multimedia Driver from the ASIO device field. Then, select ASIO Control Panel and Advanced settings.

Figure 2.8
The Windows ASIO Multimedia Setup dialog box.

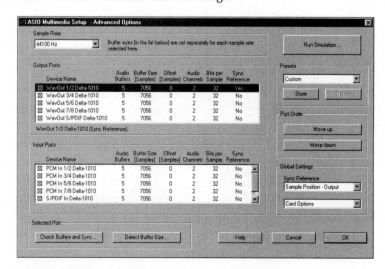

http://www.muskalipman.com

The ASIO Multimedia driver's advanced options window allows you to set preferences for your ASIO driver, test the buffer sizes, activate inputs and outputs, and determine which clock source will be used as a reference for audio synchronization.

You should start by checking the buffers and synchronization for each port on your sound card using the Check Buffers and Sync button. Once you've checked these settings, run a simulation to see if they will work on your system. This is done by using the Run Simulation button in the ASIO Multimedia Advanced Setup window. Why do you need to do this? Because just as there are many sound card manufacturers out there, there are also many ways to optimize Cubase to work with the sound card and get the most out of each one. That's especially true if it doesn't have an ASIO driver written specifically for it. By testing your sound card and making the necessary modifications, you are taking steps toward a successful recording session.

If the test fails, here are some things you might want to try, repeating the test after each modification:

- ▶ Switch between Sync Reference Sample Position and DMA Block.
- ▶ Use the Detect Buffer Size option in the Advanced Options window.
- ▶ If you are using the Sample Position Sync Reference, try increasing the buffer size manually. This will increase your latency but will reduce the stress on your computer's CPU.
- ▶ Check that no background tasks are currently running on your computer.

Figure 2.9
The Windows ASIO Multimedia Audio System Test dialog box.

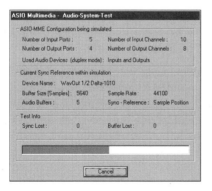

Once you are satisfied with the result of the test and wish to save these settings to retrieve them later on, you can save the parameters using the Store button in the Preset section of the ASIO Multimedia Setup Advanced Options dialog box. You might even want to look if there isn't already a preset available for your sound card before attempting to save your setup. Even if your card exists in this list, make sure to try your tested results before selecting these presets. When you run a test, it tests the sound card in your system, so the result may vary from the preset value and your system configuration. Once you save your setup as a preset, you can call it back whenever you need it. Once again, you need to use this setup only when you don't have a dedicated ASIO driver. This said, using the ASIO DirectX or ASIO DirectX Full Duplex drivers might be another alternative when you don't have a dedicated ASIO driver for your sound card. The latency time for this driver will usually be shorter than with the ASIO multimedia driver.

http://www.muskalipman.com

Clicking OK in the Audio System Test Dialog will bring you back to the ASIO Multimedia Setup Advanced Options dialog box. This will show you at a glance which ports (inputs and outputs) are active and which are not. It also shows you which input port will serve as a synchronization reference.

For a more in-depth description of this feature, the Cubase online help file titled "Getting Into Details" provides information on the ASIO Multimedia Setup window.

Running Other Audio Applications Simultaneously

There is not much to say about running other non-audio related applications simultaneously, besides the fact that if you are running applications that require memory and CPU power, these resources won't be available to you in Cubase. Some background applications might start doing a hard disk scan in the middle of a recording. A good example of this would be Find Fast, an applet that comes with Microsoft Office. Any background memory or hard-disk-intensive applications should be disabled when using Cubase. A good rule of thumb to follow is to not run other nonessential applications when running Cubase to improve your performance. If you want to find out what is running inside your Windows system, press Ctrl+Alt+Del. This will bring up the Close Program dialog box that shows you what application is currently running. You can end tasks by selecting them in this dialog box and clicking on the End Task button if you have to. Nothing you do in this dialog box can harm your system in any way. Note that once you reboot your system, the applications that were running before you ended them will be back in business. So, changing the settings for these applications is a good idea. The more icons you have in the bottom right corner of your taskbar, the more applications are running in the background, using valuable resources. Make sure you keep those to a minimum. The situation is different if you try to run another audio-related application.

To run audio-related applications simultaneously with Cubase, you will need a sound card that provides a multi-client driver. What is a multi-client driver? Basically, it is a driver that allows different applications shared access to the sound card. Think of it this way: A single-client access is like going to the grocery store and having only one cash register open. Everybody has to line up and wait their turn to pay for their groceries. A multi-client driver is like having two or three cash registers opened, where people can go to a second or even a third cash register if the first is busy.

When Cubase is loaded, it generally takes over the controls of the sound card, leaving it unusable for other applications that would need it as well to run simultaneously, such as a third-party virtual sampler or one of Steinberg's partner software developers, Propellerheads.

If you don't have a multi-client driver, there are ways around it, but with some limitations. Steinberg provides an engine called Rewire that lets you share audio resources between Steinberg and Propellerheads products, like Rebirth and Reason. This is discussed in Chapter 8. If you have an audio application that loads automatically and would like to prevent this from happening, you can uncheck it from the list found in Start > Programs > Accessories > System Tools > System Information > Tools > System Configuration Utility > Startup.

For other types of software, such as Nemesys' GigaStudio or GigaSampler, you will have to load this software before and set Cubase as your default sequencer from within the GigaStudio or GigaSampler environment. Once this is done, you can launch Cubase from the Sequencer button within GigaStudio or GigaSampler. If you have problems doing this, try disabling audio outputs in GigaStudio that you wish to use in Cubase (for good measure, keep outputs 1 and 2 available for Cubase) and disabling audio inputs and outputs that you wish to use in GigaStudio. This way, some outputs are used by GigaStudio and some by Cubase.

When running such a setup, you are imposing a huge load on your computer resources and are also testing many compatibility issues between the different manufacturers of software and hardware. In a perfect world, everything would work, but this ain't Kansas! If you are experiencing difficulties, here are a couple of places to look for information:

- ▶ Try visiting Steinberg's site to see if there is any additional information on the issue you are having.
- ▶ Try visiting your other software manufacturer's Web site as well; it also might have some answers for you.
- ▶ Check on your sound card manufacturer's Web site to see if you have the latest drivers for your sound card, and take a look at the support, troubleshooting, or FAQ section to find additional help.
- ▶ Use discussion forums to share your problems with others; chances are, someone else had the same problem you have and might have a workaround for you.

Hardware Setup

Obviously, your software is not alone in this. Without hardware, your Cubase software CD would be a very expensive coaster! It is important that your hardware configuration matches the needs of Cubase. This implies that you have a computer that meets Steinberg's recommended configuration, which includes processor types, RAM, operating system, video display adapter, and CD-ROM drive. But within those specifications, there are some hardware settings that you can apply that will make your operation run more smoothly.

Hard Drive Configuration

Your hard drive is your recording tape. When recording digital audio on it, you are basically using it as a big storage device for this audio, like a magnetic tape would do in an analog studio. Although your hard drive is not prone to produce bending, degradation, or hiss like analog tape would, it does have its own problems to look out for.

http://www.muskalipman.com

Hard drives come in many sizes, many speeds, and many configurations. If you are planning to buy a new hard drive to record digital audio, you should ultimately use this drive ONLY for audio. Why? Because audio files usually are large files. This is not true for system files or other files required by your applications. When you are recording these large files, your system will look for free space on your hard disk to store them. If it has to find little corners here and there on your disk to place them, it will slow down your writing ability, limiting the number of audio channels you can read or write. This is mainly due to disk fragmentation. When using a disk or a partition on a disk only for digital audio recordings, you reduce the amount of disk fragmentation produced by small files that are written by your operating system or by applications you run on a day-to-day basis. If you can afford it, the best solution is, of course, using a separate hard disk dedicated to your audio recording. And, preferably, this disk would be on a different E-IDE or SCSI port from your system disk. This would allow faster access to the information on your disk, avoiding any issues or degradation of performance due to shared resources. With the price of hard disks going down, it's an investment worth making if you are using Cubase as a virtual studio environment for your digital audio recordings.

Disk fragmentation is another performance-robbing phenomenon. If you write on your disk frequently, you should do this at least once a week—yes, once a week. If you are using Cubase as your main working environment for your studio, defragmenting should be done after each recording session. This will prevent your disk from unnecessary head movement during intense writing or reading sessions and accelerate the process. You will find a disk defragmentation tool in Windows under System Tools or by following these steps:

1. On your desktop, double-click on the My Computer icon.
2. Right-click on the disk drive you wish to defragment and select Properties from the drop-down menu.
3. In the Properties dialog box, click on the Tools tab.
4. Click on the Defragment Now button to begin the defragmentation process. It is best to not use your computer while this process is going on, so a good time to do this is before going to bed. It doesn't take long to do (it can take anywhere from ten minutes to a couple of hours, depending on the size of your hard disk, the speed of your computer, and the available disk space on your drive).

If you are using a Macintosh computer, you will need to use Norton Utilities' Speed Disk to do this. Simply run Norton Speed Disk from its icon, select the drive, and proceed to take a coffee break while this is being done.

The Disk tools available in the Properties dialog box allow you to run a Scandisk as well before doing a disk defragmentation. If you haven't checked your disk for lost clusters in a while, it would be a good idea to run Scandisk before defragmenting it. If you decide to run a Scandisk on your system, select the disk you wish to scan, choose Standard or Thorough from the Test Type options, then check the Automatically Fix Errors option box. This will repair damaged links and lost clusters automatically.

Figure 2.10
The Windows Disk Tools dialog box.

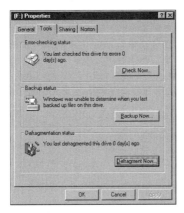

Figure 2.11
The Scan Disk utility provided in Windows.

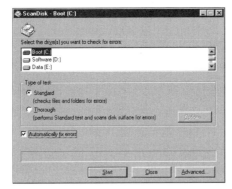

Hard Drive Types and Performance

Now that we've covered how to take care of a disk, let's look at what kind of disk you should get.

Hard disks spin at speeds between 5,400 rpm and 15,000 rpm. The faster your disk spins, the more information you can get out of it in a fixed amount of time. What you should look for in a drive is a minimal access time or average track-to-track seek time, which is how much time it takes the heads to move from one cylinder to another. When accessing arbitrary data, first the heads must seek the correct cylinder, then wait until the correct sector spins under the heads, and then read the data. Thus, a small seek time is good, and a fast disk rotation speed is good. A sufficient number to look for is 8 to 9 milliseconds. If it's shorter, it will take less time to find the information.

Another parameter to look out for is a sustained data transfer rate, but not a peak data transfer rate. When using digital audio files, your disk will be reading a sustained stream of information; that's why peak indicators don't matter much, because it is more likely that you will have multiple files of audio data being fed from the disk to the software. If you want to be able to transfer twenty-four channels of digital audio at 44.1 kHz, 16 bits, you will need a minimum of 2 MB of sustained data transfer. Now, this is the minimum. What you want to look for is at least two to three times that data transfer, so around 5 to 9 MB per second. Remember that you might have other applications running in the background accessing the hard disk and that twenty-four channels will come and go pretty quickly when working on a project.

http://www.muskalipman.com

SCSI drives and E-IDE drives today are fairly equal in performance. You might get a 10 percent to 15 percent increase in data transfer rate on a SCSI drive with the Ultra Wide 3 format, compared to the Ultra DMA 33 drives, but the price difference is not worth it. The more recent technologies such as ATA/66 and ATA/100 drives will render even greater performances. FireWire drives are quite nice as well, if you can spare your arm and leg over its purchase or if you are also doing video editing. My advice on this is to evaluate your needs for the next six months and make an educated decision based on those needs. Six months from now, drives will be cheaper, the technology will evolve, and you will be able to re-evaluate your needs then.

If your E-IDE hard drive uses DMA or Ultra DMA (UDMA) technology, you should enable this option in your system configuration to improve its performance. You should, in fact, stay away from any drive that does not support DMA for digital audio recording. This affects, among other things, the MIDI-to-audio timing.

To activate the DMA setting for your hard drive:

1. Right-click on your desktop the My Computer icon.
2. Select Properties from the drop-down menu.
3. Click on the Devices Manager tab in the Properties dialog box.
4. Click on the little plus sign (+) next to Disk Drive and select the proper disk drive.
5. Select Properties at the bottom of the dialog box.
6. Select the Settings tab in the drive's dialog box.
7. Check the DMA checkbox option to activate the DMA capabilities of your drive.

Figure 2.12
If your drive does not support the DMA setting, this box will not appear. This is the case for older drives or for SCSI devices.

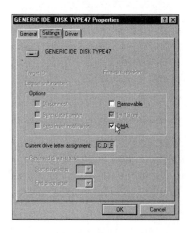

Video Display Adapters

Chances are, if you have a PCI video card and a PCI audio card, you might have some clicks and crackles once in a while in your sound as you are moving a window or as the screen refreshes. This is interference caused by the video card. Your display adapters use a fair amount of system resources. There are ways to improve this performance, just by changing some settings for your display that will not affect the way you are used to working on other applications. You might also want to stay away from very fast gaming cards and video adapters with TV inputs and outputs, since they are known to cause timing problems. If you are using an AGP card, you have less chance of running into this problem, but here are some tips regarding video display optimization:

▶ Remove the screen saver option. If you know you are going to be away from the computer for a while, simply turn your monitor off. Screen saver activities may cause glitches during playback or recording as they kick in to access system resources.

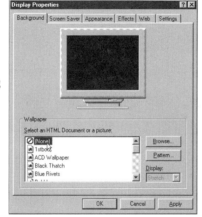

Figure 2.13
Tweaking your video display settings is a good way to free up some computer resources without disturbing your working habits or uninstalling software.

▶ If you have a PCI video card (it doesn't make much difference if you're using an AGP video card), reduce the graphic acceleration by changing the graphic settings in your system's performances. To access this panel, right-click on My Computer, select Properties, select the Performance Tab, then click on the Graphics button. Bring down the sliding cursor one notch to the left and restart your computer (Figure 2.14). If this doesn't solve the problem, repeat step by step until the acceleration is completely disabled. If the problem still exists, fully reenable acceleration. Graphic acceleration on a PCI card is by the video display adapter, but sometimes this can cause glitches in other peripherals if the display adapter is working too close or near its full potential all the time.

▶ Reduce the amount of color display to 16-bit or even 8-bit if you don't use your computer for anything else but digital audio. You can do this by right-clicking on your desktop and selecting the Properties option at the bottom of the list. Then, select the Settings tab and reduce the colors to 256.

http://www.muskalipman.com

▶ Remove any wallpaper images from your computer's desktop. They may personalize your computer, but they also take some space in your memory. Take space, bad; free space, gooooood!

Figure 2.14
The Advanced Video Settings dialog box.

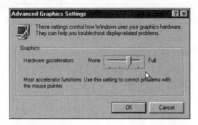

TIP

The graphic acceleration of a PCI graphic card can hinder performance when you are using audio-intensive applications; this is why the graphic acceleration can be brought down a bit. If your sound still crackles when the display is being refreshed, try bringing it down one step lower. Repeat the test until you have no more crackle or until you reach the point where you have no graphic acceleration. If it still crackles, the video card is not your problem!

Hooking Up Your Equipment

There are many ways to hook up your equipment to your computer, and it all depends on what you want to do and what type of equipment you wish to hook up. On this topic, there are two major problems you want to avoid:

1. Having too much sound, what is normally called a feedback loop.
2. Having no sound at all.

The following diagrams represent simple, yet effective, ways to hook up your equipment. Obviously, there are many more combinations, and you should try drawing out one for your own studio to help you organize your wiring effectively.

The first diagram shows a very modest MIDI setup, using the audio outputs of the keyboard to feed the self-amplified speakers. An alternative to this, especially if you want to record the MIDI coming out of your keyboard into a digital format, is to hook up the audio outputs of your keyboard to the inputs of your sound card and the outputs of your sound card to the inputs of your speakers. The way the diagram is shown, this allows you to use the sound card's input for an acoustic instrument or a microphone. Remember that microphones have a low impedance output (microphone inputs) and that, normally, your sound card's inputs are high impedance (line inputs). You will probably need a microphone pre-amplifier if you wish to use it in this way and avoid using the microphone inputs on a sound card.

The MIDI input of the keyboard would go in the MIDI output of the computer, and the MIDI output of the keyboard would go in the MIDI input of the computer.

The way you connect your audio outputs depends on the audio system at hand. If you have powered monitors, you would hook up the audio outputs of your computer or keyboard directly to them, sending the left signal to the left speaker and the right signal to the right speaker. If you are using an amplifier, you would do basically the same thing, but you would send the signal to the amplifier first, then distribute the audio signal from the amplifier to the speakers.

Figure 2.15
Simple setup without any mixer for a single-source monitoring.

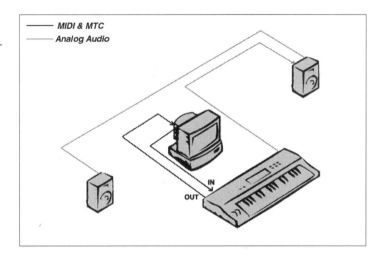

In the second diagram, a small desktop mixer has been added. This will be necessary if you are using more than one audio source (in this case, the keyboard and sound module). This way, you can have as many audio sources as your mixer has inputs. You then feed the output of your mixer into your computer. This can be a bit tricky if you have only one set of outputs on your desktop mixer. Most desktop mixers will have a different volume control for monitoring and master outputs. You should take the audio outputs of the computer and feed them into a separate pair of inputs that can be routed to a signal path that doesn't go back into itself (in this case, the computer), like a tape return, for example. If you have direct outputs or buses on your mixer, use those to send the signal to your computer rather than using the main outputs. This way, you can monitor independently the sound going to the computer and the sound coming from the computer without having the computer go back into the mix.

Notice that the MIDI Thru of the keyboard is used to echo the output of the computer into the sound module.

http://www.muskalipman.com

Figure 2.16
Simple setup with a desktop mixer for multiple-source monitoring.

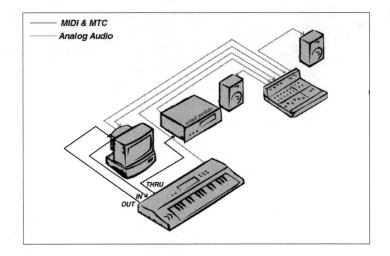

The third diagram shows a setup using a multiple input/output sound card without the use of a mixer. This would allow you to use the Cubase mixer as a mixing table. This is not the most flexible way to work, but if you are on a budget and can't afford a mixer, it's a good compromise.

You need to send all the audio outputs to separate audio inputs on the sound card and a pair of outputs from the sound card to speakers for monitoring. A MIDI patch bay has been added to help with the MIDI patching, but this is not necessary. To remove the MIDI patch bay from this setup, you will need to send the MIDI Thru of your keyboard to the MIDI In of the sound module and the MIDI Thru of the sound module to the MIDI In of the drum machine, making the keyboard and computer front and center in your MIDI routing.

Figure 2.17
Setup for a MIDI studio using a MIDI patch bay and multiple input sound card without any mixer.

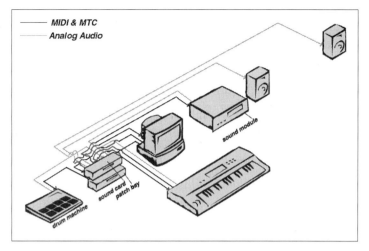

The fourth, and final, diagram shows a setup using a simple digital in/out sound card that feeds and receives information through digital transfer from the digital mixer. As in the second diagram, you might want to utilize an extra pair of audio outputs to monitor the output of your computer without sending it back into the signal of the mixer, once again creating a feedback loop.

Figure 2.18
Setup for a MIDI or audio studio using a digital mixer and a sound card providing digital inputs and outputs.

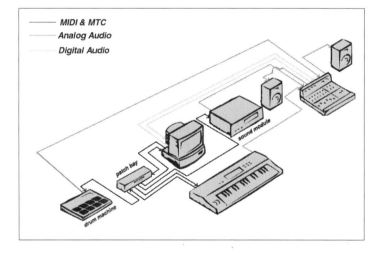

http://www.muskalipman.com

Backing Up and Folder Management

Let's discuss the art of saving files and folders in case something goes wrong. Yes, it is an art. Why so? Because it takes as much dedication as art does, and most people think it's useless anyway—until their system crashes in the middle of a session and their clients realize they don't have any way of getting back these precious performances.

There are two kinds of computer users: those who have lost information and those who will lose information. So, backing up your information on CD-Rs, removable media drives, DAT tapes, or any other kind of safety should not be an option for you—it should be mandatory.

The easiest and probably most affordable way to make backups is by saving your files to a CD-R. To do this effectively, you have to be organized and know where all your material is. That's why you have to establish a system when recording MIDI and digital audio information for your projects.

One way of doing this is by creating a different folder for each project or client. If your project includes different songs or tracks, you can then create sub-folders for every song in your project folder. Finally, you can create a sub-folder for MIDI, comments (text files that contain notes on the project and so on), and audio data, and a third one for your final mixes. This way, all your material is neatly placed and easily retrievable in case your hard disk decides to go south.

When you record digital audio, Cubase will always ask you where you want to save your files, either when you create a new song file or when you enable an audio track for recording.

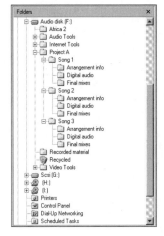

Figure 2.19
You can use Windows Explorer in Windows or Launcher in Macintosh to create additional folders and sub-folders to store your information.

3
Navigating the Arrange Window

Now that you have Cubase installed and running correctly, it's time to delve into *using* it. The heart of Cubase is the Arrange window, which is the main window that appears when you launch Cubase. The Arrange window is customizable, so it might look different from the one displayed in Figure 3.1, but the areas and type of information you will find here remain the same for all arrangements.

Understanding how the Arrange window works and what you can do in it is crucial to your work in Cubase VST—that's why I'm going to spend an entire chapter making sure you understand all the nuances associated with it. Anything you do outside this window (but inside Cubase) will always be reflected in some way in the Arrange window. It might not appear at first glance, but it will certainly affect its behavior. For example, if you delete a file in another window, such as the audio pool, it will show up in the Arrange window if the audio part you deleted in the pool is used in the arrangement. If you change a MIDI channel, that change will be reflected in the Arrange window. It is your main working area.

Let's start by looking at different parts of the Arrange window (see Figure 3.1 on the following page), examining what they do, and learning how you can use them to not only monitor your work but also to make sure your arrangements sound the way you want them to.

Figure 3.1
The Arrange window.

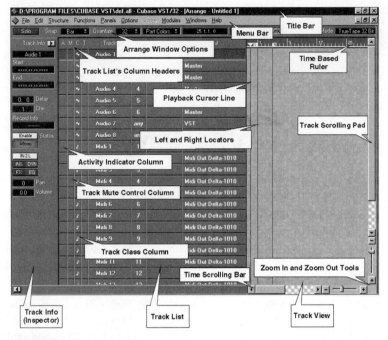

The Arrange window is organized into three main sections:

▶ **Track Info**—Also known as the Inspector, this area displays a selected track's setting information. It can be collapsed, so if you don't see it, click on the arrow in the lower left corner of the Arrange window. The Track Information area offers not only valuable information for each track but information about selected parts within that track as well. It adjusts itself depending on the selected track in the Track View or Track List pane. If no parts in the active track are selected, this area will show you the Track properties. On the other hand, if a part *is* selected, the information that will appear in the Track Info area will reflect the selected part instead of the whole track. When you click on the arrow next to the Part Info title (see Figure 3.2), the expanded functions appear as in the right portion of this figure.

Figure 3.2
The left side of the figure shows the normal track info area of a selected part on a MIDI track.

- **Track List**—The center area of the Arrange window displays a summary list of all your tracks. You can customize the Track List area to reveal more information about each track, such as Track Classes, MIDI activity, Mute, Channel, and Instrument assignment. You can also stretch this area by dragging its right edge to the right or hide it by dragging the right edge to the left. You add tracks by double-clicking in an empty space in this area, delete tracks by selecting them and pressing the Delete key on your keyboard, and move tracks by dragging tracks above or below their current position in the Track List area. Finally, you can copy tracks (including all the parts on that track) by holding the Alt key down when you drag a track to move it.
- **Track View**—The right area of the Arrange window displays parts that you record or import to the arrangement. Double-clicking on these parts will open up the appropriate editing window corresponding to the part's events. You can also use this area to move or copy parts and assign parts to different tracks.

Above these sections, spanning across all the regions, are the Arrange window options. These let you control global settings for the arrangement. So, let's look at this a little bit before you start working.

Configuring the Arrange Window Options

The area above the Track Info, Track List, and Track View areas of the Arrange window gives you control over how parts can move in your arrangement once they are recorded with the Snap option and how they will be recorded when enabling the Auto Quantize (the AQ button on the Transport bar) feature using the Quantize options. The Part Colors option will help you to group certain types of parts from others by assigning them specific colors. Basically, the settings in this area of the Arrange window affect all the tracks in your arrangement, including the Solo button, which mutes all tracks except the one that is currently selected. Other tools in this area help you when working on arrangements.

Snap

The Snap function allows you to create a virtual magnetic grid in the Track View, using the Ruler as a guide and the drop-down menu as a precision selection tool. When using the Snap option, you can draw or you can move a part that will snap to the selected value. Imagine that every subdivision of a beat has the potential of becoming a magnet. When you turn the Snap option on and select a Snap value, that beat, sub-beat, or bar becomes magnetized. So, when you insert or move a part after the Snap option is turned on, the part will "snap" only to these values. It is important to understand that the placement of a part is restricted to its beginning (left side). A part will not snap at its ending. Let's say, for example, you set the Snap value to Bar. If you decide to draw a part, you will be able to draw only a part that is the length of one bar or several entire bars. Selecting the Snap value 1/2, meanwhile, will allow you to draw a part of a length that can be divided by half bars (for example, half a bar, a bar, a bar and a half, and so on).

Figure 3.3
The Snap option drop-down menu.

To turn the Snap option off, simply select Off from the drop-down menu. The next five values—Bar, 1/2, 1/4, 1/8, and 1/16—refer to bar and measure subdivisions, where Bar would snap to every bar, 1/2 would snap to every half note, and so on. These options work only when your Time Ruler display is set to use Bars and Beats. The last two options—Frame and Second—work when your Time Ruler display is set to SMPTE time display (Hours:Minutes:Seconds:Frames). Note that the Snap value continues to work even if you choose the time display, and events will still snap to Meter values assigned in the Snap field. You can toggle your Time Ruler between Bars and Beats and SMPTE by clicking in the Time Display Ruler or in the field that displays your cursor's position, which is located to the right of the Part Colors option.

TIP
If you are working with video and are synchronizing to timecode, you might need to change the SMPTE time format for your arrangement. To change the SMPTE format, select Synchronization from the Options menu and change the value in the field called Frame Rate.

Quantize

Quantizing information means that you set a virtual grid to which notes or events cling. When you are recording MIDI information, your notes might be recorded a little bit before or a little bit after a beat. This is done because humans are not as steady and consistent as the timing in Cubase. Sometimes this is a good thing, and sometimes it isn't. So, when you want to make sure that everything falls into place, or falls exactly on the beat, you can use the quantize function to nudge MIDI events to their closest quantize value. For example, if you set your quantize value to 4, every note you record when playing on your keyboard will cling to the closest quarter note in the bar where you recorded your MIDI information. Setting your quantizing value higher will split the grid into more subdivisions for each bar in your arrangement.

Quantizing MIDI events affects the way MIDI events are played back, but it does not affect your recorded material; thus, it is not changed permanently unless you apply the Freeze Quantize function found in the Functions menu. Try experimenting with it by setting a quantize value, listening to it, then undoing it if you don't like the result. Repeat with other quantize values until you find the one that is appropriate for your arrangement. The Undo Quantize keyboard shortcut is "U." Remember this one—it'll come in handy when you are testing different Quantize modes and values.

To activate Quantizing when you record, you must activate the Auto Quantize button on the Transport bar. This is done by activating the AQ button. Once activated, every note you record will be automatically quantized to the value set in your Arrange window's Quantize field. Remember that quantizing information while recording can be helpful if you have a hard time keeping up with the beat and wish to have a very precise recording. It does take the human feel out of a performance, however.

Figure 3.4
When you click on the Quantize option field in the Arrange window option bar, the Quantize While Recording values appear.

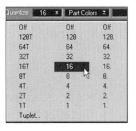

Figure 3.4 shows three columns in the quantize drop-down menu. Each column represents different quantize settings:

- ▶ The first column lets you quantize to tuplets. Tuplets are uneven subdivisions of beats. The most common tuplet would be three, where each quantize value would represent one third of a beat. This is good for a swing feel or waltz song, because it divides each beat in three, which is common to these musical styles.

- ▶ The center column represents straight quantize. This means that your quantize value will always be divisible by two—half notes, quarter notes, eighth notes, sixteenth notes, and so on. Most mainstream music uses this type of quantizing value.

▶ The third column is for dotted note quantize. Dotted notes are typically equal to a straight quantize and a half; for example, a quarter note and a half. Ragtime and some classical music genres use this type of rhythm, although usually a quantizing value will not be used on all notes but, rather, on certain lines in a song or arrangement. The keyboard shortcuts to change the quantize value are the numbers on your QWERTY keyboard, where 1 is a whole note, 2 a half note, and so on. Pressing the period changes to dotted values and T to triplets.

Part Colors

Figure 3.5 shows you a simple little option that lets you define colors for each part in the Arrange window's Track View section by clicking on the Part Colors option. If this item is checked, the files and segments will be displayed with the colors of their respective parts. You can click on a part or select a track, then use one of the colors in the Part Colors option to apply it to your selection. Although adding colors to parts might help you in organizing your events on tracks, they will not add anything to the events because they are merely visual references.

Figure 3.5
The Part Colors drop-down menu.

This option can be very useful when working with many tracks. You can group tracks by color or assign a name to each color so that you know what is what later on. For example, your rhythm section can be different shades of green, your wind section different shades of blue, and so on.

To create your own custom colors and associated color names:

1. Click on the Edit option at the bottom of the Part Colors option drop-down menu.
2. Select a color to edit in the Part Colors area.
3. Type in a new name for that color, as shown in Figure 3.6.

Figure 3.6
In your Arrangement window's Track View section, you can customize colors and add names to reflect what each color should represent.

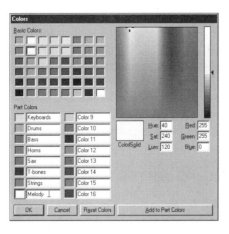

4. If you wish to change the default color, change the color using the color picker option.
5. Repeat the previous steps for another color if you want to create more custom colors and associated names.
6. Click OK when you are done.

Now that you have created custom colors and part names associated with these colors, you can use these with parts in your arrangement. To assign a color to your part, select the part and then select from the Part Colors drop-down menu one of the Part Colors you have just created.

Markers

Markers are used to define different sections of your arrangement and make it easy to go back to that section later in your work. The Marker option is separated into two functions: The button labeled Marker allows you to reveal the saved regions right above the Time Ruler (as shown in Figure 3.7), and the arrow beside it reveals a list of saved markers (or regions). Cubase treats the markers as a beginning point and an end point of a region, using the left and right locators as region boundaries.

Figure 3.7
The Marker button reveals the regions created previously and allows you to create new regions.

The second function of the Marker option lets you pick and move to an existing marker within your project. Selecting a marker from a saved list moves the left and right locators to these coordinates in time. If you enable the Loop Playback function, as shown in the Transport bar header later in this chapter, it will move the playback line to the beginning marker (or left locator) and play until it reaches the end marker (or right locator) for that region, looping this region until you select another Marker setting from your previously created Marker list. Figure 3.8 shows me picking a marker named Verse 1. Note that if you click on the measure listing rather than on the name of the region, the playback line will move to that bar. The left and right locators will remain in their current positions. This is helpful when the markers are set for the entire song, or even for another area, and you want to start playback from an area before the locators.

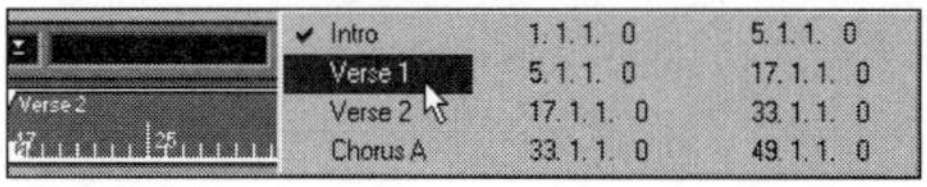

Figure 3.8
You can navigate easily using the region markers by selecting them from the drop-down menu.

To create a region using markers:

1. Press the Marker button. The Region display bar appears over the Time Ruler display.
2. With your left mouse button, click on the Time Ruler where you want your region marker to begin.
3. Now, click with the right mouse button in the Time Ruler where you want your region marker to end.
4. Click with your left mouse button in the space near the beginning of your region. When the white box appears, type in the name you wish to give your region.

Once you've created markers, you can use the arrow next to the Marker button and select it from the menu (see Figure 3.8). Cubase will move to that marker and set the left and right locators to this region. The playback line will not move from its current position when you change your locator position this way. It must be moved to the left locator after selecting the region to play from that position, since it does not automatically move to the left locator. Pressing 1 on the numeric keypad will move the Playback cursor to the left locator. Also, pressing Alt+P will move your left and right locator to the beginning and ending of the selected Marker region.

To edit region markers:

1. Press on the Marker button to reveal the Region display area over the Time Ruler display.
2. Right-click anywhere except on the Time Ruler display and hold your mouse button down. A toolbox will appear.
3. Select the Pencil tool, shown in Figure 3.9.
4. Drag the beginning or the end of the region you wish to modify to the new desired length.

Figure 3.9
Use the Pencil tool from the toolbox (top of figure) and then modify your region (bottom of figure).

To erase a region marker:

1. Press on the Marker button to reveal the Region display area over the Time Ruler display.
2. Right-click anywhere except on the Time Ruler display and hold your mouse button down. A toolbox will appear.
3. Select the Eraser tool. This looks like an eraser in your toolbox and is next to the Selection tool.
4. Click on the region's name you wish to erase.

Link Editors

The Link Editors button allows you to select a part and have it displayed in the editing window. Selecting another part will update the editing window by placing the newly selected part in it. Instead of having to double-click on a part to open its edit window, close the window and then double-click on a second part to open its edit window again. This function is called Link Editors, because it links the selected part in the Arrange window to the editing window.

To use the Link Editors button, click it to enable it. Then, double-click the part you wish to edit and select another part in the Arrange window to load this part in the edit window. You can modify all the parts of the same type through the associated editing window. If you want to edit audio parts after editing MIDI parts, you will have to close the editing window for the MIDI part first and then open the audio part's editing window. From that point on, you proceed in the same way; clicking on audio parts in your Arrange window will load the audio part in its associated editing window, and clicking on other audio parts in the Arrange window will refresh the editing window with the newly selected audio part.

Record Mode

The next Arrange window option you can control is the Record mode. Record mode lets Cubase know whether the arrangement or song file will use 16-, 24-, or 32-bit recording mode for its audio content. If you are using Cubase VST or Cubase VST score, you will have two choices here: 16-bit or 24-bit recording. If you are using Cubase VST/32, you will have two additional choices: 32-bit and 32-bit TrueTape recording. All audio files in a song or an arrangement will thereafter use this bit depth to record and playback audio.

- ▶ **16-bit recording** is compatible with every sound card and uses 2 bytes of information for each recorded sample.
- ▶ **24-bit recording** is compatible with 24-bit capable sound cards only. This format uses 3 bytes of information to store each recorded sample. Note that certain 20-bit cards might work in 24-bit mode. Check your manufacturer's documentation before trying it to make sure of what is supported and how it handles the information.
- ▶ **32-bit recording** is compatible with 24-bit capable sound cards only. This format uses 4 bytes of information to store each recorded sample.
- ▶ **32-bit TrueTape recording** is compatible with 16- and 24-bit-capable sound cards. Like the standard 32-bit recording, it uses 4 bytes of information to store each recorded sample. This format simply adds floating point information to the file. TrueTape also enables you to use the VST TrueTape panel in the Panel menu. This will allow you to add a tape saturation effect by increasing the level of your input without creating any digital clipping.

NOTE
Remember that using 24-bit recording uses 1.5 times more space than a 16-bit recording and that a 32-bit recording uses twice the space of a 16-bit recording. Make sure you have enough space on your hard disk when starting your project.

The Transport Bar

The Transport bar is a multitask floating bar that allows you to scroll through your arrangement, set recording modes, set cycling mode for playback and recording, and see what tempo the song is playing at or its time signature. Finally, it allows you to monitor MIDI activity, as shown in Figure 3.10.

To view or hide the Transport bar, select Show or Hide Transport Bar from the Window menu or press the F12 key on your keyboard. To center the Transport bar on your screen, you can also press Ctrl+Shift+Alt+F12. This section steps you through the options available on the Transport bar.

Figure 3.10
The Transport Bar.

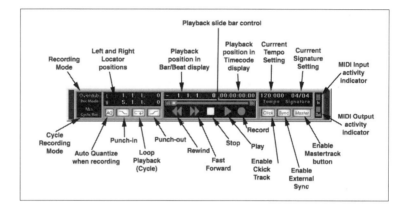

Cycle Recording

The Cycle Recording option works best when you are recording in Cycle mode. To activate Cycle mode, press the Cycle button. Each time the loop starts over at the left locator mark, this is called a lap; as runners finish their lap around the track, you do the same and start another one.

 Cycle Recording operates differently when recording MIDI than it does when recording audio. If you are recording MIDI information, you may use one of four modes: Mix, Add, Normal, and Punch. These four modes can be selected by clicking on the Transport bar over the Cycle Rec section, as shown in Figure 3.11, and apply only when recording MIDI.

Figure 3.11
Clicking over the Cycle Rec section in the Transport bar toggles between the different cycle recording modes.

Here are the differences between each Cycle mode:

- **Mix**—Using Mix mode cycle recording will allow you to add newly played MIDI information each time a lap is recorded onto the already existing information from a preceding lap. For example, you can record the kick of a drum set the first time around, then the snare, and, on the third lap, add the hi-hats. This is by far the most common cycle recording mode you will use when building percussion or drum tracks. Each time you start a new lap, the additional information will be added to the previous information in the same track.

- **Add**—On the other hand, if you want to try different things but not add them on the same track, you can use the Add cycle record mode. This does the same thing as the Mix mode, but instead of mixing all the MIDI information on the same track, it adds a MIDI track with the same properties as the first track every time it starts a new lap, as shown in the Figure 3.12.

Figure 3.12
When you use the Add Cycle Rec mode, it will create a new track for every lap it records, renaming each lap with a Take number (tk1, tk2, tk3, etc.).

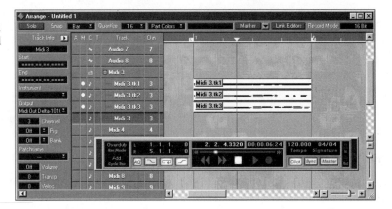

- **Normal**—This recording mode allows you to start fresh every time a lap is completed, removing what you previously recorded before you begin a new lap. You might want to use this if you are trying to get a live feel for a difficult part and repeat the section until you get it right. Otherwise, using the Add mode gives you the flexibility of selecting the "best of" from different takes. It is up to you to decide which mode works best.

- **Punch**—This mode will delete what you had recorded in a previous lap as soon as you start playing in Punch mode. This function works best when the cycle recording mode is not active.

To effectively use the Cycle Rec and Punch modes:

1. Select the Punch option from Cycle Rec.
2. Deactivate the Cycle Recording button, as shown in Figure 3.13.
3. Set the left locator on the Transport bar where you want the punch-in to occur and your right locator where you want the punch-out to occur. When you press the Record button on the Transport bar, Cubase will start playing the arrangement and will automatically start recording only when it hits the left locator and will go back to playback mode when it passes the right locator.
4. Activate the Punch-in button and the Punch-out button on the Transport bar (see Figure 3.10).
5. Position your cursor where you want the playback to begin and start the playback.

In Figure 3.13, the playback begins at Bar 1, Beat 1; the punch-in (or recording) occurs at Bar 2, Beat 1, and punch-out (or back to playback mode) at Bar 3, Beat 1 on Track MIDI 3.tk3. Notice that both the Punch-in and Punch-out buttons are selected on the Transport bar (each sides of the Cycle Recording button).

Figure 3.13
The Punch Cycle Rec mode at work with all the settings on the Transport bar.

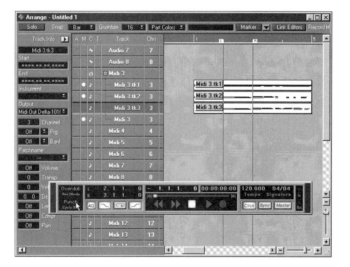

While recording using any of the Cycle Rec modes found on the Transport bar, you can click on the Cycle Rec area (see Figure 3.14) to display a menu with four additional options. These are Key Erase, Delete Sub Track, Delete Last Version, and Quantize Last Ver. Note that if you stop the recording, this menu will no longer be available. You have to be recording, preferably in cycles, for this menu to appear.

Figure 3.14
The option menu found while recording in Punch mode option.

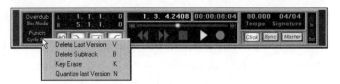

Key Erase is useful when you want to erase certain keys you just played by mistake. Let's say you are recording a drum track—C1 is your kick, D1 is your snare, and F#1 is your hi-hat. While playing, you accidentally played on the C#1 and G#1 keys. While still recording, press on those two keys (C#1 and G#1) and then select the Key Erase option from Cycle Rec. There you go: The C#1 and G#1 keys are gone from your recording.

To illustrate the three other options here, let's take another look at Figure 3.12. If you select the Delete Sub Track as you are recording one of the laps in cycle recording, it will delete all the information you just recorded in that lap but leave it available for you to edit or add notes to later on in that take. In Figure 3.12, this would mean that the part called "Midi 3.tk3" would not exist, but the track would still be there. Delete Last Version will allow you to delete everything you did during the last lap where you recorded something. In Figure 3.12, that would be the track after "Midi 3.tk3." Finally, using the Quantize Last Version option will quantize everything you recorded in the last take you recorded, leaving every other take unquantized.

Recording Mode

The Recording mode, or Rec mode, on the Transport bar allows you to set one of two recording modes when recording audio or MIDI information: Replace and Overdub. Both of these modes work when recording in either Cycle mode (in loop mode, the Cycle button is active) or normal mode (in nonlooping mode, the Cycle button is disabled). In Cycle mode, Cubase plays the arrangement from the left indicator to the right indicator, then loops back. What happens to the recorded information when it loops back depends on the recording mode found over the Rec mode area in the toolbar.

If you are in Replace mode, it replaces what was previously recorded by what you are about to record the second or third time around. When in Overdub mode, it keeps what you had recorded in the previous run and creates another recording, adding to the same part the second and third time around, or for any number of times you record over this section.

Here's an example. You are in Replace mode and have set your recording to cycle between the left and right locator. You play a kick drum until the playback line hits the right locator and starts over again at the left locator. Now, you play the snare until it reaches the right locator again. You stop the recording. Because you were in Replace mode, your kick drum has been replaced by the snare. If you repeat the same exercise in Overdub mode, you would have both the kick and the snare playing in the recorded part. Because the Replace mode replaces the recording every time the playback line returns to the left locator, you should use the Replace mode with great precaution. It is easy to forget that you are in Replace mode and erase previously recorded information for a track without realizing it. Since Cubase does not have multiple undo and redo functions, it might be hard to go back to a previous state after a couple of edits like this.

Start and End Play Locators

These are also called Left and Right locators, and they represent the beginning and end of a region when in Cycle mode. If you are not in Cycle mode, they don't influence anything. To move one of these locators, you can either click with your left mouse button on the Time Ruler to change the left locator point and the right mouse button to move the right locator point, as shown in Figure 3.15; or you can enter a numerical value in the field to the right of the "L" or "R" option on the Transport bar by double-clicking on the number and entering the desired location, as shown in Figure 3.16.

For example, entering the number "5" would set the locator to Bar 5, Beat 1. Cubase assumes that if you don't enter a beat and click value, you want to get the first beat of the bar number you entered. If you do want to go to another beat or click value, you must enter them as they would appear in the locator; for example, 5.3.119. You can also left- or right-click on a number to decrease or increase it to the next value in the bar and beat. To start your playback at any of these locations later on, simply click on the letter of the locator position (either L or R) on the Transport bar and Cubase will jump to that location in the timeline. You may also use the keyboard shortcuts: Press the "1" key on the numeric keypad to move your playback line to the Left locator and the "2" key to move it to the Right locator.

Figure 3.15
Move locator points by clicking in the Time Ruler bar.

Figure 3.16
Move locator points by editing the Transport bar locator field.

TIP
You can reverse the locators, putting the Right locator before the Left. Using this with the Cycle mode active will allow you to skip the area between the locators. Here's an example: Position your Left locator at Bar 9.1.000 and your Right locator at 5.1.000. Enable the Cycle Playback/Record mode button on your Transport bar and move your playback line to the beginning of the song. Now, press Play. Cubase will play the song from the beginning up until Bar 5.1.000, then skip to Bar 9.1.000, and continue playing. This is very useful when you want to preview what a Global Cut edit (removing bars found between these two locators) would sound like.

The actual Start position and current location of the playback line are displayed on the Transport bar, right above the Transport bar's controls (see Figure 3.10). The left value over the controls represents the playback position in Bars:Beats:Ticks value. The right value indicates the playback position in Hours:Minutes:Seconds:Frames format.

Transport Controls

The controls in Cubase are similar to any controls on a regular recording machine: Rewind, Stop, Play, Record, and Fast Forward. Above these controls is a slider that plays two main roles. First, it provides you with an idea of where you are in the arrangement, and second, the controls allow you to click and drag the slider bar's handle to anywhere you want while playing to move your playback line to that location. There is one little thing that this control panel has that a normal tape deck doesn't have: keyboard shortcuts.

Cubase uses the numeric keypad of your computer as a control panel, making use of almost all the numbers and symbols in the numeric keypad. Below is a breakdown of these shortcuts. Remembering them will help you effectively control your playback instead of using your mouse to stop, play, or enable record all the time. Note that the numbers refer only to the number keys on your numeric keypad, not to the numbers above your "qwerty" keyboard.

Table 3.1
Keyboard Shortcuts on Numeric Keypad for the Transport control panel and some locator shortcuts.

Function	Numeric Keypad
Stop	0 or Spacebar
Play	Enter
Rewind	PageUp
Fast Rewind	Shift+PageUp
Fast Forward	PageDown
Really Fast Forward	Shift+PageDown

Activate Recording	*
Go To Left Locator	1
Set Position To Left Locator	Shift+1
Go To Right Locator	2
Set Position To Right Locator	Shift+2
Increase Tempo	+
Decrease Tempo	–
Toggle Cycle mode	/
Store Locator Points	Shift+3 to 9
Recall Locator Points	3 to 9

If you can remember these simple shortcuts, you will be able to easily navigate through your arrangement without having to aim your mouse at the button on the Transport bar.

Tempo Settings

The tempo setting displayed on the Transport bar shows you the tempo value that the arrangement will play at when the Master Track button is not enabled or, if you enable the Master Track button, it will show you the current tempo of the Master Track. This allows you to record your material at a tempo at which you feel comfortable playing. It also allows you to hear your arrangement played without tempo changes that could make recording new events a little more difficult. When you want to hear the arrangement played at the speed at which it should be played, you simply click on the Master Track to set the correct playback speed. We will be covering the Master Track later in this chapter.

To increase or decrease the tempo on the Transport bar, simply left-click on the tempo itself to decrease and right-click to increase the speed. You can also nudge the tempo with the numeric keypad's plus and minus keys. You can see the tempo setting area in Figure 3.10. If this is too slow for you, double-click in the field and type the value you wish to enter. Note that if you click on one of the decimal values in the tempo, the increments will be smaller. For example, if you left-click on the second decimal, the value will decrease by one hundredth of a beat. This is, on the other hand, not true for the integer value. To increase or decrease the tempo by 10 beats per minute at a time, you have to shift-click or shift-right-click on the value. Again, as an example, shift+left-clicking on a tempo of 76 would reduce it to 66.

The Master Track

The Master Track is a special hidden track that holds your tempo changes, key signatures, and hitpoints, which are nifty little reference points that you can use to synchronize audio, MIDI, and time reference elements found in video. So, if you are working on a movie project and need to create a score for a scene with musical elements that should lock with visual elements, these hitpoints can be aligned automatically with bars and beats to make your life a little easier. We will get back to this in Chapter 12 when discussing methods of working with synchronized video.

All the tempo changes that you make in the Master Track List or Graphic Master Track editing window will play back when you activate the Master Track button on the Transport bar. However, the time signature will be heard even if the button is not activated. This is logical, since your time signature needs to be activated in order for MIDI elements to lock with bars and beats throughout the arrangement.

You can view the Master Track List editing window by selecting it from the Edit Menu, and you can access the Master Track Graphical editing window in the same menu or by double-clicking on the Master Track button, as shown in Figure 3.17.

Figure 3.17
The Master Track Graphical editing window.

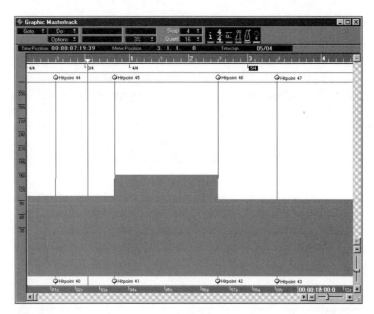

To change the tempo in the Master Track:

1. Select List Master Track from the Edit menu. The List Master Track editing window appears.
2. Double-click on the current tempo value in the Value column, as shown in Figure 3.18.
3. Type in the new tempo value.
4. Close the window and activate your Master Track button.

To add a new tempo change, time signature, time, or meter hitpoint (we'll get into that in Chapter 12) in this window, you can select the appropriate event you wish to add from the first drop-down menu, position your playback line at the desired location, and click the In button found on the toolbar, next to the Event Type selection (where you choose which type of event you want to add).

If your Master Track is set to a different tempo, you should see the tempo toggle from one setting to another when activating or deactivating the Master Track button on the Transport bar.

Figure 3.18
Adjusting the tempo in the List Master Track window.

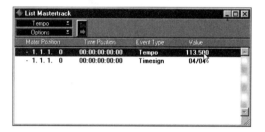

Signature Settings

The signature setting located to the right of your Transport bar allows you to view the signature setting for the current location of the playback line. If you want to simply change the setting for the whole arrangement, you can double-click on the setting and type in the new value. On the other hand, if you want to add a different signature setting or change this setting—let's say, at Bar 55—you need to use the List Master Track editing window found in the Edit menu.

To add or change a setting using the List Master Track window:

1. Launch the List Master Track window from the Edit menu.
2. From the List Master Track window, select Time Signature, located in the first drop-down menu in the upper left corner of the window. This menu contains the elements that you can add to the Master Track.
3. Using the Transport bar, position your playback line in the bar where you want to add a signature change. You can also use the playback line's current location indicator on the Transport bar and double-click the field to enter the desired location of the insert. You can modify your time later by double-clicking in the Time Position column for the desired signature.

4. Click the Insert button (or In button), as shown in Figure 3.19. Cubase will add a time signature with the same value as the previous time signature at the first beat of the bar you selected. You can't add a time signature change in the middle of a bar.

5. Double-click on the time signature under the Value column to change it, and type the desired signature value.

6. Continue entering signatures if you need to do so, then close the window when done.

Contrary to tempo changes, time signatures are not activated only when the Master Track button is on. They are ALWAYS activated.

Figure 3.19
Entering new time signatures in the List Master Track editing window.

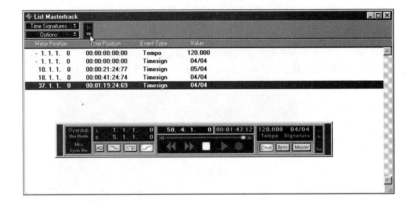

Time signatures are a way to divide music into bars and beats. The upper value above the divider refers to the number of beats in a bar. So, if you have a time signature of 3/4, it means that you have three beats per bar; 7/8 means you have seven beats per bar. The lower value below the divider line refers to the value in length of these beats. So, again, if you have a time signature of 3/4, each of the three beats will last one quarter note. In a 7/8 time signature, each of the seven beats will last for one-eighth of a note.

Here's a little exercise for you: What would a 4/2 represent? Stop reading, and think about it before you continue ... The answer is: You will have four beats, each a half-note in value. Obviously, you can subdivide each beat in subvalues, but the click track will play four clicks for each bar. In a song that plays at 120 bpm (beats per minute), this would be 4 seconds per bar, or one second per beat, whereas a 4/4 bar would last 2 seconds at the same tempo, each beat lasting half a second.

Chances are, if you are into pop, rock, jazz, techno, or any other contemporary style, 95 percent of your tracks will use a 4/4 time signature. But, just for fun, try some unusual time signatures and see if you can come up with an interesting melody or rhythmic line.

MIDI Activity

The MIDI activity display allows you to see if there is any MIDI activity being sent to Cubase or being sent by Cubase to external devices. This is a good way to test your MIDI input and output connections when setting up your system. Note that MIDI metronome information will not be displayed in the MIDI output meter.

If you are not seeing any MIDI activity when sending messages from an external controller, try changing the settings in the MIDI System Setup window available through the Options menu (see Figure 3.20).

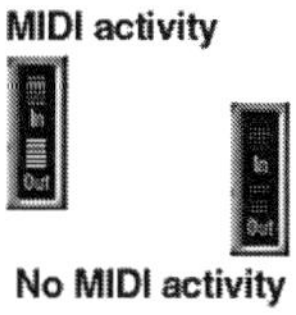

Figure 3.20
The MIDI activity monitor.

If you are not seeing any MIDI activity when playing back messages, chances are there is no MIDI present in your arrangement or coming from the MIDI Input port. To identify a solution to a problem, you first need to isolate the cause. The MIDI activity meter allows you to do this quite well. For example, if your external instruments are not receiving MIDI data, try loading a Virtual Instrument (VST Instrument) and route your MIDI track to that MIDI port. If you hear the MIDI going into the VST Instrument or if you see MIDI activity, your problem is probably somewhere else, such as a MIDI connector, the system setup, or a faulty MIDI interface. If you have previously activated the Multirecord function, found in the Options menu, the MIDI Thru will not work, either. This is not a problem in itself, but rather something to keep in mind when troubleshooting your problem. Another aspect of MIDI Thru to keep in mind is that Cubase will disable it when an audio track is selected.

The Toolboxes

In every editing window, including the Arrange window, you will find a toolbox when you right-click (or option+click on a Mac) somewhere in the appropriate window. Because these tools are important to use if you want to make the most of Cubase, it is important to understand what each icon in the toolset accomplishes.

Following are tables describing each icon for each toolbox and what it does in that particular editing window. Remember that each toolset is available when you right-click (or option+click on a Mac) anywhere in the area of the window where events can be edited:

Table 3.1
The Arrange Window Toolbox.

Tool Icon	Tool Name	Use this tool to:
	Pointer (default tool)	Select events
	Eraser	Erase events
	Speaker	Monitor audio events as a scrubbing tool and trigger tool or monitor MIDI events as a note trigger
	Pencil	Draw events, notes, modify part lengths and controllers
	Scissors	Split parts, notes, audio segments, tied notes
	Mute	Mute selected events
	Match Quantize	Match quantizing points between MIDI and audio events or to scale match MIDI chords
	Zoom	Zoom in or out of a selected area

Tool Icon	Tool Name	Use this tool to:
	Glue Tube	Glue selected parts or selected notes together
	Volume	Change the monitoring volume of a MIDI track without affecting the recorded mix automation
	Transpose	Transpose individual MIDI parts
	Groove	Apply a Groove to a part
	Group Selection	Select parts across tracks by dragging a box and move or copy the selected information
	Pan	Change the monitoring pan of a MIDI track without affecting the recorded mix automation
	Logical	Apply logical presets to parts
	Stretch	Resize a part and make its content fit to the new length

Table 3.2
The Audio Editor Window Toolbox.

Tool Icon	Tool Name	Use this tool to:
	Pointer (default tool)	Select events
	Eraser	Erase events
	Speaker	Monitor audio events as a scrubbing tool and trigger tool or to monitor MIDI events as a note trigger
	Nudge	Move an event to the next snap or quantize value
	Pencil	Draw events, notes, modify part lengths and controllers
	Scissors	Split parts, notes, audio segments, tied notes
	Line Draw	Draw controller lines such as audio fades, velocity changes, and so on
	Mute	Mute selected events

Table 3.3
The Key Edit And List Edit Window Toolbox.

Tool Icon	Tool Name	Use this tool to:
	Pointer (default tool)	Select events
	Eraser	Erase events
	Speaker	Monitor audio events as a scrubbing tool and trigger tool or monitor MIDI events as a note trigger
	Nudge	Move an event to the next snap or quantize value
	Pencil	Draw events, notes, modify part lengths and controllers
	Paint	Paint a series of MIDI notes using the quantizing value as length for all events
	Line Draw	Draw controller lines such as audio fades, velocity changes, and so on
	Mute	Mute selected events

Table 3.4
The Drum Edit Window Toolbox.

Tool Icon	Tool Name	Use this tool to:
	Pointer (default tool)	Select events
	Eraser	Erase events
	Speaker	Monitor audio events as a scrubbing tool and trigger tool or to monitor MIDI events as a note trigger
	Nudge	Move an event to the next snap or quantize value
	Stick	Similar to Pencil tool, but specific to drum tracks. Draw events and notes
	Paint	Paint a series of MIDI notes using the quantizing value as length for all events
	Line Draw	Draw controller lines such as audio fades, velocity changes, and so on
	Mute	Mute selected events

Table 3.5
The Graphical Master Track Window Toolbox.

Tool Icon	Tool Name	Use this tool to:
	Pointer (default tool)	Select events
	Eraser	Erase events
	Pencil	Draw events, notes, modify part lengths and controllers
	Scissors	Split parts, notes, audio segments, tied notes
	Nudge	Move an event to the next snap or quantize value
	Line Draw	Draw controller lines such as audio fades, velocity changes, and so on

Table 3.6
The Score Edit Window Toolbox

Tool Icon	Tool Name	Use this tool to:
	Pointer (default tool)	Select events
	Eraser	Erase events
	Speaker	Monitor audio events as a scrubbing tool and trigger tool or monitor MIDI events as a note trigger
	Note	Insert notes in a score
	Cut Flag	Change the way notes are tied together in a score layout
	Layout	This tool is available only in Page Layout mode of the score. Change the position (layout) of notes in a score
	Nudge	Move an event to the next snap or quantize value
	Scissors	Split parts, notes, audio segments, tied notes
	Rest	Add rests in a score
	Glue Tube	Glue selected parts or selected notes together
	Display Quantize	Add or display quantize values in the score
	Zoom	Zoom in or out of a selected area

Table 3.7
The Controller Edit Window Toolbox.

Tool Icon	Tool Name	Use this tool to:
	Pointer (default tool)	Select events
	Eraser	Erase events
	Pencil	Draw events, notes, modify part lengths and controllers
	Line Draw	Draw controller lines such as audio fades, velocity changes, and so on

Now You Try It

Here are the exercises you will find on the Web site for this chapter:

- ▶ Change the Snap and Quantize value of the Arrange window and move a part to see how these settings affect the changes you make on part positions.
- ▶ Assign different colors to parts.
- ▶ View, add, and edit markers.
- ▶ Modify the Transport bar.
- ▶ Change the locator positions using the Transport bar and the Time Ruler.
- ▶ Change the tempo in the Transport bar.
- ▶ Change the tempo in the List Master Track editor.
- ▶ Change the time signature in the List Master Track editor.

You will find these exercises at **www.muskalipman.com/cubase**.

Simply follow the instructions on the Web site before starting the exercises.

You can refer to this chapter to find out how to do these exercises, but try doing them without peeking first, just to see how comfortable you are with these principles. If you don't remember how to do a task, refer to the appropriate header in this chapter.

You will need to have the Universal Sound Module and the VB-1 VSTi installed on your computer to use the file provided for these exercises. If you do not have these VST instruments installed, you can always use a General MIDI-compatible device, assigning Channel 1 to play a Bass sound, Channel 2 to play a Lead Synth sound, Channel 3 to play a Strings sound, Channel 5 a Piano sound, and Channel 10 to Drums.

4

Setting Up Your MIDI Recording

In the previous chapter, you learned about the different parts of the Arrange window and how they affected your navigation in an arrangement. Here, you are going to look a little more closely at those tools and find out how to use them in a MIDI recording environment. One of these tools is VST Instruments, or VSTi for short.

A decade ago, MIDI sequencers were just that, MIDI sequencers. Then came the integration of sound into sequencers, making them part MIDI sequencer, part hard disk recorder. Now, with Virtual Instruments, Cubase brings a whole new meaning to the term "Virtual Studio Technology" (VST). You see, with virtual instruments, you use the computer to emulate synthesizers and samplers, which normally are external pieces of hardware that you have to purchase separately. This is a great new way for musicians to work on a budget. So, I guess if you've been eating white bread and peanut butter and just plain-sauce spaghetti for the past couple of years to pay for that spiffy-looking synthesizer, you're probably not too happy to see this one coming. Don't get me wrong—working with external sound modules is not on its way out, since they offer a wide range of different sound colors and using VSTi in a live performance might still be a little tricky if you don't like moving your computer and all its peripherals around too much. But if you're on a budget, they're great.

Let's take a look inside to find out more about setting up your MIDI recording session and using these virtual synthesizers to create some music.

http://www.muskalipman.com

Track View

Track View is also known as Part View, because this is where all your parts for each track appear. You've seen in Chapter 3 that you can add colors to the different parts in this view. You can also add a grid to help you align things along each track. To do this, select from the Edit menu Preferences > General. Once in the General Preferences dialog box, click the Arrangement button and then check the Draw Grid option (see Figure 4.1). Note that this grid does not affect your snap or quantize value in any way.

Figure 4.1
The Grid option will add vertical and horizontal lines in your Track View.

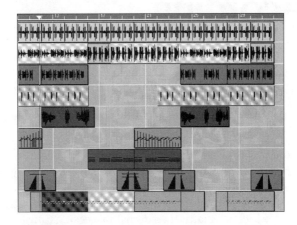

Most editing functions of parts will occur in the Track View. When you right-click in this part of the dialog box, a toolbox will appear showing you a set of tools that were described in Chapter 3. You will use them as we go along. But for now, the most important tool is the Selection tool (the pointing arrow).

On the bottom right corner, you will find two sliders with a little plus and minus sign at each end. These are your vertical and horizontal magnification tools. Use them often to zoom in and zoom out of an area. The keyboard shortcuts for the zoom tools are described in the following table

Table 4.1
Zoom tool keyboard shortcuts.

Shift+H	Zoom in vertically
Shift+G	Zoom out vertically
H	Zoom in horizontally
G	Zoom out horizontally

Track List

This area shows you seven kinds of information for each track: track states, track identification, instrument settings, MIDI routing settings, MIDI filters, part appearance, and Rocket information. To make any of the columns visible or invisible, you can click in the header section of the Track List and a pop-up menu will appear, as shown in Figure 4.2. Check any of the columns you wish to see in your Track List.

Figure 4.2
The Track List column setup pop-up box. Check elements to display them in your Track List.

The following is a short description of the columns you can display in your Track List view.

- **Track Activity**—If events are being played or recorded, activity for a track will be displayed in this column. The header column for this is "A."

- **Mute Enable**—Allows you to mute a track or a series of tracks. When a track is muted, a dot appears in the column. The column header for this is "M." To mute a track, simply click next to that track in the Mute column.

- **Track Class**—Each track can be one of several classes or types of tracks available in Cubase. The two most common are MIDI and Audio. But, as you will discover in the next pages, there are nine classes altogether. The column header for this is "C." To select a class for a track, left-click in the Class column and choose from the drop-down menu.

- **Time Lock**—A track can be time locked, which means that it doesn't matter if you change the tempo setting, because the events on this track will stay locked with time. This is particularly useful when you are working on a score or soundtrack for a movie or visual project. The column header is "T." To time lock a track, click in the track's Time Lock column. A small padlock will appear in that column.

- **Track Name**—This is a name you can give to a track. It's simply a way to identify the content of that track, but it does not affect the content of the track itself. When you give a name to a track, it will appear in the Track Info portion of the Arrange window at the top of the column. The column header is "Track." To enter a name, double-click on the default name that appears in that column and type the name you want.

- **Instrument**—An instrument is a device that Cubase refers to. This can be an external piece of hardware or a VST Instrument. Once you've configured an instrument, you select patch names from the Track Info section, or, if your Instrument column is visible, you can select the instrument from there. The column header is "Instrument." To select an instrument, click in the column for the track to which you wish to add an instrument and select an option from the pop-up menu.
- **Channel**—This is the channel setting for MIDI tracks or audio tracks. The column header is "Chn." To change the channel in the Track List, click in the column for the track you wish to change and select one of the sixteen channels available, or the "any" setting if you wish to record more than one MIDI channel on this track.
- **Output**—Once you have events on a track, you can change the output port of these events. The MIDI and audio track output options depend on your Cubase configuration as mentioned in Chapter 2. The column header is "Out." To change the output of a track, click in the column for the track in which you wish to change outputs and select from the pop-up list that appears.
- **Volume and Pan**—You can adjust the global volume and pan levels using these controls. Obviously, if you add automation later on, these values will change as Cubase reads the mix track. The column headers are "Volume" and "Pan," respectively. To change the volume or pan, click on the slider and move it to the desired position.
- **Patchname**—Like the Instrument column, this is the name of a patch for a designated instrument. The names that appear here will depend on the instrument setup, which will be discussed later in this chapter. The column header is, appropriately, "Patchname." To change or add a patchname, click in the column for the track you wish to modify and select one of the names that appear in the pop-up menu.
- **Program**—Again, if you set up an instrument, program numbers can be entered to send program change values to your instrument. If you haven't programmed an instrument, you can still send a program change using this column, but the numbers that appear here might not correspond to the correct patch number in your instrument. The column header for this one is "Prg." To add or change a program, double-click in the column for the track in which you wish to insert a program number and enter the desired number. You can also left-click or right-click to decrease or increase the value in this field.
- **Transpose**—The Transpose column allows you to transpose all MIDI data for the track or selected part. This transposition will not affect how notes are displayed in your score, but it will redirect notes to the transposed values when sent through the output of your MIDI port. The column header for this information is "Transp." To transpose MIDI events in a track, click in the Transpose column and a little keyboard will appear. By default, the value will be a "C" note. Selecting the "E" key will transpose your events a major third up; selecting the "A" key will transpose your events a minor third down.

- **Velocity**—The velocity value works like the Transpose filter, except that it adds or reduces a fixed value for all notes that are played in the selected MIDI track. For example, if you set your Velocity column for track 8 minus twelve (–12), all MIDI events will play at the velocity they were recorded at −12. This value is relative to the MIDI format, where −127 is the lowest value and +127 is the highest value. The column header for this field is "Vel." To modify the velocity for a track, either double-click in the column for the track you wish to modify and enter the desired amount or left-click to decrease the value and right-click to increase it.

- **Delay**—This is another MIDI filter, which adds a delay time before the MIDI event or makes events play before their actual attack if the value is set to a negative value. This is useful to add feel to a track by offsetting it a bit in relation to other tracks. The values that can be added here will move the actual event by up to two-sixteenths after or before the beat. The column header for this is called Delay. You can't modify this value in the Track List, but you can see if the track is offset or not. To change the value, you will need to enter it in the Track Info section.

- **Length**—The length value is also a MIDI filter that allows you to increase or decrease the length of each MIDI event in a track by a percentage value. The increments go from 25 percent to 200 percent by steps of twenty-five at a time. For example, if you played a series of quarter notes, then changed the length to 200 percent, all notes would play as if they were recorded as half notes. Inversely, if you set the value to 50 percent, every note would play as if you had recorded eighth notes. The column header here is "Len." To change the value of the length field, you can simply left-click to decrease or right-click to increase that value.

- **Banks**—This, as well as patchnames and instruments, refers to how your external or virtual MIDI instrument is set up. Some instruments use banks and programs to determine what sound they play. If this is the case, you can use the column to assign a bank value to your track. The column header is also called "Bank." To change the value, either left- or right-click to decrease or increase the value or double-click to enter the desired value.

- **Compression**—The Compression column is yet another MIDI filter feature. It is used to compress or expand the dynamic range of MIDI instruments by transforming their velocity level like an audio compressor would do. For example, you can set your filter to 50 percent to decrease the velocity by half. This decreases the difference between the velocities of the notes and also decreases their velocities overall. To bring the track up to the original volume, you can compensate by changing the velocity column. The header for this column is "Cmp." To change the value, either left- or right-click to decrease or increase the value or double-click to enter the desired value.

- **Appearance**—This allows you to change the appearance of parts in a track. There are two options that you can check when this column is displayed: N and E. When "N" is checked, the names of parts on the track will be displayed. When "E" is checked, the events for the parts on the track will be displayed. The header for this column is "N-E." You can also modify the appearance of all tracks and parts by selecting Part Appearance > Show Name and Show Events from the Options menu.

▶ **Rocket Local**—This feature is available when working with the RocketPower capabilities of Cubase. When you are using RocketNetwork and sharing files or exchanging ideas with someone else over the Internet, you are logged on to a server. You can play files locally or through the Internet connection. This column allows you to set a track to play from local files or from remote tracks from a remote computer. This feature is useless if the RocketPower button is not enabled or if you are not connected to a RocketNetwork server. The column header here is "L." To set a file to play from Local, click in this column for the track you wish to play from your computer.

NOTE
Modifications made in the Track List section will not only appear in the Track List but in the Track Info as well. If you don't like working with the Track List and prefer working with the Track Info, you can keep the Track List column to a minimum and keep the Track Info column displayed to make your modifications as you select the track. The only disadvantage to this is that you can see the details for only one track at a time when relying only on the Track Info, since it displays only the properties for the selected track.

Creating Track List Views

As you can see by the amount of information that can be displayed in the Track List view, sometimes being able to see certain information and other times seeing other information can be handy. That's why you can create and edit Track List views and save them for later use. These views will keep in memory which information you want to see, and you can recall it whenever you need to.

To create a Track List view:

1. Start by adding the columns you wish to see in your Track List.
2. Alt+click in the column header section and select Store View from the pop-up menu.
3. Enter the name under which you want to save the preset for the list view.
4. To retrieve a view, Alt+click again on the column header section and select the desired view from the list, as shown in Figure 4.3.

Figure 4.3
Save and recall Track List views.

Track Classes

A class is attached to every track in Cubase (see Figure 4.4). This determines what kind of information you can put on this track. There are nine Track Classes from which to choose. The most obvious ones are MIDI and audio tracks, but let's look at them to see what their purpose is.

Figure 4.4
Cubase Track Classes available through the pop-up menu.

To change the class of a track, you simply need to click in the "C" column and pick the class that you want.

Audio Track

This is used exclusively for audio events such as recorded or imported audio material from the audio pool. The track can contain mono, stereo, or multiple audio channels if the track is set to "Any." You can add VST or DirectX effects to audio tracks and use the VST Channel mixer to automate volume, pan, and effect parameters in real time for any of these tracks. The sampling rate and number of available audio channels for this track class are determined by the audio system setup properties (Options > Audio Setup > System).

The default editing window for this Track Class is the Audio Editor window. Recorded audio events are saved in separate files in a folder you designate when enabling the first track for recording. Subsequent tracks will be recorded in the same folder.

MIDI Track

This is for MIDI note and controller events linked to a melodic or rhythmic instrument, with the exception of drum or percussion tracks. You can use MIDI tracks for drum tracks, but there is a specific class for this that is more suited for the information contained in these tracks. MIDI tracks will contain MIDI note events, controllers such as velocity, modulation wheel, pitch bend, and so on. It can contain volume and pan control if you add it directly to the part when editing it, but you can also use Mix Tracks to adjust these values. MIDI tracks can also contain MIDI filters, as discussed in the Track List View section.

The default editing window for this Track Class is the Key Editor window. Recorded MIDI events are saved with the arrangement file itself.

Drum Track

Drum tracks are similar to MIDI tracks. The only difference is that the edit window will reflect certain particularities of rhythmic parts, such as short notes, a tighter grid, and some tools just for drums and percussion. You can't stretch note values in the edit window of a drum track.

The default editing window for this Track Class is the Drum Editor window (see Figure 4.5). Since recorded drum track events are MIDI events as well, they are also saved with the arrangement file itself.

Figure 4.5
The Drum track editing window.

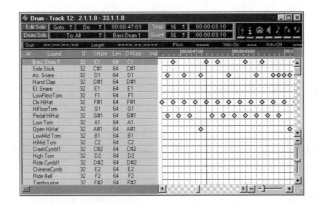

Folder Track

Folder tracks are used to group a series of tracks together to clean up your arrangement. Folder tracks don't contain any MIDI or audio parts themselves but instead hold the content of other tracks. Once tracks are assigned to a folder, you can hide the folder and name it to know what content lies beneath. Note that folder tracks are different from group tracks in that they contain the contents of a whole track or series of tracks and cannot be used to change the structure of a song later on.

Folder tracks are automatically created when recording in cycle mode with the Cycle Rec function set to Add. Folder tracks will be discussed further in Chapter 6.

Figure 4.6
A folder track displaying a collapsed tree.

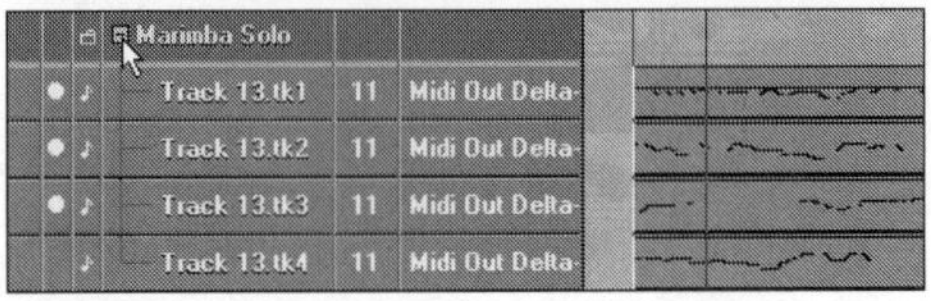

Figure 4.7
A folder track displaying an expanded tree, revealing the MIDI tracks inside.

Mix Track

When you are done recording tracks, or need to adjust volume and pan settings, you can create a mix track where audio and MIDI automation will be stored. You can't record audio events or MIDI note events in a mix track, only automation values. This also includes effects automation like Send and Insert levels and parameters, On/Off switches, and EQ parameters. You can't, however, automate DirectX effects.

When you record your automation on a mix track, you create events that will appear in that track. You can create a different mix track to try different mix settings—just make sure to mute all but one mix track at a time if you want to make sure of what you are hearing.

The default editing window for the mix track is the Controller editing window, shown in Figure 4.8. All the parameters that can be automated will appear on the left of the screen. When there are automation values recorded, a dot appears next to the name of that parameter once the list is expanded. Note once again in Figure 4.8 that automation has been recorded for the Karlette Feedback 1 and the Pan 2 parameters. Mix tracks will be further discussed in Chapter 11.

Figure 4.8
The mix track editing window.

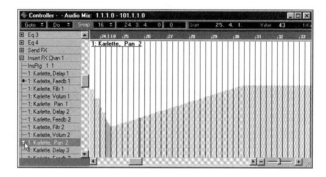

Group Track

You've completed a recording session and you want to build different arrangements using already placed events on different tracks, so you can copy and paste all the parts where you want them or you can create groups for song sections—for example, a chorus, a verse, a bridge, and so on. Once your groups are created, they contain different parts from different tracks. Then, you create a group track where you drag the desired group on the Track View area of your choice in the group track (see Figure 4.9). This will display a single part that will play back all the events that are part of that group at that point in time.

Figure 4.9
Dragging groups to a group track will insert a copy of the contents of the group in the group track.

One little thing about groups: You can group only MIDI events, not audio. Group tracks will be further discussed in Chapter 6.

Tape Track

If you own an analog or digital multitrack recorder with synchronizing capabilities, you might be able to control it with Cubase using tape tracks. From here, you can control which track will be in record-ready mode or which track will play back. If you don't have an external tape recorder or a MIDI machine-controllable device, this type of track will not serve you in any way.

Chord Track

This type of track does not contain any MIDI or audio information. Rather, it contains chord values either to be added as a lead sheet track in a musical score or used as guides for another type of class—style tracks. When you create a chord track and record chord progressions, you can apply these chord progressions to style tracks.

Style Track

Have you ever wanted to have a band playing with you? That's exactly what style tracks are. Style tracks, like mix tracks, chord tracks, and tape tracks, don't contain MIDI events per se. They actually contain a style file that generates interactive accompaniments for a predefined set of chords or events that you would play in real time. To get a better idea of how it works, try loading the Styldemo.all file provided with your copy of Cubase in the Style folder. Style tracks are discussed in greater detail in Appendix C.

Programming Mutes and Solos

Whenever you are writing a song, you might want to try different things, like, for example, having a shaker play during the bridge or having an electric guitar play during the solo instead of the saxophone. If you don't want to delete the tracks and just want to switch from one to the other while listening, you can program mutes and solos.

To record mutes and solos:

1. Click in the Mute column to activate the mute for the tracks you wish to mute or select the track you wish to solo (this should be the only one without a mute on it) and click on the Solo button in the upper left corner of the Arrange window.
2. Press Shift+Alt+F2 to store the mute or solo in this memory.
3. If you want to mute another series of tracks or solo another track, repeat Step 1, but to store another mute or solo setup, use the next memory spot: Shift+Alt+F3.
4. Continue entering mutes and solos into memory using the next Function keys (F2 through F11).

To recall mutes and solos, simply press the Shift key with the corresponding Function key (F2 to F11) that contains your recorded set of mutes or soloed track.

Recording Mutes and Solo

Now, if you want to have muted and soloed tracks change during playback, you can record these changes, provided you followed the previous steps to record your mutes and solos.

To record mute and solo changes during playback:

1. Select the Record Tempo/Mutes from the Options menu.
2. Select or create a MIDI track to record your mute and solo changes. This has to be a MIDI track, not a mix track.
3. Press the Record button or asterisk key (*) on the numerical keypad to begin recording.
4. As the arrangement plays, recall the memories you have previously entered to record during playback. You can also mute or unmute tracks individually and record this action.
5. Stop the recording when you are done and play the arrangement back to see if your track mutes change during playback.

http://www.muskalipman.com

Track Info

The Track Info area, also known as the Inspector in Cubase's documentation, gives similar details for tracks as the Track View area. The difference is that you get even more information here, and you always see the information pertaining to the selected track instead of all the track at once. By using a combination of Track View and Track Info data, you get a great deal of control over what's going on in a single glance. Well, maybe two glances.

This said, some Track Classes give you more stuff to try out than others. For the sake of keeping things flowing, the following sections will look at some parameters for the MIDI class tracks and the rest will be covered as we go along in the following chapters. Just a little something to keep you coming back for more.

One thing that's quite important to understand about Track Info is that whatever is displayed in this area reflects the selected track, taking into account that you have not selected any parts in that track. However, when you select a part in that track, the title at the top of the Track Info section changes to Part Info. This means that it now displays information for that part, which includes specific changes you might have made to the selected part, such as a program change or some additional MIDI filtering. So, make sure that you don't have any parts selected when making modifications to the Track Info area if you want to modify the entire track and also make sure the part is selected and the title for this part appears in the top section of the Track Info area, as shown in Figure 4.10.

Figure 4.10
The Track Info area changes to the Part Info area when a part is selected in the active track.

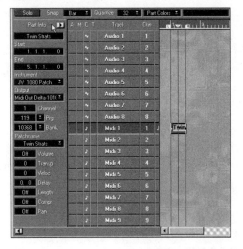

Setting Up Instruments

An instrument in Cubase is a combination of MIDI output, MIDI channel, and name assignments for both the machine and the patch inside the machine. By setting up instruments to reflect your studio's setup, you don't have to remember what instrument is hooked up to what MIDI port. You could even have your instruments in a different room and not have to worry about front panel buttons anymore—unless, of course, you want to modify some of the instrument's parameters. The first thing you need to do if you want to use instruments is to name them. So, let's set up General MIDI instruments.

> General MIDI is a convention adopted by manufacturers to define a bank of 128 instrument sounds and reserve MIDI Channel 10 for drums and percussion. Since its inception, MIDI has been a standardized language for relaying performance and control-related data. However, the basic instrument sounds that are reproduced by almost any electronic music setup will invariably change from one setup to the next (and often even within the setup whenever patch settings are changed). In one setup, MIDI data that is being transmitted over Channel 5 might trigger an upright bass sound, while another setup might have Channel 5 designed to trigger an entirely different device that might output a "Zaxxon spacegun from hell."

This lack of conformity has brought about a single set of standardized MIDI patch settings that have come to be known as General MIDI. This standardized series of sound settings has been defined so that common and popular instrument sounds are mapped to various program change numbers. For example, calling up General MIDI patch #1 will always call up a piano.

Table 4.2
General MIDI sound set groupings.

Program #	Instrument Group	Program #	Instrument Group
1-8	Piano	65-72	Reed
9-16	Chromatic perc.	73-80	Pipe
17-24	Organ	81-88	Synth Lead
25-32	Guitar	89-96	Synth Pad
33-40	Bass	97-104	Synth Effects
41-48	Strings	105-112	Ethnic
49-56	Ensemble	113-120	Percussive
57-64	Brass	121-128	Sound Effects

To create an instrument:

1. Click on the Instrument field in the Track Info area.
2. From the pop-up menu, select Setup Instrument, as shown in Figure 4.11.

Figure 4.11
The Setup Instruments pop-up menu. Previously configured instruments will appear in this menu.

The Setup Instruments dialog box appears with the MIDI channel for the selected track already present in the channel field. If you want to modify this, left-click to decrease the value, right-click to increase.

3. Type in a name for your instrument. For example, if you are using General MIDI sound tables, you could enter "GM." On the other hand, if you have a rack-mounted synthesizer or keyboard controller that you would like to use, type in the name.

NOTE
You can also set up instruments using Studio Modules, which are discussed in Appendix C. This will give you greater flexibility over some more complex performances, patches, and MIDI channel settings for your instruments.

4. You can enter an extended name for your instrument. For example, GM instruments are separated into categories, like Bass, Keyboards, Guitars, and so on. So, if you always use Guitar sounds on Channel 2, enter it in this field. If you don't know what instrument goes on what channel at this point, leave it blank.
5. From the Patchname Source field, select the Patchname Script from the drop-down menu. This will allow you to select predefined patchnames for GM instruments.
6. In the Patchname Device field, select the GM Voices option from the drop-down menu, as shown in Figure 4.12.

Figure 4.12
The list shown in the Patchname Device field depends on the option you select in the Patchname Script field.

7. Click OK to confirm your instrument setting. If, instead of a GM instrument, you would like to set up a Roland GS, Yamaha XG, or any other instrument, you would proceed in the same way, selecting the corresponding Patchname Device instead. Now that you have properly configured your instrument, you can select a patchname for that instrument.

8. Under Patchname in the Track Info, select one patch for the instrument you just set up. Because we created a GM instrument using the Patchname Script, all the patches for this instrument are organized in groups, as shown in Figure 4.13.

Figure 4.13
The patchname layout reflects the selected Patchname Script in the instrument setup.

TIP

If the name of your keyboard or sound module doesn't appear in the list when you want to assign a patchname script to your instrument, you can download a free utility from Steinberg's Web site (**http://service.steinberg.net/webdoc.nsf/show/download_e**) called Scriptmaker. This utility will allow you to create custom Patchname Scripts for your instrument.

Once your instruments are created, you can select them from the instrument list in the Track Info when the Studio Module is activated and you have added this instrument to the list of Studio Modules. Because an instrument is assigned to a MIDI port, you can have up to sixteen instruments for that port. If, instead of selecting a MIDI channel (as Channel 1 is selected in Figure 4.12), you decide to set the MIDI channel properties to "Any" (or check the All Channel option) for that instrument, a default name will be given to each MIDI channel in the extended name field. If, later on, you decide to add an extended name for that channel's instrument, you may do so by selecting the instrument and adding the name through the Instrument Setup dialog box once again. When you select that instrument later, the channel reference in the extended name will be replaced by the extended name you entered, as shown in Figure 4.14.

Figure 4.14
This shows the GM instrument definition set to Any Channel, where Channel 10 has been renamed Drums.

Play Parameters

Play Parameters do not affect the recorded material. They affect only the way it plays back. It's kind of like looking at yourself in a distorted mirror at the county fair. You do not actually have a big head, small neck, big belly, and small legs, as seen in the reflection. You simply appear like that in the mirror. MIDI playback parameters are similar. They transform the data going out. This said, you would understand that, because they don't affect the MIDI data, the Play Parameters will not appear in the MIDI editors. If you want to keep the Play Parameters and be able to edit them in a MIDI editor, you have to use the Freeze Play Parameters option from the Functions menu.

In Figure 4.15, you can see before and after looks at Freeze Play Parameters for MIDI velocity levels. What was done? If you look in the left part of the figure, you can see the Part Info to which two Play Parameters filers were applied—compression and velocity. First, 50 percent compression was added to the MIDI data, which cut the original velocity by half. Then, a value of 50 was added to the velocity.

Figure 4.15
A look at Freeze Play Parameters velocity levels, before (top) and after (bottom).

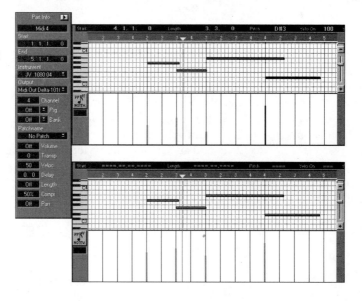

Here is a table showing the velocity values for these four notes and how these filters affected them:

Table 4.3
How Play Parameters filters affect MIDI events.

Play Parameter	Note 1	Note 2	Note 3	Note 4	Comment
Before filters					
Velocity Value	50	70	35	100	Recorded velocities
Compress (50%)	25	35	17	50	Heard velocities after filter
Velocity (+50)	50	50	50	50	Added to the previous velocities when heard
After filter	75	85	67	100	Resulting velocity that can be heard. These are the values that will be stored IF you select the Freeze Play Parameters option from the Functions menu.

Here's another table quickly describing what each Play Parameter does and its possible values:

Table 4.4
Description of Play Parameters.

Name	Possible Values	Effect on MIDI events
Volume	Off to 127	Changes the volume level.
Pan	Off, L64 to R63	Changes the panning.
Transpose	−127 to +127	Each value corresponds to a semitone. Positive values transpose notes higher, negative values transpose notes lower. You can also transpose a group on a Group Track.
Velocity	−127 to +127	Adds or removes the value from the MIDI events' velocity for the selected track or part.
Delay	−2.2560 to +2.2560	Moves the MIDI events in a track or a part forward or backward in time by as much as two sixteenth notes and a sixteenth triplet note.
Length	Off, 25% to 200%	Stretches or reduces the length of a MIDI track or part by its corresponding value.
Compression	Off, 25% to 200%	Compresses the velocity of a MIDI track or part by its corresponding value.

http://www.muskalipman.com

NOTE

Notes played before Bar 1 and Beat 1 in a part that has been delayed with the Delay Play Parameter using a minus value will not be played. The same thing applies if the delay moves the events beyond a loop cycle when playing in cycle mode.

Adding a Shadow MIDI Track

Sometimes, one instrument isn't enough to get the sound you really want. One method of dealing with this is to create a copy of a track and assign it to another MIDI channel playing another instrument. Another way of doing this is to use the Multi Out feature in Cubase. This will create a "shadow" track that can have its own Play Parameter settings but will keep the same volume setting as the original track. Because it is a shadow track, you can't shadow just a part, so if you want to double up a part, you should use the copy-and-paste technique.

To add an additional MIDI output:

1. Expand the Track Info area by clicking on the expansion arrow next to Track Info.
2. From the first field at the top of the expanded section, click on Multi Out and select the Add Out option.

An additional track has been added under the track's name, which has the same name as the track but is preceded by a little plus (+) sign, as shown in Figure 4.16. You can modify any Play Parameter for that shadow track and assign it another instrument.

Figure 4.16
A shadow track has the same name as the track it shadows, except that it has a plus sign before it.

If you want to delete or mute that shadow track, simply repeat the steps mentioned above, but in Step 2, instead of selecting the Add Out option, select either Delete Out or Mute.

Program Changes

Program changes are ways to make your instrument change sounds before a track begins or change the sound along the way. There are many ways you can add program changes to a track or part. One way is to open the List Editor and add a program change event in the desired location with the appropriate patch number as the program change value. The advantage of using this method is that you can add a program change anywhere inside a part. Because you just saw how to set up our instruments, this would seem like the obvious choice, since selecting a number that has no real meaning is not as intuitive as selecting the actual name of the patch. The only disadvantage here is that you can't change the patch halfway into a part, since program changes made when using the Part Info's Instrument and Patchname changes will always occur at the beginning of a part. So, let's look a little more closely at this second method of making program changes.

To make a program change using an instrument's patchname field:

1. Make sure no parts in the track are selected. You can see if this is the case by looking at the title in the Track Info. If it says Part Info, a part is selected.
2. Select the patchname from the defined instrument's patchname list.

That's it. Now, if you want to add a program change along the track, just select the part where you want the program (or patch) to change and repeat Step 2 from the above list.

TIP

Some MIDI instruments will stop playing for a short while when they change sounds. If your first note begins at the very start of a part, where a program change occurs, chances are you won't hear that first note. To prevent this from happening, you can set the program change to occur slightly before by changing the Play Parameter Delay setting (Edit > Preferences > MIDI > Playback window). The value represented here is the time before the actual program change occurs. Make sure this delay will not cause the change to occur as the sound is still playing from a previous part and not too late to cause the instrument to miss the first note in the new part.

When a program change is added in the Track Info area, any part created on that track will have the corresponding program change command embedded at the beginning of that part, but it will remain invisible in the List Editor. If you glue the parts together, the embedded program change will disappear. If you select a patch in the Track Info while a part on that track is selected, a program change command will be embedded in that part only. Things can get very confusing.

To prevent this confusion, you may use one of two techniques: You can perform a Freeze Play Parameters on a part, which will embed the program change and make it visible in the List Editor, or you can create a short dummy part at the beginning of each track and apply the patch just to that part to avoid any instrument choking at the beginning of your arrangement.

MIDI Volume and Pan Control

MIDI volumes and panning are handled much the same way as program changes. You can add MIDI volume or pan controls at the beginning of each track by using the corresponding Play Parameter for a MIDI track or add a controller at the beginning of a MIDI part. But here ends the comparison. Unlike program changes, volume and pan controls are part of the mix and you will probably want to change the values quite often. That's why you can use two other alternatives to enter volume and pan controls: the Midi Track Mixer and the Controller Editing window. The choice is yours, depending on how you like to do things.

Figure 4.17
You access the MIDI Track Mixer Window by selecting it in the Panels menu.

In the MIDI Track Mixer, you will find one strip of mixer for every MIDI track in your arrangement. Therefore, this mixer is dynamic in the sense that if you delete a MIDI track, the MIDI Mixer channel will disappear as well. Each strip contains a Mute and Solo button, pan control, volume fader, input level, and numerical level indicator that displays information for volume and pan controls when you are editing them, plus additional information on the MIDI channel, track number, and so on. Each mixer strip also has an extended button function, which allows you to use MIDI processing when you have GS- or XG-compatible instruments in your setup.

To record volume or pan changes:

1. Begin by enabling the Write button in the upper left corner of the window, as shown in Figure 4.17.

    If you want to hear and see the actions you record, you will need to enable the Read button as well. Otherwise, your actions will be recorded, but nothing will appear to be moving, nor will you hear anything during playback. Notice that Cubase will automatically create a mix track for you when you activate the Write button.

2. Position your locator at the position where you want to begin recording volume and pan automation.

3. Press Play on the Transport bar or the Enter key on your numeric keypad.

4. Move the volume faders or the pan lines above the volume faders for the desired tracks.

   If you are in cycle mode recording, you will find that the automation gets overwritten each time you start a lap for every change you make. This means that if you don't touch the fader for two bars, then move it again, this information is recorded. The next time you pass over that portion, if you decide to move your fader during those two bars and leave it a new position, the beginning of the mix will stay identical, but the remainder of the movements will be recorded over the first laps movement's.

5. If you want to record mutes and solos, you can do so as well in this window. Once you are done, disable the Write button.

You will probably notice some jerky movements in the volume or pan control changes once in a while. This is because you might change a fader position too quickly, move a fader while not in Read mode, and so on. Use the Controller Edit window to edit the mix track, thereby correcting mistakes that might have been recorded. To launch this window, double-click on the mix track containing the mix automation or click the mix track and select Controller from the Edit menu (refer to Figure 4.8).

To edit MIDI automation using the Controller editor:

1. Click on the plus (+) sign next to the MIDI channel you want to edit if the tree is not already expanded.
2. Select the MIDI controller you want to edit to have the control changes appear in the right part of the window.
3. Right-click in the controller part of the window (the one with the actual control changes) and select the appropriate tool; if you want to erase a controller, select the Eraser. If you want to add a control, select the Pencil tool; and if you want to smoothen a ramp or draw a ramp (like a fade in or fade out), select the Line tool.
4. If you want to add only one control change, like bringing the volume level from 87 to 64, just click and drag the mouse to the desired level. If you want to draw a series of new controllers, keep the Alt key pressed as you draw in the new control points or control line. The same thing needs to be done when using the Eraser tool.
5. Once you are done, close the window, or you may repeat these steps on another MIDI channel.

What Is a VST Instrument (VSTi)?

VST Instruments are definitely not to be confused with Instrument configurations, mentioned previously in this chapter. VST Instruments—VSTi, for short—are software-based synthesizers that use the ASIO 2 protocol developed by Steinberg to generate or output their sound through the computer's sound card. They are, in essence, software within software since they run as separate entities within Cubase VST. This opens up a whole world of exciting possibilities for any music enthusiast as well as for hardcore music veterans.

VSTis are activated through the VST Instrument option found in the Panels menu. From there, a panel appears in which you will find installed VSTis on your computer (see Figure 4.18); you can select the VSTi that you wish to activate. To install a VSTi, follow the instructions provided to you by the manufacturer of the plug-in.

Figure 4.18
The VST Instruments panel will display active and installed VST instruments.

Once loaded, by default, it is also activated. You can always deactivate a VSTi without unloading it by pressing the red button next to the number for the VSTi in the VST Instruments panel. When a VSTi is loaded and activated, an additional MIDI port will appear when you click on a MIDI track output setting. In Figure 4.19, the Neon VSTi has been loaded so it is now available as an output device. This means that you can use one of sixteen additional MIDI channels, not to mention that you can also load more than one instance of a VSTi in memory. VSTi MIDI outputs are handled in the same way as a regular MIDI output device.

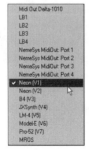

Figure 4.19
All VSTis that are loaded will appear as an additional MIDI output. Notice that there are two instances of the Neon VSTi, providing thirty-two extra MIDI channels.

There are many ways to change settings or edit a VSTi.

- ▶ Click the Edit button for the VSTi track at the bottom of the Track Info section. (Note that this is available only for MIDI tracks, not drum tracks, in version 5.0).
- ▶ Click the Edit button on the VST Instruments panel. To view this panel, select it from the Panels menu.
- ▶ Click the Edit button on top of the VSTi channel strip in the VST Channel Mixer window (see Figure 4.20). To view this panel, select it from the Panels menu.

Figure 4.20
The Edit button in the VST Channel Mixer opens the VSTi for editing.

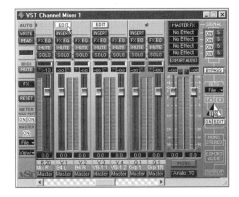

As you can see in Figure 4.20, loaded VST Instruments have their own channel strips in the VST Channel Mixer window. If your VSTi has stereo outputs, it will have two strips, and if it is mono, it will have only one. The reason VSTi doesn't appear in the MIDI Mixer window is that, even though it is a MIDI device, it uses the sound card as an output device. Therefore, it is handled much the same way as a normal digital audio signal.

The editing parameters vary from one VSTi to another. But what stays common throughout these instruments is the fact that you can create presets and save them. To save or load a single patch or instrument, select Save Instrument or Load Instrument from the File field on the VSTi panel, as shown in Figure 4.21. To save or load a bank of patches or instruments, select Save Bank or Load Bank from the File field on the VSTi panel, also shown in Figure 4.21.

Figure 4.21
The File menu on the VSTi allows you to save and retrieve instruments (single presets) and banks (multiple presets).

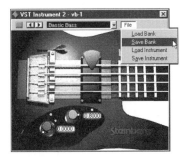

Finally, you can also automate changes you make on VSTi controls in real time. You do this the same way you would record any MIDI information—by selecting the VSTi MIDI track, pressing record, and manipulating the VSTi's controls. This will create MIDI System Exclusive messages that will appear in the MIDI part of the VSTi track.

VSTis included with Cubase

Steinberg provides you with four VST Instruments when you purchase Cubase VST 5.0 and above versions:

- **Neon**—A simple sixteen-voice polyphonic synthesizer.
- **VB-1**—A four-voice polyphonic virtual bass simulator using physical modeling parameters.
- **LM-9**—A nine-voice polyphonic drum machine.
- **Universal Sound Module (USM)**—A multi-timbral, ninety-six-voice polyphonic General MIDI device simulator that comes with some seventy megabytes of sampled waveforms.

The most recent VSTi provided by Steinberg, the Universal Sound Module, allows you to create arrangements or listen to arrangements using General MIDI sounds and presets even if you don't have a GM device in your studio. This is very useful when working on a project that requires you to edit or listen to MIDI files that were recorded or will be played back on systems that have GM-compatible devices. The GM standard is basically a set of presets that abide by a strict rule of names and numbers. All 128 sound patches on GM modules are the same. For example, sound number 1 is always a piano, sound number 9 will always be a celesta, and so on. The quality of the sound might be different, but the type of sound remains constant. Using GM sounds and program changes assures you that if you set a piano sound on Track 1, when it plays back on another system using GM sounds, it will still be a piano playing on Track 1.

The USM is not the only way you can have a VSTi play more than one instrument at a time. You can open multiple instances of the same VSTi to create a multilayered instrument or simply have different instances of the same VSTi playing different sounds. This would allow you to add different effects (and effect automation) to the same VSTi, because Cubase will create an additional set of audio mixer channels for each instance of this VSTi.

Obviously, Steinberg is not the only one developing VSTi's. You can find additional resources and links to some manufacturer's Web sites in Appendix E.

VSTi and Latency

Because VST Instruments play through your sound card, the latency factor plays a great role in how effective the instruments will really be. Since latency introduces a delay between the time a sound is played and the time a sound is heard, the shorter that delay is, the more realistic the experience will be. Make sure your system is configured properly, as outlined in Chapter 2, and always use the ASIO driver provided by your sound card manufacturer. If you have a latency that is equal to or greater than 25 ms, you might find it disconcerting to play a VSTi, since there will always be this delay between the moment you hit the keys on your keyboard and the moment you hear the sound. The smallest theoretical latency would be 0 milliseconds, but in reality, you can expect at least a 1.5- to 3-millisecond latency, which is pretty good. So, to get a good experience with VSTi, try setting your sound card driver preferences (if you have a dedicated ASIO driver for your sound card) and Cubase to have latency between 1.5 and 10 milliseconds.

Step Recording

Step recording is meant for the rhythmically challenged, for less-than-proficient keyboard players who have great ideas but just need some help entering them into a sequencer, and for creating rhythmically complex patterns, such as machine-like drum fills using sixty-four notes at 120 bpm. Step recording means that you can enter notes or chords one by one without worrying about timing. This is done in the Drum or Key Edit window.

To record MIDI in Step Recording mode:

1. Select or create a MIDI or drum track.
2. Create an empty part in that track using the Pencil tool or by clicking on an existing part to select it.
3. Select the Edit or Drum editing window from the Edit menu and open it.
4. Enable the Step Recording button in the editing window's toolbar. It's the one that looks like a foot (see Figure 4.22). The MIDI input connector is automatically activated (also shown in Figure 4.22).
5. Set the Quantize number, which determines the length of the recorded event. In the example (Figure 4.22), this value is set to 8.
6. Set the Snap number, which determines the space between the recorded events. In the example, this value is set to 4.
7. Position your playback line where you want to begin your recording. You can move the playback line by clicking where you want it to be in the ruler.

8. Play a note or a chord on your controller keyboard.

   The notes will be recorded as you play them, at the length you set the Quantize value, and spaced evenly at the value set by the Snap field. Cubase will record the velocity at which you are playing the notes or chords, so try to enter the notes at the approximate velocity you want them to play back. When you let go of the notes on your keyboard, the playback line will advance to the next Snap value in time. Pressing another note or chord will insert a new series of events at that point.

9. If you want to move forward or backward in time, use the left and right arrows on your keyboard. The insertion point where the notes will be added is displayed in the editing window's Status bar. In Figure 4.22, this number is 3.1.1 or Bar 3, Beat 1, Tick 1.

10. If you want to insert an event between two other events, activate the Insert button in the Editor's toolbar (it's the last one to the right), position your playback head where you want to insert a note or a chord, and simply play the note or chord.

Figure 4.22
MIDI Recording in Step mode in the Key edit window.

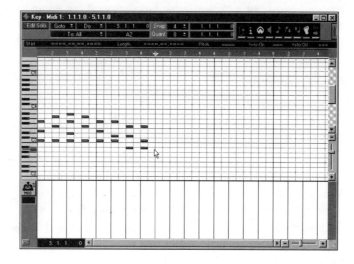

Realtime Recording

Recording a MIDI track in realtime is at the heart of a MIDI sequencer. That's why this process is quite simple. Some of the recording modes were discussed earlier, in Chapter 3, so you can refer to the appropriate section if you are not sure what they are.

When recording MIDI in realtime, you have an option on the Transport bar that allows you to automatically quantize recorded events to the value set in the Arrange window's Quantize value. To enable this setting, press the "AQ" button on the Transport bar. If you would rather not quantize when recording, you can always quantize or groove quantize later.

Before you begin your recording, make sure you have selected the right MIDI track and the right recording mode and have activated or deactivated the Cycle mode in the Transport bar. Once these precautions have been taken, you are ready to start recording.

To help you keep the beat while you are recording, you can activate the Click button on the Transport bar. To change the options for the Metronome, select the Metronome option in the Options menu. This will bring up the Metronome options dialog box, shown in Figure 4.23. You can change the settings for precounting—the number of measures the metronome will count before it actually starts moving the playback line—and you can change what source will generate the click. If you are using a MIDI instrument other than a drum on Channel 10, for example, you might want to change the MIDI channel used for the click track. You can also activate the audio click, which will send a beeping sound through your speakers. When you are done, click OK and start recording.

Figure 4.23
The Metronome setup window.

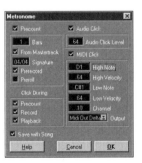

Remember that you can start recording by clicking the Record button on the Transport bar or by pressing the asterisk key on your numeric keypad.

MIDI Filtering and Mapping

Cubase allows you to filter out certain MIDI events. For example, if you don't want to record System Exclusive messages while you are recording a performance, you can filter out these events. This will reduce such data as Aftertouch, Pitch Bends, and System Exclusive messages are known to clog MIDI data streams.

To filter out unwanted MIDI information while recording:

1. In the Options menu, select MIDI Setup > Filtering.
2. In the MIDI Filter dialog box, check the types of messages you don't wish to record. You can also filter out MIDI channels by pressing the corresponding MIDI channel button in the lower section of the dialog box, as shown in Figure 4.24.
3. Click OK when you are done.

Figure 4.24
The MIDI Filtering setup window.

Another process that you can apply is MIDI mapping of controller messages. The best example of this is Breath Controllers used with MIDI instruments. You might have an instrument that supports this feature but not have the Breath Controller device itself. You could use Cubase's mapping features to convert Modulation Wheel controller messages into Breath Controller messages. To do this, open the MIDI System Setup window under the Options menu. In that dialog box, assign the MIDI controller message you want to remap in the Controller Map section of the window. When you use the Modulation Wheel the next time, Cubase will send Breath Controller data to your Breath Controller-compatible MIDI device.

Now You Try It

Here are the exercises you will find on the Web site for this chapter:

- ▶ Add a name to track and to a part in a track.
- ▶ Launch a VSTi and assign it as an instrument in a track.
- ▶ Set a patchname from the Play Properties for a VSTi.
- ▶ Create a shadow track.
- ▶ Assign different Play Properties (Transpose, Pitch, Velocity, Delay, and Pan).
- ▶ Add a program change at the beginning of a part.
- ▶ Change the Track Class of a MIDI track to a drum track.
- ▶ Record a track of your own using Auto Quantize.

You will find these exercises at **www.muskalipman.com/cubase**.

Simply follow the instructions on the Web site before starting the exercises.

You can refer to this chapter to find out how to do these exercises, but try doing them without peeking first, just to see how comfortable you are with these principles. If you don't remember how to do a task, refer to the appropriate header in this chapter.

You will need to have the Universal Sound Module and the VB-1 VSTi installed on your computer to use the file provided for these exercises. If you do not have these VST instruments installed, you can always use a General MIDI-compatible device, assigning Channel 1 to play a Bass sound, Channel 2 to play a Lead Synth sound, Channel 3 to play a Strings sound, Channel 5 a Piano sound, and Channel 10 to Drums.

5
MIDI Editing Windows

MIDI editing is where Cubase earned its first stripes as professional software, and it continues to do so by adding great flexibility to any MIDI editing parameter. In this chapter, you will learn how to use the many editing windows available to edit MIDI events, including the Key and Drum editors, the List editor, and, finally, the MIDI Controller editing window for fine-tuning event controllers such as Pan, Volume, Velocity, Pitch Bends, and so on.

You can use any of the editing windows to try out different things. If you don't want to keep the changes you made in an editing window, you can press the Escape key on your keyboard to cancel the operations. Otherwise, if you are happy with the results, closing the window in any other way will save and update the modifications you made. However, keep in mind that Cubase offers only one undo level. This means that you can undo the last operation you did, and that's it. This is why using editing windows, where you can cancel all the edits you have performed, is the safe way to edit your events.

The Editors

Before we begin talking about editors, it is important to understand that each Track Class has its own associated editing window.

Events are, therefore, associated with an editor by default. You can change this in some cases; and in other cases, there is no way to get around it. The associated editor displays events that are appropriate to the track's class, so it is optimized for the events recorded in its window. Using another editor would not allow you to manipulate the information as easily anyway. However, you can edit events in a nonassociated editor by selecting the part(s) in the Arrange window and selecting the desired editor from the Edit menu.

There are seven editors to choose from in Cubase VST:

- **Edit**—Uses the piano roll analogy, where events appear along a strip moving from left to right as you play the events. The pitch is determined by the vertical position on the scrolling events, and the position in time is determined by the horizontal position of these events. The longer an event, the longer the box in the scroll, as in a piano roll. The first events in a part being edited appear at the left of the piano roll, and the last events in that part appear at the right of the piano roll.
- **List**—Uses a table representation where it displays the raw MIDI data for any edited parts (more on that will be found in subsequent sections).
- **Drum**—Uses the piano roll analogy as well, like the Edit window, but with a small difference: There are no lengths to events; only trigger times (note on positions) are displayed.
- **Score**—Uses a traditional music staff display to edit your MIDI parts.
- **Controller**—Allows you to view all the controller events in a graphical format. This window is useful for editing continuous and noncontinuous controller events, as will be discussed in more detail later in the book.
- **Graphical Master Track**—Like the Edit editor, it allows you to see a graphical representation of tempo changes, meter changes, and hitpoints. This is the editor to use to make visual changes to your Master Track.
- **List Master Track**—This window is the equivalent of the List editor for the Graphical Master Track editor: It allows you to see, in table format, the changes that will occur in your Master Track.

This said, let's take a look at Table 5.1, which lists the default editing windows for each track class:

Table 5.1
Default editing windows for each track class.

Track Class	Default Editing Window
MIDI track	Edit window (Key Edit)
Drum track	Edit window (Drum Edit)
Audio track	Edit window (Audio Edit)
Mix track	Mixer
Chord track	Score window

You can change these default settings by going to Edit > Preferences > General > Editors next to the Editor drop-down menu.

TIP

If you have MIDI and audio volume or pan events in your tracks, you should use the Controller editing window rather than using the default Key Edit. The Key, Audio, or Drum Edit windows will show only MIDI events and one controller at a time, whereas the Controller Edit window will display audio events related to your mix as well and will allow you to view more than one controller. Also, it will display controllers containing events in a specific way, which makes it easy to spot where you should go.

The tracks inside a folder track will open in their respective editing windows. Group tracks and style tracks are not associated with any editing window and can't be edited as events in editors.

You can also notice that the Edit window changes names depending on the track class (Key, Drum, and Audio editing windows are all found under Edit in the Edit menu). The content and functions in these Edit windows are similar in many ways, yet some differences in the type of event will warrant specific editing functions.

The first part of this book addresses MIDI issues and the second part addresses audio issues. Because of this, note that the Audio editor will be discussed further in Chapter 9.

Toolbox Options

Toolboxes were introduced in Chapter 3. Now, let's take a look at how these tools work and discuss the options associated with certain tools in the editors. When a tool has different options, you can usually access these options through key and mouse-click combinations. For example, Alt+mouse-click will do something different than a simple mouse click.

Using the Pencil or Drum Stick Tool

The Pencil tool in the Key Edit window and the Drum Stick in the Drum Edit window offer similar options. The difference with the Pencil tool is that you can drag a note to determine the length of that note, whereas the Drum Stick tool will repeat the event using the Q value to determine the spacing and the Len value to determine the Length between each event in the Drum Edit window.

To create notes using the Pencil tool in the Key Edit window:

1. Set the Quantize and Snap values you wish to use. Quantize determines how long each note will be, and Snap determines the spacing between the notes.
2. Right-click in the Edit window to select the Pencil tool.
3. By default, all events will be inserted at a Note On velocity of 127. If you want to enter notes using different velocities, press Shift as you are drawing notes to enter velocity values of 96, Ctrl for values of 64, and Shift+Ctrl for values of 32. Note Off velocity will always be set at 64.
4. Click where you want to add your note. If you click and drag, you can draw longer notes than the value you set in the Quantize value, but these notes will snap to the Snap value.

Events are always created with the same MIDI channel as the part you are editing.

Once you have inserted notes using the Pencil tool, you can modify their length by clicking on the note and dragging it farther to the right to lengthen the note or dragging it to the left to shorten that note. If you don't want to accidentally add new notes, hold the Alt key down while you perform this function. This will prevent Cubase from inserting new notes, but it will allow you to modify existing events. Remember that notes will always snap in length to the Snap value.

If you wish to edit more than one note at a time, you have two options available: modify the relative length or make all events the same length.

To modify the length of multiple events:

1. With the Pointer Selection tool, drag a box over the events you want to edit. The selected events will appear in black.
2. Right-click in the Edit window to select the Pencil tool.
3. If you want all notes to be the same length, simply drag one of the selected notes to the desired length. If you want them to keep their proportional length, press and hold the Ctrl key as you lengthen or shorten the events. Remember that you can use the Alt key as well to disable the accidental insertion of new notes.

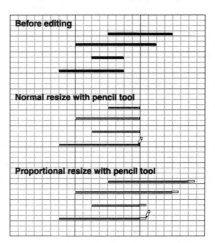

Figure 5.1
Editing multiple events with the Pencil tool.

As you can see in Figure 5.1, when you use the Ctrl key to resize events, the length is modified proportionally instead of bringing all the events to finish at the same place.

The Pencil tool has some limitations—you can change only the end of an event or events using this tool. If you want to modify the beginning, you should use the Line tool as described in the following section. You can also modify continuous and noncontinuous controllers with the Pencil tool. This will be described in the Controller editor section of this chapter, but keep in mind that whatever you can edit in the Controller editor for MIDI and drum tracks, you can also modify in the Controller part of the Key or Drum Editor window, as shown in Figure 5.2.

Figure 5.2
Editing noncontinuous controllers using the Pencil tool in the Key Edit window.

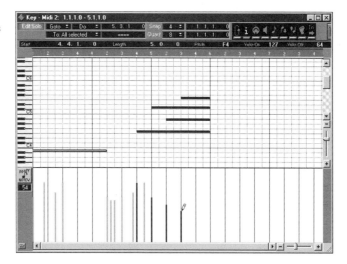

Using the Line Tool

The Line tool, like the Pencil tool, allows you to edit the end of notes or events, and it allows you to edit the beginning of events as well. This tool is best suited for multiple-note edits and start-note edits.

To edit events using the Line tool:

1. With the Selection tool, drag a box over the events you want to edit. The selected events will appear in black. You don't have to select the events, since the Line tool will edit all the notes in its path. Selecting the events is just a way to see if you will be affecting only these specific notes or not. If you notice that some unselected notes have been edited, undo the last operation and start over.

2. Right-click in the Edit window to select the Line tool.

3. If you want to edit the end of the selected events, align your Line tool, and click and drag a line in the direction and angle you want to edit the events (as shown in Figure 5.3). If you want to edit the start of events instead, keep the Alt key pressed as you draw the line.

http://www.muskalipman.com

Figure 5.3
Editing multiple events using the Line tool in the Key Edit window.

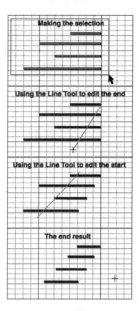

The Line tool also allows you to create linear fades in continuous controllers. This will also be discussed further in the Controller Editor section of this chapter.

Using the Paint Tool

The Paint tool is an alternative to the Pencil tool. Its purpose is to add events as well, but the difference is that you can click and drag along the two axes—entering a new event as soon as you drag beyond the Snap value set in your editing window or as soon as you move your cursor above or below the note you just created. Again, the Snap value determines the spacing between the notes, and the Quantize value determines the length of each note. Here are some options associated with the Paint tool:

In the left portion of Figure 5.4, a Pencil tool was used to draw an event by dragging it from Bar 10 to Bar 11. In the right portion of the same figure, you can see below the original note that the Paint tool was used in the same way, clicking and dragging from Bar 10 to Bar 11. This time, however, we added eighth notes at quarter-note intervals, which represents the set Quantize and Snap values above in the toolbar.

Figure 5.4
The difference between adding events with the Pencil tool and the Paint tool.

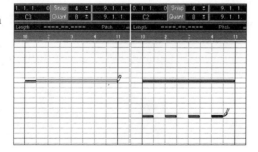

▶ When the Insert button is selected in the Edit window toolbar, you can move in time and change notes, but you can't create chords. Notes that are inserted as you move up or down will push the other notes to play later in time.

▶ Holding the Alt key as you draw the events will create a Note On velocity of 32.

▶ Holding the Ctrl key as you draw the events will create a Note On velocity of 64.

▶ Holding the Shift key as you draw the events will create a Note On velocity of 96, but it will also restrict your movement to the horizontal or time axis.

Using the Nudge Tool

You can use the Nudge tool to move an event forward or backward in time to the next or previous Snap value set in the toolbar. This can also be applied to multiple events if you select them previously with the Selection tool.

To Nudge an event to the next Snap value:

▶ **Moving the previous Snap value**—Right-click in the Edit window to select the Nudge tool from the toolbox and click on the event you wish to nudge one Snap value to the left.

▶ **Moving the next Snap value**—Right-click in the Edit window to select the Nudge tool from the toolbox and Ctrl+click on the event you wish to nudge one Snap value to the right.

The procedure is the same with multiple events selected. The nudge reference will be defined by the first event in time for the selection.

Using the Mute Tool

The Mute tool is an alternative to deleting events. Let's say you want to try different things, but aren't quite sure if you want to delete events. You can use the Mute tool to mute them instead.

To Mute events, right-click in the Edit window and select the Mute tool. To mute a single event, just click it with this tool. To mute a series of events, drag a box around them to select them and then click on one of the selected events with the Mute tool. Muted events appear grayed out on the piano roll or drum track display.

To unmute a single event, click it a second time with the Mute tool. Once you are satisfied with the result, you can either delete the muted events or unmute them by using the Unmute All option in the Do menu.

Erasing Events

You can erase events by using one of two methods: You can use the Eraser tool on single notes and selected notes, or you can select events using your Pointer tool and pressing either the Delete or Backspace key on your keyboard.

If you want to delete events in a specific area of the window, you can use the To and Do menu combination. Let's say you want to delete events in a part between 1.1.0 and 3.1.0, or Bar one, Beat 1 and Bar 3, Beat 1. You can create a loop area. Select the To Looped Events from the To menu, then select the Do Delete from the Do menu.

http://www.muskalipman.com

Toolbar Options

The MIDI event editing window's toolbar offers you a series of buttons, menus, and positioning information. At the far left of the Edit toolbar, you will find the Edit Solo button (see Figure 5.5). This function allows you to play only (solo) the selected part displayed in the window, muting all other tracks so that you can clearly hear what you are editing.

Figure 5.5
The Edit window toolbar.

The next option in the toolbar, the Goto drop-down menu, allows you to move to different parts, events, or selected events in your window. It is mainly a positioning function and does not affect your events in any way.

Below the Goto menu is the To menu, which allows you to affect certain events that are selected in a loop or cycle mode. By default, this option is set to All and will meet most of your needs, as this will modify events that you select in the piano roll or drum edit below. If you wish to modify events using the Do menu, here you should select the events that it will be applied to by using the To menu. So the Do and To work together. For example, you could create a loop, select events, then choose the To Looped Selected Ev. option, and then select Do Delete. This would delete events that are selected within the looped area only. If you press the Delete key of your keyboard, all selected events, regardless of the To menu setting, would be deleted.

Here's another way of looking at this: The Do menu applies the option you choose in the drop-down menu to the events defined by the option you selected in the To menu. For example, you choose the To Cycled Events, and then you select the Tambourine note, as shown in Figure 5.6. Now, you select the Do Fixed Note option. This changes all the events in the cycle defined by your left and right locator to the note you had selected—in this case, the Tambourine. You can see the result in Figure 5.7.

Figure 5.6
The events before applying the Fixed Note option in the Do menu.

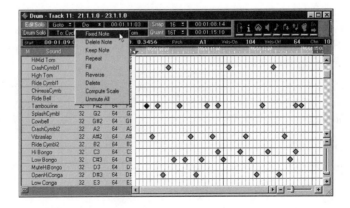

Figure 5.7
The events after applying the Fixed Note option in the Do menu.

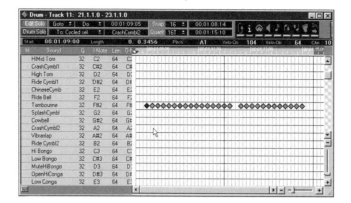

Use Fixed Note, Delete Note, or Keep Note to respectively move all notes within a range to the same value of the selected note, delete, or keep only the note or notes that are selected. The area this will affect depends on the option you selected in the To menu.

To use Fixed Note, Delete Note, or Keep Note:

1. Select the note (or notes) for the Fixed note option you wish to either move other notes to, delete all notes that are similar to, or, inversely, keep by eliminating all others, depending on which Do function you wish to apply.
2. Select the appropriate option in the To menu.
3. Select Fixed Note, Delete Note, or Keep Note from the Do menu.

Use Repeat to repeat a selected note or series of notes until the end of a part.

To use Repeat:

1. With your Pointer tool, click in the Edit window's time display at the beginning of the desired loop and drag it to the end of that loop area (see Figure 5.8). Make sure that your loop selection starts and ends at a bar line, unless you don't mind that the loop area doesn't loop well between bars.

Figure 5.8
Click and drag an area in the time ruler to create a loop region within a part.

2. Select either Looped Events (or Looped Selected Events, if you want to loop only selected events) from the To menu, as shown in Figure 5.9.

Figure 5.9
The To menu options.

3. If you want to loop only selected events—for example, specific notes or instruments in a drum track—select them with the Selection tool.
4. Select the Repeat option from the Do menu.

Figure 5.10 shows that the events included in the loop have been copied repeatedly until the end of the part. The copied events are displayed in the same shade here to better see the difference between the original pattern and the copied pattern. Following the selected loop, you can see that the pattern has been copied at equal intervals in time. This interval is equivalent to the duration of the selected loop.

Figure 5.10
The result of a Repeat option.

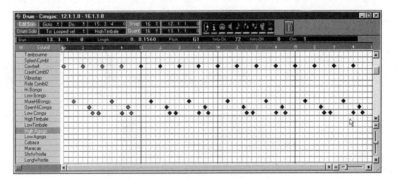

Use the Fill option in the Do menu when you want to fill the part, the cycle, or the loop area with a selected note. The duration of the note is determined by the Quantize value and the spacing is determined by the Snap value.

To use Fill:

1. Select one of the three following options in the To menu: All Events, Looped Events, or Cycled Events. This function works only with these options.
2. Select the appropriate Quantize value to determine the length of the notes and the Snap value to determine their spacing.
3. Click on a note or drum instrument you wish to use as the fill note.
4. Select Fill from the Do drop-down menu.

Use Reverse if you want to reverse the order of events in the range defined by the To menu. The Delete function works exactly the same, except that it deletes the events that are in the same range.

Use Compute Scale when you are working with MIDI events and are planning to create a score out of this track. This option will calculate what would be the scale for this section, optimizing the score layout later. This function is available only in Cubase Score or VST/32 and later versions of the software.

Finally, the Unmute All option allows you to unmute events as defined in the To menu. This is useful if you had previously muted notes with the Mute tool from the toolbox.

Next to the Do menu, you have a box displaying the current position of your cursor (the horizontal axis). Underneath that is the note or instrument corresponding to your cursor's position (the vertical axis). Use these boxes to quickly identify the position of an event in the graphic display below.

To the right of the position indicators, you will find the Snap and Quantize options. These options perform the same function as the Snap and Quantize options in the Arrange window, but since you are in an editor window, you can have an independent setting here and use these settings to define fill values as seen above. You can also modify these values to correspond to specific edits you are doing in the window. For example, if you would like to add notes to a part by drawing them in the Key Edit window, using the Snap and Quantize values will enable you to draw these events only at the specified quantized value.

Following the Snap and Quantize values, you have the loop area information display. If a loop area is selected, the begin and end position will appear here. As you have seen earlier, you can click and drag along the Time Ruler of the Edit window to create a loop area. You can also modify the begin and end points by manually entering the values in these fields. To enter a value manually, simply double-click on the appropriate field.

http://www.muskalipman.com

The next series of buttons are On/Off toggles that serve different purposes; Table 5.2 summarizes what these buttons do.

TABLE 5.2
Edit Window Toolbar Buttons.

Button	Button Name	Button Function
	Loop	Enables or disables the loop function in the Edit window.
	Info Line	Displays or hides the Info line below the toolbar.
	MIDI connector	Enables MIDI editing using the controller keyboard to select notes.
	Monitor	Enables the monitoring of MIDI events through the track's MIDI output port when the event is selected.
	Pitch	Works with the MIDI controller. When enabled, it gives the pitch value of the note you play to a selected event in the Edit window.
	Note On/Velocity	Works with the MIDI controller. When enabled, it assigns the Note On velocity parameter of the note you play to the selected event in the Edit window.
	Note Off/Velocity	Identical to Note On/Velocity button with the exception that it assigns the Note Off velocity instead.
	Step Recording	Enables the Step recording option. When selected, the MIDI editing button becomes enabled as well. See the section on step recording in Chapter 4 for more details.
	Insert	When enabled, it will add whatever event you play on your controller keyboard or with the Pencil tool at the position corresponding to the next Quantize value following the playback line.

The last menu on the Edit window toolbar is the Color menu. This allows you to assign colors to different events in your Edit window. You can assign different colors to a choice of Channels, Pitch, Velocity, or Parts. Each setting will color the corresponding selection differently for different values. For example, if you select Pitch, every C2 note will be the same color, and a B2 will be another color, and so on. This is useful when working with multiple channels in the same Edit window or if you need to edit a harmony structure and have a hard time aligning which note should be played with the keyboard on the left-hand side of the Edit window or the drum instrument if you are using a drum track.

The Info Line

If you need to quickly determine the start position or the velocity value of an event, the Info line will be your greatest ally. You can display the Info line by enabling the Info Line button on the toolbar.

To modify a parameter for a note using the Info line, select the note or group of notes and then use one of two methods:

1. Double-click the value you wish to edit and type in the new value.
2. Left-click on the appropriate value to decrease it or right-click to increase it.

If you select a range of MIDI notes or drum events, changing a value will affect all the values for the selection in proportion to the first value changed. Figure 5.11 shows selected events, with 127 as the value displayed for the velocity. In Figure 5.12, the velocity has been changed to 80 and all subsequent events in the selection have been reduced proportionally, rather than simply adjusted at 80.

Figure 5.11
Before modifying the selected events in the Key Edit window.

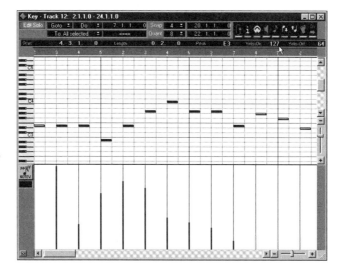

Figure 5.12
After modifying the selected events in the Key Edit window using the Velo-On value in the Info Line.

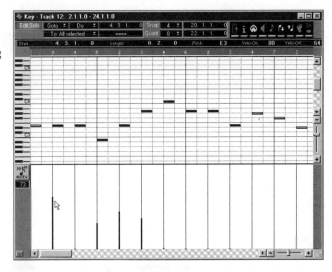

If you want to have all the values set to 80, as in the previous example, you can hold the Alt key down when clicking on the value or double-clicking on it to type in the new value. You can also select a series of events in the editor and move them with the arrow keys (left and right) on your keyboard while holding the Ctrl key down.

By using these two methods of editing single notes or a group of notes in the Info line, you can modify start times of events, their length, their pitch, their note on and off velocities, and their MIDI channel.

TIP

By default, when you are editing events in the Edit window, or any other window for that matter, the Follow Song option is enabled. This allows you to see the events as they are being played in Cubase. The window refreshes the display as the playback line moves forward. However, when editing or fine-tuning specific events in a window, this follow option might become annoying as the screen moves just as you were about to replace an event. To disable this function, press the F key on your keyboard or unselect Follow Song from the Option menu.

You can also enable the Stop Follow Song After Scrolling option by going to Edit > Preferences > General > General tab, to stop following the playback line once you use the horizontal scrollbar. This is a way of telling Cubase that you are editing a specific part and that you don't wish to see where the playback line is.

Editing Multiple Tracks

You can edit more than one track of the same class at a time in the Edit window. When selecting parts on different tracks in the Arrange window and activating the Edit window, you will be able to edit the parts for all the selected tracks at once.

If you have assigned different colors to different parts in the Arrange window, you will be able to see the parts' colors in the multitrack editing.

To edit more than one track at a time:

1. Click on the first part you want to edit in a track.
2. Shift+left-click on the next part you want to edit in another track.
3. Press Ctrl+E or select Edit from the Edit menu.

The editing window will appear with multiple tracks displayed, as shown in Figure 5.13. The active part is displayed with its part color and black borders around each event in the window. The title of the Edit window also reflects which part is active. The other parts are visible but inactive. They have the same color as the one you assigned to them in the Part Colors, but the borders are gray.

Figure 5.13
The Edit window can display more than one MIDI or drum track at a time.

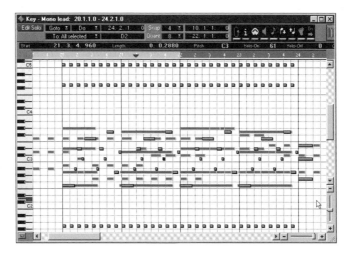

If you have more than one track visible in the Edit window, you can switch from one track to another by clicking on an event for that track in the Edit window. When step recording in a multitrack window like the one in Figure 5.13, you should always make the track where you want to step record active before enabling the Step Record option. You can, on the other hand, select events on more than one track at a time in the Edit window. Applying changes to selected events in a multiple track edit follows the same rules as if you were working with only one track at a time.

Editing MIDI Controller Events

There are two types of MIDI controller events: continuous and noncontinuous. Continuous controller events are events that occur continuously throughout the part, without being attached to a specific note event. The best example of a continuous controller event would be the Main Volume or Pan controller. These types of MIDI controllers can occur at any time. In the Edit window (Key or Drum editing), if a continuous controller has been added (a volume change, for example), this is displayed as a continuous line throughout the part, as shown in Figure 5.14. To display the controllers in the Edit window, you can click on the Show Controllers button in the lower left corner of the window.

Figure 5.14
The Main Volume control is a continuous controller and is displayed as such in the Edit window.

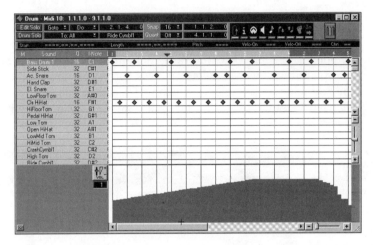

Noncontinuous controllers are attached to Note On or Note Off events such as velocity. These are displayed as vertical lines beneath each Note On event, as shown in Figure 5.15.

Figure 5.15
The Key Edit window displaying noncontinuous controllers.

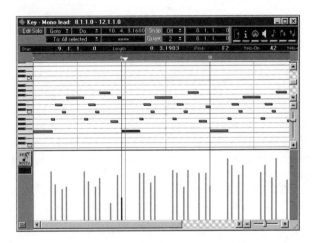

As mentioned earlier in this chapter, the Edit window is a good place to edit Note or Drum events as well as noncontinuous events. However, when it comes to editing continuous events, the Controller Edit window is more appropriate because it displays all the controllers on the left-hand side and also displays which controllers have data recorded on them.

Editing controllers in the Edit window is very similar to editing Note events. You can use the Pencil tool over a velocity controller, for example, to increase or decrease the value. To choose which controller you wish to edit, you select it from the controller selector box in the upper left-hand side of the Controller editing area of the Edit window. A pop-up menu will appear, allowing you to choose the controller of your choice.

You can edit controllers with the Pencil tool or the Line tool if you want to change the values, by simply pointing and clicking where you want to make the change or dragging a line over the area you want to affect, as shown in Figure 5.16. On the left-hand side of that figure, you can see a freehand modification of the velocity controller using the Pencil tool, and on the right-hand side, you can see a line modification of the same velocity controller using the Line tool. Note that the line in the freehand figure was added to illustrate the movement, but Cubase does not actually draw a line in freehand editing.

Figure 5.16
Modifying noncontinuous controller events in the Key Edit window.

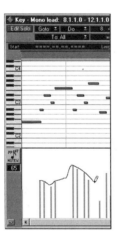 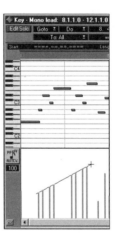

Modifying continuous event controllers will be covered in the section called "Controller Editor."

Drum Edit Window

What you have just read about the Edit window applies for the most part in the Drum Edit window as well. There are, however, some differences. The Drum Edit window treats every single drum or percussion instrument with its own parameters. For example, you can set a different Q value for the kick drum and the hi-hat. The Q value determines the spacing between each entered event. This does not affect the general Snap value you set in the Drum Edit window, but it affects the frequency at which events will be added when using the Drumstick (same as Pencil) or Paint tool. You will notice that the Drumstick tool has also replaced the Pencil tool, but they play a similar role in both editing windows.

Try this out by creating a drum track. Set the Q value for the kick drum at 4 and the hi-hat's Q value at 16. Now, use the Paintbrush tool to draw events on these instruments by simply dragging it from left to right, holding the mouse button down. You will see that a kick is added on every beat and a hi-hat on every sixteenth note.

Another small difference is that when you add an event with the Drumstick tool, clicking on it a second time will remove it, unlike with the Pencil tool, which will usually edit the note by dragging the event to make it longer or shorter. Because you can set an individual length for each instrument in a drum track, you can't extend the length in the event display area. There is a very simple reason for this treatment: Most percussive sounds are, by nature, quite short or without any sustained material, and they also are not looped. So, it really doesn't matter if you extend the event, since most instruments will play the sound until the end and the MIDI Note Off event's position will have little or no effect on this note, no matter how long you hold it. Unlike a guitar or keyboard note, the position of the attack, or Note On event, is more relevant in this case than the actual end of the event.

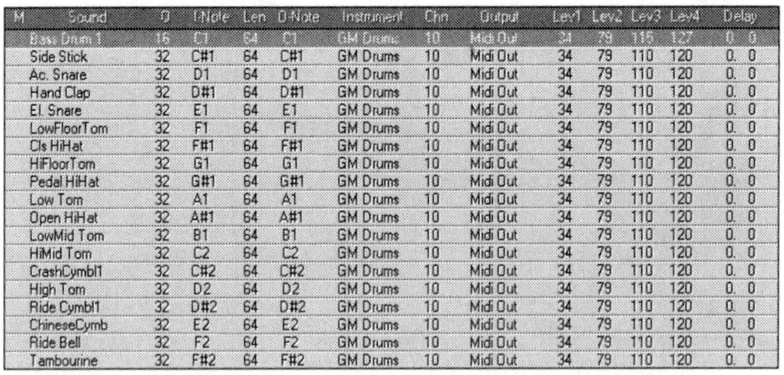

Figure 5.17
The event controller columns in the Drum Edit window.

M	Sound	Q	I-Note	Len	D-Note	Instrument	Chn	Output	Lev1	Lev2	Lev3	Lev4	Delay
	Bass Drum 1	16	C1	64	C1	GM Drums	10	Midi Out	24	79	115	127	0, 0
	Side Stick	32	C#1	64	C#1	GM Drums	10	Midi Out	34	79	110	120	0, 0
	Ac. Snare	32	D1	64	D1	GM Drums	10	Midi Out	34	79	110	120	0, 0
	Hand Clap	32	D#1	64	D#1	GM Drums	10	Midi Out	34	79	110	120	0, 0
	El Snare	32	E1	64	E1	GM Drums	10	Midi Out	34	79	110	120	0, 0
	LowFloorTom	32	F1	64	F1	GM Drums	10	Midi Out	34	79	110	120	0, 0
	Cls HiHat	32	F#1	64	F#1	GM Drums	10	Midi Out	34	79	110	120	0, 0
	HiFloorTom	32	G1	64	G1	GM Drums	10	Midi Out	34	79	110	120	0, 0
	Pedal HiHat	32	G#1	64	G#1	GM Drums	10	Midi Out	34	79	110	120	0, 0
	Low Tom	32	A1	64	A1	GM Drums	10	Midi Out	34	79	110	120	0, 0
	Open HiHat	32	A#1	64	A#1	GM Drums	10	Midi Out	34	79	110	120	0, 0
	LowMid Tom	32	B1	64	B1	GM Drums	10	Midi Out	34	79	110	120	0, 0
	HiMid Tom	32	C2	64	C2	GM Drums	10	Midi Out	34	79	110	120	0, 0
	CrashCymbl1	32	C#2	64	C#2	GM Drums	10	Midi Out	34	79	110	120	0, 0
	High Tom	32	D2	64	D2	GM Drums	10	Midi Out	34	79	110	120	0, 0
	Ride Cymbl1	32	D#2	64	D#2	GM Drums	10	Midi Out	34	79	110	120	0, 0
	ChineseCymb	32	E2	64	E2	GM Drums	10	Midi Out	34	79	110	120	0, 0
	Ride Bell	32	F2	64	F2	GM Drums	10	Midi Out	34	79	110	120	0, 0
	Tambourine	32	F#2	64	F#2	GM Drums	10	Midi Out	34	79	110	120	0, 0

To view the list of columns available in the Drum Edit window, drag the divider line between the Event view and the Column view to the right. There are fourteen columns, each representing a control over an instrument.

- **M**—Controls whether an instrument is muted or not. To mute an instrument, click in the instrument row in the M column. To unmute that instrument, click on the mute for that instrument once again.

- **Sound**—Represents the sound names as defined by the instrument drum map script you set up in the Track Info area of the Arrange window. In this case, the script uses the GM drum set patch script. You can change the name of a sound by double-clicking on the name for the instrument you wish to rename. You can also drag an instrument's row to change the order in which the instruments appear. Simply click on the name to highlight the row and drag it where you want it.

- **Q**—Is the Snap value used to add new events when using the Drumstick or Paint tool. The Q pop-up menu appears when you click on this value in the appropriate row and change the Q value for that instrument. The list that appears offers the same option as the Snap or Quantize pop-up lists. When changing the Q value, you do not affect the values of that area set by the Quantize or Snap values, so when you record new events while the Edit window is opened, the Quantize and Snap values have precedence over the Q value.

- **I-Note**—Stands for the Input Note value, or the note as recorded from the controller keyboard or drum machine. This will be important to understand when we discuss the Drum Map feature in the next section. To change this value, left-click to decrease the value, right-click to increase the value, or double-click to enter a new value.

- **Len**—Sets the length of events entered by the Drumstick or Paint tool. Because most percussive instruments play the sound until the end of the sample, no matter how long the event is held, this value plays little role in how the actual drum track will sound. To change this value, left-click to decrease the value, right-click to increase the value, or double-click to enter a new value.

- **O-Note**—Stands for Output Note Value, or the note that will play back the sound you wish to map. By default, the O-Note is the same as the I-Note, but you can remap the Input to another Output when using drum maps. Again, this will be discussed in the next section. To change this value, left-click to decrease the value, right-click to increase the value, or double-click to enter a new value.

- **Instrument**—Allows you to select an instrument from the list you have set up earlier in the Track Info area. Each note in a drum track can be assigned to a different instrument. For example, you could have the kick drum played by a GM device, the snare played by the VSTi LM-9, and so on. For this to work, you need to set your track's MIDI channel in the Track List area of the Arrange window to the Any setting; otherwise, all the sounds on the track will be played by the same instrument. To select an instrument, click on the appropriate row in the Instrument column and select one from the popup menu.

- **Chn**—Lets you select the MIDI channel you wish to assign to the instrument in a particular row. Each row can be played through a different MIDI channel. Again, for this to work, your drum track has to be set to play the Any setting in the Arrange window. To change this value, left-click to decrease, right-click to increase, or double-click to enter a new value.

- **Output**—Like the Instrument and Chn columns, lets you assign a different output for each row or note that is played in the drum part. To change the output, click on the appropriate row in the Output column and select one from the pop-up menu.

- **Lev1, Lev2, Lev3**, and **Lev4**—Different velocity level settings that you can assign to each note. Because many drum machines, samplers, and synthesizers will change the sound they play depending on the velocity at which you hit the note, you can set up to four levels of velocity for each instrument. To change this value, left-click to decrease, right-click to increase, or double-click to enter a new value. You can also set these values by enabling the MIDI connector in the Edit window's toolbar, selecting the level column for the instrument you want to edit, and pressing any key on your controller keyboard at the velocity you wish to set for this level. The value will be recorded onto the appropriate column for the selected instrument. Later, when you create events using the Drumstick or Paint tool, you can use key combinations to enter notes using one of the different levels set here. These keyboard shortcuts are:

    | Ctrl+Shift | Level 1 |
    | Ctrl | Level 2 |
    | Shift | Level 3 |

    By default, events created without a key modifier will be entered with the Level 4 value.

- **Delay**—As in the Track Info, adds a delay of up to plus or minus two sixteenth notes and a sixteenth triplet value. To change this value, left-click to decrease, right-click to increase, or double-click to enter a new value.

If you wish to set all the values in a column to the same value, you may do so by keeping the Alt key pressed as you select the column. For example, pressing Alt as you double-click in the Lev1 column for the first instrument will change all the Lev1 values to the number you enter for that column. Be careful not to do this in the Sound, I-Note, or O-Note columns, for they will all have the same sound name, or Input note. This is, on the other hand, very useful when assigning Length or Q value settings, not to mention Level settings.

Drum Maps

Because not all instruments are created equal, they all operate differently, assigning different sounds to different keys. For example, one instrument's drum setup could use all the notes in a C scale to map its drum sounds, where another instrument might use every chromatic note to map its drum set. This is fine when you know what note is playing what sound. But what if you want to try a different drum set or drum machine? Do you need to re-record all your beats because C1 is not the bass drum anymore? Well, not really. That's where drum mapping becomes very handy.

As you read in the previous section, in a Drum edit window you have two columns that display Input notes and Output notes. This is used to remap what was recorded on one note but now will play as if it were recorded on another note, remapping the event to correspond to a new drum instrument map. To do this, you can either create your own drum map or load one that has already been programmed. Cubase comes with ready-made drum maps on its CD; before you start creating your own drum map, check your CD or your Drummaps folder if you've installed them on your computer.

Drum maps are essentially a list of 128 sound names associated with Note In and Note Out events. You can have up to sixty-four drum maps loaded in a song, but you can assign only one drum map per track. For obvious reasons, if you use two tracks with the same MIDI output and MIDI channel, you can have only one drum map assigned to that instrument. Finally, you can assign only one Note In instrument per note name or note number, but you can have more than one Note In assigned to the same Note Out. There are two ways to load drum maps into your song or arrangement.

▶ Select File > Open, look in your Drummap folder, and set your File of type field in the Open dialog box to load *.drm files, or Drummap files. Choose the drum map you wish to open from one of the files available.

▶ From the Drummap field in the Track Info area, select Load Map from the drop-down menu. Once you load a drum map, it will appear in this box to be selected later on. Cubase will ask you if you want to replace the default drum map with the one you are about to load. If you choose Yes, your current default will appear second in the list of available drum maps. If you choose No, the default will stay GM.DRM (or whatever drum map you set to be the default), and the file you will load will appear following the loaded order.

Because your drum map is a way of reassigning the keys you play to other keys at the output, remember that each note in a drum map corresponds to a note number from 0 to 127. Each note number can be given a name, such as Kick Drum 1, Snare, Hi-hat, and so forth. You can then assign the played note to that named instrument, such as C1 or note number 36 to the Kick Drum 1. If you want to play Kick Drum 1 on C1 and your sound module has it on C2, you then assign the I-Note as C1 (note number 36) and the O-Note as C2 (note number 48). Table 5.3 will help you keep track of note numbers and their corresponding note names in Cubase.

To enter a name for an instrument, double-click in the appropriate row in the Sound column and type the desired name.

To change the I-Note, you can click the MIDI monitor button, then the Pitch button in the toolbar. This will allow you to enter the pitch by using your controller keyboard. Click on the I-Note column header to activate the header and play the desired input note on your keyboard. Then, click on the O-Note column header to activate the header and play the desired output note on your keyboard. This is easier than entering individual values in the columns.

Once you have set your instrument sounds, you can proceed to saving your drum map by selecting the Save Map option from the Drummap menu in the Track Info area of the drum track (see Figure 5.18). If you use this drum map often, you can save it in the folder called Library Files, which is one of the Cubase VST subfolders. This will allow you to select it from the File > Open From Library menu. The Library folder is a special folder Cubase uses where you can store frequently used files like drum maps, key command setups, mixer maps, songs, and other files associated with Cubase.

Figure 5.18
Saving your drum map through the track's Drummap menu.

Later on, if you feel you have loaded drum maps that you don't wish to use anymore, you can select the Remove Unused from the Drummap pop-up menu, shown in Figure 5.18.

Table 5.3
Note Number and Name Table.

Note No.	Note Name	Note No.	Note Name	Note No.	Note Name	Note No.	Note Name
0	C-2	32	G#0	64	E3	96	C6
1	C#-2	33	A0	65	F3	97	C#6
2	D-2	34	A#0	66	F#3	98	D6
3	D#-2	35	B0	67	G3	99	D#6
4	E-2	36	C1	68	G#3	100	E6
5	F-2	37	C#1	69	A3	101	F6
6	F#-2	38	D1	70	A#3	102	F#6
7	G-2	39	D#1	71	B3	103	G6
8	G#-2	40	E1	72	C4	104	G#6
9	A-2	41	F1	73	C#4	105	A6
10	A#-2	42	F#1	74	D4	106	A#6
11	B-2	43	G1	75	D#4	107	B6
12	C-1	44	G#1	76	E4	108	C7
13	C#-1	45	A1	77	F4	109	C#7
14	D-1	46	A#1	78	F#4	110	D7
15	D#-1	47	B1	79	G4	111	D#7
16	E-1	48	C2	80	G#4	112	E7
17	F-1	49	C#2	81	A4	113	F7
18	F#-1	50	D2	82	A#4	114	F#7
19	G-1	51	D#2	83	B4	115	G7
20	G#-1	52	E2	84	C5	116	G#7
21	A-1	53	F2	85	C#5	117	A7
22	A#-1	54	F#2	86	D5	118	A#7
24	C0	56	G#2	88	E5	120	C8
25	C#0	57	A2	89	F5	121	C#8
26	D0	58	A#2	90	F#5	122	D8
27	D#0	59	B2	91	G5	123	D#8
28	E0	60	C3	92	G#5	124	E8
29	F0	61	C#3	93	A5	125	F8
30	F#0	62	D3	94	A#5	126	F#8
31	G0	63	D#3	95	B5	127	G8

http://www.muskalipman.com

The List Window

The List Edit window, like the Key Edit window, allows you to modify your MIDI and audio events. The difference with the List editing window is that all the events are "listed" in rows of information and sorted by the order in which they were recorded. This is different from the Key or Drum Edit window in the sense that you can have three notes displayed at the same place in a piano or drum roll, but in the list rows, each has its own. This makes it a good place to look for glitches like note doubling (two notes playing the same channel or the same key at the same time) or consecutive patch changes that you've entered by mistake and that now make your sound module behave erratically.

This said, if you want to edit notes and change velocity levels or edit a mix, the Edit and Controller windows are better suited for these tasks. The List Edit window can display all types of events corresponding to different track classes. It does so by using certain columns of information and adapting the meaning of the value represented by the column in the function of the track class. For example, the audio tracks will use the Start Position, End Position, Channel, and Comments columns, while the MIDI and drum track classes will use the Start Position, Length, Value 1, Value 2, Value 3, Event Type, and Channel columns.

The Start, End, and Length columns are no-brainers. It's simple by now to imagine what they represent—the start time of the event, the end time of an event when this event has one, and the length of the event, when the event has a length. Where it becomes a little bit less obvious is when you look at the value columns.

Understanding the Information

Before we take a look at the values in the columns and what they mean, let's look at the different parts of the List Edit window, as shown in Figure 5.19. The toolbar offers some similarities with the Edit window. You will find some new elements, however.

Figure 5.19
The List Edit window.

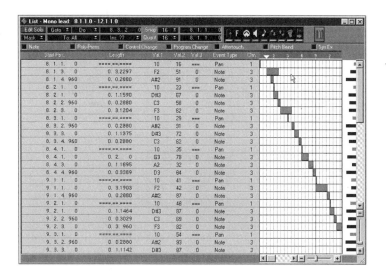

The Insert menu allows you to select the type of event you wish to insert.

The other difference in the List window's toolbar is the Filter button, represented by the letter F. This is different from the Info button in the Edit window and displays or hides a bar beneath the toolbar. This bar represents elements that you can filter from your display. They will be hidden from your view, but any modification you make can affect these events as well, unlike the Mask. But not to worry—usually, if you can see it, it's hard to erase it. To filter a type of event, click in the checkbox next to the event's name in the Filter option bar. If you don't see that bar, enable it by clicking the Filter button in the toolbar.

Below the toolbar, there are three areas giving information: the Column area, which we just talked about; the Event area in the center; and the Controller area on the right-hand side of the window.

The Controller display area shows Value 2 from the Column area. This value can be edited by using the Pencil tool. In fact, as soon as you enter the area, your tool will change to the Pencil automatically. When you make a modification to the value in this area, the change is reflected in the column titled Val.2.

Regarding the Column display area, Table 5.4 explains what each value is represented by in the Val columns depending on the track class.

Table 5.4
Description of information present for the Value columns.

Track Class	Event Type	Val.1	Val.2	Val.3	Comment
MIDI and Drum	Note	Pitch of the note	Note On velocity	Note Off velocity	Drum instrument name
	Poly Pressure	Note number	Pressure amount		
	Control Change	Controller type	Change amount		
	Program Change	Patch number			
	After touch	Pressure amount			
	Pitch bend	Fine value of bend	Coarse value of bend		
System Exclusive				The SysEx message	
Mixer	MIDI mixer	Object number	Its value		Object name and instrument setting
	Track Mixer Automation Data	Object number	Its value		Mixer object name
	VST channel mixer automation DATA	Both values will work together to specify the mixer object	Value		

Creating and Editing Events

To insert an event in the List Edit window:

1. Select the type of event you wish to insert from the Insert menu.
2. Right-click in the right area of the List window where the events appear and select the Pencil tool from the toolbox.
3. Click where you wish to insert the event. The horizontal ruler on top represents the time, and each row represents an event at that time.
4. If you wish to move your event in time, use your Pointer tool and move the event left or right by dragging it. The Column view will reflect that change.

To edit several events at once:

1. Select the first event you wish to edit in the Column display area.
2. Ctrl+click the last event in the list you wish to edit, thus selecting all the events between the two. If you wish to edit nonsequential events, Shift+click on each event.
3. Press and hold the Alt key down before you make your modifications to all the selected events. If you wish to modify a series of events proportionally, press Ctrl+Alt keys together before making the changes.

The Event Display

The Event display area shows events as they occur in time, like a Key or Drum editing window. The difference is that the vertical axis of the display shows the order in which these events occur rather than the pitch itself. If you move an event to the left, before another event occurs, it will also move up in the list as Cubase refreshes its display after you let go of the mouse.

To modify events in the Event display area, select the events you wish to move and drag them to the left or right to move them in time where you want the event or events to occur.

About Masks

The Mask menu allows you to mask selected events for editing. A mask hides unwanted events from editing, leaving what you selected as a mask for editing. This is different from the Filter function in this window, since the filter hides chosen events from display but NOT from editing. In Figure 5.19, you could select the first event and then select either Mask Event Exactly or Mask Event Type from the drop-down menu. Mask Event Exactly will mask all Pan events with the Value 1 set at 10. In this case, since the Value 1 represents the MIDI controller for Pan events, all Pan events would be selected. On the other hand, if you select the third event, Note A#2, only the Note events having the Value 1 set to A#2 would appear in your list. The Mask Event Type option masks all the events corresponding to the Event Type value. So again, if you select the third event, Note A#2, all Note events would be selected, not just the A#2 events. The other option in the Mask menu is No Mask, which removes the mask.

http://www.muskalipman.com

To edit all events in a mask:

1. Make sure the To menu is set to All Events.
2. Select the event you wish to edit.
3. Hold down the Alt key before making the modification. This will transform all events in the mask to the new value you just set.

Controller Editor

The Controller editor is an enhanced version of the Controller Area in the Edit and List windows. This editor is designed to edit non-note events: more specifically, continuous controllers for all track classes that contain controller events—MIDI, audio, and mix. The controllers are displayed in much the same way as they are in the Controller area of the Key editor's window. The difference here is that you can see all your controllers on the left side of the window, with an indicator for each controller containing recorded events. Unless you want to modify notes and controllers together, this is where you should make your modifications.

To open the Controller Edit window, select the part you want to edit using the Pointer tool in the Arrange window and then choose the Controller option from the Edit menu.

Event Types

The Event types displayed in the Controller editor window vary depending on the track class being edited. Figure 5.20 shows a MIDI track being edited. With this track class, MIDI controllers are separated into two categories: Common and Controllers. The Common controllers are the ones you will probably use the most often because, as the name says, they are common in MIDI tracks. To expand the list, click on the + sign next to the word "Common." If a controller contains data for that type of event, it will be displayed by a bullet next to the name.

Figure 5.20
The MIDI Tracks Event Type display.

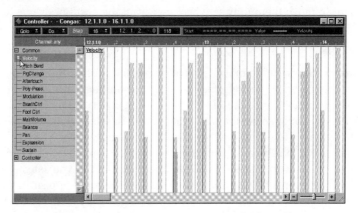

The MIDI track mixer will display a group of controllers for every MIDI track controller; typically the Pan and Volume controls, as displayed in Figure 5.21, but if the MIDI track contains extended controller events, as you can see for the Mono Lead track in the same figure, the group of controllers will contain the extended data recorded as well.

Figure 5.21
The MIDI Track Mixer Event Type display.

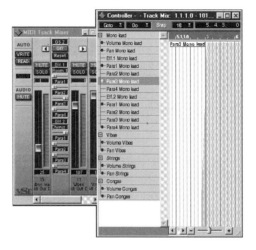

In an Audio Mix track, controller events are grouped by type of controller, time, and each group holding the events for all audio channels. The number of audio channels it holds depends on your audio system setting. In Figure 5.22, you can see that there are eight audio channels, and four of them have volume controllers recorded: channels 1, 3, 4, and 5. You will also notice that the audio waveform is displayed in the background. This will come in handy when you are editing your final mix of audio events.

Figure 5.22
The Audio Mix Track Event Type display.

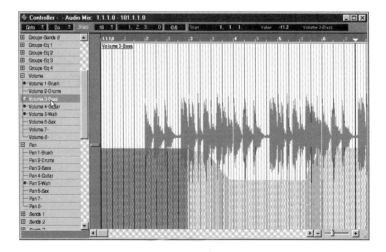

Editing Controls

To edit a controller event in the Controller Edit window, you select it in the Event Type area. It will then appear in the left area of the window. By default, the name of the controller is displayed in the upper left corner of the display. If it is not, select Show Labels from the Do menu in the window's toolbar. You can also toggle on or off the grid from that same menu.

To edit controller events, you always have to start by launching the Controller Edit window through the Edit menu and then select from the Event list the event you wish to edit. From that point on, it depends what you want to do. Here's a list of possible operations:

To modify an event already recorded:

▶ Select your Pencil tool and drag the event up or down.

To modify a series of events already recorded:

1. With the Pointer tool, drag a box over the events you wish to edit, as in the left-hand side of Figure 5.23.
2. Using the scale slider in the middle of the window, drag it down to decrease or up to increase the value of the event by a percentage value. This percentage value is indicated in the toolbar, next to the position indicator. In the right-hand side of Figure 5.23, it shows that the new values for the volume controller will be at 82 percent of the original value.

Figure 5.23
Editing a series of event controllers using the scale slider.

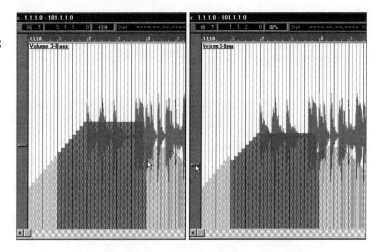

To add new controller events:

1. Select your Pencil tool if you wish to add new freehand events or the Line tool if you wish to draw straight lines, such as linear fades.
2. Hold the Alt key as you draw your new events with either the Pencil or Line tool.

To delete or erase controller events, simply right-click to select the Eraser tool from the toolbox and click on the events you wish to erase. If you want to erase more than one event, you can select the events first, as mentioned earlier.

To smooth changes between values, you can also use the Smooth option in the Do menu on the toolbar. To use the Smooth option:

1. Make a selection of events you wish to smooth.
2. Select Do > Smooth.

The Smooth function doesn't add values, it just makes the transition between events a bit smoother by comparing the data before and after and extrapolating a value in between. Remember that the Quantize value will affect when your modifications will take place. A smaller Quantize value (larger numbers) will result in a more precise change of values in terms of frequency at which these values change. This will also increase the amount of information needed to reproduce these controller changes. If you have too many controller changes at one point, your computer might start displaying inconsistencies while playing back these events. If this is the case, reduce the Quantize value to reduce the number of intermediate steps and try playing the arrangement once again.

You can reduce the number of continuous event controllers by selecting your events and then the Reduce option in the Do menu item.

http://www.muskalipman.com

Displaying Multiple Event Types

Sometimes, you will want to edit more than one event at a time. You could do it the long way by switching from one event type to the other, or you could select more than one event type by Ctrl+clicking them in the Event type area for consecutive event type editing or Shift+clicking them if they are not consecutive. Figure 5.24 shows three separate audio channel volume controller events in one window.

Figure 5.24
Displaying more than one event at a time can be useful when comparing volume changes.

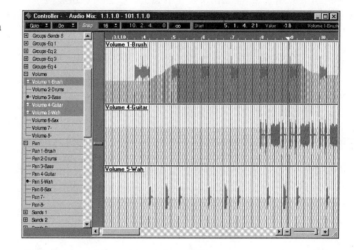

The fact that you can display more than one event, as shown in Figure 5.24, can also be useful when using the Mirror Active option from the Do menu in this window. Mirror Active allows you to select a range or all event controllers in an active track and copy them to the other tracks visible in a multi-event display. In Figure 5.24, the first layer is active, since it is of a different color. If Mirror Active were to be applied, the portion in dark from the first track would be copied to the two other tracks.

Now You Try It

Here are the exercises you will find on the Website for this chapter:

- ▶ Move events with the Selection and Nudge tool.
- ▶ Use the To and Do menus in the Drum Editor to edit events.
- ▶ Resize events using the Pencil tool and Line tool.
- ▶ Mute events.
- ▶ Edit events in the List editor.

You will find these exercises at **www.muskalipman.com/cubase**.

Simply follow the instructions on the Web site before starting the exercises.

You can refer to this chapter to find out how to do these exercises, but try doing them without peeking first, just to see how comfortable you are with these principles. If you don't remember how to do a task, refer to the appropriate header in this chapter.

You will need to have the Universal Sound Module and the VB-1 VSTi installed on your computer to use the file provided for these exercises. If you do not have these VST instruments installed, you can always use a General MIDI-compatible device, assigning Channel 1 to play a Bass sound, Channel 2 to play a Lead Synth sound, Channel 3 to play a Strings sound, Channel 5 a Piano sound, and Channel 10 to Drums.

6
Making Sense of Track Editing

Now that you know how to use the editing functions in the editing windows, we will move on to more editing options, but in the Arrange window this time. Because the Arrange window is the main work area, it is important to have tools that will let you organize the information in a way that is conducive to your creativity. This is why we will take a look at folder and group track classes. Folder tracks are used to organize tracks; group tracks are used to arrange groups, or sections, of music in a different way without having to record every instrument one by one, from beginning to end.

You will also learn how to use the Logical editor—a powerful MIDI editing tool that can perform macro tasks on your MIDI data. For example, you can use the Logical editor to create a double speed/half speed drum track, fix lengths for an entire track, and more.

Finally, you will see how you can use the locators with the functions found in the Structure menu, applying edits over the entire range of tracks in your Arrange window. This is interesting, because up until now, we have focused on how to edit parts and tracks individually. In this chapter, you will learn how to use editing functions that affect the entire arrangement, making changes to the structure of your project.

Folder Tracks

Folder tracks are different from other track classes because, like folders on your computer—which hold files—they hold the contents of other tracks. Folder tracks allow you to organize your space in an arrangement by taking, for example, all the backing vocal tracks and adding them to a folder track that you can call "Back Vocals." Once tracks are in a folder track, you can collapse the folder track as you would a tree in Windows Explorer. When a folder track is collapsed, you will see all the tracks it contains in the Track View area of the Arrange window, as displayed in Figure 6.1. To expand a collapsed Folder track, click on the plus sign next to the track's name in the List View area.

Figure 6.1
This is an example of a collapsed folder track.

Folder tracks can contain any type of tracks, including other folder tracks. You can use folder tracks not only to organize your arrangement but also to mute a series of tracks at once. All tracks that are inside a folder track will be muted when you mute this track.

To move tracks to a folder track, click on the track's name in the Track List area of the Arrange window and drag the track over the folder track. You can also select parts on different tracks and move them to a folder track. Here's how you can do this:

1. Create a track by using the Key Command, Ctrl+T, or by double-clicking after the last track in the Track List area.
2. Change the track class to Folder Track from the C column in the Track List area.
3. While your folder track is highlighted, select parts in your Track View area. You can Shift+click different parts or drag a box over the parts you wish to add to the folder track. You don't need to select all the parts in a track to add it to the folder track. Any track that has parts selected will be added.
4. From the Structure menu, select Move Tracks to Folder.

All tracks containing selected parts are added to the folder track.

When your folder track is selected, you will see a Solo button appear in the Track Info area. You can use this to solo a track from your folder track. This will not mute tracks that are outside the folder tracks but will mute only tracks that are not selected in your folder tracks. This is helpful when you want to isolate good takes if you are using the folder track to group a set of different takes.

Group Tracks

Group tracks, like folder tracks, are used to organize your arrangement. This is their only similarity. You can use group tracks to create song structures that repeat. For example, you can create a group track containing your MIDI kick drum and MIDI snare, calling this group "Loop A." You can also separate each section of your song into groups, such as Intro Beat, Verse Beat, Break Beat, Fill Beat, and so on. Once your groups are created, you can then add them to a group track and place a group where you want it to play, placing only one element instead of having to copy and paste a series of parts. Group tracks contain only MIDI tracks, so you will have to paste your audio or mix events later. A nice advantage to groups is that when you modify the part that is used in a group, the group updates all instances of that part on the group track. Let's look at how you can use group tacks.

To create a new group:

1. Make your groups visible. To do this, select Show Groups from the Structure menu or press Ctrl+J on your keyboard. This will display a Group area on the right side of your Arrange window, as displayed in Figure 6.2.

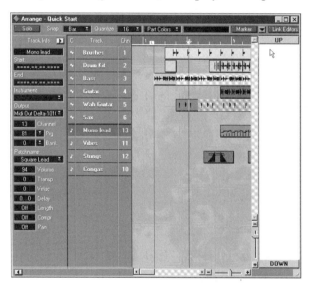

Figure 6.2
A Group area is displayed to the right of the Arrange window.

2. Select the MIDI parts you wish to use in your group.
3. From the Structure menu, select Build Group or press Ctrl+U on your keyboard. The Build Group dialog box (see Figure 6.3) will appear, prompting you to enter a new name for your group.

4. Type in the new name and click New to add this new group to your list of groups.

Figure 6.3
The Build Group dialog box.

The group you created then appears in the Group list in the Arrange window.

To add a part to an already existing group, select the group you wish to add a part to, then select the part you wish to add to that group. Press Ctrl+U or select Build Group from the Structure menu, this time clicking the Add to button instead of the New button.

You can repeat these steps to create up to sixty-four different groups per arrangement. Because a group works as a unit, you can position a group on a group track wherever you want it. All parts in a group will keep their relative position within that group and their relative MIDI channel and MIDI settings.

To use a group track:

1. Start by creating a new track by pressing Ctrl+T and double-clicking below the last track in the Track List area or by selecting Create Track from the Structure menu.
2. Change the track class to Group Track from the C column in the Track List area.
3. Drag a group from the Group List area in the group track at the desired position, as shown in Figure 6.4.

Figure 6.4
Building a group track using groups from the Group List area.

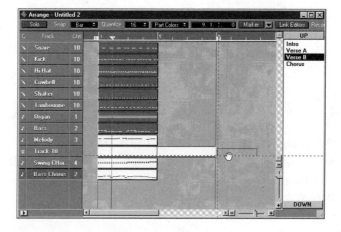

Remember to mute the tracks that are part of your groups if they are playing in their respective tracks at the same time your group track is; otherwise, some note doubling will occur and this may also choke the MIDI data stream and cause MIDI instruments to lock up. Try not to overlap groups either, because this will produce an overlap of MIDI data, which probably won't sound great.

If you change your mind about the content of a group, you can always replace the content by selecting that group and then selecting the new parts you wish to use for this group. Finally, you create a group—using the process mentioned earlier—and select the Replace option in the Build Group dialog box. The existing group will now have the new parts in it.

Suppose that hours have passed and you don't remember which part you used to create a group? Just click on the group in the Group List and all the parts you used to create that group will be highlighted. If you deleted a part from a track that you used in a group, it will no longer be played in that group, so it won't appear as being selected.

What if you want to delete a group? Drag the group outside of the Arrange window, and voilà!

Groups created in your arrangement will be saved with your arrangement. Groups created in your song will be saved with your song. So, if you are using Song files and Arrangement files, understand this: A Song file can contain many arrangements. An Arrangement file can contain only one arrangement. If you use groups created in a Song file and swap it between arrangements of the same song, they will be saved with the Song file. However, if you save an arrangement created within a Song file, but not the arrangement that contained the original groups, these groups won't appear the next time you open this Arrangement file.

NOTE
If you quantize a group, it will not only affect the group itself but all the parts included in that group. So be careful when using the quantize function, for this might influence more than you bargained for.

Logical Editing

Logical editing is another way of editing MIDI data. Using this method, you create specific parameters for Cubase to look for and then decide to change them, delete them, or move them. This is for the MIDI-savvy user, because you need to know how MIDI messages work in order to fully understand how logical editing works.

The Logical editor will affect events differently, depending on the location from which you launch it, but it will always perform the tasks in the same way. For example, if you are in the Arrange window and have not selected any parts, it will perform edits on all the parts for the selected tracks. On the other hand, if you have a part selected, it will look for and edit only events in that part. Finally, if you are in an editing window, the Logical editor will perform its modifications on the events as defined by the To menu in the editing window's toolbar for this part only. This is why you should set the To menu to reflect what you want to edit BEFORE launching the Logical editor.

You may use already created Logical edit presets included with Cubase, or you may create your own and save them as well. Logical edits are stored as separate files on your hard disk and are common to any song or arrangement.

This is how it works (refer to Figure 6.5 to see what the following example is describing): The Logical editor starts by applying a filter for which you decide a condition for a type of event. For example, if you want to transpose notes that are between C2 and G4, the event type would be Notes and the condition would be set as Values inside a range of notes you wish to modify (in this case C2 and G4). Then, you apply a function. In this example, it is a transform function. Finally, you may have to apply processing for certain functions. Again, in our example, if you want to transpose the notes between C2 and G4, you have to tell the editor how many steps you want to transpose to and in what direction—up or down. If you wanted to transpose these notes a perfect fifth (seven semitones), you would process the notes by adding 7 to the note value. All you need to do now is to click the Do It button to apply this logical edit. What will be affected by the Logical editor depends on the location from which you launched the editor and if you had selected events or not. The Logical editor allows you to edit a selected track, a selected part, or a selected range of events in a part, depending on the point from which you launch the Logical editor.

Figure 6.5
The Logical editor used to transpose notes between C2 and G4 up a fifth on Track 10.

Remember that using the Logical editor allows you to modify events in a way that would normally take much more time if done manually in one of the editors. The example above is just one of many ways you can quickly and effectively transform MIDI events, not to mention the creative aspects of the Logical editor. For example, creating a textured melody using a copy of the MIDI events, transposed a third above but using a velocity level set at 25 percent of the original version, will simply add color to this melody without having it stand out.

The following sections will allow you to get an understanding of these principles, and you can decide how you want to apply them.

Logical Editor Parameters

Let's take a closer look at the parameters found in the Logical editor. Figure 6.6 describes the different fields; following the figure are descriptions about the parameters in these fields.

Figure 6.6
The Logical editor's fields and buttons.

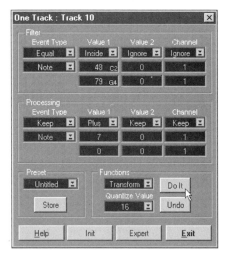

Filter

▶ **Event Type**—The top field defines the condition that will be applied. The field beneath defines what Event Type will be affected by the Logical editor.

▶ **Value 1**—Defines the conditions for events to be targeted by the filter. In the two fields below, if you need to define a range, enter the second value first; otherwise it will be disabled by the first.

▶ **Value 2**—Used to set an optional second set of conditions for filtering.

▶ **Channel**—Also optional, represents a condition for the track's MIDI Channel.

Processing

▶ **Event Type**—This and the entire row to the right of it represent the processing operators that allow you to decide whether to keep events or edit them. The field below defines what Event Type will be affected by the processing above. It is disabled when the Event Type is set to Keep.

▶ **Channel**—Use the second and third fields to set the parameters for the processing operators above. The values will influence how the MIDI data will be processed.

▶ **Preset**—Allows you to select from a list of saved files.

▶ **Store**—Click on this button if you want to save your settings to a file and use them later.

▶ **Functions**—This is the heart of the Logical editor. It determines what function to apply to the filtered events. Choosing Transform or Insert will enable the Processing section of the editor.

- **Quantize Value**—Use this field when setting the Function field to Quantize. Otherwise, this field is disabled.
- **Do It**—Click on this button to apply the function once you are satisfied with your setup.
- **Init**—Used to initialize the Logical editor.
- **Expert**—Used to toggle between the Expert and Simple modes of the editor.

About Event Type

There are two kinds of Event Type fields. First, you have the Filter Event Types, then the Processing Event Type that will apply processing on the events defined by the first Filter Event Type.

There are three Filter Event Types:

- **Ignore**—Ignores the filter altogether, passing all events through the processing. When you choose this option, the rest of the fields in the Filter section are ignored.
- **Equal**—Selects only events that correspond to a specific condition set by the field below the Filter's Event Type field.
- **Unequal**—Selects only the events that DO NOT correspond to a specific set by the field below the Filter's Event Type field.

There are two Processing Event Types:

- **Keep**—Leaves the existing values for events as they are without modifying them.
- **Fix**—Modifies the existing events as set in the field below the Processing Event Type field.

About Filter Values

There are three kinds of filter values:

- **Ignore**—Disables any condition, passing the values through the filter, processing them all.
- **Equal, Unequal, Higher,** or **Lower**—Lets you set one value in the field below the Value 1 or Value 2 Filter field. This will take the value and compare it with the condition and filter the rest out.
- **Inside** or **Outside**—Lets you specify a range of values between a higher value first, then a lower value. Everything between this range or excluded from this range in the case of the Outside condition, will be processed.

About Filter And Processing Values

You can have two sets of filter values and two sets of processing values. What these values represent depends on the Event Type you choose to process. The processing values are used to modify the events, and the filter values are conditions set to send the result to be processed or not. Table 6.1 describes the filter values.

Table 6.1
The Filter Values.

Event Type	Value 1	Value 2
Notes	Used for Note Events. The value is indicated in both number value and note value.	Represent the note-on velocity.
Poly Pressure	Indicates pressure value on a specific key, found by looking at the letters showing the pitch.	The amount of pressure for the note event.
Control Change	Used to indicate the number for the MIDI Controller.	The amount of Control Change.
Program Change	Used to indicate the Program Change number for your MIDI instrument.	N/A
Aftertouch	The amount of pressure you apply after a key is pressed.	N/A
Pitch Bend	The amount of fine-tuning in a pitch bend. This is rarely used.	The amount of coarse bend.

Like its filter values counterpart, the processing values have three types of conditions: those that ignore or, in this case, keep the values as they are; those that refer to a specific value and apply an operator to that value; and those that ask for a range of values and apply an operator to this range. In the latter case, a number corresponding to the proper Event Type is required to process the operator. Let's take a look at these processing value operators.

- **Keep**—Keeps the existing values as is, not affecting the event or having to set any number in the value fields.
- **Plus**—Adds to the existing value by the amount in the field below from the Event Type value set in the Event Type field.
- **Minus**—Removes the existing value by the amount in the field below from the Event Type value set in the Event Type field.
- **Multiply**—Multiplies the existing value by the amount in the field below from the Event Type value set in the Event Type field. You can use up to two decimals, but the result will be rounded to the nearest integer.
- **Divide**—Divides the existing value by the amount in the field below from the Event Type value set in the Event Type field. You can use up to two decimal places, but the result will be rounded to the nearest integer, just like Multiply.
- **Fix**—Replaces the existing values with the one you enter in the field below.
- **Value 2**—Replaces the numbers of the Value 1 field with the ones found in the Value 2 field.

http://www.muskalipman.com

- **Dyn**—This function is used to create a "ramp" from one value to another, such as a crescendo or a diminuendo. This function involves four parameters, a Start and an End value and a Start and an End point. If you open the Logical editor from the Arrange window, the Start and End points will be the start and end of the part or parts on the selected track. If you open Logical editor from one of the editors, the Start and End points will be one of three things: the start and end of the part, the left and right locator values, or the loop boundaries, all depending on how the To menu was set in the editor. The two value fields are used to set the initial value at the beginning of the range and the final value at the end.

- **Random**—Replaces the values with random numbers within a range specified by the two values.

About Functions

Functions are what you want to do with the events you filtered and processed. Actually, you need only to set the processing values and event types if you are using the Transform or Insert functions. To use all the other functions, you need only a filter setup.

- **Quantize**—Quantizes the events that pass through the filtered events. You can use the field below the function field to set the Quantize value. Quantizing non-note events can be used to reduce the amount of controller events in your arrangement.

- **Select**—If you launch the Logical editor from the Edit windows—Key, Drum, List, or Score—it simply selects the events that pass through the filters for future processing directly in the editor, after you have exited Logical editor. You cannot use this function if you are not launching the Logical editor from the Edit windows.

- **Delete**—Deletes the notes that pass through the filters.

- **Extract**—If you launch the Logical editor from the Arrange window, it cuts the events that pass through the filters out of the part or parts and then creates a new part or parts with the extracted events only. You cannot use this function if you are not launching the Logical editor from the Arrange window.

- **Copy**—If you launch the Logical editor from the Arrange window, it copies the events that pass through the filters out of the part or parts and then creates a new part or parts with the extracted events only. You cannot use this function if you are not launching the Logical editor from the Arrange window.

- **Transform**—Transforms the events that pass through the filters. The transformation is set by the values set in processing. This doesn't add any new events; it just changes the existing ones.

- **Insert**—Adds the events that pass through the filters. The transformation is set by the values set in processing. This adds new events to the part(s).

The best way to understand all of this is to look at some of the presets. Load them and look at how they change the values in the different parts of the window. Since the preset names are pretty descriptive, you'll get a good sense of what's happening.

Easy vs. Expert Mode

There are two modes in the Logical editor: Easy mode, which we have discussed in the previous pages, and Expert mode. Before you continue, note that the most common features can be found in the Easy mode. The Expert mode adds two new columns to the equation. These columns refer to specific time values, ranges, or location in the arrangement.

Setting Values

The Length value in the Expert Mode of the Logical editor's Filter section allows you to define a length for events that will be filtered. To set the value for this field, click near the integer value to increase or decrease this value or near the decimals to increase or decrease these decimals. The values for this field represent sixteenth notes and ticks.

The Bar Range value in the Expert Mode of the Logical editor's Filter section allows you to define a range for events that will be filtered as well. To set the values for this range, you can proceed in the same manner as for defining length—always left-clicking to decrease the values, right-clicking to increase the values, or clicking and dragging a selection in the range. The Bar Range values have the same rules as any other field in this window: If the condition you choose calls for a single value, only one value will appear as editable. The Bar Range itself displays a maximum of one bar divided into sixteenth notes and ticks.

To select a range, click and drag in the Bar Range area of the Logical editing window, as shown in Figure 6.8. Each integer represents a sixteenth note and the decimals represent ticks. The number of ticks depends on your software resolution preferences, but by default it is set to 15,360 ticks, which represents a quarter note. So, if an integer is a sixteenth note, you will have up to 3,839 ticks between each integer.

Figure 6.8
Defining a range of beats for a logical edit in the Expert mode.

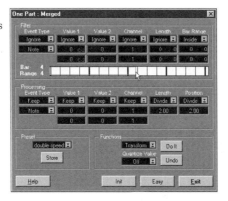

NOTE

Cubase always plays and records audio at 15,360 ppqn (pulses per quarter note), but if you don't wish to see that much detail when editing, you can set your Preferences to a lower value by going to Edit > Preferences > General > General Display Resolution. On the other hand, if you feel that your system is overloaded by information and that the graphic display seems slow, you can reduce the MROS/System Resolution to a lower value by going to Options > Synchronization. This will reduce the system's MIDI resolution and allow for smoother data transfer when you have a large amount of data being processed. Remember, though, that this reduces the overall resolution of your system, thus reducing the precision you will have over MIDI editing and timing features. You should try to leave this value (MROS/System Resolution) at 1920 ppqn if you can. The actual MIDI playback precision is determined by this value.

Quantize and Grooves

We have discussed Quantize options before. More specifically, we have discussed Note On Quantizing, which is just one form of quantizing available in Cubase VST. Cubase offers five Quantizing flavors: Over Quantize, Note On, Iterative, Analytic, and Groove Quantizing. They all serve the same purpose—to enhance your rhythmic performance. As you will see, some methods of quantizing sound more human than others, allowing for "imperfections" that will add the "feel" quality to a rhythm. Others are more mathematical in their approach and are more suited for Score editing or straight techno beats, for example. The method you choose will depend on what you wish to accomplish in the end.

You can quantize both audio and MIDI events. When quantizing MIDI events, you are quantizing MIDI note events. When quantizing audio events, you are quantizing the Q-points associated with audio events to the nearest Quantize value. If you wish to quantize an audio drum loop, you can cut the loop in smaller parts to quantize individual beats. This is not common however, because, depending on the loop itself, splitting up a loop might introduce silences or overlaps in the audio content, which would result in undesirable effects. Propellerhead offers software application called Recycle that works specifically on this problem, so you might want to look into this if working with drum loops is your thing. We will get back to audio later.

The Over Quantize function is best suited for musical content. It will move note events to the nearest Quantize value set in the Arrange window's toolbar, detecting chord structures to make sure that they stay together and aligning them to the value. If you consistently play ahead or behind the beat, it will use this fact to establish where it should set the notes when quantizing. This method of quantizing does not make events longer or shorter. To Over Quantize, choose the Quantize value from the Quantize menu in the Arrange window's toolbar; select the part, parts, or track you wish to quantize; and then press the letter Q on your keyboard or select Functions > Quantize Type > Over Quantize.

NOTE

If you select another quantizing method, this will put a checkmark next to this type in the Quantize Type sub-menu. Subsequently, when you press the letter Q, it will apply that quantizing method to the events rather than the Over Quantize method. This is a new feature in Cubase 5.0.

The Note On Quantize function works like the Over Quantize, moving the beginning of note events to the closest Quantize value. Unlike Over Quantize, though, it doesn't move the note off value, thus adjusting the length automatically to fit the new beginning. To Note Quantize, choose the Quantize value from the Quantize menu in the Arrange window's toolbar; select the part, parts, or track you wish to quantize; and then select Functions > Quantize Type > Note Quantize.

The Iterative Quantize function works a little differently than the two previous methods. In this case, you can set a window around the Quantize value. If the event is within that window, it won't be quantized. On the other hand, if it is in that window, you can set a degree of correction in percentage. This quantizing method has the same purpose as Groove Quantizing—to strengthen the rhythmic parts without being too aggressive with its modification. To Iterative Quantize, choose the Quantize value from the Quantize menu in the Arrange window's toolbar; select the part, parts, or track you wish to quantize; and then select Functions > Quantize Type > Iterative Quantize.

To modify the Quantize strength and the window around which events are not modified by the Iterative Quantize function, select Edit > Preferences > MIDI and click on the Quantize tab, as shown in Figure 6.9. You can set the strength by left-clicking to decrease or right-clicking to increase the number to the right of the appropriate line (Iterative Q: Strength Percentage). Setting the strength to 70 percent will move all events 70 percent closer to the Quantize value than they are now. You can do the same for the "Don't Iterative Q Notes Closer than [xx] ticks" option to increase the window area around the events. For example, if you set this value to 0.100, any event within that distance, before or after the Quantize value, will be ignored.

Figure 6.9
The Iterative Quantize options are found in this preference menu.

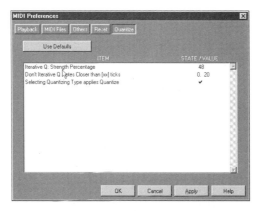

The Analytic Quantize function looks at the information and quantizes the values that are close enough to the quantizing value you set in the Arrange window. If the events are too far away, quantizing won't happen. Use this for rhythmically complex parts that could include, for example, triplets, trills, or arpeggio chords. To Analytic Quantize, choose the Quantize value from the Quantize menu in the Arrange window's toolbar; select the part, parts, or track you wish to quantize; and then select Functions > Quantize Type > Analytic Quantize.

The last type of quantizing is called Groove Quantizing. This is a bit different than simple quantizing, because it uses an external file as a rhythmic template for the part you want to quantize. Here's how it works: Let's say someone, a professional drummer, comes to your studio. He/she sets up an electronic drum kit and starts playing, accentuating certain beats, hitting others a little bit late and some a little early, creating a "groove." You obviously record these "groovy" beats as MIDI events. What you record, in reality, are Note On events and their velocity. You then save these parts as groove files and use them as models or templates for later use with your own performances. This is a very powerful creative tool as well, since you can take a beat or any rhythmic content and pass it through a groove control to get a different feeling.

What is really nice about Groove Quantizing is that you don't have to get a drummer in your studio to use this, since there are already a good number of templates to choose from on your Cubase VST CD. You can also add third-party grooves or use Groove CDs that come with some sampled sound libraries.

When using Groove Quantize, you can either select a groove from a list of presets installed on your hard disk or use the Groove Control box. The preset list can be found in the Functions menu under Quantize Type and through the GRV tool in the Arrange window's toolbox. Figure 6.10 shows you the cascading list of options available. Selecting one of the grooves available will apply that groove to your selected part or track. Remember that this works best with MIDI data.

Using the Groove Control box works the same way, but it gives you more flexibility over how the groove is applied to your selected part. You can also edit the grooves and create your own.

Figure 6.10
The Groove Preset list unfolds to reveal the grooves that are installed on your hard disk in the Groove folder.

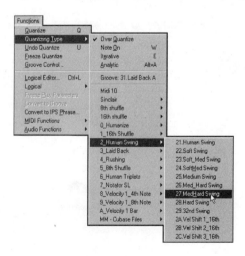

Groove Control

You can access the Groove Control by selecting it under the Functions menu. The Groove Control window allows you to apply, edit, create, and save grooves. A Groove Quantize is an extension of the quantize function, but rather than applying quantize by aligning events to a predetermined grid of bars and beats, it quantizes the events to notes that have been played by a musician and saved as a groove file. This groove file is then used as the predetermined grid, which helps to ensure that the quantizing retains the original human feeling, as described in the previous section. The Groove Control is the window that allows you to select which one of those groove files you want to apply to the MIDI events and how it should be applied.

If you don't have any grooves installed, or if they are not in your Groove sub-folder found in the Cubase VST program folder, you can set the path to the location of your groove files in the Groove Control window. Click on the Set Path button in the lower left corner of the window, as shown in Figure 6.11.

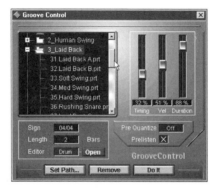

Figure 6.11
The Groove Control window.

To apply a groove using the Groove Control window:

1. Start by selecting the MIDI part or parts you wish to Groove Quantize.
2. Select the Groove Control option in the Functions menu.
3. In the left-hand side, select the folder containing the type of groove you wish to apply and then click on a groove file.
4. Start a cycled playback of the parts you wish to hear from the Transport toolbar. Note that you don't have to be in playback mode to Groove Quantize, but you can listen to the result or try different grooves as it is playing.
5. Check the Prelisten option box in the Groove Control window to hear the processing.

6. If your material is not rhythmically tight, you can pre-quantize the events by clicking in the Pre Quantize field in the Groove Control window and selecting a quantizing value. This will help you get better results out of the groove. If your events are not pre-quantized, the Groove Control might interpret the data in an undesirable way.

7. To try different types of grooves on the cycled playback, click on different grooves and notice how your music changes.

   You have three sliders in the upper right area of the window: Timing, Vel, and Duration. The Timing slider allows you to control how much of the groove will be injected into the timing of your original events. Zero percent would leave the original timing as is, where 100 percent would make the original content follow exactly the groove's timing. The Vel, short for Velocity, affects how much of the groove's velocity you want to apply to the original material's velocity. Like the Timing slider, the higher the percentage, the more control you give to the groove's velocity rather than to the original material's velocities. Note that some grooves don't have velocity values attached to them. In this case, this slider would not have any effect. The third slider is the Duration of the note, or Note-Off event. If you are Groove Quantizing beats or drum loops, this slider has little or no effect on the events, since, as mentioned earlier in the Drum Edit section, percussive instruments don't take length values into consideration.

8. Set the Timing, Vel, and Length values to their preferred values, listening to the result as they play back.

9. When you are satisfied with the result, press the Do It button in the Groove Control box to apply the changes.

You can also edit an existing groove file. Because grooves are usually shared between songs and arrangements, it is customary to leave them intact and create copies that you will edit and save under a new name. This way, you can always rely on unaltered grooves from project to project. To edit a groove file:

1. Select the Groove Control option in the Functions menu.
2. In the left-hand side, select the folder containing the type of groove you wish to edit and then drag it to a MIDI track in your Arrange window, as shown in Figure 6.12.

Figure 6.12
A part is created once you drag the groove onto a MIDI track. The part will have the same name as the groove file.

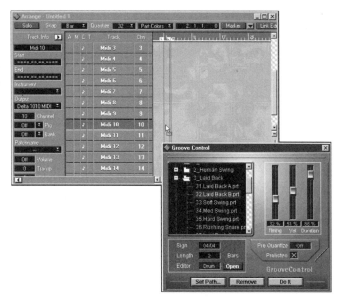

3. Select the part and edit its name in the Part Info area.
4. Once you've renamed the part, drag it back into the Groove Control's file and folder area. Now, the groove has been renamed and saved with the original groove still intact.
5. In the Groove Control window, select the editor you wish to use to edit the groove from the Edit pop-up window.
6. With your groove still selected in the list, click on the Open button in the Groove Control window. The editing window you selected opens.
7. Make the appropriate modifications to your groove using the editing tools available and discussed in Chapter 5.
8. Press Enter on your keyboard to close and save the modifications.

If you have a rhythmic part that you would like to preserve and use as a groove in other arrangements, you can save both MIDI and audio parts as grooves using the Groove Control window. Creating grooves with audio parts requires a basic knowledge of M-points, which are discussed in Chapter 10. Please refer to that section in the book to get more details.

To create a groove template file from a MIDI part:

1. Create a one- or two-bar pattern in the Arrange window. To create groove files, you can use any length, but it works best with a shorter pattern. Just make sure it works well in a loop, so that when you apply it to a longer pattern, the feel remains constant.
2. Once you are satisfied, leave the editing window if you opened one to fine-tune your pattern, select the part, and name it in the Part Info area.
3. Open the Groove Control window from the Functions menu and drag your part into the window. This will create a new groove in the root of your Grooves folder. You can also select your part and then select Convert To Groove from the Functions menu. This will do exactly the same thing. The choice is yours.
4. In the lower left corner of the Groove Control window, you can set the time signature for your groove, the number of bars that are used for your groove, and the preferred editor to edit your groove (see Figure 6.11).

If you were a Cubase user before and have accumulated grooves in pre-Cubase VST versions, you can import them by using the Import Cubase 3.xx Grooves function found in the File menu. You can also create new sub-folders in your Grooves folder to organize your grooves. Finally, you can remove grooves that you don't use by selecting the groove from the Groove Control window and clicking on the Remove button found between the Set Path and Do It buttons in this window.

Locator Functions

Locators can be used for more than just defining where a cycled section begins and ends. You saw earlier in this book that you could use the locators to set markers and define regions between these markers (Chapter 3). Locators can also be used to define edit areas in your Arrange window. By doing this, you can cut parts that overlap a specific region that you wish to use as a group, for example, or you could insert a fixed number of empty bars between two parts. This section will discuss these features and how to use them.

Cut

The Cut function using locators works the same as if you selected text and pressed the Cut button on the word processor's toolbar. The Cut Between Locator function will remove any space or part between the locator points on all tracks that contain events, including the Master Track. What was placed to the right of the right locator point is moved to the left to fill the space. The only events that won't be removed are the events on muted tracks.

To cut between locators:

1. Position your left and right locator points where you want to remove time (or bars), as shown in Figure 6.13 on the left-hand side.
2. Select the Cut At Locators function from the Structure menu.

Figure 6.13
Before (top) and after (bottom) looks at the Cut At Locator function.

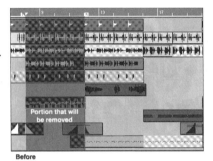
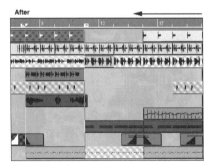

TIP

Remember that when you cut or create parts, then modify the events or parts themselves, you might have events that finish past the boundary of your part. This can be useful, but sometimes you might want the events to end at the same place where the parts end. That's when you can use the Trim Events To Part option from the Structure menu after selecting the part you wish to modify. This will move the Note Off events that occur past the part to within the boundaries of the part itself.

Insert

This is the opposite of Cut. So, if you want to add time between locators, this is the one for you. If a part begins before the left locator and follows through after the left locator, time corresponding to the length between these locators will be added to the parts. If the part begins after the left locator, it will be moved after the right locator.

To insert between locators:

1. Position your left and right locator points where you want to insert time (or bars), as shown in Figure 6.14 on the left-hand side.
2. Select the Insert At Locators function from the Structure menu.

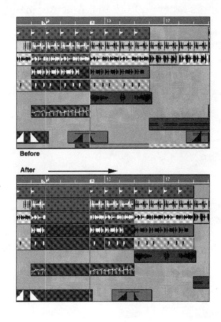

Figure 6.14
Before (top) and after (bottom) looks at the Insert At Locator function.

Split

Splitting events at locators is similar to cutting events at locators, but instead of removing the events between the locators, it simply splits the events across all tracks at the left and right locator points, leaving the content there for editing. This is also a good way to create regions for later use in the creation of a group. Another way of splitting would be to select all the events and then select the Scissors tool from the toolbox to split the selected events. This method has the advantage of working on two points at once. The only disadvantage is that it does not affect muted tracks.

To split at locators:

1. Position your left and right locator points where you want to split the parts, as shown in Figure 6.15. If you want to split at only one point, position the left and right locators at the same place in the timeline.
2. Select the Split At Locators function from the Structure menu.

Figure 6.15
Using the Split At Locators function allows you to split across all tracks at once.

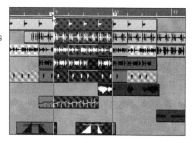

Copy

The Copy Locator Range function in the Structure menu allows you to copy all the nonmuted tracks between the locators to the position of your playback line. It will create new parts for the copied range across all tracks but will not push the existing parts and events after the copied data; rather, it will blend the old parts with the new parts.

To copy a locator range:

1. Position your left and right locator points where you want to copy the parts, as shown in Figure 6.16. If you want to exclude tracks from being copied, mute them first.
2. Set the playback line to the position where you wish to insert the copied content from your locator range. In Figure 6.16, the playback line is positioned at Bar 17.1.1.0.
3. Select the Copy Locator Range function from the Structure menu.

Figure 6.16
Using the Copy Locator Range function allows you to copy the content quickly from one area to another in your arrangement.

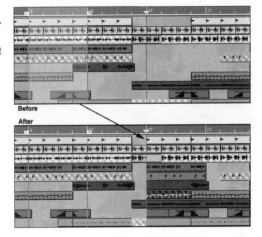

Explode

No, this is not what happens to your computer when using this function. This is a nifty tool that allows you to extract, or explode, a part containing information recorded from different channels, MIDI or audio, onto separate tracks. Let's say a client comes in with some sequences on a hardware sequencer. You transfer the file into Cubase by recording it. This will create a single track with all the MIDI events on it. Now, if you want to edit these events on separate tracks, you can use the Explode By Channel function from the Structure menu to create a new track for each MIDI channel.

Here's another example: You record a drum pattern in cycle mode, adding instruments to your pattern every time the cycle begins to get a full pattern. This is probably the simplest way of doing a drum pattern, but once all your instruments are recorded, they are all contained in the same part. If you want to assign a different Groove Quantize to the snare drum—making it laid back, for example—this could be done by selecting the snare drum events in the Drum editor and applying a groove to the selected events. Or you can use the Explode By Channel function, creating a track for every note in your pattern, as shown in Figure 6.17.

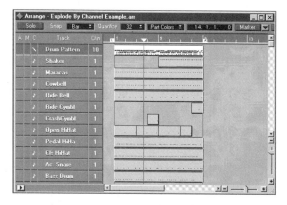

Figure 6.17
A track is created for every drum instrument in your drum pattern when you use the Explode By Channel function from the Structure menu. Each track will be given the name of the instrument in the drum map used for the original track.

You can also use Explode by Channel to extract different audio channels recorded in one track.

To explode a track by channel:

1. Position your left and right locator points to define which part of the track you wish to explode by channel. In Figure 6.17, this corresponds to the range between Bar 1 and Bar 9
2. Select the track you wish to explode by channel.
3. Select the Explode By Channel function from the Structure menu.

Merge

Merge does the reverse of Explode, merging all nonmuted tracks of the same class between the locators onto one single track. When you merge tracks that contain a MIDI transpose value in the Track Info area, this value is converted into an actual transposition of events. For example, if you have set your MIDI track transposition value to +7, a C2 note in the Key editor would be played as a G2 note. Once merged, the C2 would actually become a G2 in the Key editor. The same goes for drum track instruments. If you want to merge tracks with different MIDI channels assigned to them, you can set your merged track to Any in the Channel column of the Track List area to play the original channels. Otherwise, the merged tracks will all play on the channel you set for this merged track.

To merge tracks:

1. Position your left and right locator points to define which part of the tracks you wish to merge into one.
2. Mute the tracks you don't wish to include in the merged track part.
3. Select an empty track where you want the merge to occur. If you don't select an empty track, it will place the newly created part over the existing part and you will have to move it if you want to be able to edit the hidden part later.
4. Select the Merge Tracks function from the Structure menu.
5. Set the merged track to Any in the Channel column to hear the correct sounds on their respective MIDI or audio channels and mute the source tracks used to create this merged track to avoid any note doubling.

TIP

When you work on an arrangement, you will probably record events, move them, delete some, and mute others. This might result in some parts being left empty but still present in your Arrange window. To clean up the display and optimize your arrangement, you can use the Optimize Arrangement function found in the Structure menu. To optimize your arrangement, select the track you wish to optimize and then select the option in the Structure menu. This can be applied to any type of tracks, but remember that audio events containing silence, if recorded this way, are still events and this silence is part of the audio file; therefore, it will not be removed from the display in the Arrange window.

The Arrange Window Toolbox

The toolbox tools were discussed in Chapter 3, and you have learned to use these in the different editors in Cubase. However, the Arrange window offers sixteen tools—some you probably know how to use by now because they are common to all windows, but others are specific to this window.

First, there is the Pointer, or Arrow, tool. This is the default tool for selecting parts on a track and moving them around.

- ▶ Double-clicking on a part with this tool will launch the appropriate editor.
- ▶ Clicking on a part and dragging it with this tool will move the part. Pressing the Alt key as you move a part will create a copy of this part, and pressing the Ctrl key as you move a part will create a ghost copy of it. Where this part will be moved to depends on the Snap value for the Arrange window.
- ▶ To select multiple parts on different tracks, you can click outside a part and drag a rectangle over the parts you wish to select. Note that you don't have to include the whole part in your selection; as long as a portion of your selection touches the selection box that you draw, the part(s) will be included in this selection. If you click inside a part, you will move this part rather than creating a selection.

The Pencil tool allows you to draw a part on most types of tracks, with the exception of folder, group, and style tracks. Beyond drawing new parts, you can also use this tool to resize parts, making them shorter or longer. The Snap value will influence where the parts that you resize or draw will go in the Arrange grid window, so it's a good idea to change the Snap value before using the Pencil tool.

- ▶ To draw a part, simply click and drag your cursor on a track from the point where you want your part to begin to where you want it to end.
- ▶ To resize a part, click inside an existing part and move your cursor inward to shorten the part and outward to lengthen it. You can resize both the beginning and ending of a part. Note that if you shorten a part that contains events beyond the new length, these events will be lost.
- ▶ You can also resize multiple parts. Once you've selected the parts you wish to resize with the Pointer tool, switch back to the Pencil tool, click inside one of the parts you wish to resize, and drag the mouse to the location where you want your parts to begin or end. Holding down the Ctrl key as you resize multiple parts will resize these parts proportionally rather than bringing them all to the same end point.

▶ Holding down the Alt key as you click and drag a part to the right will create copies of the selected part(s) in the track, as shown in the bottom portion of Figure 6.18. Holding down both Ctrl and Alt down will create ghost copies.

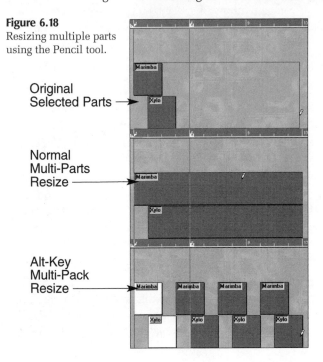

Figure 6.18
Resizing multiple parts using the Pencil tool.

Original Selected Parts

Normal Multi-Parts Resize

Alt-Key Multi-Pack Resize

The Eraser tool allows you to alter a single part just by clicking on it. Or, if the option Tools Work On All Selected Parts is checked in the Edit > Preferences > General > Arrangement dialog box, then clicking on a part that is part of a selection will delete all the selected parts in that selection. Note that when you delete an audio part, the segments in the Audio Pool will not be removed. To delete a part and its corresponding segments and files completely, hold the Ctrl key down as you erase them from the Arrange window. However, be careful, because this will erase the file from your hard disk. For more information on the Audio Pool and working with audio files, you can go to Chapter 9.

The Scissors tool allows you to split a part into two or more parts. The exact split point is determined by the Snap value in the Arrange window (see the part on the upper track of Figure 6.19).

▶ Holding down the Alt key as you click will split the part into equal parts corresponding to the first split size, as shown in Figure 6.19 (part on lower track).

Figure 6.19
Splitting a part into two or several parts using the Scissors tool.

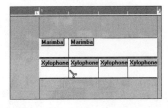

http://www.muskalipman.com

- ▶ If several parts are selected, a split will occur at the same location for every selected part.
- ▶ Holding down the Ctrl key as you split several parts will add a split in relation to their respective starting point (Figure 6.20, Bar 9).
- ▶ Holding down the Alt key as you split several selected parts will split them in equal parts as it would if you had only one selected part; the length between the splits is determined by the distance between the start point and the split point of the selected parts (Figure 6.20, Bar 17).
- ▶ Holding down both the Ctrl and Alt keys as you split several parts will split them in several parts of equal length. The length of these parts is determined by the distance between the start and split point of the part you click on to split (Figure 6.20, Bar 25).

Notice that in Figure 6.20 the scissors location in all these examples has been added to demonstrate where the split was made.

Figure 6.20
Splitting multiple selected parts using different key combinations with the Scissors tool.

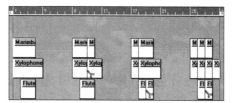

The Speaker tool allows you to listen to the content of parts in two different ways depending on the track class:

- ▶ Clicking and dragging your mouse in both directions (left or right) using the Speaker icon on a MIDI track will act as a MIDI scrub tool, allowing you to hear MIDI events for that track. The direction in which you move your mouse determines the direction in which the MIDI events are read.
- ▶ Clicking on an audio event will let you monitor the audio part from that point on until you let go of the mouse. You can't scrub the audio in the Arrange window with the Speaker tool, but if you wish to do this, please refer to Chapter 10 of this book to learn how.

The Glue or Glue Tube tool allows you to join separate parts together.

- ▶ Just click on the first part you want to glue, then on the second part. Both parts will then be joined together. If parts overlapped before you joined them, the overlapping content will be merged in the new joined part.
- ▶ Holding the Alt key down while clicking on the first part of a track with the Glue Tube tool will join all the parts from that track together.
- ▶ If parts are selected over different tracks, the Glue tool will act the same way as if there were only one part selected on one track.

The Match Quantize tool allows you to take the quantize feel of one part and apply it to another part. Here's an example: You record a MIDI track containing a kick drum. Then, you record a bass line. Quite often, the bass and the kick should keep the same feel, anticipating or delaying the same beats and accentuating the same moments as well. With Match Quantize, you can use the feel of the kick track and copy it to the bass track so that the kick and the bass follow the same "groove." To use the Match Quantize tool, select a proper Quantize value, and then with the Match Quantize tool selected, drag the part containing the source of the "feel" or "groove" information you want to copy over the destination part where you want this groove to be applied. A dialog box will appear and ask you how you want to handle the velocity information (accentuations). If you want to copy the velocity information as is in the destination, select Copy. The Merge option will keep some of the destination's velocity information if it is greater than what is being copied, and No will copy only timing information, preserving the destination's velocity. You can also use this with audio parts. This is described in Chapter 10.

The Mute tool allows you to mute individual parts rather than entire tracks. To mute a part or a series of selected parts, click on them with the Mute tool. If you wish to unmute a muted part, click on it again. Muting can be an alternative to erasing a part, especially when you want to try different things.

The Zoom tool acts as a magnifying glass. You can click anywhere in the Arrange window to zoom into that place. Ctrl+clicking will change this tool to zoom out from that location. You can also drag a box around the area you wish to magnify.

The Selection Range tool allows you to draw a selection across different tracks, independent of part boundaries. Once a selection is made, you can move this selection to a new location, create a copy of it, or use this selection to define which portion of your arrangement you would like to render as an audio mixdown.

> ▶ Click and drag a box around the range of parts you would like to include in your selection. The Snap value will determine where your region's start and end will occur.

> ▶ Hold the Alt key down as you drag the Selection Range tool to automatically span your selection over all current tracks. This is useful when you want to make a global cut of or insert bars and would like to move all your events to a new location. It is also useful when you want to render a mix of your audio tracks to an audio file for this selection.

▶ If you use this with markers, you can click on a marker (see Figure 6.21) with the Selection Range tool to select all the events in that marker's part and then drag the marker part to a new position to move it or hold the Alt key as you are moving it to create a copy.

Figure 6.21
Use the Selection Range tool to move marker parts.

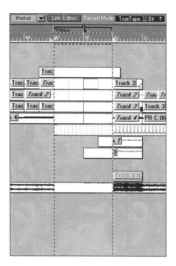

The Volume, Pan, and Transpose tools are three Play Parameters that are available in the Track or Part Info area, but for convenience, you can also use their respective tools in the Arrange window toolbox. To change either of those values for a track, select the parts first if you want to change one of these settings for more than one part; otherwise, simply click on the part with the appropriate tool (Volume, Pan, or Transpose) to perform the editing. A slider (Volume and Pan) or a keyboard (Transpose) will appear. Simply move that slider or click on the note representing the transposition amount you want to apply to the part(s), as shown in Figure 6.22. These tools apply only to MIDI or Drum tracks.

Figure 6.22
Changing the Transpose Play Parameter using the Transpose tool in the Arrange window.

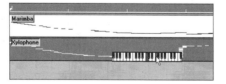

The Logical editor tool is a shortcut for using the Logical editor's list of presets. As you saw earlier in this chapter, you can apply different types of processing with the Logical editor and save these processes as presets, which appear in the Functions > Logical sub-menu. By selecting the Log tool in the Arrange window's toolbox, you can click on a part to select one of these presets without having to access the menu, as shown in Figure 6.23.

Figure 6.23
Using the Log tool to quickly apply a Logical editor preset to a selected part or parts.

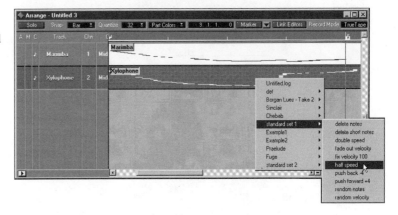

The Groove tool, like the Logical editor (Log) tool, is also a shortcut you can use to apply a Groove template to a selected part. Simply click on a part using the Grv tool to reveal the list of installed grooves to apply this groove to your part, as shown in Figure 6.24.

Figure 6.24
Using the Grv tool to quickly apply a groove preset to a selected part or parts.

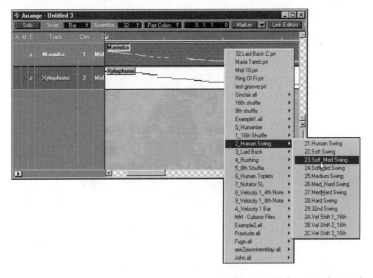

The Stretch tool allows you to time stretch events as you resize the part. This works on both audio and MIDI tracks, changing the events to fit the new size of the part. Beware when doing this on audio parts, however, because it will change the audio file(s) contained in that part. It would be wise to make a copy of the file before applying the Stretch tool to an audio part. (See more about working and managing audio files in Chapter 9.)

When applying this process, the Arrange window will display a percentage factor in its toolbar area, as shown in Figure 6.25. The top part shows you that the file is going to be stretched to a factor of 125 percent, where 100 percent is the normal speed. The bottom part is the result of that stretch. All events will keep a relative distance between them after the time stretch or compression and part resizing is applied. The Snap value will determine where your part will snap to when you let go of the mouse.

Figure 6.25
Using the Stretch tool to time stretch a part to fit its new size. The bottom part shows you the result of a 25 percent increase in length.

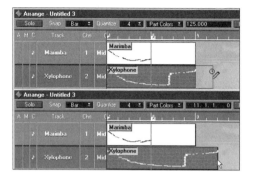

Now You Try It

Here are the exercises you will find on the Web site for this chapter:

- ▶ Create folder tracks and move other tracks into it.
- ▶ Use the Split At Locator function.
- ▶ Navigate using marker regions.
- ▶ Create groups and use group tracks.
- ▶ Apply a Groove Quantize with the Groove Control Panel.
- ▶ Make use of the Logical editor tool.
- ▶ Use the Match Quantize tool.

You will find these exercises at **www.muskalipman.com/cubase**.

Simply follow the instructions on the Web site before starting the exercises.

You can refer to this chapter to find out how to do these exercises, but try doing them without peeking first, just to see how comfortable you are with these principles. If you don't remember how to do a task, refer to the appropriate header in this chapter.

You will need to have the Universal Sound Module and the VB-1 VSTi installed on your computer to use the file provided for these exercises. If you do not have these VST instruments installed, you can always use a General MIDI-compatible device, assigning Channel 1 to play a Bass sound, Channel 2 to play a Lead Synth sound, Channel 3 to play a Strings sound, Channel 5 a Piano sound, and Channel 10 to Drums.

7
Score Editing

Creating a score with Cubase is a way of turning your MIDI sequence into a music sheet that can be read by other musicians. To accomplish this task, you will want to take what you recorded into your MIDI sequencer and convert it into musical notation. Cubase VST provides powerful tools that will help you produce professional-looking music sheets. Cubase VST/Score and Cubase VST/32 versions will help you even more by providing an additional menu with options to help you do this.

When you create and edit a song in Cubase, you create different tracks of MIDI events. Each one of those tracks can become a musical sheet. You can combine different tracks to create a more complex conductor score or create a lead sheet to give chord and rhythm indications to a group of studio musicians.

We will not cover everything there is to know about scoring in this chapter, since this could be the subject of an entire book unto itself. For a more in-depth look at the scoring capabilities of Cubase VST Score and Cubase VST/32 functions, you can read the online documentation provided with the software. We will cover the basics and some of the more advanced techniques involved in scoring with Cubase. Note, however, that if you have the basic Cubase VST version, many of the functions covered here won't apply, since most of the scoring functions are available only in the VST Score and VST/32 versions of the software. You will find all the scoring functions that are available in Cubase VST under the Do menu of the Score editor. This chapter assumes that you are using the Score or VST/32 version of the software.

Finally, this chapter will assume that you know how to enter notes in a MIDI sequencer and will focus on laying out the information in a proper way.

About Score Editing

Scoring is an art form all to itself. To understand and make the best out of the scoring capabilities of Cubase VST/32 and Cubase VST Score, it is useful to know music and music notation. What is important in score editing is that the result is legible to other musicians. It is simply a way to write down on a music sheet a standard set of notes and symbols, which is then read by musicians as they play their instruments. This is the whole purpose of creating a score. Sometimes this might mean that you will have to edit MIDI events in a way that makes the recording sound unnatural, because Cubase gives you tools to adapt what you played in a score but will not be able to interpret everything.

In many ways, the score approximates the basic MIDI information in a sequence (yes, only MIDI information can be translated into a score, not audio). A musician will, in turn, interpret this score by playing the notes or symbols that appear on the music sheet, and you will be able to play back this performance as an audio or MIDI interpretation, depending on the instrument the musician plays. Obviously, if you already have the MIDI down, you don't really need to re-record it. However, for interpretive reasons, this might be one of the useful applications for music scores. Because scores are approximations of the MIDI data, you might want to save a copy of your arrangement or song as a playable file and another copy as a scoring file; the copy you will use for scoring is well quantized and straightforward. This will help you in creating a clean music sheet without having to change the way the original MIDI tracks were recorded.

You can score only MIDI events with the scoring tools. This is very important to understand. As a result, if you are recording a song that contains mostly audio content, you will have to create additional MIDI tracks to create a score out of it.

One thing to remember about MIDI recording is that the length and precision of your MIDI events will greatly influence how the information will be displayed in the score itself. You will be able to tell Cubase how to interpret the information for an optimized layout, but to avoid having to manipulate the events extensively, you should quantize everything before you start editing your score. Figure 7.1 shows a simple melodic line that was played without quantize. On the top part, you can see how Cubase interpreted the information, creating a complex series of ties between the notes to reproduce what was played. On the lower part, you can see the same melodic line, but quantized and enharmonically corrected. This means that the "accidents," or notes that are outside the regular scale, have been adjusted as well to better reflect a correct way of scoring musical notes. This is possible because Cubase takes the MIDI events and compares them with the score settings to display the score layout. So, depending on your score settings and how you recorded your MIDI events, your result will vary.

Figure 7.1
You need to tell Cubase how you want the MIDI events to appear in the score. Here are before (top) and after (bottom) looks at a simple melodic line taken from the MIDI events as they appear above.

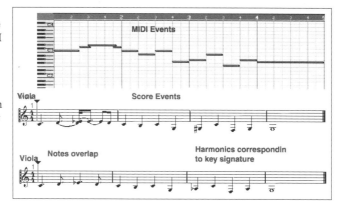

Score Edit Window

The Score Edit window, like the Key, Drum, List, and Audio editing windows, is available from the Edit menu. To launch the Score editor, select a MIDI part or track and press Ctrl+R on your keyboard or select the Score option from the Edit menu.

In the Score editor, you have two basic display modes: Page mode and Edit mode. If you are working with the standard version, you can see only the Edit mode, but the page will print with the default Page mode display. To switch from Page mode to Edit mode, select the option in the Score menu. This is a toggle option, meaning that if you are in Edit mode, the option will display Page mode to switch to that mode, and, inversely, if you are in Page mode, the option will display Edit mode. By default, Cubase will open the editor in Edit mode. The main difference between the two is that Page mode is like the Page Display mode on a word processor: It lets you see the page as it will appear once printed and includes the elements that are part of the page layout. Therefore, you can position your title, add printing elements, and so on. Another difference between the two is the tools available in the toolbox when you right-click in the editing area. You can find a description of these tools in Chapter 3.

Both editing modes display similar toolbars, so let's look at what these tools do.

Figure 7.2
The Score editor's toolbars.

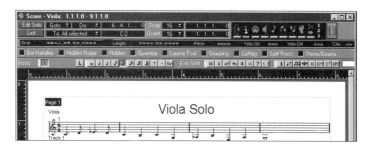

The Edit Solo, Goto, To, Position Box, Pitch Position Box, Snap, and Quantize displays in the upper toolbar perform the same functions as in other editing windows. The Link button found below the Edit Solo button works like the Link Editors button in the Arrange window: Whenever you make a staff active by clicking in the area to the left of a staff, the content found in another opened editing window will reflect the content of that activated staff. An active staff displays a thick border at the beginning of each staff line, and the Score editor's title bar shows the name of the active staff. In Figure 7.3, the Cello staff is the active one.

Figure 7.3
The black line to the left of the staff clef indicates the active staff, in this case, the Cello. Any other opened editing window will display this staff.

The toolbar is actually five separate rows:

- **Status bar**—The first section below the Title bar, this represents most of the tools found in other editing windows.

- **Info Line**—The black row with yellow text, this displays information on a selected event. To reveal or hide this row, you can click on the Info button found in the Status bar.

- **Show Invisible Filter bar**—This displays a series of checkboxes. Each checkbox is an invisible item that you can choose to see by checking the appropriate box. Invisible items are items that will not appear on printed paper. To reveal or hide this row, press the F button on the right-hand side of the horizontal scrollbar (see Figure 7.4).

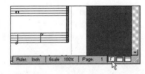

Figure 7.4
You can find additional buttons in this toolbar, like the Show/Hide the Invisible Filter Bar button.

- **Score toolbar**—The last one from the top, just above the Ruler bar, this displays many of the tools you need to insert and edit notes, rests, and symbols in your score. You can tear off these toolbars by clicking and dragging off the toolbar at the gray rectangle to the left of each section. This will create a floating tool palette, as shown in Figure 7.5. You will find more information regarding this toolbar later in this chapter.

Figure 7.5
Tearing off the Score toolbars allows you to move them around freely in your Score editor, even when the rest of the Score toolbar is hidden from view.

▶ **Ruler bar**—Shown in inches in Figure 7.2, and displayed in Page mode, this allows you only to align text elements from your score with a horizontal and vertical ruler, which are found on the top and left part of the editing window. You can change the units displayed in this Ruler bar by clicking the Ruler pop-up menu found in the lower right corner of the Score editor (see Figure 7.4). To hide the rulers, select the Off option from this pop-up menu.

Score Preferences

The Score Preferences window offers a wide range of options you can set to make your score look and react the way you want. Thirteen different categories separate these settings (see Figure 7.6). To access Score Preferences, go to Edit > Preferences > Score.

Figure 7.6
The Score Preferences window.

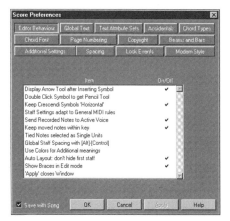

The Edit Behavior page offers a number of global settings that can be set to On or Off. To toggle an option, click on the option to add a checkmark in the on/off column. One of the options that you will find here will make your cursor change to the Pointer tool once a symbol has been inserted. This is useful when you don't insert the same symbol very often and would like to position your symbol precisely once you've inserted it. Most of the options are self-explanatory and are well documented, but if you don't know what one option does, click on the Help button at the bottom of the page to get context-sensitive help.

The global text sets font attributes for different parts of your score, including bar numbers, track names, time signatures, and so on.

The Text Attribute Sets page lets you create template text styles that you can use throughout your score.

To create a style:

1. Click on the Add button in the Text Attributes Sets window.
2. In the Attribute Set field, type a name for your style. For example, if you want to create a style for lyrics, call your style Lyrics. Whenever you add lyrics, you can apply that style to them without having to set your font, size, and attributes every time.
3. Change the font, its size, and its attributes (Bold, Italic, Underline, and so on).
4. Select a proper melisma setting. A melisma is a line that appears after a syllable when you are adding lyrics to indicate that the syllable is stretched over many notes. Figure 7.23 illustrates this. The melisma style represents the line itself, and the melisma is how the line should end. In Figure 7.23, the melisma style is solid and the end is plain. You will learn how to use melisma when looking at how to use text later on in this chapter.
5. Select a frame type if you wish to see a frame around your text.
6. Press Apply when you are done.

The style you have just created will be accessible in the Score menu's Text Attribute Sets option.

The Accidentals page lets you determine how accidental notes should appear in your score. An accidental is an altered note that doesn't belong to the key signature. The rule for accidentals is that when one appears in a bar, each time the same note appears in this bar, it keeps the accident active until the next bar. If you want to add precision to this setting by repeating the accident each time the same note appears in the same bar, you can tell Cubase to repeat the accident. The right part of this page offers you a choice of most common tensions used and a sharp or flat setting for each one. For example, if you have a Cm with a flat ninths note, you can decide to show this as either a D flat or as a C minor chord with an augmented octave (C sharp). As a rule of thumb, keep flat tensions as flat notes and sharp tensions as sharp notes. Therefore, in our above-mentioned example, a musician would prefer reading a D flat rather than a C sharp.

The Chord Types page displays different ways of showing chord symbols. How to set up this page depends on how you prefer seeing chords displayed and from which scoring school you are. Different schools of thought exist on this subject, so the choice is up to you.

The Chord Font page offers you three styles of music chords: English, with the A to G scale; French, with the Do to Si scale; and German, which is similar to the English style except that the B key letter is replaced by the H key letter and B flats become A sharps. You can select the font type and a font size for each part of the chord. Look at the sample in the window to see how the change affects the layout of the chord.

The Page Numbering and Copyright pages, respectively, allow you to set properties for positioning and content of page numbers and the copyright information in your score's page layout.

The Beams and Bars page displays properties for bar numbering and layout in your score and beam properties, such as angles of beams when tied beams are slanted.

The Additional Settings page, like the Editor Behavior page, displays options that can be toggled on and off. Here, the settings relate mostly to tuplet representation, how to handle clef and program changes, and where to position accents like staccatos in your score.

The Spacing page is where you can tell Cubase how much space you want between elements on your score layout. You can set each element to a default value, or you can change it to customize the display of your score. Like any other number value in Cubase, to change it, you left-click to decrease, right-click to increase, or double-click to enter the value manually.

The Lock Events page sets the layer position for different types of elements in your score. Use this with the Lock Layer tool in the Score toolbar. Finally, if you are writing contemporary music, you might want to use a more modern style of notation in your score layout. The Modern Style page allows you to change some aspects of your score to suit this trend. For example, if you have atonal music—this is music written without a specific key in mind—you might want to use the Accidental For Each Note option, which will tell the player that tied notes are both accidental, rather than putting an accident at the beginning of the tied notes. Because atonal music does not have the same rules for accidents as tonal music, it is important to give as many indications to the player as possible.

Page and Edit Mode

You can do most functions in Edit mode, which is the standard mode for editing. It is also the only mode available for Standard Cubase VST users. As mentioned earlier, you can toggle between Page and Edit through the Score menu's first option. The advantage of working in Page mode is that you can see how your page will be laid out and add layout graphics, text, and annotations. Figure 7.7 shows the Edit mode display, and Figure 7.8 shows the Page mode display with the additional content of title, comment, and copyright information.

Figure 7.7
The Edit mode display.

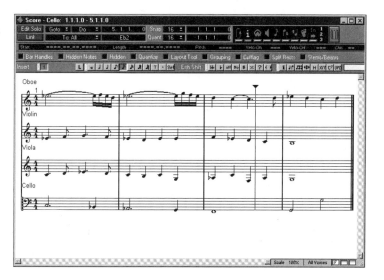

Figure 7.8
The Page mode display.

Adding Fixed Text

To add a title, comments, and copyright information to a new arrangement, double-click on the existing title in Page mode display. The default title, if you haven't saved your file already, will be Untitled1; otherwise, it will have your file's title displayed. A dialog box will appear with a pop-up menu on top, as shown in Figure 7.9. This pop-up menu has three options: Title, Comments, and Copyright. Select the option you want to fill and type the text in the field below this pop-up menu. To enter another option, like Comments, select it from the pop-up menu and type the new information. You can change the text attributes for these three pieces of information by selecting the appropriate options below. Once you are done, click the OK button.

Figure 7.9
The Score Title dialog box.

Status Bar

In other windows, the Status bar is called the toolbar, because it is the only toolbar available. In the Score editor, as you saw, there are many toolbars. The first is the Status bar because it displays status information on cursor position, cycle positions, snap, and quantize values.

To the right of the Insert button on the Status bar, you will find three numbers—1, 2, and 3. These correspond to layers that are available in your score. You can set different types of graphic, note, and text elements to your score using one of these three layers. To avoid moving something you don't want to move, you can lock out a layer from editing changes by clicking on the layer. When a layer is gray, you will not be able to modify the elements found in this layer. To assign elements to specific layers, double-click on any of the Lock Layer numbers. The Score Preferences window will appear with the Lock Event tab active, as shown in Figure 7.10. Assign each element found in this window to a layer to isolate these elements. Once you are satisfied, click Apply and then OK. When you want to edit a layer, but not the content found on the other layers, click on the numbers corresponding to the layers you wish to lock from editing.

Figure 7.10
The Lock Events options in the Score Preferences dialog box.

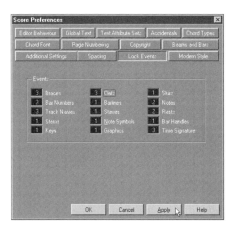

The Do menu holds many functions that are new to this window. For functions like fixes, delete, keep, and so on, please refer to Chapter 5, where you first read about them. Remember that all the functions in the Do menu will be influenced by the option chosen in the To menu, just as in the Edit and List windows. Note that all Do menu options are available in all Cubase VST versions.

▶ **Compute Scale**—Use this with Style tracks to generate chords. A special topic about this feature appears in Appendix C. This works better if you have chords recorded as a chord progression rather than a harmony rhythm track. You can also use this with the Make Chords function described below. Remember that this is most useful when used with Style tracks.

▶ **Insert Slur**—Use this function to add a slur to selected events in your score. Use slurs to indicate musical phrases. You can modify the slur's curve by clicking on one of its handles. Figure 7.11 shows a slur added to Bar 1 of the Violin line.

Figure 7.11
Example of a slur on a series of notes. In this case, the slur could be a bow indication, telling the violinist to not change bow direction while playing these notes.

▶ **Insert Quantize**—This will add a quantize value at the position of the playback head for the active track. In the Insert Quantize dialog box, choose the appropriate options to get the result you want out of the score layout. This does not affect the Quantize value set in the Score editor, but it will refine the layout for the selected notes. To view the Quantize values you added, select the Quantize checkbox from the Show Invisible Filter bar.

▶ **Insert Tuplet**—A tuplet is an uneven number of notes played in an even subdivision of time, like a triplet in a 4/4 bar, or an even number of notes played in an uneven subdivision of time, like a duplet in a 6/8 bar. The most common example of this is a triplet, where three notes take the place of two quarter notes, eighth notes, sixteenth notes, and so on, depending on the value of the triplets. Shuffle and jazz feels are often tuplet based, but they normally are not written as such. You would rather find the indication "Swing Feel" or "Shuffle Feel" at the top of the score to indicate to the musician that the notes should be played in this style. You will find many more applications of this in classical music as well, and you should be familiar with the standards used to display these specific styles when creating your scores. To add a tuplet symbol to your score, select the notes you wish to add a tuplet bracket to and select the Insert Tuplet option. In the Build Tuplet dialog box, select the number of notes over which the tuplet should span. For example, you can select three notes and select 5plet, short for quintuplet, where two of the five notes in the tuplets are silences.

▶ **Connect Dynamics**—To use this function, you must first have Dynamics symbols added to your score. Once you have done this, select the two dynamics between which you want to add a crescendo or diminuendo (increase or decrease in volume and intensity) and select this function. To add dynamics to a score, go to Score > Symbol Palettes > Dynamics. Click on the first dynamic you wish to enter and then click with the Pencil tool where you want to add it. Select the second dynamic value and insert it where you want to add it. Figure 7.12 shows a crescendo inserted with the Connect Dynamics function.

Figure 7.12
The Oboe part has a dynamic crescendo between Piano (p) to Mezzo Piano (mp).

- **Make Chords**—This function automatically creates chord symbols above the active staff. This function works best when you have a polyphony or chord structure in your score. To Make Chords, select a staff or make a selection of notes where you want to have chords, and select the option from the Do pop-up menu. You can also choose an option from the To pop-up menu to determine which events will be affected. This does not create any additional notes. Figure 7.13 shows a basic piano harmony with chords. If you have many transitional notes outside the scale, this might cause Cubase to misinterpret the chord structure, so keep it simple.

Figure 7.13
Chord Symbols appear above the active track.

- **Make Guitar Symbols**—A number of things have to be set up before you can use this option. First, you need to have a corresponding guitar symbol that matches the chord you played. For example, if you played a D minor chord, you need to have this chord in your library; otherwise, nothing will show up. To add or edit guitar symbols into your library, select in your Score menu Global Settings > Edit Guitar Lib. This will display a list of chords in your library. You can create a new one by pressing the New button. Save your new library by pressing the Save button, and remove it by pressing the Remove button. Clicking on New will create a new symbol. To edit this symbol, double-click on it and add the symbols corresponding to the new guitar chord. You will have to know how to create guitar chord structures to use this. Once you have created your guitar chords, select a staff to make it active and then choose Make Chords first to create your chords. You can edit the chords and then select the Make Guitar Symbols. Figure 7.14 shows a guitar chord progression with guitar symbols.

Figure 7.14
Guitar symbols should appear above the guitar staff. You can move the symbols by dragging them where you want them to appear.

http://www.muskalipman.com

▶ **Flip Stems**—Use this option to flip the stems of selected notes. By default, in a monophonic part, notes above the third line in the staff have stems going down, and notes below this same line have stems going up. Select the notes whose stems you want to flip and choose this option.

▶ **Group**—Use this option when you want to beam a series of notes together. Figure 7.15 shows notes that were grouped together in the first bar. To group a series of notes, select them and then choose Group from the Do menu or click the Group button on the toolbar. To ungroup notes, select the notes that are in a grouped beam and select Group again from the Do menu.

Figure 7.15
The Group function and button allow you to group different notes together under a single beam.

▶ **Auto Grouping**—This is similar to Group, with the exception that it groups notes within a bar automatically when selecting notes over several bars, rather than grouping all notes selected under one bar. To use Auto Grouping, select the notes you wish to group and choose this option from the Do menu.

▶ **Hide**—Use this function to hide elements from the score such as rests or bar lines. You can also use the Hide button on the toolbar to do the same thing. To hide something, select it and choose this function. To unhide something, check the Hidden checkbox in the Show Invisible Filter bar. Your hidden symbols will appear. Select the hidden symbol you wish to remove, as shown in Figure 7.16, and press Delete on your keyboard.

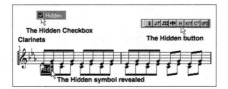

Figure 7.16
The Hide function.

▶ **Show**—If you have many hidden elements, you can use this function to reveal them all.

▶ **Multi Insert**—Use this function if you wish to insert a symbol more than one note at a time. Let's take the clarinet part you saw in Figure 7.16 and add some staccato symbols on each note. To do this, select the notes to which you wish to add symbols, then choose the palette containing the symbols you want to add by going to Score > Symbol Palettes > Note Symbols. Click on the symbol you wish to add and make sure your To menu is set to Selected Events. Finally, choose the Multi Insert option from the Do menu pop-up. In Figure 7.17, you can see that staccatos appear in the first bar.

Figure 7.17
Using the Multi Insert function allows you to add symbols to more than one note at a time.

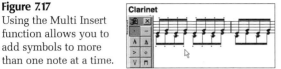

▶ **Mute/Unmute Selected**—This works like the Mute tool from the Edit window. Selected notes are muted from playback. To unmute the notes, select them again and choose Unmute Selected from the Do menu.

▶ **Build Trill**—A trill is a musical ornament between two notes. When you play a trill, a series of notes will appear on your score, which might not be what you want. To build a trill, select the notes you wish to affect and choose this option from the Do menu. Figure 7.18 shows you the different steps involved, with the original notes as they would appear before the trill and, at the bottom, as they appear once the trill has been built. Check the Help option in the dialog box to add a note in parenthesis on your staff. This will tell the player which note to trill.

Figure 7.18
Select the corresponding options in the Build Trill dialog box to create the desired trill markings.

▶ **Paste Note Attributes**—Use this function to copy properties from a selected note, including note symbols, to any other notes.

When you are in Page mode, you can use the Scale pop-up menu found in the lower right-hand corner of the Score editor's window. This allows you to zoom in your score to edit details or zoom out to see the page as a whole. This works pretty much the same way as a Print Preview function in a word processor or a display scale function in any other type of application.

Next to the Scale pop-up menu, you will find the Page display. If your score has more than one page, you can navigate through the pages in Page mode by left-clicking to go to the previous page or right-clicking to go to the next page. You can double-click to enter the number of the page you want to jump to. You can also add a key command in your Edit > Preferences > Key Command > Score window under Move to Next Page and Move to Previous Page options. For example, assign Alt+Left Arrow to move to the previous page and Alt+Right Arrow to move to the next page.

Use the three buttons following the page number in the lower right corner of the Score editor to show or hide toolbars or tool rows. The F button will toggle the display for the Filter bar, the next button toggles the display for the Score tools, and the last button hides all toolbars to reveal only the content of the score itself. Toggling this button will bring back the bars as you had them before pressing this button.

Score Toolbar

The Score toolbar's main function is to select the type of notes you want to add to a score. However, it holds many more little tools to help you lay out your page. For starters, the first button on the left is called the Voice Selector Insert button. If a track contains more than one voice, you can select in which voice within this polyphony you want to add your note. In Figure 7.19, you can see the active staff has two voices. Because the staff has two voices, you can select which voice you want to assign notes to by clicking on the number corresponding to the voice. To select a voice to add notes to, simply click on the number corresponding to the desired voice. To see more than one voice, set your staff to Polyphony mode in the Staff Settings window found under the Score menu.

Figure 7.19
The voice selector in the Score toolbar displays how many voices are available in the active staff.

Next on the Score toolbar, you will find the L button. This button, when activated, prevents you from moving objects and notes from one staff to another. Most of the time, you will want to leave this off. However, if you need to transpose selected notes very high or very low, so that they appear below or above the current staff, enable it so Cubase will not think you want to move the notes to another staff.

Following the L button, you will find note values. These are used to select the note values you wish to add to your score. When you select a note value, it automatically changes the Quantize value in your Status bar to correspond to the value of the note you selected. For example, if you select a whole note, Quantize will display "1." When you switch to a quarter note, Quantize will display a "4" value.

The enharmonic shift buttons provide a way to change the enharmonic notes in your score. Enharmonic notes are different ways to represent the same pitch. For example, E flat or Eb could be represented by D sharp or D# or even F double-flat (Fbb). The Off button turns the enharmonic shift to off and the No button hides the accidentals. If you use many accidental notes, you might want to add additional markings. For example, if you have many voices on a staff and each one plays an accidental C sharp (C#), you can select subsequent C sharp notes in the bar and click on the Question Mark button (?). This will add a helping accident. The notation rules don't require you to add this accident, but since you wish to help the musicians who are reading the score, this will provide them with additional information. Pressing the Parenthesis button [( )] will add this accidental in parenthesis.

The I button, short for "Information," will show you information on a selected element in your score. What will appear once you select the I button depends on what you select. For example, if you select a clef and press this button, the Clef window will appear and allow you to change it. On the other hand, if you select a note and press this button, the Note window will appear, allowing you to modify different parameters for note representation.

The Flip Stem button—well, it flips stems of selected notes, as discussed earlier in this chapter.

The Group button, like the Flip Stem button, was also discussed earlier in this chapter. Selecting notes and clicking this button will group them together under one beam. You can also use the Do menu functions to achieve a similar result.

The Auto Layout button is a shortcut button for the Auto Layout function found in the Score menu. If you select an entire staff, it will perform like the Move Bars option, and if no staff is selected, you will get the Bars and Staves option, both equivalent to the Auto Layout functions found in the Score menu. What this does exactly is discussed in the Layout section of this chapter.

The H, or "Hide" button, hides the selected elements from view. Also discussed previously, it is similar to the Hide function in the Do menu. To reveal a hidden object, check the Hidden Notes in the Show Invisible Filters bar. You can also select the Show function in the Do menu.

http://www.muskalipman.com

The X/Y Position button reveals the graphical position of your cursor in a horizontal (X, vertical; Y, horizontal) display in Page mode. When you click on a non-note event—the title, for example—you will see in this display the Delta X and Y coordinates of the selected object changing as you move it around the screen. Use this to fine-tune the positioning of your graphic elements on the score. The X/Y Position window also allows you to toggle between the different ruler formats: inches, centimeters, points, and millimeters. To change the format of the ruler, click on the upper left corner of the window where it says, "Measure in ...." In the last column, you have the "To Prev Staff" and "To Next Staff" values. These values represent the space between the current selected staff and the previous and following staff in the score. Double-clicking either of these values will allow you to type in a new spacing value.

The C7 button is "Make Chords," which creates a chord out of the selected notes in your score. To make chords, you will need to have a three-note polyphony to get accurate results from the Make Chords button. Once your chords are created, they will appear above the selected staff. You will find more information on chords in the following sections of this chapter.

Once you have completed your editing, it's possible your layout is not refreshed properly. If this occurs, you can force an update by clicking on the UPD button or Update button. You can also do this through the Force Update option found in the Score menu.

The last area on the Score toolbar represents the location in bars and beats of the selected non-note object. For example, if you select a chord and move it around, the display will show the location of this chord in reference to bars and beats. This is useful when you want to make sure that the chord, as in this example, aligns at the proper moment in time with the notes below. For this field to work, you can select only one non-note object at a time.

Symbol Palettes

In the Score menu, you will discover the Score Palettes option. From the Score Palettes option, you will find many palettes available to add graphical elements to your score. None of these symbols actually affects how the music is played back, but they are used to add interpretation indications for the musicians. There are ten palettes from which to choose, and they all work pretty much the same way: To add a symbol from a symbol palette to your score, click on a symbol, then click on the score where you want to add it. If the symbol needs more information, a dialog box will appear to let you enter additional fields or text as required.

Once you have a palette displayed, you can switch from one palette to another by clicking in the Title bar of the Symbol palette, as shown in Figure 7.20. This will reveal the list of palettes from which you can choose. Selecting another palette will replace the displayed palette with the new one. Holding down the Ctrl key as you make your selection will not replace the existing palette, but rather open a new one.

Figure 7.20
The Title bar of the Symbol palette allows you to switch from one palette to another from its drop-down menu.

The last palette available is the Custom palette. This allows you to store symbols you use most often from other palettes. To add symbols to the Custom palette, open it and then open the Symbol palette that holds the symbol you want to add. Hold down the Alt key as you select that symbol.

The last option on the Palette list is Flip Direction. Use this to switch from a vertical palette layout to a horizontal layout.

Some of the symbols in these palettes might be grayed out if you are in Edit mode. To activate these disabled symbols, switch to Page mode.

For a full description of each palette symbol, consult the electronic document titled "Score" that came with your software, found at Working With Symbols > Symbol Palette.

Working with Chords

You might have a harmony happening in your staff. You might also have a piano or guitar part with chords played as a harmonic rhythm track. In both cases, you can choose to add a chord symbol over the track by selecting the track and then clicking on the Make Chords button in the Score toolbar, as discussed in the previous sections of this chapter. Once your chords are created, chances are you will want to tweak them, since Cubase might not interpret them properly all the time.

Before you start creating chords, it is a good thing to set your chord display preferences in the Score Preferences window, as discussed earlier. What you set in this preference window will determine what will appear when you double-click on a chord to edit it. For example, if you set the Major chord type to display MA7 rather than maj7 or simply j7, the MA7 will appear in the Chords dialog box when you edit the chord. To access this panel, select Edit > Preferences > Scores > Chord Types. The chords you create after setting your preferences will follow the rules you set here.

The next step is to actually create the chords using the Make Chords button on the Score toolbar or by using the Make Chords button found in the Symbol palette called Other.

186 Score Editing – Chapter 7

To create automatic chords:

1. Select the track for which you want to create chord symbols and launch the Score editor. You will need to have at least three notes per chord for this function to work.
2. Select the staff over which you want the chords to appear.
3. Make sure the To menu displays the appropriate option. In other words, if you want to create chords for the whole track, this option should be set to All Events.
4. Click the Make Chords button on the Score toolbar, or select Make Chords from the Do menu in the Status bar.

To create custom chords:

1. Select the track for which you want to create chord symbols and launch the Score editor.
2. Select the Symbol Palettes > Other from the Score menu.
3. Click the Make Chords button (C7) and then click over the staff to which you wish to add a chord. It is easier if you align your pencil with the chord structure beneath it. The Edit Chord Symbol dialog box will appear, as shown in Figure 7.21.

Figure 7.21
The Edit Chord Symbol dialog box.

4. Enter the note that corresponds to the root of your chord. For example, if you played F, A, and D, this could be a D minor chord, with a root of D, or an F6 chord, with a root of F. Which chord it is depends on many things, so you will have to know a bit about harmony to make that kind of decision.
5. Next, enter the chord type. This tells the player if the chord is a major, minor, diminished, half-diminished, augmented, or a sustained fourth degree chord. If you are not familiar with these terms, you might want to use automatic chord construction, found in the Score toolbar, instead. In the example in step 4, the chord was a minor chord, so in this case you would select minor.

6. Next, add the highest tension found in your chord. For example, if you have a minor seventh and a minor ninth, add the minor ninth tension, since it is understood in scoring theory that the minor ninth will also contain a minor seventh (unless otherwise noted). On the other hand, if you have a tension on the fifth, such as a sharp fifth or flat fifth added to your flat ninth, you can type in the values manually. Figure 7.22 displays a D minor with a sharp fifth and a major seventh chord on the left. The center column displays different ways you can add the tension by clicking in the tension field, and the right column displays the result depending on the way you typed in the tension. Note that the syntax used here is useful when you have complex tensions. Normally, you don't have to type anything if you have a simple tension.

7. The last field in your Edit Chord Symbol dialog box is for the bass note. If you want the bass to play a note different from the ones found in the chord, you would select that note in the pop-up menu. If your bass plays a note that is part of the chord structure but not the root, you usually don't have to write it in. However, in the example in Figure 7.22, if you wanted the bass to play an E, which is not part of the chord structure as it appears, you would add this in the bass note.

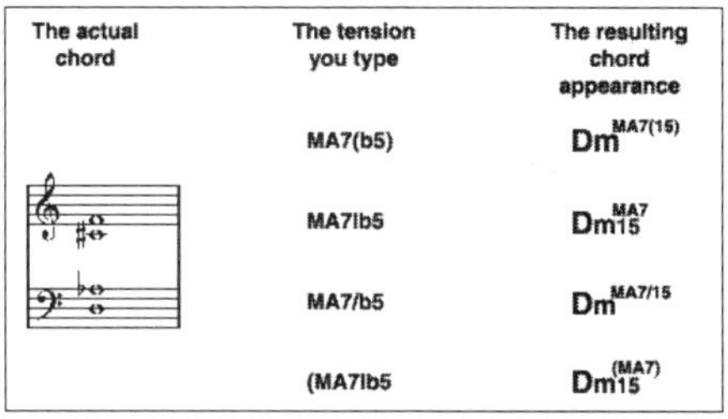

Figure 7.22
Adding text in the tension field allows you to customize the tension's layout in the chord structure.

The actual chord	The tension you type	The resulting chord appearance
	MA7(b5)	Dm^{MA7(15)}
	MA7!b5	Dm15^{MA7}
	MA7/b5	Dm^{MA7/15}
	(MA7!b5	Dm15^(MA7)

8. If your chord needs to be an enharmonic chord, like D sharp instead of E flat, check the Enharmonic Shift checkbox. The checkbox called lower root allows you to change the root note from uppercase to lowercase. This can be useful sometimes to identify a minor key from a major key, with the latter being in uppercase. By default, the root is always in uppercase and unless you always use this, leave it as is.

9. If you want to keep this chord structure for later use in your score, select the Library drop-down menu and choose Add from this menu. This will save the structure in the library of your song file once you save this file. You will notice that the root of the structure will not appear in the library. This is because you might want to use the same structure with another key later on. To use it later on, just select the root note and then select the structure from the drop-down menu.

http://www.muskalipman.com

When creating chords using the Make Chords function, Cubase will use the Quantize value set in the Score window to determine the maximum number of chords it will add. If you don't want to have too many chords, reduce the Quantize value to represent a realistic number of chords per bar. There is no fixed number of chords in a bar, but usually, this should not be more than four chords per bar; in most cases, it will be one to two chords per bar. The best way to create chord tracks is to play a MIDI track containing the chord structure played as simply as possible.

Cubase will use all the vertical notes in your layout to analyze and create these chords. If you have melodic lines or musical lines with many transitional notes, the software might interpret those notes as chords, giving you a superfluous amount of tensions and chords. So, when you create chords, select only the tracks that contain the basic harmonic structure of your song and set your Quantize value to the desired amount beforehand.

Cubase also assumes that chords are in their root positions. This means that if you play a first or second inversion of a chord—let's say a C chord played E-G-C or a second inversion G-C-E—it will interpret this as a C chord on an E bass or a C chord on a G bass. To avoid this, simply hold the Ctrl key down as you press the Make Chords button in the Score toolbar. If you find that the chords produced automatically by Cubase do not match the correct harmonic structure of your song, you can double-click on a chord and change its structure in the Edit Chord Symbol dialog box. Again, Cubase only tries to interpret the chord, but since this is often a question of interpretation and context, some chords will be wrong and you will need to edit them.

Adding Text

As you have seen previously in this chapter, there are different types of text symbols in a score layout. One of them is the fixed type text, which was discussed earlier in this chapter. Examples of fixed text are the title, comments, and copyright information found on the first page of your score. What we will explore here is how to use the other text options found in the Symbol palettes. There are three different palettes holding text elements: Other, Layout, and Global. Which symbol you should use depends on what you want to add and where you want it to appear.

If you want to add lyrics to a song, you should always use the Lyrics Symbol found in the Other palette.

To add lyrics:

1. Start by selecting the staff under which you want to insert the lyrics.
2. Select Symbol Palettes > Other from the Score menu.
3. Click on the Lyrics button in the palette. Your cursor will change to the Pencil tool.
4. Click under or over the note where you want to add the lyric and enter the first syllable for your word or enter a word.
5. Press the Tab key to move to the next note. If you have a word or a syllable that stretches over many notes, press the Tab key to move under or over the next note where you want to add the next word or syllable. When done, click outside of the box.

Once you've completed inserting the lyrics, you can adjust the melisma lines to stretch a syllable or a word over a series of notes. A melisma, as discussed earlier in this chapter, is a line that carries through several notes.

To stretch a word or syllable across several notes, click on the word or syllable you want to stretch using the Selection tool and drag the handle of the selected syllable to the right of where you want the melisma to end, as shown in Figure 7.23.

Figure 7.23
The selected word appears in reverse highlight and the handle appears as a square in the lower right corner of the highlighted word or syllable.

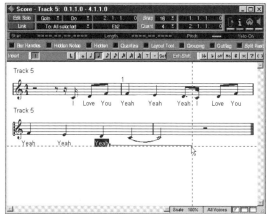

You can move lyrics up or down using the Selection tool, but you can't move lyrics to the left or right. You can also copy words or syllables by selecting them and keeping the Alt key pressed as you move the selection to a new area in your score. If you want to move all the lyrics you just entered at once, hold the Shift key down and double-click the first word or syllable in the lyrics. All elements from that set of lyrics will be highlighted and ready to move.

Your lyrics might be crammed into a small space the first time you look at them on the score. To arrange the spacing so that the lyrics don't appear too squeezed, select Auto Layout > Move All Bars from the Score menu.

If your song contains more than one verse, you can enter lyrics for the second verse as you did for the first verse. Once entered, select all the lyrics from this verse and choose Text Functions > Move To Verse > Verse 2 from the Score menu. You can add up to six different verse lyrics this way.

If you have created text attribute sets, you can select the lyrics and apply the text attribute set of your choice by choosing it from the Text Attribute Sets option in the Score menu.

You can also add simple text indications, as shown in Figure 7.24. This text was added using the Text symbol also found in the Other palette. You enter this type of text the same way you would enter lyrics. The only difference here is that you can add carriage returns by pressing the Ctrl+Enter keys. If you want to insert this text to all staves in your score at the same time, press and hold the Alt key before you click with your Pencil tool to position your text.

Figure 7.24
Adding simple text in the score's layout.

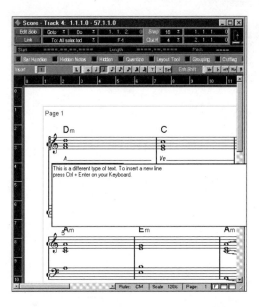

To edit any type of text, you can double-click on it and start editing the text as you would in any other word processing software. Once you are done, click outside the editing area to accept the changes and get out of text editing mode.

There are three other types of text that you can add to your score:

▶ **Page text**—This text is part of the layout of your score and is not attached to any note events on your score, so it will appear on your page when you check the Layout Layer Only option in your Score menu. You will find this type of text in the Layout palette. Holding down the Alt key when clicking to insert page text with the Pencil tool will add the text to all the pages of your score.

▶ **System text**—This is similar to the page text in every way but one: It is tied to notes and bars. So, if you move your bars or notes, the system text will also move with it. You can find the System text option in the Layout palette.

▶ **Global text**—Found under the Glob Text button of the Global palette, this type of text also belongs to the layout of your score and is similar to system text. However, global text can appear on as many tracks as you decide. To have global text appear for a staff, check the Glob column in the Layout Settings window of the Score menu, as shown in Figure 7.25. The staves with a checkmark will display the global text. Once you have made your setting in the Layout Settings, open the Global palette from Score > Symbol Palettes, make the staff where you want to add the global text active, and click on the Glob Text button. Click where you want the text to appear and type your text. Copies of this text will appear on all the staves you selected in the Layout Setting window, as shown in Figure 7.26. Notice how the sample global text in Figure 7.26 doesn't appear over one of the tracks. In Figure 7.25, the clarinet track is not selected.

Figure 7.25
Setting a track to Global will make the elements you add from the Global palette appear on this staff.

Figure 7.26
Global text appears over or below the staves, depending on where you insert the original global text. Here, the text is highlighted and ready to be moved elsewhere if you want.

TIP

You can copy and paste text from a text file (*.txt or *.doc) directly into the score as lyrics using Score > Text Functions > Lyrics from the Clipboard function. Simply copy some text from a file using the Copy function in your favorite word processor and then select your starting note with the cursor. Then, choose Score > Text Functions > Lyrics from the Clipboard, and each word will automatically be assigned to the next note in the sequence. If Cubase finds a hyphen in the text, it will treat the word as two separate ones (thus splitting the word over two notes). This is useful if you have a sheet of lyrics as a text file already. You can go through the text, hyphenating it where all of the different syllables are and then have Cubase put the lyrics to the music.

Drums and Percussion

Because you can treat drum and percussion tracks differently than other instruments, both in the track classes and in the Score layout, we will look at how you can use the drum map and note heads to customize the look of your drum track in the score.

In Chapter 5, you saw that a song can contain different drum maps and that each drum instrument has a Note In and Note Out value. In the score, this is similar; the Note In value remains the same, but instead of the Note Out, you will have a displayed note, which is how the note will appear on the staff. You can also set a different note head for each instrument in your drum kit. This way, the drummer will have an easier time reading the part.

To use the drum map and edit the displayed notes and note heads:

1. Select your drum staff in the score to make it active.
2. In the Score menu, select Global Settings > Drum map. The Drum Map dialog box will appear, as shown in Figure 7.27.

Figure 7.27
The Drum Map dialog box.

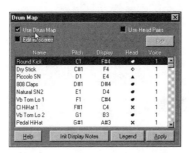

3. Check the Use Drum Map option to use the drum map associated with your drum track.
4. To change the displayed note of your drum instrument, left-click to decrease the note value, right-click to increase it, or double-click to enter the note value for an instrument in the Display column of the Drum Map window. Note that you can assign two or more instruments to the same displayed note and assign different heads to them. For example, if you have two notes that play the same instrument, like a hi-hat, you can display them both with the same note value.
5. Click in the Head column to have the Head Note pop-up menu appear. Select the desired head for that instrument.
6. If you set your drum part to play multiple parts, you can set each instrument to a different voice. To change the voice number for an instrument, use the Voice column.

Now that you have set the display note and note head values and assigned different instruments to different voices, you will need to edit the Staff Settings in the Score menu (see Figure 7.28).

Figure 7.28
The Staff Setting dialog box offers a preset list from which you can choose The Drum (or "Rythme," as shown here) preset for drum tracks.

To set up your drum track:

1. Under the Staff Mode field, select the appropriate option. If you want to use a multi-voice or polyphonic setup, allowing you to have stems going in different directions for different voices, select the Polyphonic option.
2. Select a proper Notes and Rests Display Quantize value for your drum staff, or check the Auto Quantize option.
3. Check the Deviation (Dev.) checkbox if your track has notes that are not played precisely on the beats. This option will help Cubase recognize patterns.
4. Check the Adapt box to adapt certain triplet patterns. Selecting this option will allow Cubase to look for and interpret tuplets. If Cubase finds tuplets, it will assume that there are more to be found and will adapt the layout to reflect this fact.

5. The Interpretation Flags section (Interpret. Flags) offers four options:

   Clean Lengths will lengthen shorter notes to reduce the amount of unnecessary short rests.

   No Overlaps cuts notes when one note is playing while another starts. This is useful to make the staff more legible. If you are using the Polyphonic Staff mode, this has less impact on legibility, but try it and look at the result. If you don't like it, remove this option.

   Syncopation, when active, removes displayed ties across bars.

   Shuffle displays shuffle rhythms as simple straight rhythm. This does not affect the groove but makes it easier to read. If you use this, you can simply add a global text over the drum staff indicating Shuffle mode.

6. You can also select the Rythme preset from the Preset menu. This might change some settings you just made, however, so pay attention to how the settings are before you select a preset.

7. Click on the Staff Options button. This will bring up the Staff Option dialog box (see Figure 7.29).

Figure 7.29
The Staff Option dialog box.

8. In the Switches area of the Staff Options window, select the appropriate options for your drum track. This will affect the look of beams between eighth, sixteenth, and thirty-second notes.

9. Under Drum Map, select the Use Score Drum Map option to use the drum map associated with your track. Note that this option and the one found in the Drum Map window are the same. If you checked it earlier, it will appear checked here as well; if you uncheck it here, it will be unchecked in the Drum Map Setup window as well. If you want to display your drum staff as a single line, check the Single Line Drum Staff option (see Figure 7.30). The notes below this option indicate which notes will appear on the line. Notes below the C3 in Figure 7.29 will appear below the line, and notes above C4 will appear above the line. If you don't want to see accidentals in your drum staff layout, check the No Accidentals option. Since accidentals have little or no influence on actual drum sounds, you don't need to display them. As a rule, unless you are using tuned instruments, leave this on.

Figure 7.30
A single-line drum staff.

10. In the System area of the window, set the number of system lines for your staff next to the System Lines field. You can increase or decrease the number of lines and the space between each line as well. Use the Size option to make the staff bigger or smaller.
11. When done, click on the Exit button to return to the Staff Setting dialog box.
12. Finally, click on OK to return to the Score editor.

Layouts

When you create an arrangement, write a song, or print scores, you often have a score sheet for the conductor and individual sheets for each musician. So, the drummer has a drum part, the trumpet player has a trumpet part, and the piano player has a piano part. Use Layouts to create and save layouts for this purpose. Using the same tracks, you can create a score for the conductor with specific layout settings for this type of score. You can then select an individual track from the same song and create a music sheet layout—let's say, for all the strings (violin, alto, cello, and bass)—each one using the same "Strings" layout. A layout will contain staff spacing, bar lines, and layout symbols information.

Once a layout is created, you can access it when you are in the Arrange window from the Edit menu, under Select > Score Layout's sub-menu. This selects the tracks that are part of the selected layout for you to edit in the Score editor. Layouts are created automatically when you edit a track or set of tracks in the Score editor and are saved with your song file (*.all).

To create a layout:

1. Select a track or a group of tracks for which you want to create a layout.
2. Press Ctrl+R on your keyboard or select the Score editor function under the Edit menu.
3. Make your modifications in the Score editor, such as staff settings, and add whatever global or layout symbols you need.
4. Save the result and exit the Score editor by closing the window. If you press the Escape key, just as in any other editing window, you will be asked if you wish to save the changes or not.

To access this layout after creating it, you can use one of two methods, depending on where you are. If you want to access it from the Arrange window, select Edit > Select > Score Layouts and select the layout you want from there. From the Score editor, go to the Score > Display Layout sub-menu.

To manage, edit, and apply layouts:

1. Open the Score editor and select Page Layout from the Score menu.
2. Select Layout Settings from the Score menu (see Figure 7.31).

Figure 7.31
The Layout Settings window.

Under the layout area on the left (see Figure 7.31), you can see the layouts that are in use by your current song. The current active layout is displayed in a normal font with a bullet next to it. A layout used by a set of tracks or a simple track is represented by normal text without a bullet. A layout that has been loaded using the Load button below the layout area, but is unused by the current file, displays names in italic.

To rename a layout, double-click on its name and type in the new name for it. Tracks used by this layout display a bullet next to them in the track area of this window (on the right side). If you want to remove a layout from this list, select it from the layout area and click on the Remove button. Use the Clean Up button if you want Cubase to remove any unused layouts from this window and from the song.

In the track area of this window (see Figure 7.31), tracks that are part of the selected layout on the left part display bullets. Each symbol above the track area represents an option for the track's layout setting. If you want to add a brace or bracket before the appropriate staff or staves, click next to the desired staff. You can span the brackets or braces across different staves by clicking on them and dragging them over the desired staves. In Figure 7.31, this is the case for the strings, organ, and bass part. The 4/4 sign will display the time signature in Modern Time (note that when you enable one of the staves with this option, the Modern Time signature option will be checked). Check the Name column next to the staff on which you want the Staff Name to appear. To disable all staff names, uncheck the Staff Names checkbox on the right. You can enter a long name for the first occurrence of the staff name and a short name if you want the following staves of the same track to display a different name. In Figure 7.31, the strings track will show up as STR. The Global or Glob column enables the staff to display global symbols such as global text and rehearsal marks, as discussed earlier in this chapter.

http://www.muskalipman.com

The spacing option in the right area of the Layout Settings window allows you to set the spacing characteristics for all the notes in this layout to Regular spacing, which is recommended for normal melody or syncopated material; Optimize spacing, which is recommended for chord tracks; or Equal, which will divide each note into equal amounts of space.

The Multi Rests option allows you to replace a series of successive rests on a staff with a multi-rest symbol. Set the value to the minimum amount of successive rests your staff needs to have before using the multi-rest symbol.

The Size option sets the size of all staves in this score's layout.

At the bottom of the window, you will find two buttons: Get Layout and Get Form Only. You can load a layout with the Load button, then select the Get Layout button to apply all the layout properties of the selected layout from the layout area. On the other hand, if you want only certain layout settings from the selected layout, click on Get Form Only. This will import the settings for rehearsal marks, segnos, codas, endings, all symbols from the Global palette, bar line types, and bar numbers offset value. This option will ignore every other layout setting. When you have worked on a layout from one instrument and would like to transfer these settings to another, use one of those two functions.

Printing and Page Setup

The ultimate goal in using the Score functions is to print the result on a page so that musicians can read it. When you are in Page mode, you will see a gray border appearing around your page in Page mode display (shown in Figure 7.8). The default settings for your printer will determine where this border appears.

To change the page size and margin settings:

1. From the File menu, select Print & Page Setup. The default printer setup window will appear.
2. Set the paper size and page orientation to the desired values.
3. Adjust the margin values for Top, Bottom, Left, and Right.

TIP

If you want these values to become your default values every time you create a new score, open the Def.all file, which is your default song containing all your default settings, make the changes to your margins, and save to this file.

4. Click on the Printer button at the bottom of the Page Setup dialog box.
5. Choose the printer you want to work with and click OK, or edit the printer's properties and then click OK twice.

Now You Try It

Here are the exercises you will find on the Web site for this chapter. Note that some of these steps require Cubase VST Score or Cubase VST/32. If you don't have one of these versions, just skip over them:

- ▶ Edit the Staff setting.
- ▶ Use Staff presets.
- ▶ Add chords and edit them.
- ▶ Add titles and comments.
- ▶ Add brackets to staves in the Score settings.
- ▶ Change stave names.
- ▶ Add text.
- ▶ Print your score.

You will find these exercises at **www.muskalipman.com/cubase**.

Simply follow the instructions on the Web site before starting the exercises.

You can refer to this chapter to find out how to do these exercises, but try doing them without peeking first, just to see how comfortable you are with these principles. If you don't remember how to do a task, refer to the appropriate header in this chapter.

You will need to have the Universal Sound Module and the VB-1 VSTi installed on your computer to use the file provided for these exercises. If you do not have these VST instruments installed, you can always use a General MIDI-compatible device, assigning Channel 1 to play a Bass sound, Channel 2 to play a Lead Synth sound, Channel 3 to play a Strings sound, Channel 5 a Piano sound, and Channel 10 to Drums.

8
Setting Up Audio Recording

This chapter covers the basic steps in setting up your recording session, including how to use the VST Channel Mixer window to assign dynamics, equalization, and effects to your audio channels. You will also discover how to customize the VST Channel Mixers to fit your needs and optimize your mixing experience.

Understanding how signal flows within Cubase and how Cubase interacts with your sound card's physical connection is important when recording digital audio or processing already recorded digital audio. We will look at how you can assign channels to different buses, groups, and outputs on your sound card, as well as how the effects are processed and streamed within each audio channel.

VST Channel Mixer

The VST Channel Mixer is like a mixing console for audio tracks, VST Instruments, and any Rewire-compatible software. Rewire, as you will see later in this chapter, allows you to integrate third-party software, such as Rebirth and Reason, within your Cubase VST environment by providing additional Virtual Instrument outputs. What the Channel Mixer displays is up to you, since you can customize different displays for both your Channel Mixer 1 and Channel Mixer 2 panels. Both Channel Mixers are available through the Panels menu in Cubase. There are no differences between the Channel Mixers. They are both used to do the same thing: mix your audio and Virtual Instruments. Cubase provides two Channel Mixers to allow you to set up two different sets of channels. For example, you can set Channel Mixer 1 to display audio channels, VST Instruments, and Rewire channels, while Channel Mixer 2 could be set to display your groups and Master Channel outputs. Each type of channel is displayed with a different color in your Channel Mixer. Here's a list describing each one:

- **Gray**—For audio channels. Stereo channels have locked faders, meaning that you can't move one without moving the other, unless you hold the Alt key down as you move one of the faders in an audio pair. In Figure 8.1, the first two audio channels are in stereo and the rest of the audio channels are mono. Note that the buttons above the faders are linked by a little line, and the Insert button on top is visible only for the first channel in the pair. The small Input button (In) above the faders in audio channels is used to monitor the input of the audio channel rather than the playback. This is the only type of channel that has this button. In Figure 8.1, the fader for Channel 3 is currently monitoring the input, since you can see that the button is highlighted.

- **Beige**—For VST Instrument (VSTi) channels. If a VST Instrument is stereo, the display for the channels will be similar to stereo audio channels. VST Instruments are MIDI virtual instruments. However, since they use your sound card to output the sounds they generate, they appear in the Channel Mixer rather than in the MIDI Mixer. The number of VST Instrument channels displayed depends on how many VST Instruments are loaded in your song or arrangement.

- **Red**—For Rewire channels. These follow the same type of display as VST Instrument channels. The number of Rewire channels displayed depends on which Rewire channels are active in your Rewire panel. This will be discussed later in this chapter.

- **Blue**—For Group channels. Group channels are always in a stereo pair. They are used to combine the signals coming from different channels assigned to a group. This way, you can control their overall level through one signal fader, or they can be used to send a group of audio, VSTi, and Rewire channels to a set of effects settings that is common to every one. For example, you can decide to send a series of channels to a group and assign a reverb to that group, rather than assigning the same reverb with the same setting to all the channels individually. Another use for groups is to assign different channels at different output levels and control their proportional output level through one set of group faders. For example, you could have channels 1 through 8 playing different parts of your drum kit (kick on Channel 1, snare on Channel 2, hi-hat on Channel 3, and so on), all set to their own output levels. You can assign this drum kit to a group instead of to the Master output, making this group output fader the proportional output level for all these audio channels at once. This would also allow you to assign a compressor to the drum kit as well through the Group channel. Don't worry if you don't understand this concept right away, because we'll get back to it later in this chapter.

NOTE

The number of audio channels displayed in a Channel Mixer depends on the number of audio channels available in your audio settings. If you set your Cubase properties to use eight audio channels, you will have eight audio channels in both your Channel Mixer and in your song file. If you want to change this setting, select from the Options menu, Audio Setup > System, and then change the number of channels in the Audio Performance section of the Audio System Setup window. Note that if your computer is not fast enough, having more audio channels than your system can handle will slow it down considerably. Allocating fewer audio channels may allow you to set higher values for the Memory per channel and Disk block buffer size fields in the Options > Audio Setup > System dialog box. Maximum settings for these parameters are normally recommended. If your system has limited physical memory, set only the number of channels you actually need. Remember that these settings can be changed at any time if you feel that your computer performance is hindered by these changes.

Figure 8.1
The VST Channel Mixer.

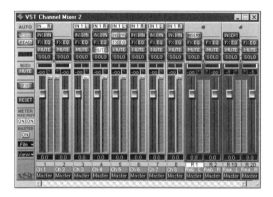

Let's look at how you can customize those two mixers, and then we'll discuss what each element can do.

To change which channels you want the mixer to display:

1. Start by opening your VST Channel Mixer from the Panels menu. Select either Channel Mixer 1 or 2.
2. Click on the View drop-down menu in the lower left corner of the window, as shown in Figure 8.1.

A list of presets will appear. This list is the default and describes which types of channels the Channel Mixer will display. For example, choosing Tracks will display only all audio channels but will hide VSTi channels, Rewire channels, and Group channels.

3. Select a preset from the list.

You might want to create your own set of channel displays in the Channel Mixer. This way, you can customize the layout and use both mixers 1 and 2 to view different types of channels, perhaps keeping all the audio channels and Virtual Instruments in one mixer and only the groups in the second mixer.

To create a customized Channel Mixer:

1. Repeat all the steps from the previous list of steps, but instead of selecting a preset with a name, choose one of the Default presets.
2. Click on the View drop-down menu and select Edit at the top of the menu. The VST Mixer Views window will appear, as shown in Figure 8.2.

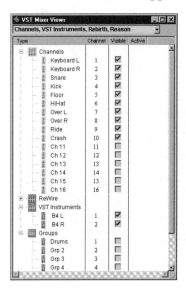

Figure 8.2
The VST Mixer Views window.

This window displays four columns:

- ▶ The first column shows a list of channel types, and under each type, the actual channels with their labels next to them.
- ▶ In the second column, you can see the channel number associated with the channel type's label. This corresponds to the channel number you assign to an audio track in the Arrange window or the order in which you assigned VST Instruments. In this case, since there is only one VSTi loaded, the channel numbers for the VSTi type are 1 and 2, representing the left and right outputs of the B4 instrument.
- ▶ The third column is where you choose to make a channel visible or not. Check the channels you wish to see in the Channel Mixer by toggling the checkmark in the Visible column.

▶ The last column, called Active, lets you activate or deactivate Rewire channels. You can't see this in Figure 8.2, but to make a channel visible in your Channel Mixer, you need to activate the channel. This applies only to Rewire channels. Activate the appropriate Rewire channels and then make them visible in your Channel Mixer by checking the field in the Visible column.

If you can't see individual channels because the Type display is collapsed, click on the plus sign next to the channel type group to expand the tree. Inversely, if you don't want to see all channels in a type of channel, click on the minus sign next to the Group type to collapse it.

You can use the VST Mixer Views window to rename channels by double-clicking where the name of the channel appears. This will allow you to edit in the field, and you can type in the new name for your channel. If you look at Figure 8.2, Group Channel 1 has been renamed "Drums." This name appears at the bottom of the fader, just below the channel number in the Channel Mixer window.

Now, let's look at each channel from top to bottom and identify the different functions. You may want to refer to Figure 8.1 from time to time or launch your Channel Mixer to understand these descriptions.

At the top of audio channels, you will find the Input channel that is assigned to that channel. This represents the physical input from which the sound comes when you record on this channel. The name displayed here depends on the name you set in the VST Inputs window found under the Panels menu, shown in Figure 8.3. If you have only a pair of stereo inputs and outputs on your sound card, you won't be able to change the input setting. However, if you have more than one input pair, you can change which input the audio comes from when recording on this channel.

Figure 8.3
The VST Inputs window.

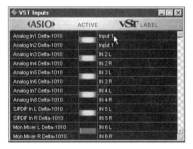

To change the input of a channel:

1. Start by opening the VST Inputs window from the Panels menu.
2. Activate the inputs you wish to use by clicking on the Active button next to the sound card's input.
3. If you want to change the name that will appear on the input's drop-down menu in the Channel Mixer, double-click on the name of the input corresponding to the input channel you wish to rename in the right column titled VST Label. Then, type the name you want to see in the Channel Mixer.
4. Open the Channel Mixer by selecting either VST Channel Mixer 1 or 2 from the Panels menu.
5. Ctrl+click on the Input button at the top of the audio channel. A drop-down menu will appear showing you a list of active inputs.
6. Select the input that you want to use for that channel from the list.

The next row of buttons on each channel in the VST Channel Mixer window has either one Insert button or an Insert button (INS) and a Dynamic button (DYN). Active buttons are highlighted. The Insert button allows you to insert an effect on this channel. An inserted effect takes the signal coming from the channel, sends it to the effect, takes the output of the effect, and sends it back into that channel. You can use either VST effects or DirectX effects as channel inserts. We will look at how this routing works later in this chapter. The Dynamics, or DYN, button available on audio channels opens only the channel settings for dynamic effects such as compressors, limiters, noise gates, and expanders. Like Insert, the Dynamics button is applied directly to the channel's output.

The next row offers two buttons: the FX, or effects button, and the EQ, or equalization button. Use the FX button to add an effect to the signal passing through this channel. Here are the differences between Insert Effects and Send Effects:

- Only one channel can use the VST effect assigned to that channel as an Insert Effect. On the other hand, you can send multiple channels to the same VST effect when using a Send Effect.
- The output of an Insert Effect is sent back directly into that channel. A Send Effect can be routed to Bus, to the Master Faders, or to Groups to redirect audio channels into a bus (to create a headphone mix, for example.) Note that this works only if you don't actually assign an effect to that Send Effect.
- You can have up to four Insert Effects per channel. You can have up to eight Send Effects per arrangement.
- Insert Effects has no channel controls over how much a signal goes into the effect; only within the effect window can you adjust the Input level. Send Effects has an independent level control for each send effect on each audio channel. There is also a separate VST Send Effects panel to control the amount of general Input level going into each send effect.

▶ Send Effects can take the signal from an audio channel pre- or post-fader. This means that when it is in Pre-Fader mode, the position of the audio channel's fader will not affect the amount of signal being sent to the send effect. However, in Post-Fader mode, the position of the audio channel's fader will influence the level of this channel's signal going into the send effect. Insert Effects doesn't have pre/post fader switches.

Use the EQ button when you want to add equalization to your channel. Equalization is a form of band filtering. You can boost or cut certain frequencies from an audio's output signal using this feature, just as you would manipulate certain frequencies using a graphic equalizer or tone controls on a home stereo sound system. How to use both the FX and EQ buttons will be discussed further in the next section of this chapter.

The next button is the Mute button, which you can use to mute the channel from playback. Below the Mute button, you will find the Solo button, which mutes all the channels except the one you selected as being solo. Use the Mute and Solo buttons to isolate certain elements, as you would use these buttons in the Arrange window. Note that using the Solo button does not influence MIDI channels, since this is the "Audio" channel mixer. To mute MIDI tracks when using Solo in the VST Channel Mixer, click on the MIDI Mute button found on the left-hand side of the VST Channel Mixer's option menu.

The area below the Solo button is a horizontal rectangle with a line somewhere in that rectangle. This is your panning control. To move the pan to the left or right, click on the line and drag it to the desired position. Notice in Figure 8.1 how the stereo channels are panned compared to the mono channels. To bring the pan back to its center value, hold the Ctrl key down as you click in the pan control area. To move your pan with more precision, hold the Shift key down as you move your cursor in the box. The value for the pan is displayed below the fader and above the channel's number when you modify the value for this option. Like most numeric values that appear in Cubase, you can also double-click in the field to type a new value.

Below the pan control, you have the fader area, which displays a fader for volume control and a playback level meter next to the fader. This becomes an input level meter when you activate the channel's input. Above the channel fader, you have a numerical display showing you the peak value for this channel. This represents the margin before clipping. The closer you are to zero, the closer you are to digital clipping. If clipping occurs, the little red dot (representing an LED) next to the peak margin indicator will light up. To reset the clip indicator, click on it.

When you move your fader up or down, the value in boost or cut will be represented in numerical value below the fader. This same area displays the pan information when moving the pan. If you move your fader above the 0.0 line, you are boosting, or increasing, the amplitude of the signal, and when you are moving the fader below the 0.0 line, you are cutting, or reducing, the amplitude of that signal. To bring your faders back to a nominal level, which is always set at 0.0, hold the Ctrl key down as you click on the fader's handle. If you want to move only one fader in a stereo pair of channel faders, hold down the Alt key as you move that fader. You can also use the Shift key if you want to increase the accuracy of your fader's resolution when moving it up or down.

If you want to toggle between a playback level meter and a recording level meter, you click on the In button found directly above the level meter. This transforms the channel's output level meter into a channel input level meter. You can monitor input levels this way without recording anything.

The channel number is displayed under the numerical display of the channel's fader. To select more than one channel, you can Shift+click on the channel number to select these channels. Selecting multiple channels can be useful if you want to save the settings you made for these channels to a separate file by using the File drop-down menu found to the left of the Channel Mixer window. Saving settings allows you to recall certain settings when working on another project or a different arrangement of the same song. Choose the appropriate option in the File menu when you want to save Channel Mixer settings.

In the left area, called the VST Channel Mixer option menu, you will find a series of option buttons and menus. The first one on the top is the Auto area with two buttons: Write and Read. If you want to record mixing automation, you need to enable the Write button. To read automation recorded, enable the Read button. You can enable both buttons to read your automation as it is being recorded. This will be discussed further in Chapter 11.

The Solo display lights up when you have enabled a Solo track, and the MIDI mute button allows you to Mute MIDI playback. The FX button is highlighted when an effect is in use. Clicking on this button will bring up the VST Send Effects window. Use this to initialize, choose, and configure your effects or control how much effect you want to send back into a mix.

The Reset button resets all the VST Channel Mixer's parameters to a default value and closes the window.

The Meter section has two options. The Hold button will hold peaks for playback and recording meter levels for each channel as a static line. The Fast button makes the playback and recording meter level react quickly to peak changes. Disabling this option will make the meter level perform as a standard VU meter found on analog or digital mixers.

The Master button allows you to see the VST Master Mixer Channels in your VST Channel Mixer. When you activate this, the Master Mixer channels will appear after the last channel on the right of your Channel Mixer. This is the same as having the Master Mixer window opened.

Channel EQ

"EQing" (pronounced "ee-queing") is part of the recording and mixing process in probably 99 percent of recordings today, and at some point in your creation process, you will find it to be a very useful tool. This said, it can be used correctively or creatively. Too much equalization and you might lose the purity of the well-recorded original sound ... then again, maybe this is what you were going for. You can use an EQ to increase or decrease specific frequencies to help the general quality of the sound, to correct certain flaws in the recording due to poor microphone performance, to remove noise generated by fluorescent lighting or air conditioning, and in more ways than this chapter will allow. In Cubase, you have four bands of parametric EQ per channel. The only channels you don't have EQ control on are the Master Mixer outputs and the buses.

Notice in Figure 8.4 that when you click on either the INS, DYN, FX, or EQ buttons from the Track Info area or within the VST Channel Mixer, the VST Channel Settings window opens, reproducing on the left side of the window the same setup as found in the VST Channel Mixer, except that here you see only one channel at a time. You will always see the option buttons found on the left of the channel fader and the Insert Effects and Send Effects settings on the right of the fader. The button you pressed to get the VST Channel Settings determines the content found beyond the Send Effects settings. In other words, if you pressed the EQ button to get here, you will get the EQ settings window. On the other hand, if you pressed the DYN button, the EQ settings will be replaced by the Dynamic settings, as shown in Figure 8.6.

Figure 8.4
The EQ settings in the VST Channel Settings window.

Each EQ band gives you control over Gain, Frequency, and Q.

- ▶ The **Gain** control is the amount of gain or reduction that you apply to a frequency. You can add or reduce from + or −24 dB.
- ▶ The **Frequency** determines what frequency will be affected by your gain or cut. You can set each band to any frequency between 20 Hz and 20,000 Hz.
- ▶ The **Q** is the control you have over the width of the frequency band you want to affect. The lower the numeric value for this field, the larger the width; the higher the numeric value for this field, the narrower the width. Narrow Qs are useful to isolate a problematic frequency, such as a 60 Hz cycle that is often associated with electrical equipment. Use wide Qs to enhance or reduce a large area of the harmonic structure of a sound, such as boosting the high end of the sound.

To assign an EQ to an audio channel:

1. You can assign an EQ to a channel from different places inside Cubase. One of them is through the Track Info area, as shown in Figure 8.5. Click on the EQ button to open the VST Channel Settings for that track. You can also click on the EQ button in the VST Channel Mixer for the same track. This will launch the VST Channel Settings window as well.

Figure 8.5
The Track Info area of an audio track displays the same buttons you will find in the Channel Mixer: Insert, Dynamic, Effects, and EQ.

2. To activate a band, click the On button in the right half of the Channel Settings window for up to four bands per channel. If you don't activate the band, the changes you make will have no effect on the sound.

3. To select a frequency, click and drag the outer gray knob above the Frequency display window for the active band. You can also double-click in the frequency display to type your frequency or click on the graph above the bands, moving the square handle next to the number corresponding to your band.

Moving this box left or right will change the frequency; moving it up or down will add or remove gain from that band's frequency. If no boxes appear, it's because you haven't activated any bands. You can kill two birds with one stone by clicking on the green line to activate the band corresponding to the area where you click and moving the box that will appear to where you want it. Notice how the graph area is split into four bands—20 Hz to 500 Hz; 500 Hz to 5,000 Hz; 5,000 Hz to 10 kHz; and 10 kHz to 20 kHz. These are the four default bands. Once activated, you can drag a band outside that band area.

4. Adjust the gain by clicking and dragging the inner green knob above the frequency display or, again, by using either the box in the graph or by double-clicking in the gain area and typing your value. You can enter a maximum value of + or −24. This corresponds to a boost or cut of 24 dB.

5. To change the Q for the band, you will need to use the Q knob found over the Q display. Drag it up to increase or down to decrease the value. You can also double-click in the Q display area to type your Q value. You can enter any number between 0 and 18.

6. Bands 1 and 4 have two additional buttons. Use the Low Cut button in the first band to use the HPF (High Pass Filter) option, which cuts everything below the frequency you set for that band; or use the Low Shelf button to increase or decrease the gain for the frequencies below the band's setting. The fourth band has the same mirror option for high frequencies. Use the Hi Cut or LPF (Low Pass Filter) to remove everything above the band's frequency, or use the Hi Shelf to increase or decrease the gain for the frequencies above the band's setting.

7. To hear the sound without the EQ active and make sure that the settings you are applying actually help your sound, you can use the Bypass button below the second band. This bypasses the EQ altogether without having to turn your bands off.

8. Once you are happy with the result, you can store your settings for later use by clicking on the Store button below the third band.

This will create a preset that you can find below the Store button. To recall a preset, click on the Preset drop-down menu and select the desired preset from the list. To rename a preset, make it active and double-click on its name to retype the new name. If you want to remove a preset from the list, select it and click the Remove button.

TIP
When you make modifications to a stereo channel, by default what you do for one channel will be reflected on the other channel in this stereo pair. If you don't want this, hold down the Alt key when making your modification to the selected channel in the pair.

Audio Channel Dynamics Control

Like the EQ settings, you can find the Dynamics settings button both in the VST Channel Mixer and in the Track Info area of the selected audio track. Unlike the EQ, though, you can have dynamic control only in an audio channel. If you want to use dynamic control on Rewire, VSTi, or groups, you will have to use the effect provided with Cubase VST called "Dynamics." This effect is very similar to the channel's Dynamic Control window.

About Dynamic Control

Before we begin discussing what this window does, let's look at what dynamic control is. (If you are familiar with this concept, you may skip this section and start reading about how to use the dynamic controls in the VST Channel Settings window.) A dynamic control in audio implies that you can modify the peaks and valleys of the amplitude of a sound by adding boundaries like a ceiling or a floor. The basic parameters of dynamic controls are:

- **Threshold**—This is the point from which a signal is affected. Signals below or above this level will not be affected depending on the type of dynamic control you are using.

- **Attack**—This determines how quickly the processing is applied to the sound. It acts like an attack part of an envelope; the value you set will determine the time it takes for the effect to go from not processing the sound to processing the sound, and it does this gradually. Longer values mean longer attack time; shorter values mean shorter attack time.

- **Release**—This determines how long the process will last once the signal has passed the threshold, has been affected by the processing, and then moves out of the threshold area. Like the attack, this is the tail end of an envelope, and the value you set determines how much time it will take before the processing ends completely. It is also a gradual process. Longer values mean longer release time; shorter values mean shorter release time.

- **Ratio**—This determines the amount of processing applied to the sound.

As you will see, there are more parameters in the Dynamic Controls window, but these are basic dynamic parameters. Cubase offers four different types of dynamic control:

- **Gating**—With the AutoGate module, you can reduce the level of low-level noises or sounds. By setting a threshold, you tell the processor to close the gate (or the amplifier), making that sound silent. When the threshold is passed, the gate opens and the sound emerges. Use this dynamic process when you want to remove a noisy guitar amplifier buzzing from a recording when the guitar player is not playing. You will still have the amplifier "buzz" when the guitar player plays, but it will be less noticeable since, hopefully, the guitar sound will hide it within its harmonics. With the AutoGate processor, you can set a specific range of frequencies to look for.

- **Auto Gain** or, in Cubase VST, the **AutoLevel** processor—This feature is very handy when you have different levels between recorded materials, because it reduces the differences between these levels. Any signal passing the threshold will be affected: Low-level sounds passing this threshold are increased and high-level sounds are decreased. Levels below the threshold are not affected, so noise is not boosted in the signal at that point.

- **Compression**—This is the core of the dynamic world. Use a compressor to reduce the dynamic range between different amplitudes. Amplitude that passes a set threshold is "compressed" at a determined ratio level, like 2:1, which means that for every two decibels that pass over the threshold level, only one will come out. Therefore, if you have a sound going in a compressor at -2 dB with a threshold value set at -20 and a ratio of 2 to 1, the resulting sound will be -11 dB instead (20 $-$ 2 = 18 dB above the threshold, 18/2=9 dB after the compression ratio is applied, $-20+9=-11$ dB).

  The attack time determines how fast the compressor reacts—for fast, aggressive percussive sounds (like kick drums, snares, and so on), the faster the better. The release time determines how long it should take before the compressor stops compressing between threshold points. Always use your judgment when setting compressor parameters, for your ears are the best tools in setting the compression process properly, as with any other dynamic effect.

- **Limiting**—This is found in two flavors in the VST's dynamic control: SoftClip and Limit. A limiter makes sure nothing goes beyond the threshold value, and it makes sure that the volume (amplitude) doesn't exceed that prespecified threshold level. Imagine that the limiter is a wall. Whenever a sound attempts to pass through this wall, it bangs into it and stays there. So, if your volume is always near the limiter's threshold, you will not pass the 0 dB limit, but you might hear some distortion. The difference between SoftClip and Limit in Cubase is that SoftClip analyzes the signal and starts limiting 6 decibels before the threshold is reached, creating a more gentle limiting curve, whereas Limit starts limiting at the threshold value you decide.

Figure 8.6 shows you a graphical display of the different types of dynamic controls found in the Channel's Dynamic Control panel. The vertical axis represents the output signal and the horizontal axis represents the input signal. Normally, the output is equal to the input; that's why a straight diagonal line represents the original signal. If you apply dynamic processing to this line, you will have a different output for each type of processing you apply on the signal. The processing type is indicated above each graphic representation.

Figure 8.6
How dynamic control affects the dynamic output of a signal.

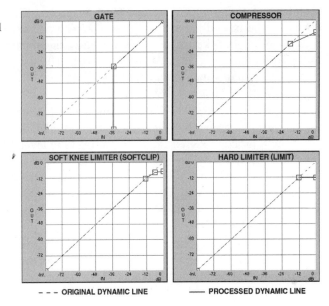

Using Dynamic Control

To access the Dynamic Control panel for an audio channel, click on the DYN button either from the Track Info area or from the VST Channel Mixer window. Figure 8.7 shows you the dynamic control in the VST Channel Settings window for any audio channel. You will find five different buttons in this window, called, respectively, AutoGate, AutoLevel, Compress, SoftClip, and Limit. These correspond to the five dynamic controls available. All the other buttons are options for these five dynamic control processes.

To activate a dynamic process, click on the desired button.

Figure 8.7
The Dynamic Control panel in the VST Channel Settings window.

To set the AutoGate process:

1. Start by enabling the AutoGate function by clicking on its button, shown as highlighted (active) in Figure 8.7.
2. Set the slider with a handle under the Trigger Frequency Range area to its Listen position by clicking on the handle and dragging it to the right. This slider has three positions: Off, On, and Listen.
3. Set your low and high frequencies to determine the range for your gate trigger by dragging the vertical handles. You can press Play on your Transport bar to listen to the range being filtered as you are modifying this range. You will then see an additional column (Labeled "R") appear in the Track List area.

This allows you to select a range of frequencies that can trigger the gate to open. For example, if you don't want to hear a singer's headphone leaking into the microphone, you might want to exclude the high- and low-end frequencies from the gate's trigger frequency range. Any frequency inside the frequency range will have the potential to trigger the gate to open, whereas the frequencies outside this range will not affect the gate, keeping it closed, as it should be in this example. The trigger frequency range is located between the two vertical lines and is displayed in green. This range will trigger your gate to open.

4. Now that you have set the range, bring the slider below the trigger frequency range to the On position.

If you have a constant low-level noise in your recording, you can use the Calibrate button under the Threshold knob found in the AutoGate function.

5. Start the playback of the song or arrangement where there are no actual instruments recorded and click the Calibrate button to determine the optimized threshold level to remove (gate) the noise from the sound. If you find that it cuts into your desired program material, change the value manually by clicking on the Threshold knob and dragging it up or down.
6. Set the attack function to Predict mode. The button is yellow when activated, as shown in Figure 8.7. This will optimize your attack speed—the speed at which the amplifier opens when the threshold has been reached.
7. Set the hold value by dragging the mouse over the Hold knob to have the gate hold the doors open for the time set in the numerical display below this button. If you set this value too high, the gate will stay open and you might hear noise from the original sound coming in.
8. Set the release to auto by clicking on the Auto button. This will determine the best release time, or, in other words, the optimal amount of time it will take for the gate's doors to close.

TIP

You can use AutoGate in Listen mode to get EQ effects resembling a very narrow band pass filter, such as a 1930s radio or telephone line simulation.

http://www.muskalipman.com

Use the AutoLevel process if you have different segments coming from different sources on your audio track. The AutoLevel will try to reduce the volume differences between uneven audio segments. For example, sounds recorded softer will sound a little bit louder and sounds recorded louder will sound a little bit softer. To enable this process, click on the AutoLevel button in the VST Channel Settings window. AutoLevel looks ahead to find these changes in amplitude.

To set the AutoLevel process:

1. Set the threshold level by clicking on the Threshold knob, found in the AutoLevel area located underneath the AutoGate area, or double-click on it to enter the value you want. This process will not affect sounds that are below this threshold value.
2. Set the vertical slider to Fast, Mid, or Slow by clicking on the handle in the middle and moving it to where you want. This will affect the speed at which the process reacts to the amplitude changes in your sound.

To enable the compressor, click on its button in the VST Channel Settings window. Below the compressor activation button, you will see a graph showing the result of your compressor settings. Below the compressor's characteristic graph is a Gain Reduction meter. This will show you how much gain is removed from the original amplitude of the sound.

You should know at this point that, no matter which dynamic process you are using, it is always a good idea to listen to the result while making your settings. So, set your playback in Cycle mode to loop the area you wish to edit.

To set your compressor:

1. Set your threshold value for the compressor like any other field in this window. Remember that the threshold is the point from which the sound will start to be compressed.
2. Set your ratio to the desired value. You can set this value from 1:1 to 8:1, meaning that for every 8 decibels passing the threshold, only one will come out.
3. Set your attack value to the desired level. This determines how quickly the compressor kicks in once the threshold has been reached. If you're not sure, experiment with this setting while listening to the track.
4. Leave or assign the Release button to Auto. This will determine the best release time. If you think of a compressor as a muscle contraction, the release time is the time it takes for your muscle to feel relaxed after a contraction.
5. The MakeUpGain knob will allow you to add gain to your output once it has been compressed. This is useful when the amount of compression brings down the sound considerably. You can set this to a value of between 0 dB of compensation up to 24 dB of gain.

The SoftClip and Limit processes do the same thing in a different way. Consequently, you should use one or the other, not both. The only thing you need to do for the SoftClip is to activate it by clicking on its button. The display underneath the SoftClip button shows you the signal below -6 dB. The SoftClip starts to limit the signal once it passes into the orange area, increasing the limiting amount as it approaches the dark red area. If the signal should stay in the dark red area, distortion will be introduced, so try to keep the level moving in the orange to red area. Note that while distortion is not the same as clipping, it is usually not desirable.

To set the Limit:

1. Click on the Limit button to activate it.
2. Set the threshold value for the limiter. This is the uppermost amplitude value your signal will reach. Any part of the sound that was recorded over this threshold setting will be limited at the output. Like with the SoftClip function, too much limiting might result in unwanted distortion.
3. Set the Release to Auto.

To turn all the dynamic processes off, click the On button in the lower right corner of the VST Channel Settings window. Clicking it once again will bring the dynamic processes back to the settings they were at before you pressed the On button. You can also use the Bypass button below the On button to bypass the dynamic processes to allow for "before" and "after" listening. This is useful to make sure the dynamic settings are correct.

The graphic next to the On and Bypass buttons shows you the actual signal flow once it enters the Dynamic Processing panel. Note that the dynamic control is inserted before the fade control in your channel.

Channel Effect Routing

Cubase VST uses two types of effects: VST effects and DirectX effects. Both types of effects can be routed in your signal in three ways: Insert, Send, and Master. They are also both considered to be virtual effects, meaning that they work like real external processing effects, except that they are not hardware based but software based. They work within the Cubase VST environment. Note, however, that VST effects, unlike DirectX effects, can be automated. Because VST effects were designed to work well within the VST environment, whenever you have the same effect available in both VST and DirectX formats, it is suggested that you use the VST effects version, because it will use fewer computer resources than the DirectX one.

You can set up to four different insert effects per audio channel. Figure 8.8 shows you the actual signal routing. Note that the only control over the amount of wet/dry signal ratio you have is within the effect's window itself. The term "dry" refers to a signal without processing, and the term "wet" refers to a signal that contains processing, such as reverb, for example.

Figure 8.8
The Insert Effects signal path.

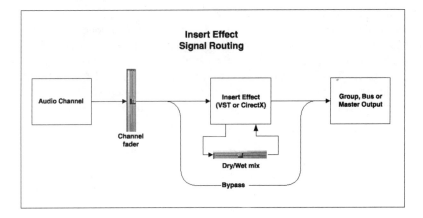

To use and set an effect using Insert Effects:

1. Select the track from the Arrange window or the channel from the VST Channel Mixer that you wish to send to Insert Effects.

2. Click the INS, or Insert, button in the Track Info area if you are in the Arrange window or the same button above the channel's fader in the VST Channel Mixer. The VST Channel Setting window will appear. In the Inserts section of this window, you will find four sets of controls corresponding to each assignable insert effect.

3. Start by clicking on the Insert Effect Selector to select the effect you wish to use, as shown in Figure 8.9.

Figure 8.9
The drop-down menu shown here might vary depending on the VST and DirectX effects that you have installed on your system. Notice that your DirectX effects will appear in sub-menus at the bottom of the list.

Setting Up Audio Recording – Chapter 8   217

4. Click the On button for the insert effect you just selected to activate it.
5. If you wish to edit the effect's parameters, click the Edit button next to the insert effect's On button. This will open the effect's editing window, as shown in Figure 8.10.

Figure 8.10
The effect's setup window opens when you click on the insert's Edit window. What control you have over the effect depends on the effect itself.

6. Once you have modified the effect's parameters, you can leave the window open or close it. These parameters will stay valid until you change the effect in the Insert Effects section of that channel.

We will discuss different effect parameters in more detail in Chapter 11.

You can also use up to eight different send effects per channel. Figure 8.11 shows you how the signal is routed. In this type of effect routing, the control you have over how much effect is being added to the signal is much greater than with insert effects. If you look at this figure, you can see that the signal can be taken from either the pre- or post-fader point. This means that the position of the channel's fader will influence how much of the signal goes into the effect if you are in post-fader mode (default) or will have no effect if you are in pre-fader mode. We will discuss how to change these settings later in this section.

Figure 8.11
The Send Effects signal path.

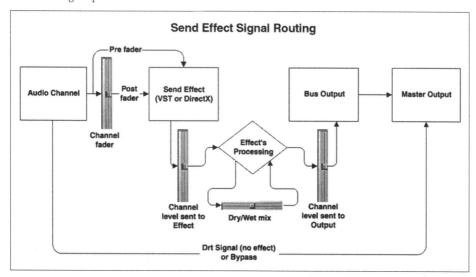

http://www.muskalipman.com

Send effects can be routed to different buses. Buses are extra faders, or outputs, in your VST Master Mixer window that you can use as additional fader controls for, among other things, sending a signal to an external effect. You can have extra buses only if your sound card has more than one stereo audio output stream available. These can be either physical outputs (as is the case of the Delta 1010, for example) or they can be virtual channels handled by the sound card's own mixing panel (as is the case with the Echo Mia and Creamware Pulsar, for example). Once past the channel fader, the signal is sent through another level control called the Channel Sent Level. This controls how much of the channel's signal you want to send to the effect. In the VST Channel Settings window, this is the blue knob found under the On and Pre buttons for each send effect. Where you send the actual effect is assigned by the drop-down menu found underneath the Channel Sent Level knob. Inside the effect itself, you have the same controls as you had with the insert effects. This is because you are using the same effects but in a different routing scheme and as different instances of the effect. Finally, you have one last control over how much of the effect output you want to send to the mix (either the Master or Bus faders).

Let's look at how to assign and set up a send effect:

1. Select the track from the Arrange window or the channel from the VST Channel Mixer that you wish to send to the effect.
2. Click on the FX button to activate the effect setup window. The VST Channel Settings window will appear.
3. In the Panels menu, select the VST Send Effects option or click on the blue FX button on the left of the VST Channel Setting window.

   This will bring up the VST Send Effects window. This is where you assign which send effects you want to use. Unlike the VST insert effects, you have eight effects active per arrangement.

4. Click on the field where it says No Effect to choose the desired effect from the list. Note that the list appearing here is the same one that appeared in the Insert Effects drop-down menu.
5. Click the red On button to activate that effect, as shown in Figure 8.12.

Figure 8.12
The VST Send Effects control window.

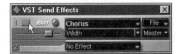

6. To edit this effect or choose a preset for it: Click the Edit button to the right of the On button in the same window. When you are done, you can close the effect's window and the settings will remain active.
7. Adjust the amount of signal you want to send to the mix from the VST Send Effects window using the horizontal slider found under the On button. This will add or reduce the amount of effect sent back into the mix. Note that if you have more than one channel using this same effect, moving this fader will influence the return of this effect for all channels passing through it.

8. If your buses are active, you can assign the output of the effect to a specific bus rather than to the Master output. Do this by selecting the appropriate bus in the drop-down menu where it says Master on the right side of the window, below the File drop-down menu. If you don't have other active buses, you can send your send effect only to the Master output.
9. Back in the VST Channel Settings window, activate the Pre button if you wish to take the signal before the channel fader or leave it inactive to take the signal after the channel fader.
10. Adjust the amount of signal going into your effect by clicking and dragging the blue knob under the On and Pre buttons for the send effect you wish to use.

Since you can have up to eight send effects per channel, they all have the same sets of controls. Later, if you want to bypass an effect, you can click the Bypass button found in the Send Effects section of the VST Channel Settings. If you have more than one effect assigned and would like to bypass only one of the effects, click on the On button instead. This will temporarily deactivate this channel from the Send Effects. When reactivating it, the original settings will still be there.

If you wish to add another send effect to a channel, repeat steps 4 through 10 from the previous list, selecting the second send effect from the VST Send Effects window. Remember that if you are going to use the same effect on more than one track, it is recommended that you use Send Effects rather than Insert Effects. This will be easier on your processor, because it has to calculate only the output of one effect rather than multiple instances of the same effect.

VST Master Mixer

The VST Master Mixer is your main output. Depending on how you set up your system or how many outputs your sound card has, you will generally use the two main outputs of your sound card to monitor the output in your sound system. If you have more than two outputs (and probably inputs), you can use these additional outputs as buses. Let's say your sound card has eight inputs and eight outputs. You can assign outputs 1 and 2 to the Master output. This is your monitor mix output, or what you want to hear in your speakers. Outputs 3 and 4 can be used by Bus 2, 5 and 6 by Bus 3, and 7 and 8 by Bus 4. This way, you can send four different pairs of signals to an external multitrack recorder—external effects, different monitor mixes, and so on.

As you saw earlier, you can also use the buses to send effects to an external effect or to a headphone amplifier.

The Master Mixer also has up to four different assignable effects. These Master Mixer Effects are very useful for final dynamic control over the entire mix, or noise reducing effects. Since master effects are applied to any channel going to the Master output, you probably won't want to use anything else here.

http://www.muskalipman.com

Figure 8.13 shows you a diagram of how the audio routing works and where the Master Mixer's outputs fit into all this. The Master output and the Bus outputs don't send the signal simultaneously to all the outputs of a sound card. Look at Figure 8.13: You can assign the Master or Bus outputs to any outputs on your sound card, one stereo pair at a time. Therefore, the physical outputs on your sound card can be used to monitor anything you configure within the VST Master Mixer window.

Figure 8.13
Cubase VST's Master Mixer and Buses routing.

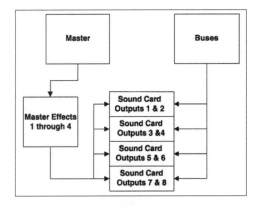

The Master Mixer has four master effects, and each will be sent to the sound card's output assigned for the Master Mixer faders. Only one sound card output can be assigned at a time, but when you switch from one output to another, the rest of the buses will also follow this setting. For example, if you set your Master Mixer to outputs 1 and 2 on your sound card, these outputs will not be selected in the Bus output selector. This is covered in the following header.

To assign a master effect into your mix:

1. Launch the VST Master Mixer window from the Panels menu.

Under the Master FX, you will find four fields. If you have not yet selected Master Effects, they should all display "No Effects."

2. Click on the first field and select an effect from the drop-down menu. The list of effects here is similar to the Send and Insert effects.

3. Click the On button to the right of the effects name to activate it (see Figure 8.14).

Figure 8.14
The VST Master Effects window.

http://www.muskalipman.com

4. To edit the effect's parameters, hold the Ctrl key down as you press the On button or select the VST Master Effects option from the Panels menu and then click the Edit button next to the Master Effects you want to edit.
5. To add another effect to the Master Mixer, repeat steps 2 and 3.

If you want to monitor the mix in mono to be certain there are no phase cancellations in your mix, you can press the Mono button below the Master Mixer faders. Below this button, you will also find a drop-down menu offering a list of available outputs to which you can assign the Master Mixer. These are the sound card's physical outputs used to monitor your arrangement. If you don't have multiple outputs on your sound card, only one pair of stereo outputs will be available here.

You can bypass Master Effects by clicking the bypass button in the VST Master Mixer window, as shown in Figure 8.14. You can also click the "S" button to solo an effect. Toggling the On button for each effect will temporarily activate or deactivate the master effects individually.

Finally, the Export button below Master Effects will be used later to export everything that is passing through the Master Mixer to an audio file on your computer. This will be discussed in the last chapter of this book.

VST Audio Bus System

Figure 8.14 show a setup with four buses and one master in this case. This is because there are ten outputs on the system used to create this figure. The total number of buses available depends on the total number of physical outputs available on your sound card. Therefore, if you have twenty-four outputs, you will have a total of eleven buses plus one Master Mixer, because each bus is a pair of two outputs.

Working With Inputs

Just as you can have more than two outputs available if you have more than two physical outputs on your sound card, you can activate more than two inputs at a time if you have more than two physical inputs on your sound card.

To enable inputs:

1. Select the VST Inputs option from the Panels menu.
2. Click the green button in the Active column next to the inputs available on your system.
3. To deactivate an input, click the Active button once again. Figure 8.15 displays the active inputs (in a bright green on your screen).

Figure 8.15
The VST Inputs window.

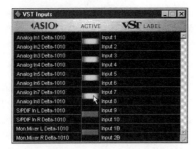

The columns to the left of the Active column represent the ASIO name given to each input by the ASIO driver of your sound card. In the right column, you can see the VST Input Labels. You can rename these labels by double-clicking on the name and typing a new one. The name that you type for a label will then be reflected in the VST Channel Mixer's audio channel's inputs at the top of the channel's strip, as shown in Figure 8.16.

Figure 8.16
The Input labels displayed in the VST Inputs panel are the same as the labels displayed both in the VST Channel Mixer and in the Track Info area of the audio channel (not shown here).

To change the input of an audio channel in the VST Channel Mixer, hold the Ctrl key down as you click the Input button (if you click directly on the letter L or R, you don't need to hold down the Ctrl key) and choose the desired input from the pop-up menu.

To activate the Input monitoring, make sure the In button above the channel's level monitor in the VST Channel Mixer is activated. It should be a bright yellow when active, and you should also see the input level of your signal coming in rather than the output signal going out.

Working with Outputs

Outputs, like inputs, are dependent on the sound card's physical connections. As discussed earlier in this chapter, you can assign different outputs to buses in the VST Master Mixer window. Each bus has its own physical output. Below the buses fader, you will find a drop-down menu offering you a list of available outputs. A checkmark next to the output's ASIO name indicates the current selection for that bus. If you select an output that is already assigned to another bus, the other bus will switch to the output that was previously used by the output you are using. Here's an example: If Bus 1 (the Master) uses outputs 1 and 2, and Bus 2 uses outputs 3 and 4, switching Bus 1 to outputs 3 and 4 will force Bus 2 to use outputs 1 and 2.

To change the label of a bus, click in the bus label, as shown in Figure 8.17, and type in your new label for that bus.

To activate a bus, click the Active button below the bus label. The first bus in Figure 8.17 is active and the others are not. Once you activate a bus, it becomes available in output assignment menus for audio, Rewire, VSTi, Audio Channel sends, and Group channels.

Note that the first bus is always your Master Mixer fader. This is why, by default, your first bus after the Master Mixer is labeled Bus 2.

All your bus settings are saved with the song file (*.all), but if you change your ASIO driver in the Options > Audio Setup > System window, Cubase will prompt you with a warning telling you that the bus settings will be lost.

To route a channel to a bus, select the appropriate bus from the pop-up menu found under each channel. This is set by default to Master.

If you want to use your Bus outputs to route a send effect to an external effect, do so by selecting the Bus output from the VST Channel Settings window, as shown in Figure 8.18. The Bus outputs you activate in the VST Master Mixer window determine the buses available in this list.

Figure 8.18
Assigning send effects to a Bus output instead of a virtual effect can be used to route your signal to an external device.

To return the effect into your mix, you can assign an audio channel to another set of inputs and then record the signal coming from the external effect on a track in Cubase VST. You can use send effects to send a signal to a headphone amplifier as well.

Master Effect Routing

The master effects found in the VST Master Mixer are routed directly into the signal path of the Master Mixer. This means that they operate in much the same way as an Insert effect. They are pre-fader, so the position of your Master Mixer faders has no consequence on the output of the effect. Since it is applied to all audio channels passing through the Master Mixer, the type of effect you use here should be limited to dynamic control over the entire mix and noise reduction processes. This doesn't mean you can't use reverb on the entire mix, but if you do so, understand that you won't be able to prevent any audio channel from passing through this reverb, including channels that are already assigned to reverbs through send effects, for example. If you want to save a file as streaming audio content for the Web, you might want to use a final brickwall equalizer to limit the frequencies of your mix before converting it to RealMedia, QuickTime, Windows Media, or MP3 files.

Rewire

Rewire is a software-based technology that lets you share application resources inside your computer—more specifically, Rewire-compatible ones. Developed by Propellerhead and Steinberg, most products sold by either company will be compatible with this technology.

What Rewire does is quite nice, and it's simple to use. It patches the outputs of one software application into the inputs of another software application and synchronizes them. This has the same effect as a VSTi, except that Rewire instruments or Rewire software applications are not running inside Cubase, as a VSTi is. When you activate Rewire channels in Panels > Rewire, you add these channels to the VST Channel Mixer. This allows all Rewire-compatible applications to share the same sound card, assigning each Rewire instrument a different output if you want, and also providing a common transport control and timing base; you can control playback for all applications from Cubase.

To use Rewire:

1. Launch Cubase first. It is important that your other Rewire applications are launched after Cubase.
2. In the Options menu, make sure the Play in Background option is selected.
3. In the Panels menu, select Rewire.

    The Rewire Panel will appear, as shown in Figure 8.19. What will appear in this panel depends on the Rewire-compatible applications installed on your computer. In this example, Rebirth and Reason are installed.

Figure 8.19
The Rewire activation window.

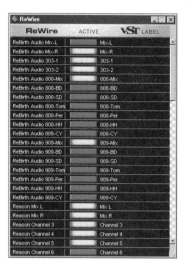

4. Click the green buttons in the Active column next to the channels you wish to activate in Cubase.

5. If you wish to rename a channel, click in the VST Label column and type in the label you want to use.

6. Launch your Rewire application.

At this point, the transport bars in both applications are linked together. This means that you can start and stop your playback within any application, and the others will follow. If you record events, this will be recorded in the application that is active, or, in other words, the recording will take place in the application you pressed on the recording button. So, recording is independent, but playback will follow. If you use Cycle playback or recording, all applications will follow this loop. When you have a loop playing in Reason, for example, this loop will stay looped. Cubase VST always sets the tempo setting when Master Track is active. If you change the tempo in Cubase's Master Track, the other applications will follow the lead. If you are not using Master Track, you can change the tempo setting in either application, and the playback will reflect it. In other words, if you start playback at 100 bpm in Reason and Cubase is not set to play the tempo from Master Track, it will play at 100 bpm.

All Rewire channels that are not muted when you export your mixdown from the Export Audio button in the VST Master Mixer window will be included in this output file.

One thing to look out for is the sample playback rate. Make sure both applications are set to a compatible sampling rate. If your Rewire application doesn't support Cubase VST's sampling rate, the Rewire application might not play the right pitch.

Now You Try It

Here are the exercises you will find on the Web site for this chapter. Note that some audio files have been included with the Song file, making the download a little bit longer. Efforts were made to keep these files to a minimal size by using short samples and VSTi instruments included with Cubase VST.

- ▶ Assign and adjust the Channel EQ.
- ▶ Use dynamic controls on Drum tracks.
- ▶ Route audio channels to groups.
- ▶ Assign, adjust the parameters, and route a send effect.
- ▶ Assign and adjust master effects.
- ▶ Customize your VST Channel Mixer view.

You will find these exercises at the following Web address: **www.muskalipman.com/cubase**.

Simply follow the instructions on the Web site before starting the exercises.

You may refer to the passages in this chapter to find out how to do these exercises, but try doing them without peeking first, just to see how comfortable you are with these principles. If you don't remember how to do a task, refer to the appropriate section of this chapter.

As with exercises in previous chapters, you will need to have the Universal Sound Module installed on your computer to use the file provided for these exercises. Unlike in previous examples, you won't be able to use GM instruments. The exercises use the VST Channel Mixer as a reference for the exercises, and GM instruments use the VST MIDI Mixer channels instead.

9
Working with Audio Files

You saw in the previous chapter how to set up your VST Channel Mixer and enable inputs and outputs. Here, you are going to learn how to set up tracks for your audio recordings. Once the tracks are recorded, parts are created. In these parts, you will find audio segments. These segments are portions of audio files you save on your hard disk. To manage all this, you will use the Audio Pool.

The Audio Pool is an audio file management system inside Cubase where files are the equivalent of files in an Explorer or Launcher window. However, unlike Explorer or Launcher, files also contain segments, which are regions found in a file that can be used in an arrangement. Every time a portion of a file is used in an arrangement, a segment is created under the file in the Audio Pool.

Each file that you record in Cubase is stored separately on your hard disk. However, you might not be using all the information (or audio) contained in that file. This is why you create segments in Cubase. You can have as many segments as you want per file and as many files as you want per pool, but you can have only one pool per song. Every arrangement in a song file will share the song's Audio Pool. Learning how to use this pool will help you manage disk space and share files from one project to another.

Finally, we will look at how Cubase handles different types of files you might want to import in your arrangement.

Audio Recording

Preparing your recording session in Cubase implies that you will want to configure your system in a way that will let you hear what is already recorded, while sending a feed to a headphone amplifier, and then recording only what the musician is playing—all while making sure the levels are OK. You have seen in the previous chapter how to use buses. This implied that you were using a multi-input/output sound card. We'll discuss the simple solution and the multiple solution here. The simple solution involves a single two-input/output setup with no mixer. The multiple solution involves a multi-input/output setup with a hardware mixing board as an option, for more flexibility.

To set up a recording using only two inputs/outputs:

1. Start by connecting your musical instrument or microphone to the input or inputs of your computer. Since you are connecting directly into the computer, you first need to establish the kind of connectors your sound card is using. If they are line inputs, they will accept high-impedance instruments such as keyboards or line out of a guitar amplifier. If your sound card uses microphone inputs with low impedance, you will need to use an external preamplifier. If you have a consumer sound card (such as a SoundBlaster), you might want to consider using only the line inputs, using a preamplifier rather than connecting anything in the microphone inputs. The quality of those connectors is not always up to par with the quality of sound you wish to record, and they might introduce some undesirable artifacts into your sound. You can also use a Direct Box to convert high-impedance line signals into low-impedance balanced microphone signals to fit professional microphone inputs, if you have them on your sound card. This will probably offer the best sound quality, especially when using instruments like guitars and basses.

2. Select the first available audio track in the arrange page or create an audio track in your arrangement by pressing Ctrl+T on your keyboard, by double-clicking below the last track in your arrangement, or by selecting Create Track from the Structure menu.

3. Change the class of the track to Audio. By default, your track's output will display Master. Leave it there for now, but you can change the output of the audio channel if you need to do so by selecting a different output at the bottom of the audio channel's fader in the VST Channel Mixer.

4. Open the Track Info area in the Arrange window to view the track's parameters.

5. Under the Channel option, select the audio channel or channels you wish to use for this recording. If you select a set of two channels (stereo), you will get a choice of channel pairs, excluding any channels that have already been allocated to a stereo pair, and your recording will be stereo. You can change this before you start recording, but once a mono track contains mono content files, you won't be able to record stereo files on this track anymore, because a channel or set of channels are assigned to this track. Once a track is set to mono or stereo, you can change which channel it uses, but with certain conditions: only odd-numbered tracks can be changed from mono to stereo, and only if the next even numbered channel is available. So, if you are using channel 1 and want to use another channel in a mono setting, you can choose channel 2. However, if you want to start your recording as stereo, you will either need to have channel 2 available or select another pair of odd/even numbered channels, like 3/4, 5/6, 7/8, and so on.

6. Ctrl+click the Input selector (but if you click the letter L or R, you won't have to hold down the Ctrl key), as shown in Figure 9.1, to select the input from which to record the audio. In this case, the recording is mono, so you can select either the left or the right input of your sound card.

Figure 9.1
You can also select the input for your recording in the Track Info area or the VST Channel Mixer window.

If you previously opened a new song file, Cubase prompted you to select a folder to store audio recordings. If this is the case, Cubase won't ask you to select a folder again but will assume you want to save the audio where you assigned it when creating the new song file. In any case, it might be a good idea to create a folder structure before you start recording in order to organize your files properly.

7. Click the Enable button in the Track Info area.
8. Select the appropriate folder to save the audio recording files. This will bring up a window prompting you to select a folder in which to save the recorded material, if you did not tell Cubase as you were creating a new song where you wanted to save the audio files. You should establish a logical system for your files, saving your recordings in the same folder where you will save the song or arrangement file or on a separate disk but in a folder structure that will make sense to you throughout your project.
9. From the Panels menu, select the VST Channel Mixer panel.
10. Click on the Input meter level button for the channel you will be using. When you play a couple of notes, you should see some input coming in the audio channel's input meter. If not, check your connections.
11. Adjust your input levels by doing one of the following: Change the gain on your instrument or use your sound card's interface to control the input levels. You don't want to clip and you don't want to come in too low, either. Optimally, the level should be set as high as possible without overloading the input.

NOTE

The input level meters found next to the channel faders in the VST Channel Mixer have absolutely no effect whatsoever on the input level. If you want to change the input level, you will need to use your sound card's interface or adjust the level coming from the instruments themselves.

Also, if you are noticing a high latency (delay between the time you play the instrument and the time you can hear it), you can switch the ASIO Direct Monitoring option found in Options > Audio Setup > System to Global Disable.

12. Back in the Track Info area, under the Record Info field, type the name under which you want to save the file. For example, if you are recording the solo guitar, call it "solo guitar."

You can always rename the file later on, but it is a good habit to get into, since names that don't mean anything to you now will be even more confusing when you decide to work on this project in a couple of weeks. See the section on "How to Use The Audio Pool" later in this chapter to learn how to rename files once they have been recorded.

13. Choose the appropriate recording mode in the Transport bar and set your locators correctly if you are recording in Cycle mode.

Press Record when you are ready to record your track.

When done, Cubase might prompt you to confirm the recording, as displayed in Figure 9.2, if you have unchecked the Options > Audio Setup > Confirm Record option. This said, it would be a good idea to keep this option checked to allow you to name the files yourself after a recording. This will give you more control over the names of the files and which files have been saved. Enter the name you wish to give to the new file and click on the Confirm button. Pressing Skip or Skip All in the Confirm Record dialog box will cancel your recording.

Figure 9.2
The Confirm Record dialog box will display the name and channel for each recording you did, asking you to confirm.

If you have a multi-input sound card, the easiest—and most relevant—method is to record each performer on a separate track, recording a separate audio file for each.

To set up recording using more than two inputs:

1. Repeat steps 1 to 5 from the previous list for all the tracks you wish to record simultaneously. For example, if you are recording drums, bass, guitar, and vocals, create four tracks. Mono recordings will use one channel, stereo recordings will use two channels, and the "any" setting will display a list of available channels from which to choose. Figure 9.3 shows a drum track set to "any," with four individual inputs active. The number of simultaneous inputs you can have depends on two things—the number of physical inputs on your sound card and the number of VST inputs you activate in the Panels > VST Inputs window. Each channel will create a separate file on your system.

2. In the VST Inputs window, activate the additional inputs you wish to use by clicking on the Activate button next to that input.

3. Under Options > Multirecord menu, make sure the Active option is checked. You will then see an additional column appear in the Track List area. This is the Record Enable column.

4. In the Track Info area, Ctrl+click on the Input selector (if you click the letter L or R, you won't have to hold down the Ctrl key) to select the inputs from which to record the audio on each track.

5. While still in the Track Info area, click the Enable button for each one of them. Note that you will not have to tell Cubase in which folder to save the audio content every time, only the first time. If Cubase doesn't ask you, it's because you already told it where to save the audio content when creating the new song.

Figure 9.3
The "any" setting allows you to select on which channel you wish to record audio.

6. Open the VST Channel Mixer from the Panels menu.

NOTE

In the example in Figure 9.3, the drum track will use four channels. If you want these four channels to come from separate inputs on your sound card, you will have to select them in the VST Channel Mixer's Input Selection drop-down menu.

7. In the VST Channel Mixer, activate the input level meter above the channel's level meter.
8. Adjust your input levels so that they don't clip or come in too low, as mentioned previously. Remember that the faders in the VST Channel Mixer will play no role in the input level.
9. Set your recording mode in the Transport bar and start recording.
10. When you are done recording, press the Stop button on the Transport bar or press the spacebar on your keyboard.

Cubase will prompt you to confirm all the recordings. In the example found in Figure 9.3, you should get one file for the vocals, one for the bass, one for the guitar (stereo), and four for the drums.

If you want to send a signal to headphone amplifiers so that the musicians can monitor what is recorded or being played in your arrangement, you can use the send effects routed through the buses on your multi-input/output sound card. This way, you can use up to four separate stereo headphone feeds since you have eight send effects, which are all mono sends.

Selecting a Recording Resolution

Before you start recording, you should know that it is a good idea to set your recording resolution to avoid having different files with different resolutions playing at the same time in your arrangement. This will take less processing time away from more important tasks. Remember that the higher the bit-rate or word length, the more dynamic range your sound will have. The downside of this is that it will take up more space on your hard disk. Nevertheless, if you are serious about sound quality, you should record as high a resolution as you can get, not to mention using a high sampling rate to capture all those crisp harmonics.

TIP

On this note, if you are using a digital mixer or another digital device to record your material—such as DAT, DA-98, or ADAT—there's no point in recording with a resolution higher than the highest resolution in all the other digital equipment in your setup. For example, if your digital mixer's digital output supports only 16-bit word length, anything you record in more than 16 bits will be superfluous, since what is being sent by the mixer uses only the first sixteen bits of that binary word.

This said, if you have 24-bit or above VST effects or DirectX effects, having a higher resolution file can help in making use of this higher resolution processing, especially in the case of TrueTape 32-bit recording. However, CUBASE VST/32 can't add relevant sound information that is not there to begin with.

▶ To change the resolution of your recording, click on the drop-down menu found in the Arrange window next to the recording mode.

▶ To change the sampling frequency of your arrangement, select the Options > Audio Setup > System window. You will find a field called Sample Rate, which offers the supported sampling frequencies of your sound card.

Controlling Your Input Levels

As mentioned previously, the faders next to the VST Channel Mixer's input level meters have no effect on the input level of your recording. Aside from using your sound card's input level interface, you can adjust the input level from the source instrument or by passing your signal through a preamplifier. Since a good input level is important, it is recommended that you make sure to work this out before recording signals that have a low-level input level.

The VST TrueTape emulator will allow you to add up to 24 dB of gain to your 32-bit TrueTape recording. However, it is not meant to boost your signal as a preamplifier would but rather to emulate the tape saturation created by an analog multitrack tape recorder. Yes, this works only with 32-bit sound. To bring up the VST TrueTape control panel, select this option from the Panels menu. To control the level of input saturation you wish to have, move the cursor to the right, as shown in Figure 9.4.

Figure 9.4
The VST TrueTape window available when recording in 32-bit or 32-bit TrueTape mode.

You will notice that as you bring the drive level of the TrueTape slider to the right, the meter level in the VST Channel Mixer will also increase—and might clip. It is very difficult to have actual digital distortion when using 32-bit floating-point recording; clipping, in this case, will sound more like an analog saturation, which is the whole purpose of the 32-bit TrueTape control panel.

The Audio Pool Window

The Audio Pool window is like Windows Explorer or the Apple Launcher. It is your audio file management window. All audio recordings from your songs and arrangements are displayed in your Audio Pool. If you are in a song file, working on more than one arrangement, the pool will hold all the audio files that are used by all the arrangements belonging to that song.

You can also save an Audio Pool to use it later in another song or arrangement, importing it in the existing Audio Pool of that file.

The Audio Pool also allows you to view your audio files and corresponding segments, edit them, and import them in your Arrange window to create new audio events in parts.

To access the Audio Pool, press the Ctrl+F keys on your keyboard or select it from the Panels menu.

Files, Segments, and Audio Events

To understand how the Audio Pool works, you have to understand the difference between files, segments, and audio events, or audio parts.

- ▶ **File**—Refers to an audio file on your hard disk. This file can be a WAV, AIFF, or MP3 file. A file is added to the Audio Pool when you record and save an audio recording; when you import a file using the File > Import option; or when you use the import function inside the Audio Pool's File drop-down menu.

- ▶ **Segment**—Refers to a portion of a file that is used or not used in your song. You can have as many segments per file as you want. Segments are always linked to their files, since they are a way for Cubase to define a starting point and an end point from which to play within a file. Segments are created automatically when you record an audio file and then split it inside the Audio Editor or Arrange window.

- ▶ **Audio event**—Refer to segments that you import from the Audio Pool to create a new part in your Arrange window. In other words, audio events are inside audio parts; and you can have more than one audio event playing inside an audio part. Audio events are created automatically when you drag a file or a segment from the Audio Pool into the Arrange window.

Figure 9.5 displays the relationship between the file, the segment, and the audio event. You can also see in this figure the hierarchy between a song file, arrangements within that song file, and how the Audio Pool is shared between arrangements from the song file.

Figure 9.5
How Cubase handles audio from the Audio Pool in a song file.

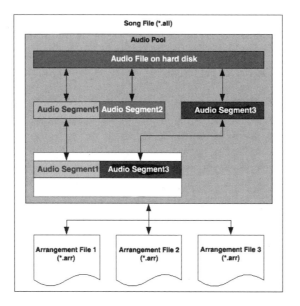

Headings and Columns

You will find two heading rows inside the Audio Pool. The first one displays information about the file, while the second one displays information about the segments from that file. To hide or view these headings, select Show Headings from the View drop-down menu in the Audio Pool. This will display the heading rows. To view all the information pertaining to the audio segments and audio files, select the Show Info option in the View drop-down menu of the Audio Pool or click on the "I" button in the Audio Pool's toolbar, as shown in Figure 9.6.

Figure 9.6
The Heading rows display information on the audio content of your Audio Pool.

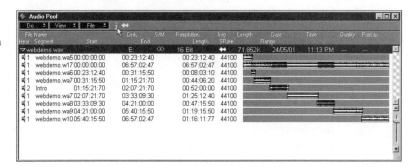

In this first row:

- ▶ **File Name**—Represents the name of the file on your hard disk. By double-clicking on the file name displayed in this column, you can rename that file. Renaming the file inside the Audio Pool allows Cubase to find this file when you want to access it later. If you rename a file from the Explorer window or from the Launcher in a Mac, Cubase won't be able to find it and will prompt you to look for this file.

- ▶ **Disk**—Tells you on which disk the file is located. Double-clicking on the letter of a disk will prompt Cubase to ask if you want to refind this file on your hard disk. This can be useful when you edit the file using an external wave editor like Wavelab, Sound Forge, or CoolEdit Pro and then rename it. If Cubase can't find the file in its original location, it will display three question marks instead of the name of the drive. Clicking on these question marks will allow you to browse your hard disk to find it and reassociate this new location with the Audio Pool.

- ▶ **S/M**—Displays a single circle when a file is mono and an intersecting pair of circles when a file is stereo.

- ▶ **Img**—Displays a small waveform icon if the file contains an image file associated with it. An image file is simply a graphic representation of the audio data contained in that file. It is not part of the audio file itself, but is a separate file with an OVW extension. If Cubase can't find that image file, it will display a small question mark between brackets. Clicking on the question mark will enable a rescan of the file and create a new image file on your hard disk if needed. If you move the audio file from its original location, but fail to move the image file, you will have to regenerate the image file.

- ▶ **Length**—Shows you the size of this file on your hard disk.
- ▶ **Date** and **Time**—Show you the creation date and time of this file.
- ▶ **Quality** and **Post As**—Refer to the RocketPower functions. Because RocketPower works over the Internet, you can set different qualities for sharing and distributing your audio or receiving audio other people send you. You then see what these qualities for the files on your system are, and set the quality of files posted to a server. These columns will stay empty if you are not using RocketPower.

In the second row, you will find the Segment information columns. If you can't see segments, click on the little arrow to the left of the file's name to expand the file's list of associated segments:

- ▶ **Hear**—Represented by a little speaker icon, this allows you to audition your segments by clicking on the speaker icon. You will hear the segment play from the beginning. Next to the speaker icon, you will see a number. This number corresponds to the amount of times this segment is present in the arrangement. If no numbers appear, it means that the segment is not being used.

TIP
To expand all the files at once, hold the Alt key down as you click on the arrow. To collapse them, repeat this operation again.

- ▶ **Segment**—Shows name and file type. You can double-click the name of a segment to rename it.
- ▶ **Start, End,** and **Length**—Correspond to the time the segment begins playing in the file, the time the segment stops playing, and the length of time between these two points.
- ▶ **SRate**—Stands for the audio recording's sampling rate (or sampling frequency).
- ▶ **Range**—Shows you a graphic display of the portion the segment plays within the full length of the file. The size of the file will always span from the left to the right of the gray area. Think of it as a relative display. The segment will appear in its relative place. In other words, the file might be five minutes or five seconds long, but the portion it will take will always correspond to 100 percent of the range area, whereas the segments will appear where they occur within that 100 percent.

Customizing the View

You can choose to view the information with greater or lesser detail by selecting different options. To show or hide the resolution, length, date, and time, click on the "I" button in the Audio Pool's toolbar or the Show/Hide Info from the View menu, also in the Audio Pool window. If you prefer to hide the information column headers, select Hide Info (or Show Info, if you want to see them) from the View menu.

To better associate segments with their parts in the Arrange window, you can choose the Show Part Colors option from the Audio Pool's View menu. If you assigned colors to parts, they will appear in the Audio Pool as well.

To turn the audio waveform display off or on, click on the Audio Waveform button in the Audio Pool's toolbar. You will still see a box around the portion taken by a segment, but you will no longer see the waveform displayed.

You can also use the vertical zoom bar on the lower right side of the Audio Pool's window to zoom in or out of the information displayed in this window. All waveforms inside the segment will adjust themselves proportionally to their new sizes. When you stretch the window to the width of your screen, the waveform display also expands, showing you more details.

The format displayed in the Start, End, and Length columns can be set to display samples, timecode, or bars and beats. To change the format, select the appropriate option from the View menu in the Audio Pool's toolbar. Note that the format displayed will carry the same properties as the rest of your arrangement. In other words, if you have tempo changes, if you change your timecode format, or if you record using a different sampling frequency, these changes all will be adjusted consequently in the Audio Pool.

Finding information sometimes might require viewing this information in different ways. You can sort your audio files and segments by name, date, or size by choosing the corresponding option in the View menu.

The Order Segments option in the View menu sorts the segments in their order of appearance in the file.

How to Use the Audio Pool

It was mentioned earlier in this chapter that the Audio Pool resembles Explorer under Windows or Launcher under Macintosh, in that it is used to manage audio files on your hard disk. However, the Audio Pool allows you to do software-specific operations such as purging unused segments, exporting and importing files, and generating wave displays as you create new segments. Every time you make an operation on audio files inside the Cubase environment, either through the Arrange, Audio Editor, or Wave Editor, this will be reflected in the Audio Pool. If you make modifications on audio files outside the Audio Pool—or outside of Cubase, for that matter—these changes might not be displayed correctly inside the pool itself. Since the Audio Pool will have an easier time finding files that you have modified if it is done from within the software environment itself, it is better to modify these files within this window rather than outside of the Cubase environment. This said, you can copy, rename, and remove any unused files inside your Audio Pool.

File and Segment Usage

When using a segment in one of the arrangements you are working on, a number appears next to its speaker icon. If any of the segments under a file is in use, you can't remove the file from the pool without losing the connection to the file. On the other hand, if some of your files contain segments that are not being used, you can purge them from your Audio Pool by selecting the Purge Segments from the Do menu in the Audio Pool. This will remove any unnecessary segments from your pool.

If you want to find out where your files are on the hard disk, you can right-click or Ctrl+click on a file's name in the Audio Pool to reveal the path to the file. In Figure 9.7, you can see that the file called Guitars1.wav is on the G drive in the "Demo Song" folder inside the "audio" sub-folder. You can click on the Find Target option from the popup menu to open the Explorer window that contains the content of this folder.

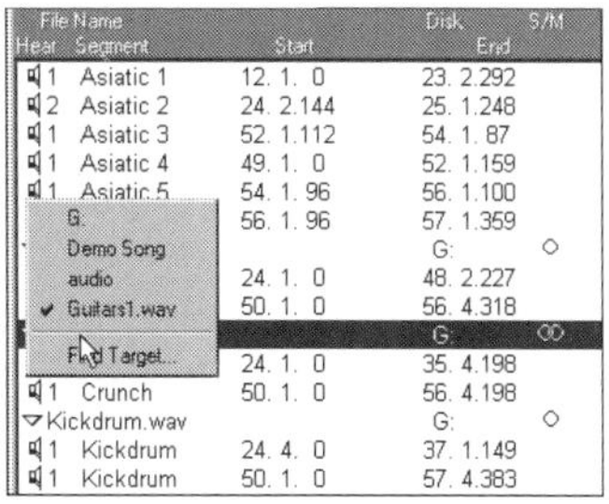

Figure 9.7
This context menu displays the location of your file on the hard drive.

Audio File Operations

One of the operations you can do in the Audio Pool is renaming a file. To do this, double-click on it and type in the new or edited name. When you want to apply some processing to a file but would rather keep the original file intact, you can duplicate that file by selecting it and choosing Duplicate File from the File menu. This method allows you to make modifications to the audio file while preserving the original intact, rather than using the copy-and-paste function in Explorer or Launcher.

You can delete files from the Audio Pool by clicking or shift-clicking on multiple files and by pressing the Delete or Backspace key on your keyboard. This action will delete the file only from the pool. If you want to delete it both from the pool and from your hard disk, hold the Ctrl key down when you press the Backspace key. On the other hand, you might find that it is more useful to delete only unused files. This is done automatically when you select the Delete Unused Files option from the Audio Pool's File menu.

If you erase the default segment created when you record or import a file in the Audio Pool, you can generate a new segment from this file that will play from the beginning of the file to its end. Select the file and choose Duplicate Segment from the Do menu in the Audio Pool.

When files are missing from your pool, it might be because you renamed the file outside the Cubase environment or that you moved it to another location without telling Cubase where it can be found. Unfound files are usually displayed with three question marks in the Disk column. To find them, click in that column to prompt the Find dialog box. Locate the folder where Cubase can find the file and click Open to accept the new location.

You can also decide to replace a file with another file while keeping the segments intact. An example of this application might be that you edited a file in an external editor and optimized it for use in Cubase. If the file hasn't been modified in time—meaning that it is the same length as the one you want to replace—you can click on the Disk letter in the Disk Column to find the file, and then select the new file. This will replace the old file reference with the new one, conserving the segment's positions. If the files are not the same length, the segments in that file will no longer be relevant.

As mentioned earlier, Cubase displays audio files by creating a waveform display of that file, which it keeps in a separate file. To refresh or generate that waveform if it is missing or if it doesn't correspond to the content anymore, click on the waveform icon in the Img column. When you rename a file within the Audio Pool, its image file is also renamed automatically, but this is not the case if you rename a file outside the Cubase environment. You can also turn the automatic waveform file creation process off if you don't want to see the waveform appearing in your Arrange window after recording. This can be useful when you are in a recording session, since it can take a couple of seconds, even minutes, to generate these image files, depending on their length. To do this, uncheck the Use Waveform option in the Options menu.

Segment Operations

In the Audio Pool, you can listen to segments in two ways. The first is by holding your cursor on the speaker icon next to the segment's label. This will play the segment from the beginning, stopping when you let go of the mouse button. The second is to hold your mouse button down on the waveform display. This way, you can point anywhere in the segment to hear the segment play from that point on.

You can rename segments the same way you would rename a file, by double-clicking on the segment's label and entering the new name or the edited name for that segment. You can also use the Alt+N keyboard shortcut.

Duplicating a segment is also quite easy, although it is different from duplicating a file. Simply select the segment you wish to duplicate and choose the Duplicate Segment option from the Do menu in the Audio Pool. Remember that duplicating segments does not take more disk space, because they always refer to the audio file. If you are duplicating a segment to use many times in the arrangement, you are better off copying a part in a track referring to a segment rather than crowding your Audio Pool.

Sometimes, you might want to adjust the Start and End points of a segment within the Audio Pool. To resize a segment using the waveform display:

1. Select the segment you wish to edit in the Audio Pool.
2. If you want to change the start or end, hold the Alt key down as you click and drag the start or end to its new location. If you want to change which part is played in the file without modifying the length of the segment by simply moving the segment's position, hold the Ctrl key down as you click and drag the segment to its new location.

Figure 9.8
The options available when you want to modify segments inside the Audio Pool.

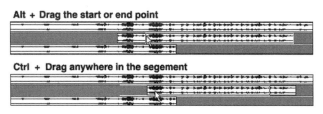

Notice in Figure 9.8 how the segment being modified (shown by box around edited area) in the upper portion of the figure stays in place but the beginning is being repositioned. The lower part of the figure shows the Ctrl option as the segment is being moved (shown by box around edited area) with its length preserved.

Once you've created your audio tracks and need to clean up your segments, the best way to do this is by using the Purge Segments option in the Do menu. This option will remove any unused segments in the Audio Pool. When you delete segments that are being used in the Arrange window from the Audio Pool, they will be removed from both the Arrange window and the Audio Pool. You can't undo this operation, so be careful when using it. Since segments always display how many times they have been used in an arrangement, it is easy to spot them from the Audio Pool.

Audio files take up a lot of space on your hard disk. When you record, you probably have lots of stuff recorded that you are not using in any arrangements—time before a musician starts playing, errors and retakes that aren't quite good enough, and so on. When you create segments to remove these elements from your editing window, you don't erase the information these elements take on your hard disk. They are simply hidden from view. You can remove them from your Audio Pool by selecting the segments and deleting them, but they will remain on your hard disk. You can use a function called Erase Unused in the Do menu. This function will edit the file on the hard disk to reflect only the segments that are being used in your arrangement. Obviously, if you are using the same file in another arrangement, it might be a good idea to copy it before proceeding.

To use the Erase Unused function:

1. Click on the unused segments or shift+click multiple entries. If you want to erase all unused segments from a file, you can select the file instead of the segments in that file.
2. From the Do menu, select Erase Unused.
3. Click Compact to continue or Abort to cancel.

Cubase will remove the audio information that is not used in the arrangement, therefore reducing the space used on the disk. It will tell you how much space will be saved by doing this, as shown in Figure 9.9.

Figure 9.9
Erasing unused segments from your audio files can save some hard disk space.

Cubase will then proceed to create the file once you select the Compact option.

In the preceding example, you erased only the unused segments from one file, but you can also erase all the unused segments in your arrangement. To do this, select all the files (you can use the keyboard shortcut Ctrl+A) before selecting the Erase Unused function from the Do menu.

You can also see where your segments are in an arrangement by selecting the segment in the Audio Pool, then selecting the Find Parts option from the Do menu. This will select the part in the Arrange window.

Importing and Exporting Audio from the Pool

As you will see later in this chapter, you can import files from your hard disk from the File menu's import function. Since we are talking about the Audio Pool, let us address how it is done from within this window. Note that only WAV, AIFF, and MP3 files can be imported directly in the Audio Pool. If you want to import Mixman or Recycle files, please refer to the corresponding section in the following parts of this chapter.

To import audio files from within the Audio Pool, select the Import Audio option from the File menu in the Audio Pool. You will need to locate your file on the hard disk, select it, and then click the Open button to complete the operation. If the file is big, it might take some time to create the waveform file, but once it's done, the newly imported file will appear in your Audio Pool.

You can also use the import function with the Ctrl or Shift keys when selecting more than one file to import at a time. Shift+clicking files will select continuous files, and Ctrl+click will select noncontinuous files in your Explorer window.

If you want to keep a segment as an audio file all by itself, you can click on the segment to select it, then choose the Export Segment option from the Do menu in the Audio Pool. A window will appear asking you to confirm your choice; you will then be prompted to enter the new name for the segment you want to save as a file.

Dragging Segments into Other Windows

One of the nice things about the Audio Pool, besides being able to manage your audio content, is that it allows you to share this content between different arrangements. You can click and drag segments from the Audio Pool anywhere in an audio track in your Arrange window, Audio editor, or Wave editor.

To drag a segment into another window, make sure both windows are visible, then click on the segment's name from the Audio Pool and drag it to where you want it: the Arrange, Audio editor, or Wave editor window.

When you drag a segment into the Arrange window, a part is created to house the segment. You will have to drag the segment into an audio track for this to work.

When you drag a segment into the Audio editor, the segment will be positioned according to the snap value in the Audio editor. The segment also has to be of the same type as the audio being edited in the Audio editor. For example, you won't be able to drag a stereo file if the track containing the part that is being edited is set to Mono. On the other hand, if your track is set to "any" in the Channel column, you will have to choose which "lane" you want to put your dragged segment on . A lane in the Audio editor corresponds to the audio channel used to play back the audio content. If you use a lane (or channel) already being used by another segment on another track, you will not be able to hear the audio content, because only one audio event at a time can play on each lane (or channel).

Archiving Files

There are two archiving functions in Cubase: Prepare Archive and Prepare Master.

The Prepare Archive function found in the File menu in the Audio Pool's toolbar will save a copy of either all the audio that is being used in one of the arrangements or all the audio that is being used in all of the arrangements of a song file.

To use the Prepare Archive function:

1. Select the Prepare Archive function from the File menu in the Audio Pool.
2. Select the folder where you want to save your audio content (Figure 9.10). Note that this will create a copy of your audio content, so you will need sufficient space to save these files.

Figure 9.10
Choose an appropriate folder destination for your file archive.

Cubase will then ask you what you want to save.

3. Select Referenced to save only the audio files that are being used in the active arrangement. Select All if you want all the audio that is being used in all the arrangements found in the song file.

The Prepare Master function—also found in the Audio Pool's File menu—is similar to a macro command in the sense that it applies different processes. In fact, the Prepare Master will start by extracting only the segments that are being used in an arrangement (like the Purge Segments function). It will then proceed to erase all unused portions of the audio files (like the Erase Unused function). Finally, it will create an archive of the resulting audio files in a folder (like the Prepare Archive function).

To use the Prepare Master function, you can use the same steps as for the Prepare Archive function, simply selecting the Prepare Master function instead. Cubase will warn you that this action cannot be undone, but since this process is nondestructive—your original files won't be affected—it doesn't matter that much. What will happen, however, is that all the links to your audio files will be updated, and your segments will be updated to reflect these new changes. This said, as a precaution, it might be a good idea to save your song or arrangement before you use the Prepare Master function.

Saving Your Audio Pool for Later Use

When you save a song or an arrangement, the Audio Pool is saved with it. However, if you wish to use an Audio Pool in another song or arrangement, you can save it as an individual file and load it in another file. Since Audio Pools don't contain audio files themselves but rather references to these audio files, they don't take much space on your hard disk. You will want to make sure not to move the audio files that are used in that Audio Pool; otherwise, your pool will point to nothing and you will have to manually search for the missing links.

To Save an Audio Pool, select this option from the Audio Pool's File menu. A dialog box will prompt you to enter a name and a location in which to save the pool. Once a pool is saved, you may import it into another Audio Pool using the File > Load Pool option in the Audio Pool's toolbar. The loaded pool's content is added to the existing pool in your project.

Importing Audio Files

Because you sometimes might want to use prerecorded material in your song or arrangement, Cubase allows you to import this material in two different ways. The first is to simply drag WAV, AIFF, or MP3 files from the Windows Explorer (or the Mac Launcher) into a track or below the last track in Cubase to create a new track. The second way is to click the File menu's Import option, and then the Audio File option from the sub-menu. Note that when importing MP3 files, Cubase will create a WAV or AIFF copy of this file on your hard disk rather than using the MP3 file directly. Just remember that WAV and AIFF files can be much larger than their MP3 counterpart.

You can also import two other types of files, described below.

Recycling Files with Recycle

Recycle files are generated by software called Recycle, which is also developed by Propellerhead. The purpose of Recycle is to cut drum loops into smaller parts, allowing you to reuse these samples at different tempos without changing the pitch.

NOTE

In order to import Recycle 2.0 or above versions, you will need to have at least Cubase 5.05 for Windows or 5.01 for Macintosh.

You import Recycle files the same way you would any other type of files mentioned above, but instead of selecting the Audio File option in the sub-menu, you would select the Recycle File in that same sub-menu, as shown in Figure 9.11.

Figure 9.11
The Import sub-menu

Once your Recycle file is loaded, don't remove the original file. If you remove this Recycle file, Cubase, which usually refers to it when playing the imported version, will no longer be able to locate it. A number of segments will be imported in your audio track, as displayed in Figure 9.12.

Figure 9.12
The Recycle file creates segments for each beat in your loop.

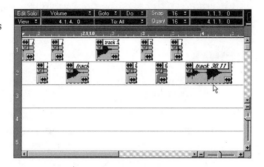

About Mixman

Mixman is another type of file that you can import in Cubase through the Import option in the File menu. Mixman is a similar application to Recycle in the sense that it allows you to manipulate loops and play them at different speeds without altering the pitch. Cubase imports Mixman Tracks (TRK) files, which are the building blocks used to create songs in Mixman. Each track is usually a sample.

To import a Mixman file:

1. Select the Mixman Trk option from the Import sub-menu. The Import Mixman window will display import options, as shown in Figure 9.13.

Figure 9.13
The Mixman import options

2. Find the folder containing your Mixman files.

   In the Import window, Cubase displays the original tempo of the track and the tempo of your song. When you import a Mixman track, it will convert this file to play at your song's tempo. Unlike Recycle files, you won't have an audio segment for each instrument, but rather a single sample.

3. Select the Pitch Shift option you wish to apply to your sample. If you don't want the sample to pitch shift, uncheck the Auto checkbox and leave the Half-Steps field at 0:00.

4. In most cases, you will want to leave the Time Stretch Auto function checked. This will determine the right amount of time stretching for your Mixman sample to fit at the project's tempo setting.

5. Click the Play Converted button to hear the result before importing. If you want to compare it with the original, click the Play Original button.

6. Press Create File to import the Mixman track into your arrangement. This file will appear on the selected audio track at the left locator position.

If you change the tempo of your song or arrangement, the tempo of the Mixman file will not follow this change. You will need to reimport it at the new tempo setting.

Now You Try It

Here are the exercises you will find on the Web site for this chapter. Note that for this chapter, some audio files have been included, with the song file making the download a little bit longer. Efforts were made to keep these files to a minimal size by using short samples and VSTi instruments included with Cubase VST.

- Import MP3 files into the Audio Pool.
- Import Recycle files into the Audio Pool.
- Create and use segments from the Audio Pool in the Arrange window.
- Rename segments in the Audio Pool.
- Save your Audio Pool.
- Set up Cubase for a mono or stereo recording.

You will find these exercises at **www.muskalipman.com/cubase**.

Simply follow the instructions on the Web site before starting the exercises.

You can refer to this chapter to find out how to do these exercises, but try doing them without peeking first, just to see how comfortable you are with these principles. If you don't remember how to do a task, refer to the appropriate section in this chapter.

As with exercises in previous chapters, you will need to have the Universal Sound Module installed on your computer to use the file provided for these exercises.

10
Audio Editing

As with MIDI, audio has its own editing environment. Actually, audio has three different editing environments: the Audio Pool, which was discussed earlier; the Audio editor; and the Wave editor. Each allows you to do different types of operations on your audio files. As you saw in the previous chapter, the Audio Pool allows you to manage files and segments. In this chapter, you will see how to place these files, or rather segments in this case, and arrange them in the Audio editor. Table 10.1 will help you to understand better when and why you would choose one editor over another:

Table 10.1
Differences between the different Audio editors.

What you want to do is:	Then you should use the:
See a list of files you have recorded	Audio Pool
Remove unused segments or unused files from your arrangement	Audio Pool
Create new files from segments you've created	Audio Pool
Save all the references to audio files you use in an arrangement	Audio Pool
Move audio segments around in your parts	Audio editor
Change the length of your segments	Audio editor
Arrange segments on different audio channels	Audio editor
Add hitpoints and adjust Q-points	Audio editor
Adjust in time imported Mixman or Recycle files	Audio editor
Create a volume or pan automation on a segment (nondestructive)	Audio editor
Repeat segments throughout the part	Audio editor
Normalize the level of your audio files	Internal Wave editor
Edit audio segments while having an overview of the file itself	Internal Wave editor
Make precise changes to several audio segments	Internal Wave editor
Create a destructive (modify the original audio file) fade	Internal Wave editor
Change the pitch or time-stretch an audio file	Internal Wave editor
Master files for CD distribution	External Wave editor
Convert files for Web distribution	External Wave editor
Check for clips and pops and fix noisy recordings	External Wave editor

The major difference between the two is that the Audio editor is mainly a nondestructive environment, and the Wave editor is mainly a destructive environment. This means that in the first, you rarely modify the actual content of the audio file on your hard disk, whereas in the latter, you are applying different audio functions that will affect the audio file on your hard disk. You also have the choice to load the Wave editior included with Cubase or launch another external program (such as Wavelab from Steinberg or Sound Forge from Sonic Foundry) as your default Wave editor.

The Audio Editor

The Audio editor is a nondestructive audio editing environment that will let you edit segments in audio tracks. Like the Key, Drum, and Score editors, you can have access to the Audio editor by double-clicking any audio parts in the Arrange window. It is nondestructive in the sense that no matter what you do in the Audio editor, the files to which segments refer will not be affected. The only exception to this is that if you select an audio segment and press Ctrl+Backspace, the audio will be permanently erased from your disc. However, this is not something you would be likely to do accidentally. What you modify in reality are visual parameters or reference points: the position of a segment on a track, the channel through which this segment will play, the start and end positions of the segment within a file on the hard disk, and so on. It's like MIDI data for audio: The editing itself does not contain the audio content, only pointers to the audio content, and it will always need to refer to the audio files.

The Audio editor is similar to the other editors you saw in Chapter 5. You will find a toolbar in the top part of the window with similar menus and buttons as in the Key and Drum editing windows. Most of the functions in these menus will be discussed in detail in this chapter. Note that the Goto and To menus, as well as the Snap, Quantize, and Position Indicators menu, are the same as in the other windows, so please refer to the appropriate description in Chapter 5 if you need to refresh your memory.

The Loop, Information, Speaker, Insert, and Part Color icon buttons in the toolbar also act in similar ways as previously described (see Figure 10.1). The Speaker and Meter/Time icons, on the other hand, play different roles, which are addressed here.

Figure 10.1
The Audio editor window.

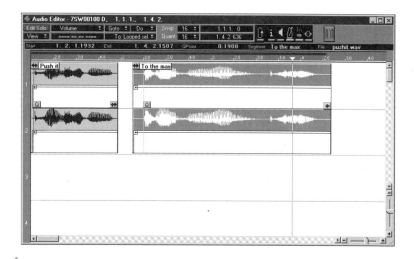

The left margin of the Audio editor displays numbers that represent the output channels used by the track to play the audio content. Each number is separated by a line. The area in each line represents a lane on which you can put audio events. If you do not see the numbers in the left margin, select Lane Info from the View menu in the Audio editor.

The lower right corner displays both a vertical and a horizontal zoom bar so you can adjust your magnification level.

Let's look at the vocabulary and the hierarchy system used in the Audio editor.

Events, Lanes, and Segments

As was discussed in the Audio Pool section of the previous chapter, when you record audio, you save it as a file on your hard disk. You also saw the relation between files, segments, and events in parts. This is where you can actually see how they interact. When you double-click on an audio part in the Arrange window, you launch the Audio editor. This window will display the content of one part. Inside that part, you will have different boxes containing a waveform. These are called audio events. Audio events use segments created from an audio file or files to play the content inside the waveform. Therefore, in a part, you will have audio events that will play segments from different files.

Now that you have assigned an audio channel setting for each track in your arrangement, the Audio editor will reflect these settings as well. If a track is mono, when you open the Audio editor, you will see the audio event placed in that part on the first lane on top. The number for that lane corresponds to the number of the output channel. The subsequent lanes will also have the same number, since this is a mono track. You can add other audio events on the subsequent lanes and place them in time. All audio events in this part will play on several lanes but will come out of the same audio channel. The only rule is that only one audio event can play on a channel at a time. If you overlap events, the lower lane with the same audio channel will always take over that channel and play until the end of the audio event in that lane. In Figure 10.2, you can see that segments are placed across three different lanes, but each lane is playing on Channel 1.

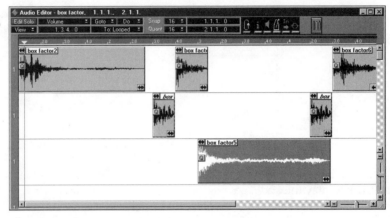

Figure 10.2
Audio Events in a mono track playing in different lanes but through the same channel.

To view what will actually happen and how the overlapping events will sound, you can select the By Output option from the Audio editor's View menu, as shown in Figure 10.3. As you can see, the events that were overlapping in Figure 10.2 are displayed one on top of another in Figure 10.3. This might be useful when you want to use a punch-in/punch-out approach, replacing a bad take with a better one and placing the event you want to hear over the event you don't want to hear. However, in this case, some parts of the sound will be cut off.

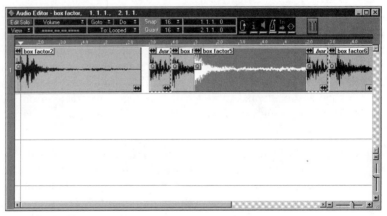

Figure 10.3
Audio Events in a mono track displaying one lane per channel output.

When you are editing a stereo track, you will have two lane numbers corresponding to the left and right side of your audio, and the numbers will reflect your settings in the track's channel column. The principle is the same for mono and stereo files. Overlapping events will compete for the outputs.

The last type of audio track is the one set to play on "any" channels. In this case, each lane can be a separate channel. You will see the channel numbers in the left margin of the window. You will have as many channel numbers as you have channels in your Arrange window. So, let's say you set up Cubase to use eight channels—you will have lanes 1 through 8, and then these lanes are repeated over and over again. Since each lane is playing on a different channel, you will still hear overlapping events. There is one caution note to be added here: If another track is using channels that you are trying to use in the track you are editing in "any" channel mode, overlapping events will be cut off. To avoid this, you can select different events in the Arrange window and select the Audio editor from the Edit menu to open several parts at once in a single editing window, as shown in Figure 10.4.

Figure 10.4
Opening several parts at the same time in the editing window allows you to see which channels are used and which ones are free.

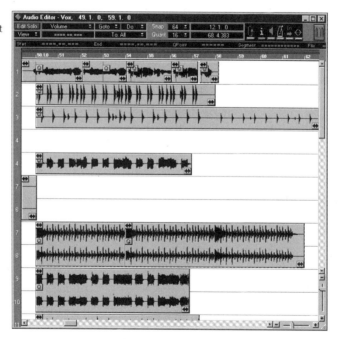

As you can see in Figure 10.4, some channel numbers are repeated because different tracks are sharing the same channels. To view only one channel per lane, select the By Output option from the View menu in the Audio editor.

Customizing Your View

The View menu, as mentioned above, allows you to set each lane by output rather than repeating lanes with the same channel number. It also allows you to customize the information displayed for audio events in the Audio editor. Here are some options available in this menu:

- ▶ Waveforms will display the waveform of the segment in the audio event on each lane.
- ▶ Names will display the name of the segment in the upper left corner of each audio event.
- ▶ Handles appear in the upper left corner and lower right corner of each audio event. Use handles to modify the start and end insets of segments for audio events. If you don't want to see these handles, uncheck this option in the View menu to hide them temporarily. You will still be able to trim the segments by dragging the area where the handles would appear normally.
- ▶ By Output will display only one lane per audio channel available, showing you if events are overlapping in each channel.
- ▶ Lane Info toggles the display of the channel number in the left-hand side of the Audio editor's window.
- ▶ Dynamic Events reveals additional controls you can have over each event, such as volume, pan, and match point. You will find discussions on these controls later in this chapter. By default, these events are not displayed, so you will have to choose this option from the View menu to display it.

Another way you can customize how the information is displayed is by using the Time/Meter button in the Audio editor's toolbar. This button will display, when in Time format, equal spacing between each second. The button will look like a clock when you are displaying the ruler in Time format. Use this when you are working with visual cues and need to have a better look at time subdivisions. On the other hand, if you are working mostly on music-based content, use the Meter format, which displays measures (or bars) in equal spacing format. A Metronome icon will be visible when you are in Meter time display.

You can also toggle the display between timecode and bars/beat format by clicking in the position indicator that is located to the right of the View menu in the toolbar. The actual timecode format displayed depends on your song's setting.

Importing Audio

You can import audio in the Audio editor by dragging files from the Audio Pool into the editor or by dragging a file from an Explorer or Launcher window. The only rule that applies to files you drag into the Audio editor is that stereo files can be dragged into stereo tracks—therefore, stereo channels—in the editor. You can import mono files into mono tracks. As for importing audio in tracks that are set to play on "any" channel, you will be able to place stereo files in lanes that are paired together as stereo channels and mono files in lanes that are not paired with any other channels. So, for example, if you already have a mono track that uses Channel 1 a stereo track that uses channels 3 and 4, and a third track that uses the "any" setting, you will be able to place mono files on channels 1 and 2 of this track and stereo files on channels 3 and 4. When importing a file into a track that is set to "any," it is important to notice where you are placing your file. More specifically, notice on which lane, because a lane might be used by another track and this will affect your playback.

When you import a file by dragging it directly from your desktop, Cubase will add it automatically to the Audio Pool and will create a default segment there. Another consideration is that the files have to be recorded at the same sampling frequency as the frequency of your arrangement. Failing to do so will result in your file playing at the wrong pitch. You can import files of 16- or 24-bit resolution if you are using Cubase VST and Cubase Score, and 32-bit resolution if you are using the VST/32 edition of the software.

To Import a file directly in the Audio editor:

1. With your Audio editor opened, set the Snap field to the desired value.
2. Right-click to select the Pencil tool from the toolbox.
3. With the Pencil tool, click in the appropriate lane at the position where you want to insert the new audio file. Try to avoid clicking on another event unless you want the two events to overlap.
4. A dialog box will appear, asking you to select the file from your hard disk. Find the file and select it. If the file type you are looking for is not displayed, change the file type in the appropriate field of the import window.
5. Click the Open button to complete the import process.

http://www.muskalipman.com

Auditioning Audio

Being able to listen to the audio events in the Audio editor is a great way of finding problems and fixing them. You have three ways of listening to events in the editor: Audition, Scrub, and Monitor.

The Audition function allows you to hear the event you click on at the location you click until you let go of the mouse button. To use this function, right-click anywhere in the editor to select the Speaker tool from the toolbox. Make sure the Scrub button in the toolbar is not active; otherwise, you will be in Scrub mode rather than Audition. The Scrub button looks like two arrows pointing left and right. When active, it is green. Click anywhere in an audio event to hear the event. Once you let go of the mouse button, the playback head will go back to where it was before.

The Scrub function allows you to scrub the audio as if you had a shuttle wheel on a video or audio deck. Dragging your cursor to the left after you click will play the audio event backwards, and dragging your cursor to the right will play the audio forward. The speed at which you drag your mouse will influence the speed at which the file is read. Enabling the Scrub function is similar to enabling the Audition function. The only difference is that you have to enable the Scrub button in the editor's toolbar (it's the last one to the right). Click anywhere inside an audio event with the Speaker tool and hold your mouse button down as you move left and right.

The Monitor function allows you to monitor different changes you make to the audio event, such as when you modify the start or end insets or when you change the Q-point's position. A Q-point is an audio quantization point that you can use within a segment to align audio events with Quantize values. This will be further described in the following sections. The Monitor function is a way of getting feedback from Cubase when doing these modifications without having to switch from the Pointer tool to the Speaker tool. To use the Monitor function, enable the Speaker button in the editor's toolbar. The next time you change the Q-point or insets of an event, Cubase will play the event for a fixed amount of time to reflect the new length or Q-point position and then proceed to refresh the screen. If you want to change the time it will play after you made your modification, Ctrl+click on the Speaker button on the toolbar. A pop-up menu will appear, offering you four choices, as displayed in Figure 10.5.

Figure 10.5
Changing the Monitor time setting in the Audio editor.

Editing Audio Events

Editing audio events can be done in a few different ways. First, you can use the info line under the Audio editor's toolbar. This gives you information on a selected event. You will find the start and end time of the event, the location of the event's Q-point, and the audio event's corresponding segment and file name. To change any of these values, click on an event to select it, then double-click the value you wish to edit in the info line and enter the new value as you would for any other field. If you don't see the info line, click on the I button in the window's toolbar. When selecting multiple events, you can quickly edit them using this method, but modifying the end inset will be proportional to the event's length. Figure 10.6 shows you an example of this, where you see three selected events before (top) and after (bottom) changing the end insets.

Figure 10.6
Editing multiple events using the info line.

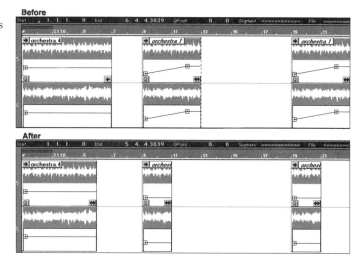

If you change the selected event's segment or file name by double-clicking on it, these changes will also have an effect on the pool's segment and file names.

Another way you can edit audio events is by changing the start and end insets of these events. The insets are references used by Cubase to define a segment within a file. You will find such inset control handles in the upper left corner and lower right corner of each audio event on a lane. Modifying these insets will modify the corresponding segment in both the pool and the Arrange window. To view the handles that will allow you to modify the start and end insets, select the Handles option from the editor's View menu. There are two types of handles for both start and end insets:

▶ If the upper left corner of an event displays an arrow pointing to the right, it means that you can move the inset only forward in time, because you are at the beginning of the file and no other audio information exists beyond that point. Similarly, if the lower right corner of an event displays an arrow pointing to the left, it means that you can move the inset only backward in time, because you are at the end of the audio file and there is no more audio data beyond this point.

▶ If either the upper left or lower right corners of an event display a double-sided arrow, it means that you can move the inset to the left or right. If you move the start inset to the left, you will lengthen the segment accordingly; if you move it to the right, you will shorten the segment accordingly. The reverse is true for the end inset—moving it to the left will shorten the segment and moving it to the right will lengthen it.

Figure 10.7 shows you different combinations of inset handles.

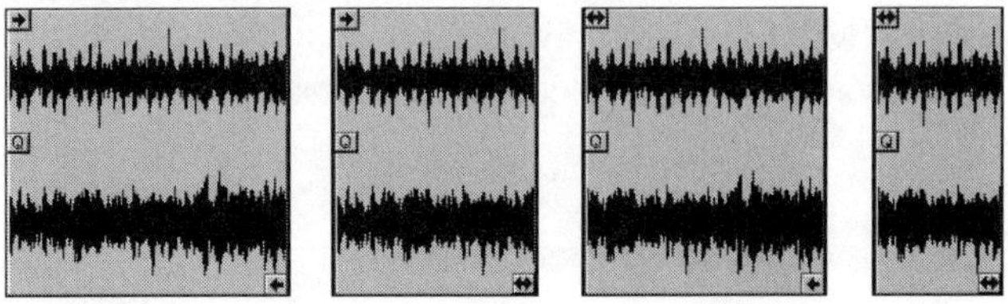

Figure 10.7
Use event handles to modify the start and end insets of a segment.

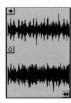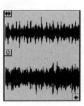

To modify the start or end insets properly, you need to select an appropriate Snap value from the editor's toolbar; otherwise, you won't be able to change the inset the way you want it. Once you have set the Snap value, select the Pointer tool from the toolbox, then click and drag the inset handle to the desired location. You might also want to use the Snap to Zero option found in the Options > Audio Setup sub-menu. This will allow you to change the insets without ending the segment in the middle of an audio signal, therefore creating a pop as the sound card interprets the change between the end of the audio segment and the content that follows as being far apart. Because the insets modify only the points between which a file is read, you can always unhide a portion of that file by moving the insets once again. This is nondestructive editing at its best.

Now that you know how to move the insets, you are ready to move, copy, cut, and delete the actual event in a part. This is similar to editing MIDI events in the sense that you are modifying playback instructions rather than actual audio data. Remember that every time you make a modification, the Snap and Quantize values will have an influence on the result.

▶ **To move an event**—Using the Pointer tool, click on the event and move it to the desired location. To move several events at once, Shift+click on the events you wish to move simultaneously. Once your events are selected, you may choose to restrict the movement vertically or horizontally by keeping the Shift key down as you are moving your events. For example, if you start moving horizontally, your movement will be restricted to up and down.

▶ **To copy an event**—You have two choices: create a real or a ghost copy. A real copy is independent of, yet identical to, the original segment copied, whereas a ghost copy is dependent. When you make a change to any of the ghost copies or to the original that has ghost copies, all other copies will reflect this change as well. To create a real copy, hold the Alt key down while clicking the event you wish to copy and drag it to the new location. It is a good idea to rename real copies to avoid confusing them with ghost copies. To create a ghost copy, hold the Ctrl key down while clicking the event you wish to copy and drag it to the desired location. When the name of the segments appear in the editor, you will notice that ghost copies are written in italic and their borders are dotted. If you make changes to the start or end insets of a ghost copy, this will convert the ghost copy into a real copy unless you hold down the Ctrl key as you modify the insets. When a real copy is created after editing the insets of a ghost, a new segment will appear in the Audio Pool as well.

▶ **To mute an event**—Right-click in the editor to select the Mute tool and then click on the event you wish to mute. If you choose to erase muted events later, you can select the Erase Muted option from the Do menu in the Audio editor. Once again, this operation is nondestructive.

▶ **To split an event**—Right-click in the editor to select the Scissors tool, then click on the event where you wish to split. If you are not happy with the splitting point, you can always zoom in and modify the insets for the newly created segments. You may also want to check the Snap to Zero option found under Options > Audio Setup. If you wish to automatically delete the portion to the left of the split, hold the Alt key down as you split. For the portion to the right, hold the Ctrl key down as you split. You can also use Snip Loop in the Do menu. Use this option when you want to split an event and keep only the audio found between the loop area in the Audio editor. To use Snip Loop, start by creating a loop area in the Audio editor and then select this option in the Do menu. This will split all events in the Audio editor at the start and end of the loop area.

▶ **To delete an event**—Right-click in the editor to select the Eraser tool, then click on the event you wish to delete. If you wish to delete a file from the disk as well, select the event with the Arrow tool, then hold the Ctrl key down as you press the Backspace key. As with the Key and Drum editors, you can use the To and Do menus together to keep only selected events.

When editing multiple tracks at once in the Audio editor, you might prefer to use the traditional cut, copy, and paste method rather than clicking and dragging events one by one. To copy or cut several audio events on different tracks, start by selecting them, then use the Cut (Ctrl+X) or Copy (Ctrl+C) functions from the Edit menu. To paste them, position your playback cursor at the location where you want to insert the content of the clipboard, click in the Lane Info to make the destination lane active (the lane number will become green), and then select Paste (Ctrl+V) from the Edit menu to complete the operation.

http://www.muskalipman.com

About Q-Points

A Q-point is a quantize reference used by Cubase to "snap" audio events to a meaningful Snap or Quantize value. I say "meaningful," because an audio event may start long before the actual sound in the event starts. To compensate for the difference between the audio event starting point and the actual moment in the event that you would like to use as a quantize or snap reference, a Q-point is added. You should position this Q-point at the most significant strong point in your audio event in order to have a "meaningful" quantize or snap. An example of this would be the start of a kick drum in a drum loop.

Figure 10.8 shows you a situation where the Q-point line arrives after the event has begun. When you later quantize this audio event, it will use the Q-point's position to determine if the event needs to be moved and to where.

Figure 10.8
The Q-point in the Audio editor.

To move the Q-point of an event, click and drag on the letter Q in the middle of the Q-point line for the appropriate audio event. If you don't see the Q-point, select the Handles option from the View menu in the editor's toolbar.

About M-Points

M-points are markers added to an audio event. These markers appear at significant places in the audio event, usually where beats or subdivisions of these beats occur, such as eighth notes, for example. Each marker not only holds timing information but also velocity information, as displayed in Figure 10.9. You can see that the lines under the audio waveform display appear when there are beats in the drum loop. You will find small square handles along these lines to identify the relative velocity of each marker.

Figure 10.9
Using match points in the Audio editor.

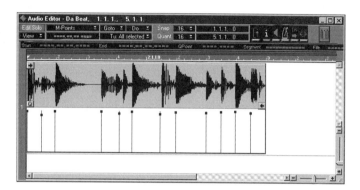

You can use the M-points or match points to:

▶ Change the tempo to match an audio beat.

▶ Change an audio beat to match a tempo.

▶ Create a Groove template from the timing and velocity of an audio event.

▶ Match the quantizing of MIDI parts to audio parts.

▶ Match the quantizing of audio parts to MIDI parts.

▶ Match the quantizing of an audio part to another audio part using the Snip function.

To view M-points:

1. In the menu to the right of the Edit Solo button in the Audio editor, select M-points.
2. In the View menu, select Dynamic Events to add a checkmark next to it.

To create M-points:

1. Select the audio event in your editor.
2. From the Do menu, select Get M-Points. The Get Match Points window will appear, as shown in Figure 10.10.
3. Set the Sensitivity value to the desired amount. The higher the number, the more sensitive Cubase will be to peaks, and it therefore will create more M-points.
4. Set the Attack value to the desired amount. Again, the higher the number, the more Cubase will need attack amplitude in the audio event to generate an M-point.
5. Set the Maximum Number of Events Per Second to the desired amount. For example, if you have a loop that plays at 120 bpm, each beat will last half a second. So, two beats last one second. If you want to subdivide the M-points into sixteenth notes, you would set this value to 8 when playing a file at 120 bpm.
6. If you are not sure what to put in these fields, press the Default button to reset the values in the fields.

Click Process to generate the M-points.

Figure 10.10
The Get Match Points window.

To edit M-points once they are created:

▶ **To add an M-point**—Right-click in the editor and select the Pencil tool from the toolbox, then Alt+click where you want to add the M-point in the M-point display area under the waveform.

▶ **To change the velocity of an M-point**—With the Pencil tool, click on an M-point and move it up or down to the desired velocity.

▶ **To move an M-point**—Click on the velocity handle with the Pencil tool and move it to the left or right, where you want it. If you find that the M-point jumps to an undesired Snap value, change the Snap value or set it to Off to move freely in the event.

▶ **To erase an M-point**—Right-click in the editor and select the Eraser tool, then click on the M-point handle you wish to delete.

Now, let's say you have a drum loop that's playing at a certain speed and you would like the song to play at that same speed. To do this, you can use the M-points and the Graphical Master Track window to find the appropriate tempo to match your loop.

To set a song to match the tempo of an audio event:

1. Start by adding manual M-points on significant portions of your audio event. This could be the first quarter note of each bar, or on every quarter note, for the first couple of bars. There's no need to do more than a few bars, unless your segment is very long and the tempo varies quite a bit from beginning to end. In that case, you should have a few M-points throughout the entire segment. If your material is long and varies in tempo significantly, you won't be able to get every single beat to fit exactly, but try to get the important points in your audio to match properly.

TIP
Often, music will have tempo variations at the beginning and near the end. To avoid getting bad tempo match-ups, try matching M-points past the beginning and before the ending.

2. Select your audio event and choose the Match Audio And Tempo from the Do menu. The Graphic Master Track window will open with your audio segment displayed in it.
3. In the Options menu, select the Show Hitpoint Matches option. This will draw pointed lines coming up from the M-points. The idea here is to match these lines with their corresponding beats in the bars and beats ruler above, as shown in Figure 10.11. As you can see in this figure, the first line matches with Bar 1, but as you look further in time, the lines don't match up anymore. Hitpoints are merely markers in a timeline that you can use to adjust timing. They will be discussed further in Chapter 12.

Figure 10.11
Matching the tempo of a song with M-points from an audio event in the Graphic Master Track window.

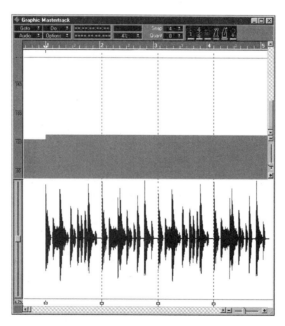

4. Go to the slider found to the left of the audio waveform display in the lower left part of the Graphic Master Track window and move it up or down to align the lines with the appropriate beats above in the ruler.

   If you find that the scale of the slider bar is too small and you can't move beyond a certain point, click below the slider where you see a percentage value. A pop-up menu will appear that will let you select a higher percentage. This is the amount of stretch or compression of time you apply to the tempo.

5. Once you are satisfied with the alignment of the M-points to the bars and beats, select the Slider to Tempo option in the Audio drop-down menu of the Graphic Master Track window. The lines will become full instead of dotted when a perfect sync occurs. That will be your cue to stop trying to modify the tempo further.

The tempo of your song is adjusted to reflect this audio event. Remember that this will work when you activate the Master button on the Transport bar, since the tempo you just changed is the Master Track tempo. If your Master button is disabled, the correct playback tempo will be activated only when the Master Track is also active or if you set the normal playback tempo to the same value as in the Master Track.

To set an audio event to the song's tempo:

- Repeat steps 1 through 4 from the previous list. In Step 5, instead of selecting the Slider to Tempo option, select the Slider to Time Stretch option.
- Try not to time stretch your audio by more than 5 percent, because this process actually adds or removes samples from your audio recording. Too much of this might add undesired artifacts in your sound.

You can also use the M-points of an audio event, such as a drum loop, to create a Groove template to be used later with MIDI events.

To create a Groove template from an audio event:

1. Select the audio event from which you want to extract a groove.
2. In the Do menu, select Get M-Points and adjust the values in this window. Click Process when done.
3. Fine-tune the M-points by moving them if they need to be moved, adjust the velocity levels, and add or remove M-points that don't seem to match crucial events in your audio segment.
4. Select Match Audio and Tempo from the Do menu to open the Graphic Master Track editor.
5. Select the Show Hitpoint Match from the Options menu of the Graphic Master Track editor.

6. Move the slider at the bottom left of the Graphic Master Track window to find the right tempo for this audio event as described earlier, if you haven't done this before.
7. In the Audio drop-down menu, select the M-Points to Groove option to generate the Groove template file.

This will generate a *.prt file in your default Groove folder. If you open the Groove Control window from the Functions menu, as you scroll down your list of grooves you will find that the groove you just created had the same name as the part you were just editing.

Quantizing Audio

There are two ways you can quantize audio events: change their relative position in the part or actually quantize the data inside the event using M-points as a quantizing reference. The latter option will, in fact, modify the audio file on disk to match the new quantizing you apply. When you quantize an audio event's relative position in the Audio editor, you quantize the Q-point to the nearest Quantize value. Since you have only one Q-point per audio event or segment, you can adjust only one reference to a Quantize value. This does not change your audio data in any way. If you wish to quantize an audio event using more than one Q-point, you can split up your audio event into multiple segments. An easy way of doing this is to use the M-points, once again, as a reference.

To split up an audio event using M-points to quantize this event without modifying the audio data (see Figure 10.12):

1. Select your audio event and create M-points for it using the Get M-Points function as described earlier.
2. Fine-tune your M-points so that they correspond to something meaningful.
3. In the Do menu, select the Snip at M-Points function.
4. Adjust the insets of the newly created segments. The insets are the little handles at the top left and bottom right corners of the audio segment that determine where your segment begins and ends in the audio file.
5. Set the Quantize value to the desired value.
6. From the Functions menu, select the Quantize Type and then the appropriate type from the sub-menu.

Figure 10.12
Create audio segments using M-points.

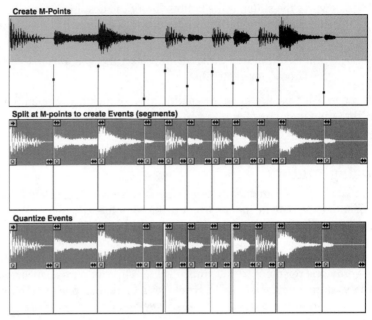

If you want to quantize the audio event using the M-points and modify the audio data on disk, repeat steps 1 and 2 in the previous list. Set your Quantize value as usual, then select the Quantize at M-Points from the Do menu instead of the Snip at M-Points option. Cubase will render the new file and replace the old one on your disk

TIP

Since true quantizing of audio events affects the audio file on your disk (destructive editing), it would be wise to make a copy of this file beforehand so that you can use the unquantized version later in another context or revert to this file if needed. You should also know that if there is a large stretch factor when you quantize, audio artifacts will be audible during playback due to lack of information in the original audio file to extrapolate accurate information between these large gaps. So, try to quantize the audio when only small amounts of quantizing need to be applied.

Cubase does many things very well, but in this respect, the time stretching and pitch shifting algorithms are not its best features in terms of output quality. If you do a lot of tempo matching and pitch shifting work with loops, you might be better served by other applications, such as ACID from Sonic Foundry, whose main goal is exactly this type of work: aligning beats and pitch shifting loops to make them play in the same scale.

About Match Quantizing

When you add M-points to audio parts, you add quantizing information that allows you to create Groove templates, as you saw earlier. This means that if you can create a groove out of an audio file, you can also apply the timing of an audio part that contains M-points to a MIDI part or to another audio part.

To apply the timing of an audio part to a MIDI part:

1. In the Arrange window, right-click to select the Match Quantize tool from the toolbox. As shown in Figure 10.13, this will transform your cursor into the letter Q.
2. Click and drag the audio part you wish to use as the timing model over the MIDI part you want to affect. Your cursor will become a hand when you drag the part. A dialog box will appear, asking you if you want to copy the accent values from the original audio part, merge them with the MIDI part, or not include them at all.
3. Select the appropriate option to complete the timing transfer.

Figure 10.13
Using the Match Quantize tool in the Arrange window.

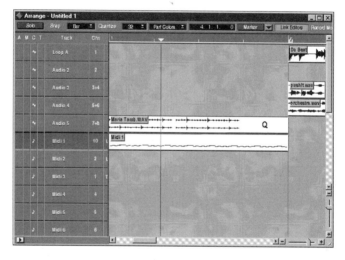

This will take the feel (timing and velocity information) of the audio part and apply it to the MIDI part.

You can also copy the M-point quantizing from one audio part to another. To do this, start by creating M-points for both audio parts. If you want to use only a portion of the audio part as a source for this process, you can split the part as well. Repeat the same steps as you did for MIDI parts. This time, the dialog box will ask you if you want to use Dynamic Time Stretching, which would change the length of the destination to the length of the source. Since, in this case, you want to use only the M-points as a feel or Groove Quantize template, select No. This will modify your audio file, so if you want to try this out, make a copy of your file beforehand.

Fitting Audio Events to Loop Area

Sometimes, you might just want to take an audio event and stretch or compress it so that it fits within a given number of bars. Drum loops are a perfect example of this. You have seen in the previous headers of this chapter how to adjust the tempo of a song or arrangement to fit an audio file. This is fine and dandy when all of your loops are playing at the same speed. However, sometimes you might want to adjust an event to fit at the right tempo without worrying too much about the tempo that's already in place. That's when you would use the Fit Audio To Loop Range option.

To use the Fit Audio To Loop Range:

1. In the Audio editor containing the audio loop you wish to fit within a given number of bars, create a loop area above the ruler bar, as shown in Figure 10.14.

Figure 10.14
Creating a loop area in the Audio editor.

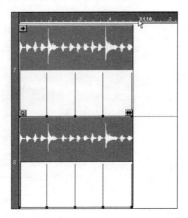

2. Select the audio event you wish to transform.
3. Select the Fit Event To Loop Range in the Do menu of the Audio editor. A dialog box will appear, asking you what you want to do: change the tempo, change the audio, or just cancel this operation. When you select tempo, it will change the tempo to fit the audio content found in that cycle. When you choose audio, it will process the file to make it fit perfectly inside this loop area. Again, this will modify your audio file, so make a copy of it prior to applying this process.
4. Select the appropriate option to process the file.

Audio Envelope Controls

Up until now, we have only discussed the M-points as being dynamic events displayed when the Dynamic Events option is selected in the View menu of the Audio editor. There are two other dynamic events you can display in this area: volume and pan. To select which one you want to see, select one of the three options in the menu next to the Edit Solo button in the editor's toolbar. The name of the dynamic control displayed is visible in this field. If you can't see any dynamic events, select the Dynamic Events option from the View menu in the editor's toolbar.

You can have control over the audio segment for both the volume and pan envelopes. This means that when you modify the volume envelope in a segment, any ghost or regular copies of this same segment will be affected.

The audio's volume and pan controls, being tied to the segments, will be independent of the VST Channel Mixer automation you can create, since the VST Channel Mixer's control is over parts in an audio channel rather than to a segment in a part.

To add and modify volume or pan controls:

1. Make the pan or volume control visible by selecting the Dynamic Events option in the View menu of the editor, then select the appropriate option in the menu next to the Edit Solo button.
2. Right-click in the Audio editor's window to select the Pencil tool from the toolbox.
3. To change the volume level, click in the box that appears at the 0 dB level and move it up or down to change the volume. You can't go beyond 0 dB, so if you want to boost your signal, use the VST Channel Mixer. To change the pan position, Alt+click in the Dynamic Events area to add a handle at the beginning of the audio event.
4. If you wish to add additional handles for the pan or volume levels, hold the Alt key down as you click on the line with the Pencil tool.
5. To move your handles in time without changing the value, click on the handle while holding the Alt key down. To move your handle's value without changing its position in time, click on the handle while holding the Shift key down.

By default, the audio event on top when overlapping with another audio event in a lane of the Audio editor will be the only one heard. You can, however, create a linear or algorithm crossfade between these two overlapping or adjacent events. You can also create a simple linear or algorithmic fade at the beginning or ending of an event.

To create a crossfade between two adjacent or overlapping events playing on the same audio channel:

1. Right-click somewhere in the Audio editor to select the Crossfade tool (identical to the line tool) from the toolbox.
2. Click near the position where you want to start the crossfade and drag your cursor to the position where you want the crossfade to end. As shown in Figure 10.15, the Create Crossfade dialog box will appear.

Figure 10.15
The Create Crossfade dialog box.

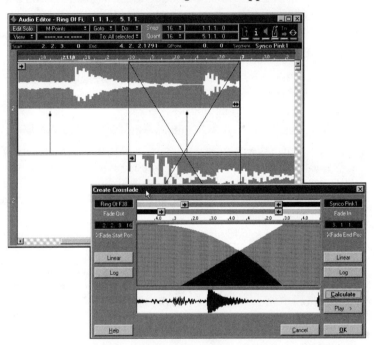

The left portion of the Create Crossfade dialog box shows you the audio event at the beginning of the fade. This will be the event that will fade out. The window displays the name of the event and the position where the fadeout begins for this event. Below this information, you will find two buttons: Linear and Log, which represent either linear fade or logarithmic fade.

3. Select the Linear or Log button, depending on the type of curve you want the first event to use as a fadeout type. In Figure 10.15, this is set to Log. The right portion of the Create Crossfade dialog box shows you the audio event at the end of the fade. This will be the event that will fade in. The window also displays the name and start of the fade-in position for this event.

4. Select the Linear or Log button, depending on the type of curve you want the second event to use as a fade-in type. In Figure 10.15, this is set to Linear.
5. Click the Calculate button to calculate the crossfade. This is necessary to enable the Play button to listen to the result before committing to it.
6. Once Cubase has finished calculating the crossfade, click the Play button to listen to the result. This will play the crossfading portion of the audio events. Above the crossfade graphic area, you can see two lines with arrows pointing inwards. The top line represents the start and end insets for the fade-in event, and the bottom line represents the start and end insets for the fade-out event. After listening to the result of the fade, you might want to adjust the positioning of these insets if you don't feel the crossfade is right.
7. Move the insets to the left or right by clicking and dragging the arrows for the fade-in or fade-out events. The actual space where the events are both represented in a dark gray color is the area where the files are overlapping.
8. If you made changes, press Calculate again to listen to the result; otherwise, click the OK button to proceed.

This will create a new audio file and a corresponding segment that will appear over both previous events. To make sure these three events don't move apart, creating drops in the audio signal, they are automatically grouped together.

TIP

When using crossfades, you will notice in the graphical display of the Create Crossfade window that a "valley" occurs, depending on the fade types you use. This valley is the point at which one event is fading out before the next event starts fading in. This will also create a drop in your sound level that can be noticeable. If this is what you want, then do nothing, but if you would like to have a constant output level, use the algorithm fade type for both the fade in and fade out. This will give you a more natural sounding transition and a constant output level. If you still have a valley, you can adjust the insets for the overlapping sections.

Creating a simple fade in or fade out is done in the same way as you would a crossfade, with the exception that there is only one audio event playing or displayed in the Create Fade dialog box. Repeat steps 1 through 4 from the crossfade list above to create a fade. You need to select only one audio event for this type of operation. Figure 10.16 shows you what the Create Fade dialog box looks like.

Figure 10.16
The Crossfade dialog box when you select only one audio event to fade from or fade to in the Audio editor.

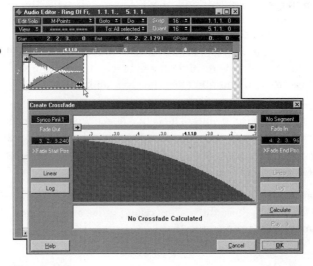

About Audio Functions

Audio functions are different processing functions that you can apply directly to the audio files, parts, events, or segments from the Arrange window, the Audio editor, the Audio Pool, or the Wave editor. Most of the operations in the Audio Functions menu are applied to the whole audio file, unless you select a specific part in the Internal Wave editor. These options are found under the Functions menu in the Audio Functions sub-menu and they include the following options (see Figure 10.17):

Figure 10.17
The Audio Functions Option menu.

▶ **External Wave editor**—Select this option to set a default External Wave editor. The difference between a Wave editor and an Audio editor will be explained in the following section of this chapter. Settings in this window include which External Wave editor you want to use and where this editor can be found on your system.

Figure 10.18
Setting up the External Wave editor.

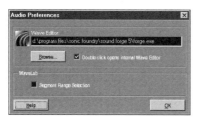

▶ **The Launch External Wave editor** and **Launch Internal Wave editor**—These options, respectively, launch either the External Wave editor you set in the External Wave editor option above or the Internal Wave editor included with Cubase VST.

▶ **Reverse**—Flips the waveform from beginning to end, making the file play backward. Use this to create reverse tails, which is a very effective way of bringing in new material in a crescendo-like fashion. A classic example of this would be the reverse cymbal smash effect.

▶ **Silence**—Transforms your audio data into digital silence. This brings all the bits in the selected audio file—or portion of file if you are in the Internal Wave editor—to a single zero value, or pure silence.

▶ **Fade In and Fade Out**—Unlike the Crossfade function, this creates a fade in or out over only the selected area in the Wave editor. In the Audio editor, this will span the range of the selected segment (or audio event). You can also make a custom fade curve by using the Fade Dialog option found in the same menu.

▶ **Quieten**—Reduces by half the volume of an audio segment, audio part, or audio file.

▶ **Normalize**—This will ask you to enter the value to which you want to set the highest amplitude level (volume) in decibels. Cubase will then scan the selected file, look for the highest peak in that file, and then increase or decrease the amplitude of the file in relation to the value you entered. For example, if you entered −1 dB and your highest peak is at −4 dB, it will bring everything up by 3 decibels. However, this does not change the proportional dynamics of the audio data. It will raise or lower everything, including noise levels, because it does not process the audio data in any other way.

▶ **Pitch Shift**—Unlike a standard sampler, you can change the pitch of a recording without changing the speed. When you select this option, the Pitch Shift dialog box will appear, as shown in Figure 10.19. You can set the pitch value by left-clicking to decrease, right-clicking to increase, or double-clicking to enter the desired pitch change value in the Semitones: Cents field. Check the Format Mode option when using melodic instruments for greater sound quality. Uncheck the Exact Length option if you also want a more natural sounding result. If you find this does not work well for your timing, check it and try it again. You can also adjust the gain and the accuracy of pitch-shifted material. The rule here is that you will want to use more sound accuracy unless your audio event is rhythmically intensive. Finally, select the best quality unless you have a slow computer and can't be bothered.

Figure 10.19
The Audio Function's Pitch Shift dialog box.

▶ **Time Stretch**—Also unlike standard samplers, you can change the time without changing the pitch. When you select this option, the Time Stretch dialog box will appear, as shown in Figure 10.20. You can set the Time Stretch value in one of four ways: by entering a new time value (in timecode format); by entering a start BPM and resulting BPM value; by entering a new number of samples; or by selecting a stretch factor value from 0.5 to 2.0. When you select any of these methods, the other methods will calculate themselves automatically to correspond to the value you have entered. As with the Pitch Shift function, you can emphasize the importance of length by checking the Exact Length option and emphasize rhythm over sound in the Accuracy slide bar. You can also determine the quality of the process by selecting Fast, Standard, or Best quality.

Figure 10.20
The Audio Function's Time Stretch dialog box.

▶ **Fade Dialog**—This option is similar to the Fade In and Fade Out functions in everything but one small detail: You can also draw your fade curve by clicking and dragging your cursor in the graphic display area, as shown in Figure 10.21. To reset this area, click one of the four buttons found to the right of this window.

Figure 10.21
The Audio Function's Fade Dialog window.

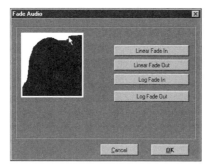

Wave Editors

Wave editors give you greater control over the actual treatment of the audio file itself. Unlike the Audio editor, you can paste audio data and add DirectX effects directly and save them to the audio file (in the case of the External Wave editor). This is, however, a destructive process, in the sense that the audio on your hard disk is modified, unlike with the Audio editor.

You can use one of two types of Wave editors: Either use the built-in Wave editor that comes with Cubase or link Cubase to external wave editing software such as Wavelab, Sound Forge, or CoolEdit. As you saw in Figure 10.18, you can set the path to the External Wave editor through the Audio Functions menu. Checking the Double click opens internal Wave editor option in this window will launch the Internal Wave editor whenever you double-click on an audio event from the Audio editor or on an audio segment in the Audio Pool. Otherwise, double-clicking on these events will launch the External Wave editor set in the Audio Preferences window found in the audio functions described in the previous section.

The second option in the Audio Preferences window pertains to how Cubase handles segments when using Wavelab. It's important that you check the Segment Range Selection box only if you are using Wavelab. Otherwise, the application will load but will not understand what to do with these segments. What this option does, in reality, is select the segment in the file you double-clicked on to open the External Wave editor.

Built-In Wave Editors

The Built-In Wave editor (see Figure 10.22) is similar to other editing windows found in Cubase. You will find the Do menu that contains the same audio functions found under the Functions menu in the Audio Functions sub-menu. The File menu in the Wave editor lets you select which file from the Audio Pool you wish to load in the editor. The Segment will display a list of segments available for that file. The field next to the Segment menu displays the position of your cursor in the window.

The next four buttons are your Wave editor's transport buttons. The Play button plays the segment from the current location until the end of a selection if a selection is made or until the end of the segment. You need to hold the mouse button down on this button, unlike the normal Play button on the Transport bar. The Loop button will loop the playback of a selection you make in the window. The next two buttons will bring your playback head to the Start Inset point or the End Inset point for the loaded segment in the Wave editor. The next two fields display, in samples, the position of the first selected sample and the position of the last selected sample.

Below this toolbar, you will find the Ruler bar in Real Time format (hours:minutes:seconds: milliseconds). You can use this Ruler bar to position your playback head without losing a selection in the waveform display area below. This brings us to the waveform display area. This area shows you the loaded segment and its Start and End insets. Any selection you make within that waveform will be shown in reverse highlight. We'll look at how to make selections in the next few paragraphs.

As you can see in Figure 10.22, there is an overview bar above the horizontal scrollbar and below the waveform display of the Wave editor. The boxes to the left and right (gray on your screen) indicate the portions of audio from the file that are outside the segment's range. The box that is blue on your screen shows the area of the file currently displayed on screen. The reverse highlight in the overview represents the current selection within the audio segment.

To zoom in or out in time, use the zoom bar in the lower right corner of the window. As in the other editing windows, the G and H keys are shortcuts to this tool (G for zoom out, H for zoom in).

Figure 10.22
The Built-In Wave editor.

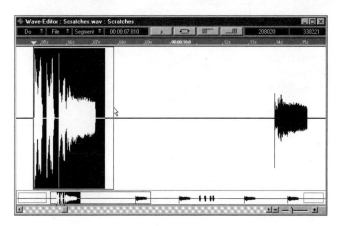

Table 10.2 lists the different operations available in the Wave editor. Most of these operations relate to a selection or the actual insets of a segment. Once you understand how to make or modify a selection, you can apply any of the functions found in the Do menu. To know what these functions are, go back to the section on Audio Functions earlier in this chapter.

Table 10.2
Working with selections and segments in the Built-In Wave editor.

To:	Do:
Make a selection	Click at the position where you want your selection to begin and drag over the area you wish to select.
Change the end point of a selection without changing the beginning	Hold the Shift key down and click near the end of your selection and drag the end to its new location.
Change the beginning point of a selection without changing the ending	Hold the Shift key down and click before the start of your selection and drag it to its new location.
Change the segment's insets	Click on the Inset markers in the waveform display and move them to their new location.
Change the portion of audio displayed in the waveform area	Ctrl+Click and drag in the overview area to draw a box over the area you wish to view.
Move the viewing area	Click in the box representing your viewing area in the overview display and drag it to the left or right to move your display in time.
Convert a selection into a new file on the hard disk	Make a selection and choose the Selection to File in the File menu of the editor.
Convert a selection into a new segment in the Audio Pool	Make a selection and choose the Selection to Segment in the Segment menu of the editor.
Select all audio between the insets of the segment	Press Ctrl+A.
Select all audio in the file displayed	Press Ctrl+A a second time. This will toggle the selection.
Change the file displayed	Select the desired file found in the Audio Pool from the File menu.
Change the segment displayed	Select the desired segment found for the loaded file from the Segment menu.
Move the segment within the file while preserving the segment's length	Right-click in the Wave Editor to select the Hand tool, click inside the segment and drag it to a new location in the file.

External Wave Editors

The External Wave editor can be an application that can read a WAV file (or AIFF file if you are on a Macintosh computer). You would probably want to use an external editor if the editing functions found in the Internal Wave editor don't correspond to your needs.

Cubase offers a few options in regards to your configuration. This will determine two aspects of the Cubase environment's behavior: You can set which application to use as an external editor and you can also set your preferred environment to be the Internal or External Wave editor. You saw in the previous section, "Wave Editors," that you can set Cubase to launch the Internal Wave editor as default editor when double-clicking on an audio event. You can also launch an External Wave editor by holding the Ctrl key down when you double-click on your audio event. Inversely, if you uncheck the option to launch the Internal Wave editor when double-clicking, holding the Ctrl key down when double-clicking would launch the External Wave editor instead.

There are some sound card issues that might occur when using an External Wave editor that you need to know about.

- ▶ If you are using an MME audio driver rather than a proprietary ASIO driver with your sound card, Cubase will not release the sound card to an external editor if the Play in Background option (found in the Options menu) is active. You will need to uncheck this option in order to hear anything at all. You might have to save your Cubase file and quit Cubase to release the audio outputs if this is the type of driver you are using.
- ▶ The Play position in Cubase must be outside the range of the wave being edited, or else the external editor will be unable to save edits to the file being edited.
- ▶ With a multi-output sound card equipped with an ASIO driver, Cubase will always grab the first two outputs (1 and 2) of your sound card. You should set your external editor to use another output pair to avoid conflicts. You will, however, need a multi-client ASIO driver in order to use the sound card in more than one application at a time. You might want to consult your sound card documentation to see if it is, in fact, a multi-client sound card. And, if so, check what the default settings are so that you can make the necessary adjustments to allow more than one application to access your sound card at a time.

If your External Wave editor is Wavelab or Wavelab LE, you can check the Segment Range Selection option in the Audio Preference window (see Figure 10.18). This will select the range of the segment you are editing when opening the file in Wavelab. Uncheck this option if you are not using Wavelab as your external editor. If you are using Sonic Foundry's Sound Forge version 5 or above, Sound Forge will tell you that there were some errors when loading the file. This is due to its inability to deal with Cubase's segments. You can ignore this message and proceed to the editing, since this is not crucial to the audio editing process.

When you are editing an audio file in a Wave editor, you are making destructive edits. Therefore, any changes you make in this file will change the audio data on the hard disk. If, for some reason, the changes you make modify the length of the audio file, any segments you had will be offset. Since segments are, in reality, time pointers telling Cubase that the segment begins here and ends there, when you change the audio file's length, you are changing the relationship the audio data has to its segment time markers used by Cubase.

To avoid this, make a copy of your file before exporting it to an external application. If you decide to save your file under a new name inside the audio editor, you can use the Refind option in the Audio Pool to replace the old file with the new file. This will automatically rebuild the waveform image file and leave the segments where they were. If you don't change the name of your file and haven't changed the length of it either, you should only have to save the changes in the external editor, close the file, and return to Cubase. The update is automatic, as it will refresh the waveform display when you make Cubase the active window once again if the Use Waveforms option is checked in the Options > Audio Setup sub-menu.

If you want to edit only one of many segments in a file, you can use the Export Segment option found in the Do menu of the Audio Pool. This will create a new audio file containing only the audio found between the start and end point of this segment.

Now You Try It

Here are the exercises you will find on the Web site for this chapter. Note that for this chapter, some audio files have been included with the song file, making the download a little bit longer. Efforts were made to keep these files to a minimal size, by using short samples and VSTi Instruments included with Cubase VST.

- Edit audio events inside the Audio editor.
- Adjust the length of audio segments in the Audio editor.
- Adjust Q-points and Quantize audio segments in the Audio editor.
- Repeat selected events in a part.
- Work with M-points.
- Split a segment using M-points.
- Create a fade-in in the Wave editor.
- Normalize an audio file in the Wave editor.

You will find these exercises at the following Web address: **www.muskalipman.com/cubase**.

Simply follow the instructions on the Web site before starting the exercises.

You can refer to the passages in this chapter to find out how to do these exercises, but try doing them without peeking first, just to see how comfortable you are with these principles. If you don't remember how to do a task, refer to the appropriate header in this chapter.

As with exercises in previous chapters, you will need to have the Universal Sound Module installed on your computer to use the file provided for these exercises.

11
Mixing

Mixing a recording is an art form unto itself—the art of listening. Being a great musician doesn't mean you're going to be a great mixing engineer, and being a great mixer doesn't mean you will be a great musician. So, with this out of the way, let us look at the tools you will be using to try to get the most out of your recording, no matter what your specialty is. When you listen to a recording, you hear instruments that are too loud, others that are too soft, some too edgy, and others too dull.

The goal is to get everything in perfect balance. This is done by adjusting the intensity level of each track; making space for each instrument by panning them in the stereo field; improving their presence by adding—but mostly cutting—frequencies with EQ to allow each instrument to have its own place in the ear's range of frequencies; controlling their dynamic range by using compression if necessary; and, finally, by adding color and tonal textures with effects. The mixing process inside Cubase is not unlike the traditional mixing process in the sense that external mixer desks have many of the same features as Cubase offers. Where Cubase shines is through its integration of traditional mixing techniques and the addition of realtime effect processing and automation.

Cubase provides support for VST effects that come with the program or those bought as plug-ins, and it also provides support for third-party DirectX effects (under the Windows environment). These can produce the same result as VST effects but are a little more CPU intensive than their VST counterpart because they were written using different standards. Since VST plug-ins have been written for Cubase (but are also compatible with Logic), this type of plug-in will be more effective inside Cubase than DirectX. On this note, be aware that to use DirectX effects, you will need to have a DirectX-compatible computer and the latest DirectX support available. You will also need to install those third-party DirectX effects on your computer.

TIP
Make sure to consult Steinberg's Web site to find out which DirectX version you need and to verify that the other plug-ins you have support the same DirectX drivers. DirectX technology applies only if you have the PC version of Cubase.

Because Cubase is a multitrack recorder and a MIDI sequencer, you will have two different windows under which you can control your sounds: the VST Channel Mixer and the MIDI Track Mixer. The first will be used to mix audio, Rewire, and VSTi tracks. The second will be used exclusively to mix MIDI tracks.

We have discussed these mixers before, so their options should be familiar to you by now. Until now, though, we have looked at how to move faders or pans, adding effects, but not how to automate these movements. Unlike traditional mixers, Cubase VST allows you to record most of the manipulations you will make inside these two mixing environments, including, to a certain degree, effect automation.

VST Channel Mixer Automation

VST Channel Mixer automation affects the way audio events are played, and the computer is responsible for this processing, whereas MIDI automation is processed by the MIDI instrument. Audio mix automation also allows you to record quite a few more parameters than are available in MIDI mix automations. There are two sets of automation that you can apply: Channel setting automation and Global setting automation. The Channel setting affects the channel, and the Global setting will influence any channels that are routed through this setting. Here's a list of what you can automate in the VST Channel Mixer:

Table 11.1
Parameters available for automation in the VST Channel Mixer

Channel settings	Global Settings
Volume	Master volume controls
Pan	Master Send Effect levels
Mute	Program selection of Send Effects
EQ Bypass button	The first sixteen parameters for each Send Effects
The settings for up to 4 EQ modules	Program selection of the Master Effect
Effect Send activation switch	The first eight parameters for each Master Effects
Effect Send levels	
Effect Send pre switch	
Effect Send bypass switch	
Insert Effect program selection	The first fifteen parameter settings for each Insert Effect

Although Cubase allows you to record automation for the Insert Effect parameters, you will be limited to the first thirty-two audio channels, eight groups, and sixteen VSTi or Rewire channels. If you hit these limits, you're into some serious automation and should think about trying to simplify things by using successive sub-mix steps.

Before heading into the automation section itself, let's point out that you can set the levels and pans of audio channels in the VST Channel Mixer without using automation, just as you would on a normal mixer desk to monitor your tracks appropriately. As long as the Write or Read buttons (found in the upper left part of the VST Channel Mixers) are not activated (pressed), the faders, pan, and any other effect settings will stay at the same position.

Recording and Playing Your Mix

To record your mix automation using the VST Channel Mixer:

1. Open the VST Channel Mixer (Ctrl+Asterisk [*] is the shortcut key).
2. Activate the VST Channel Mixer's Write button, as shown in Figure 11.1.

Figure 11.1
Activating the Write button in the VST Channel Mixer to record the mix automation.

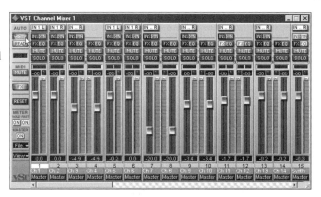

3. Position your playback cursor and press the Play button on the Transport bar (or Enter on the numeric keypad).
4. Move the appropriate faders, knobs, switches, and so on (this includes any parameter mentioned in Table 11.1).
5. Stop the playback.
6. Deactivate the Write button and listen to your automation. Since the Write button also records automation when Cubase is stopped, this might introduce unwanted automation values.

TIP

You can take advantage of the fact that Cubase records automation even when it is stopped by recording a series of automation values at the location of your playback line. Simply position your playback line where you wish to record this series, activate the Write button, make the changes in the automation, and deactivate the Write button when you are done. This will add all the parameter changes at the location of your playback line to create a dramatic change—such as effects turning on and off—in the automation at this point.

Cubase will create an additional mix track containing an audio mix part in which your mixing automation events can be found. This will be a separate track from your MIDI Track mix part. Once you add new automation, these automation additions will append the existing audio mix part rather than create a new one.

Remember that you can record automation in more than one step, so limit your automation to one channel at a time. Some might argue that this is hard to do, since you don't know how loud or soft the other channels will be. The idea is to start your automation by setting approximate values, then refine as you go along, but you don't have to take my word for it. Try a method that you like and stick with it if it's working for you. The goal is to feel comfortable with the mixing process. Re-ordering your tracks according to sound types (melody, harmonic rhythms, bass, drums, and so on) might help you to focus your attention on how the sounds blend together rather than searching in the VST Channel Mixer to find where your things are. Sending these groups of instruments to different group faders might also help in the mixing process.

To send a channel to a specific group, select the desired output group for the channel under the channel's fader in the VST Channel Mixer. When you change the output of that group later, every channel assigned to that group will be affected.

To hear your mix automation when you play back, activate the Read button in the VST Channel Mixer and unmute the mix track containing your audio mix part. When you start playing your arrangement, Cubase will play any automation you recorded up to that point. It might be a good idea to activate this button right after you record your automation the first time, since you won't be able to hear the automation unless the Read button is active. You may also mute the automation from the Arrange window by muting the mix track containing your audio mix automation events.

Editing Your Mix

To edit your audio mix automation:

1. Double-click on the part containing your automation on the audio mix track (make sure you are choosing the audio mix track, not the MIDI mix track). This will launch the Controller editor window. This window, discussed in Chapter 5, displays the audio controllers differently than the MIDI controllers. The left side of the window displays the different parameters grouped by controller categories, as shown in Table 11.1, and the actual channel for these controllers is visible when you click on the plus sign next to a parameter. The controller values are displayed in the right side of the window.

2. Click on the parameter's channel that you wish to edit in the left side of the window. If you can't see individual channels, click on the plus sign next to the audio parameter to reveal the individual channels for these parameters.

3. To edit a single value, right-click in the right-hand area of the window to select the Pencil tool and click where you want to make the change. To add more controller changes (automation), keep the Alt key down as you click in this area (see Figure 11.2).

Figure 11.2
Editing audio mix automation information for the audio volume controller.

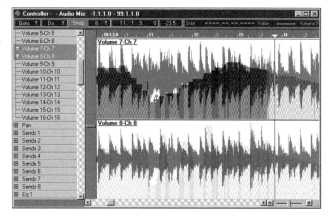

4. To erase automation values, right-click in the right-hand area of the window. The controller values appear as before. Select the Eraser tool.
5. Click on the values you wish to delete.

When editing automation for effect parameters, you will not see the audio waveform displayed in the background, as in Figure 11.2. These parameters will look more like MIDI controllers being edited than audio event controllers, but the result is the same. Another difference between an audio channel automation and an effect parameter automation is that effects are sorted first by channel and then by parameter (see Figure 11.3), whereas the volume, pan, Insert Effect level, and other level controls are sorted by type and then by channel. Explore the Controller editor of an audio mix on your own to get an idea of how this information is laid out.

Figure 11.3
VST Effects plug-in automation as displayed in the Controller Editor.

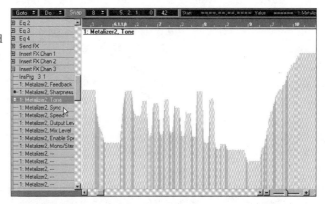

Remember that when you are editing events in the Controller editor, the Snap value will determine the spacing between each inserted automation value. To save the changes you made to your automation, simply close the editing window.

MIDI Track Mixer

The MIDI Track Mixer is a window that offers you control over volume and pan MIDI controllers. Furthermore, if you have a Roland GS- or Yamaha XG-compatible sound card or MIDI instrument, you will be able to control additional parameters specific to these General MIDI protocols.

To access the MIDI Track Mixer, click on Panels > MIDI Track Mixer. The MIDI Track Mixer window will appear, as shown in Figure 11.4.

Figure 11.4
The MIDI Track Mixer window.

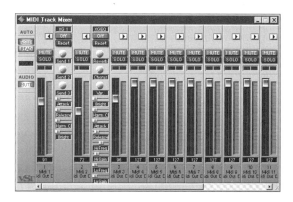

Although the MIDI Track Mixer allows you to control volume and pan like the VST Channel Mixer does for audio, it handles these parameters in a different way. Instead of actually modifying the volume of the sound, it sends a MIDI controller parameter message to the MIDI device so that it plays at the proper settings. For example, when you raise the fader in the MIDI Track Mixer to 100, it sends out a MIDI Controller 7 message to the appropriate MIDI device, telling it to set this controller to the value of 100.

TIP
You might wonder what the difference is between a MIDI Track Mixer volume controller and the Track Info's volume controller parameter. In fact, they are basically the same. The difference is that whenever you set a Track MIDI volume change, this is reflected in the MIDI Track Mixer. But the reverse is not true. For example, if you record a MIDI track volume automation, the values entered in the MIDI Track Mixer will not be reflected in the Track Info's MIDI volume field. As for volume changes you enter when a MIDI part is selected, these will not appear in the MIDI Track Mixer. This can get a little confusing, so use the MIDI Track Mixer when you want to have more control over the MIDI volume changes or when you want to add volume changes somewhere other than at the beginning of a track or a part. The same applies to MIDI pan changes. To avoid confusion when you do this, make sure to remove any previous MIDI volume or pan control changes that you might have added in the Track Info area.

The Controls

The MIDI Track Mixer window has the following controls (from left to right and top to bottom in Figure 11.4):

- ▶ Two automation buttons that allow you to write and read MIDI automation.
- ▶ A button that allows you to mute audio tracks when mixing or automating MIDI tracks. It offers sixteen mixer channels for each hardware MIDI output port (since VSTi and Rewire are handled by the VST Channel Mixer, they do not appear here). Each one of these channels offers the following controls:

  An arrow button that expands the channel to reveal a set of additional controls for XG- and GS-compatible instruments. You can choose one of the sets of controls available from the field's drop-down menu at the top of the channel's strip. In Figure 11.4, channels 1 and 2 are set to XG-compatible instruments. Note that these extra controls are useless if your instruments do not support these protocols. No matter which extended panel you use, there will always be an Off and Reset button below the extended panel selector. The Off button will set the values of this channel to the lowest possible value without sending a MIDI message, and the Reset button will set all the values to a default position.

- ▶ The Mute and Solo buttons allow you to mute or solo individual MIDI tracks. This will not affect audio tracks, so if you want to solo a MIDI track and mute all other audio tracks, use the Audio Mute button to the left of the window.
- ▶ A pan field displays the position of the MIDI pan controller. When you click and drag the green line in this field, the position of this field is displayed in the numerical value indicator found below the channel's fader.
- ▶ The channel's fader controls the MIDI volume controller value. This value is shown, by default, in the numerical value indicator below the channel's fader.
- ▶ To the right of the channel's fader, you will see the velocity meter of the MIDI instrument playing on this channel.
- ▶ The numerical value indicator, as mentioned above, displays either the pan or volume value when you change it. If you have entered a value in the Track Info area for this MIDI track, it will be displayed here. Remember, though, that any automation you add in the MIDI Track Mixer will not be reflected in the Track Info area of this track.
- ▶ At the bottom of each channel, you will see the channel's number, the track's name, and the MIDI output port's name.

MIDI Automation

MIDI automation is pretty straightforward, but you have to be aware of certain issues. Since the volume and pan automation are not updated in the Track Info area, and vice versa (as mentioned above), except for the track volume, it is advisable to use only one method of recording pan and volume information to avoid confusion later. To add volume and pan changes to tracks and parts using the Track Info and Part Info area, refer to the section called ``MIDI Volume and Pan Control'' in Chapter 4. The following text will describe how to record, playback, and edit MIDI automation using the MIDI Track Mixer.

To record MIDI automation:

1. Opening the MIDI Track Mixer by selecting it from the Panels menu.
2. Position your playback cursor to the location in your arrangement where you would like to start recording automation.
3. Click the Write button in the MIDI Track Mixer to enable the MIDI automation.
4. Press the Play button in the Transport bar to begin playback and move the MIDI faders and pans appropriately. Since you can write more than one automation, it is best to keep your focus on one channel at a time, stopping between takes to listen to the result before recording the next channel.
5. When you are satisfied, disable the Write button and enable the Read button. You should always disable the Write button when you are finished recording your automation, because Cubase will record any changes you make even if the arrangement is not playing. If you decide to record over a section, leave the Read button active so that Cubase will read previously recorded automations.
6. Start the playback to listen to your recorded automation. If you want to add automation, reactive the Write button and start again, as described in Step 4. If you want to record over a previously automated controller, click and hold your mouse on that controller to write over it. Since you can undo the most recent recording, it is a good idea to deactivate the Write button between takes to avoid recording an automation by mistake. All your automations will be recorded on a special mix track.

    You will have two automation tracks if you automate both audio and MIDI. The default name for the audio mix automation will be "Audio Mix," and the default name for MIDI mix automation will be "Track Mix." If you delete the part containing your automation on this track, or if you mute the track, the automation will not be heard. In fact, if you delete the automation part, you will lose the automation.
7. When you are happy with the automation, don't forget to deactivate the Write button for a last time and leave the Read button on to hear this automation.

To edit your MIDI automation using the Controller editor:

1. Double-click on the part containing your automation on the mix track (make sure you are choosing the MIDI mix track, not the audio mix track). This will launch the Controller Editor window. As seen in Chapter 5, the controller window displays the MIDI controller's names on the left side of the window and the controller values on the right side of the window.
2. Click on the MIDI channel you wish to edit on the left side of the window. If you can't see individual controllers, click on the plus sign next to the MIDI channel to reveal the individual controllers.
3. Select the controller under the MIDI channel you wish to edit.
4. To edit a single value, right-click in the right-hand area of the window to select the Pencil tool and click where you want to make the change. To add new controller changes (automation), keep the Alt key down as you click in this area (see Figure 11.5).

Figure 11.5
Editing MIDI automation in the Controller editor.

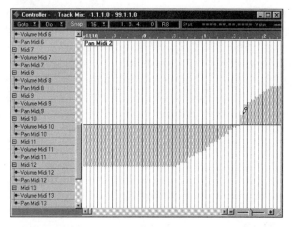

5. To erase automation values, right-click in an empty space and select the Eraser tool.
6. Click on the values you wish to delete.

For more information on editing in the Controller editor window, please refer to the section called "Editing Controls" in Chapter 5.

If you want to troubleshoot an automation operation you've made, remember that the Controller editing environment will add a black dot next to the MIDI parameter containing MIDI automation values. Since this is a very visual environment, it is sometimes easier to edit volume automation, for example, in this window. You will be able to see jumps in volumes or pans that can create an awkward jump in sound due to mistakes made while recording the automation.

TIP
To see more than one controller at a time inside the Controller editor, hold down the Shift key as you click on the MIDI controller in the area on the left. This will split the Controller editing area to the right in as many parts as you select controllers.

You may also copy the events inside a MIDI Track Mix part somewhere else in your arrangement window. This can be useful when you have the same elements but don't want to have to repeat the automation process. To do this, simply cut the mix track part you wish to copy (or move), and then Ctrl+drag it to a new location in the same track to create a ghost copy, or Alt+drag it to make a new copy. If you simply want to move it, just drag it to the new location.

Working with Effects

Why use effects? There are probably as many reasons to use effects as there are effects available. However, in some cases, depending on the style of music you are creating, less is more. Effects can be used to enhance certain parts or to drastically alter the tonal qualities of recorded tracks. A good rule of thumb is to try to make your music as interesting as possible without using effects, then add subtle colors to your music with these effects. Obviously, using effects is not always about adding subtle colors—it can be used as a very powerful creative tool as well. That's why more and more effects are available. Designing your sounds with VST effects when producing pop or techno music, for example, is not only an option but an integrated part of these musical styles. This said, you should use effects as you see fit for the type of production you are doing.

Cubase offers two different sets of VST effects: earlier effects that were available before version 5.0 and more recent effects available since version 5.0. The difference between the earlier versions and the more recent effects (VST 2.0 standard) is that the newer effects support MIDI timing information and have more effective algorithms. A whole new selection of VST 2.0 Effects are also included with Cubase VST. Cubase sends MIDI timing information to a VST plug-in that requests it. This can be used for tempo-based delays or MIDI control over pitch shifting and harmonizers. Both types of VST plug-in effects can be found in any drop-down menu where you can select effects. This includes the VST Channel Mixer, VST Master Mixer, VST Send Effects, VST Master Effects, and the VST Channel Settings panel. The earlier VST plug-ins will be found in their own submenu in this drop-down menu, as shown in Figure 11.6.

Figure 11.6
This list shows the VST and DirectX plug-ins that are installed and available on your system.

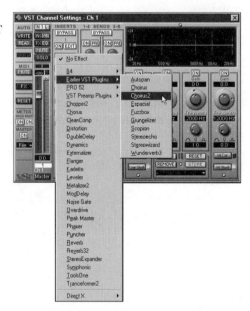

Normally, Cubase will install VST plug-ins in a VST plug-ins folder found in the application folder. However, if you have other VST plug-ins installed somewhere else on your computer, you can assign a path to them from Cubase in order to share these plug-ins between applications. To set the path to this alternative folder, select Options > Audio Setup > Shared VST Plug-ins Folder. A dialog box will appear, asking you to specify a path to the alternative VST plug-in folder. Click the Browse button to look for the folder, select i, and click the Select button to assign it as your shared plug-in folder.

NOTE

You will notice that all the effects discussed here are realtime effects. This implies that the computer is processing the effect as the sound is being heard, which requires a great deal of processing power from your computer. The more you add effects that need processing in realtime, the more you will need a powerful computer.

This is also quite different from the audio functions found in the Functions menu. You might also find DirectX effects similar to these functions (such as time stretching and pitch shifting, for example), but unlike DirectX plug-ins, Functions are not processed in realtime and will replace the audio file on your hard disk. In this case, the choice would be yours. If you find a similar effect that processes the audio in realtime and you have the computer that can handle it, go for it. Otherwise, use a copy of the audio file and apply a corresponding function to it in non-realtime.

Because we already discussed how to route the effects using the VST Send Effects, the VST Master Effects, and the Insert Effects in Chapter 8, this chapter will discuss different parameters available in the VST plug-in effects and how to use DirectX effects.

You can access these effects through the INS or FX buttons in the Track Info area of the audio track for which you want to assign the effect. Once inside the VST Channel Mixer, you can choose the appropriate effect from the drop-down menu, as shown in Figure 11.6. If you want to edit an effect parameter found in an Insert Effect, click the Edit button next to the appropriate Insert Effect. If you want to edit the effect's parameter for a Send Effects, choose Panels > VST Send Effects to bring the VST Send Effects panel into view and click the Edit button next to the appropriate effect.

When working with effects, you might want to recall some of the parameter settings you make to effects. It is possible to save both individual effects and banks of effects and later recall these effects. The way Cubase handles these settings is simple: It saves effects and banks of effects (set of effects parameters) into separate files, with the FXP extension for effect programs and FXB for effect banks.

To save and recall effect programs or banks:

1. With the VST Plug-in Effect window open, choose an empty or default setting before you start modifying the plug-in's parameters.
2. Make the necessary adjustments to your effect's parameters.
3. When satisfied with the effect's parameters, double-click on the name's field in the top portion of the plug-in's window. In Figure 11.7, this is where it says "Init 1."
4. Type the desired name for the effect's setting.
5. Click on the arrow to the left of the file's pop-up menu in the effect's dialog box.
6. Choose Save Effect if you want to save only this effect to a file on your hard disk, or choose Save Bank if you want to save all the settings of the effects currently loaded.
7. A dialog box will appear, asking you to specify a location and a name for the file. Select a destination folder. This should be inside your VST plug-in folder if you want to use it later. Type a name for your file.
8. Click the Save button in the dialog box to save the bank or the program to file.
9. The next time you wish to recall this effect in another song, simply select Load Effect or Load Bank from the File pop-up menu in the VST plug-in's dialog box.

Earlier Effects

All the VST plug-in effects using a VST 1.0 standard are found in a sub-menu called Earlier Effects in the effects menu, as shown in Figure 11.6. The list of earlier effects includes the following plug-ins:

▶ **Choirus** and **Choirus 2**—Chorus and flanger are effects that you can use to add depth to a sound. A delay is added to the original sound that is continuously varied through time by a low frequency oscillator (LFO). Both effects will render identical results, but Choirus 2 uses a different algorithm that requires more processing power. See Figure 11.7.

Figure 11.7
The Choirus 2 effect dialog box.

▶ **Scopion**—This is an oscilloscope that analyzes the left or right side of a stereo input signal and displays the waveform contents in realtime. It would make sense to use this as a master effect, since it doesn't do anything to your sound, but rather, lets you see how it reacts through time. See Figure 11.8.

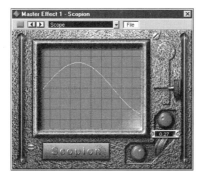

Figure 11.8
The Scopion effect interface.

▶ **Autopan**—Makes your signal move from left to right (or right to left). To get the full benefit of this plug-in, use it in pre-fader mode and turn the volume fader of your track down. Otherwise, you will hear the original signal and the Autopan signal together, reducing the perception of the effect. See Figure 11.9.

Figure 11.9
The Autopan effect dialog box.

▶ **Espacial**—This is a mono channel input reverb that you can use to add ambiance and room tone to your audio signal. It is best suited for send effects, where you can control the amount of room tone or reverb sent back to the channel's output. See Figure 11.10.

Figure 11.10
The Espacial effect dialog box.

- **Electro Fuzz** or **FuzzBox**—Reproduces the effect of a guitar distortion pedal. This doesn't mean you have to use it with a guitar, but the transistor distortion effect is what the engineers at Steinberg were going for. This effect uses a mono input and can be used both as an insert effect or send effect. See Figure 11.11.

Figure 11.11
The Electro Fuzz effect interface.

- **Stereoecho**—A mono delay that uses two separate delay settings for the left and right outputs, creating a stereo effect. For best results, use this effect as a send effect. See Figure 11.12.

Figure 11.12
The Stereoecho effect dialog box.

- **Stereowizard**—Enhances the stereo field of a stereo audio signal by widening it field. For best results, use it as a master effect to widen your mix. You could use this on a mono signal, but the effect might cancel some frequencies. If you use this on a mono signal that's been processed by a stereo effect, such as the Stereoecho or Wunderverb 3, you will have a better result than simply taking a mono signal copied on two channels and panned left and right. See Figure 11.13.

Figure 11.13
The Stereowizard effect dialog box.

Mixing – Chapter 11   297

▶ **Wunderverb 3**—This is another mono input reverb that you can use as a send effect. The advantage of Wunderverb 3 is that it uses very little processing power. See Figure 11.14.

Figure 11.14
The Wunderverb 3 effect interface.

▶ **Grungelizer**—Simulates vinyl recordings by adding scratches, hums, noise, and distortion into your signal. Use this effect when you want to recreate the feeling of an old record. This effect can be used as any type of effect routing, since it depends on the result you wish to have. See Figure 11.15.

Figure 11.15
The Grungelizer effect interface.

http://www.muskalipman.com

Available in Cubase 5.0

Cubase 5.0 introduced the ASIO 2.0 protocol, which, as mentioned above, includes MIDI synchronization features. The parameters used in these plug-in effects are similar to the ones used in the earlier versions of the software. But because the ASIO 2.0 plug-ins allow MIDI synchronization, some new parameters are introduced into the plug-in's interface, allowing you to use the tempo of the current song to control the speed of some effects and how other effects will handle their parameters in sync with MIDI timing.

Table 11.2 lists the VST plug-in effects included with Cubase, the effect type, and parameters. Following this table are descriptions of each parameter and how it affects the sound.

Table 11.2
List of ASIO 2 VST Plug-ins.

Effect Name	Effect Type	Parameters
DoubleDelay	Delay	Mix, Feedback, Tempo Sync popup 1 and 2, TmpSync knob 1 and 2, Pan
ModDelay	Delay	Mix, Feedback, Tempo Sync popup, TmpSync knob, Time, DelayMod
Karlette	Delay	Delay, Volume, Damp, Pan, Feedback, Dry/Wet, Sync
Chorus	Chorus/Flanger	Mix, Freq, Delay, Stages
Flanger	Chorus/Flanger	Mix, Tempo Sync Popup, TmpSync knob, Shape Sync knob, Feedback, Rate, Depth, Delay, Stereo Basis
Symphonic	Chorus/Flanger	Mix, Delay, Depth, Rate, Tempo Sync popup, TmpSync knob, Stereo Basis
Distortion	Distortion	Input, Output, Shapes, Contour, Drive, Factory Presets
Overdrive	Distortion	Input, Output, Bass, Mid, Hi, Drive, Speaker Simulation
Chopper2	Pan	Mix, Input, Output, Speed, Tempo Sync Popup, Sync button, Stereo/Mono button, Waveform buttons, Depth
Reverb (and Reverb 32)	Reverb	Mix, Roomsize, PreDelay, Reverb Time, Damp, (Filter Lo and Hi Cut, Mix)
Metalizer2	Filter	Mix, Sharpness, Tone, Feedback, Speed, Tempo Sync popup
Tranceformer2	Filter	Mix, Pitch, Speed, On button, Waveform buttons, Stereo/Mono button, Tempo Sync Popup
Phaser	Filter	Mix, Feedback, TmpSync knob, Rate, Tempo Sync Popup, Stereo Basis
Dynamics	Dynamic	All the same parameters as found in the VST Channel Mixer, with the exception of SoftClip and Limiter. A routing button has been added to choose the order in which you want the different dynamic processes to be applied. Refer to Chapter 8 for a description of the parameters involved in this plug-in.

VST Plug-in Parameter Descriptions

Because many parameters are similar from one plug-in to another, you will find—in alphabetical order—a list of the parameters and a description of their effect on the sound. Many of these parameters have different names but play similar roles in different plug-ins, affecting the sound within the context of that plug-in. The best way to truly understand how they affect the sound and how they can be used in a creative environment is to try them out and apply them on an audio signal, changing the values and observing the effect they have on the sound. To get a visual feedback, you can assign the Scopion plug-in to the VST Master Effect and leave the Scope visible as you apply a plug-in. You will notice how the actual waveform changes as you apply the plug-in and change a parameter.

- ▶ **Bass, Mid and Hi**—These three parameters allow you to boost or cut their respective frequency ranges by plus or minus 15 decibels, changing the tonal quality of the effect.

- ▶ **Contour**—Acts as a lowpass filter, influencing the tonal quality of the effect (in this case, the distortion). Higher values will add a bassy and boomy color to your distortion. The top part of Figure 11.16 shows the Contour parameter set to 100 percent and the bottom part set to 0 percent.

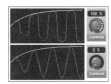

Figure 11.16
The Contour parameter found in the Distortion plug-in.

- ▶ **Damp**—Determines how much of the high frequencies you want to cut from a reverb tail. The higher the value, the more you cut high frequencies, dampening or dulling the reverb's tail.

- ▶ **Delay**—The time value in milliseconds at which a delay is introduced in the signal before the next occurrence of that signal. Depending on the effect, this can influence the speed or depth of a delay. The top of Figure 11.17 shows the Delay parameter set to 100 milliseconds and the bottom part set to 6.8 milliseconds. These values might change from one plug-in to another, but the effect of this parameter is similar.

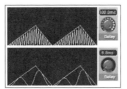

Figure 11.17
The Delay parameter found in the Chorus, Flanger, Karlette, and Symphonic plug-ins.

http://www.muskalipman.com

- **DelayMod**—Determines the delay before which a modulation of the signal occurs. It is set as a percentage value.
- **Depth**—Determines the depth or amount of modulation a waveform will have when applied to a signal. This will influence the amplitude of the signal through time, where higher values will create wider and more pronounced effects. The top of Figure 11.18 shows the Depth parameter set to 100 percent and the bottom part set to 21 percent.

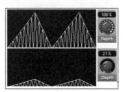

Figure 11.18
The Depth parameter found in the Chopper2, Flanger, and Symphonic plug-ins.

- **Drive**—Determines the amount of harmonic distortion or overdrive you add to your audio signal depending on the effect you are using. The top of Figure 11.19 shows the Drive parameter set to 100 percent and the bottom part set to 0 percent.

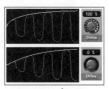

Figure 11.19
The Drive parameter found in the Distortion and Overdrive plug-ins.

- **Dry/Wet**—This parameter affects the mix between the dry, or original, signal and the wet, or processed output, signal. When the slider is set to wet, it's setting the wet value to 100 percent and the dry value to 0 percent. Inversely, when the slider is set to dry, it sets the dry value to 100 percent and the wet value to 0 percent. You can set this to any value between those two extremes to get the desired mix ratio.
- **Factory Presets**—This is different than presets you would select from the effect's saved preset list. They correspond to different algorithms used to calculate the distortion's shape. Choose one of the five available presets and then tweak the other parameters to get the distortion quality you want.

▶ **Feedback**—Determines the amount of effect that should be reintroduced into the effect itself. This also influences the density of the effect. This value is usually set in percentages. The top of Figure 11.20 shows the Feedback parameter set to 100 percent and the bottom part set to 16 percent.

Figure 11.20
The Feedback parameter found in the DoubleDelay, ModDelay, Karlette, Flanger, Metalizer2, and Phaser plug-ins.

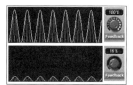

▶ **Filter Hi/Lo Cut**—These two parameters will allow you to change the tonal qualities of the effect by adding or cutting the high and low frequencies, respectively. Playing with the high frequencies will change the brightness of the reverb, while the low frequency adjustments can serve to reduce rumble caused by reverberating bass lines. This can help with the low-end definition of your sound.

▶ **Freq or Rate**—Determines the modulation frequency or the modulation rate of an effect in Hertz. The higher the value, the higher the modulation frequency (or rate) will be for the given effect. The top of Figure 11.21 shows the Rate parameter set to 5 Hz and the bottom part set to 0.10 Hz. These values might change from one plug-in to another, but the effect is similar.

Figure 11.21
The Rate parameter is found in the Flanger, Symphonic, and Phaser plug-ins, whereas the Freq parameter is found in the Chorus plug-in.

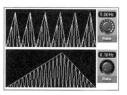

▶ **Input and Output**—Determine, respectively, the amount of signal going into the effect and the amount of effect going out to the VST send effect or back into the VST Channel if used as an insert effect (similar to the Wet/Dry or Mix parameters). The Input plays the same role as the VST send effect's Send knob. When used as an insert, use the Input to control how much of the signal you want to send into the effect.

▶ **Mix**—Sets the ratio between dry sound (original sound) and wet sound (the effect). The higher the value, the more effect you will hear from the output.

▶ **On button**—Available in the Tranceformer2 plug-in, this allows you to switch the Pitch parameter on or off (see Figure 11.22). When set to off, the speed of the modulation is the only frequency that will affect the sound, whereas when this button is set to On, the Pitch parameter interacts with the Speed parameter, creating a more pronounced and intricate effect.

Figure 11.22
The On/Off button found in Metalizer2 plug-in

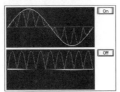

▶ **Pan**—Determines the pan position of an effect in the stereo field.

▶ **Pitch**—This is another parameter that determines the pitch of a modulating frequency. The higher the pitch, the faster the modulation. In the Tranceformer2 effect, this is combined with the Speed parameter, which, in turn, adds a second modulation frequency to the pitch to create a complex dynamic filtering effect. The top of Figure 11.23 shows the Pitch parameter set to 5,000 Hz and the bottom part set to 1 Hz.

Figure 11.23
The Pitch parameter found in the Tranceformer2 plug-in.

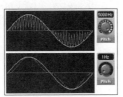

▶ **PreDelay**—Determines the time it takes for the first reflection of the sound to be heard. Small pre-delay values will usually have a more natural effect on the sound, and larger values will blur the attacks of a sound. The top of Figure 11.24 shows the PreDelay parameter set to 100 percent and the bottom part set to 1 percent.

Figure 11.24
The PreDelay parameter found in the Reverb 32 plug-in.

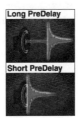

▶ **Reverb Length**—Sets the time the reverb will take before it can't be heard anymore. The top of Figure 11.25 shows the Reverb Length parameter set to 100 percent and the bottom part set to 1 percent.

Figure 11.25
The Reverb Length parameter found in the Reverb and Reverb 32 plug-ins.

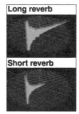

▶ **Roomsize**—Determines the size of a reverberating room, affecting the density of the effect. The higher the value, the larger the room. The top of Figure 11.26 shows the Roomsize parameter set to 100 percent and the bottom part set to 1 percent.

Figure 11.26
The Roomsize parameter found in the Reverb and Reverb 32 plug-ins

▶ **Routing**—This parameter is available in the Dynamics plug-in and allows you to change the order of the process in which the signal passes through when you apply more than one dynamic process. In Figure 11.27, the Routing parameter is set to 1-2-3.

Figure 11.27
The cursor points at the Routing setting in the Dynamics plug-in window.

- **Shape Sync knob**—Changes the shape of the modulation waveform, affecting the color of the modulation. The top of Figure 11.28 shows the Shape Sync parameter set to 0, the middle part set to 8 and the bottom part set to 16. Intermediate values will result in intermediate shapes for the modulating waveform.

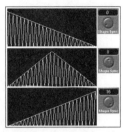

Figure 11.28
The Shape Sync knob parameter found in the DoubleDelay, ModDelay, Flanger, Phaser, and Symphonic plug-ins.

- **Shapes**—The shape selection influences how a signal is processed. This parameter is used only with the Distortion plug-in and influences how quickly the distortion is added to the sound. Figure 11.29 displays the three shapes you can choose from when adjusting this parameter. The first one on top shows a linear approach, the middle one shows a hard clip approach, and the third one at the bottom shows a soft knee curve approach. The shapes displayed here might not be the same in all plug-ins, but how they affect the sound is similar in each.

Figure 11.29
The Shapes parameter found in the Distortion, Chopper2, and Tranceformer2 plug-ins.

- **Sharpness**—The sharpness of an effect plays a similar role to the Q parameter in an EQ, allowing you to make a filtering band narrower or larger. The top of Figure 11.30 shows the Sharpness parameter set to 100 percent and the bottom part set to 0 percent.

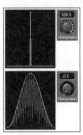

Figure 11.30
The Sharpness parameter found in the Metalizer plug-in.

▶ **Speaker Simulation**—This is an On/Off button that simulates the output of a guitar amplifier when on, cutting frequencies that would normally not appear in a guitar amplifier (see top part of Figure 11.31).

Figure 11.31
The Speaker Simulation parameter found in the Overdrive plug-in.

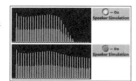

▶ **Speed**—This parameter is similar to the Freq and Rate parameters in the sense that it determines the frequency of a modulation, which affects the modulation's speed. The Speed parameter is available in the Chopper, Metalizer2, and Tranceformer2 effects and can be set, when the Sync button is activated, to a Quantize value similar to the Tempo Sync pop-up menu. When the Sync button is deactivated, you can set the speed of the modulation to a specific frequency.

▶ **Stages**—Introduces additional occurrences into the original source of the audio signal. The value corresponds to the number of times these occurrences are introduced. More stages (also called Taps) will produce a denser effect.

▶ **Stereo Basis**—This parameter allows you to expand the stereo field of the effect's output. The top of Figure 11.32 shows the Stereo Basis parameter set to 100 percent (full stereo) and the bottom part set to 0 percent (center).

Figure 11.32
The Stereo Basis parameter found in the Flanger, Phaser, and Symphonic plug-ins.

▶ **Stereo/Mono button**—Allows you to toggle between stereo or mono mode. The stereo mode will send the effect in the left and right channel, effectively panning the effect.

▶ **Tempo Sync Popup**—This is a pop-up menu that lets you set which tempo subdivision to use to introduce a tempo-based delay equal to the value selected. This delay will be in sync with your current MIDI tempo. The values available are the same as your Quantize or Snap values. The smaller the Sync value, the slower the occurrences. The default value for this popup menu is No Sync.

▶ **Time**—Can be used when the Tempo Sync is set to No Sync, meaning that you introduce a fixed amount of time for a delay to occur rather than a tempo-based delay. The values are in milliseconds.

- **TmpSync**—Multiplies the Tempo Sync value in a tempo-based effect by a factor of 1 to 10. Smaller factors will result in faster pulses, and higher factors will result in slower pulses. The top of Figure 11.33 shows the TmpSync parameter set to X1, or a multiple of 1. The middle part is set to X5, or a multiple of 5. The bottom part of the same figure is set to X10 for a multiple of 10. Intermediate values will result in intermediate multiples of the Tempo Sync pop-up menu. Note that this type of MIDI sync parameter is typical of ASIO 2.0 plug-ins.

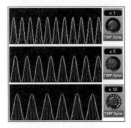

Figure 11.33
The TmpSync (Tempo Sync) parameter found in the Chopper2, DoubleDelay, Metalizer2, ModDelay, Flanger, Phaser, Symphonic, and Tranceormer2 plug-ins.

- **Tone**—The tonal quality of a sound refers to the modulating frequency added to an audio signal. This parameter is available in the Metalizer2 effect. It adds a low tone when the value is set in the lower scale and will increase the number of frequencies (pitch) as you turn the knob to a higher value. The top of Figure 11.34 shows the Tone parameter set to 100 percent and the bottom part set to 1 percent.

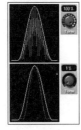

Figure 11.34
The Tone parameter found in the Metalizer2 plug-in.

- **Volume**—Affects the volume of the Delay parameter in the Karlette plug-in.
- **Waveform buttons**—Allow you to select the shape of the modulating waveform for an effect.

Most of these parameters can be automated during the VST Channel Mixer automation process, which was discussed earlier in this chapter. This means that you can dynamically modify a parameter as the sound plays and record these changes to reproduce them during playback.

DirectX Effects

For the Cubase end-user, DirectX allows you to share effect plug-ins between applications. If you have purchased DirectX-compatible plug-ins for another audio software product, this means that you can share these effects with Cubase.

To work, you will need to install both DirectX and the actual plug-ins on your Windows-based computer. You can get a copy of the most recent DirectX software at **http://www.microsoft.com/directx**. Since DirectX is not just for Cubase, you should not install it inside your Cubase folders but in a common program or shared folder.

Once your DirectX software is installed, you can install your DirectX-compatible software, such as DirectX effects plug-ins. These plug-in effects can be anywhere on your computer, preferably inside a common folder for easy access.

To activate DirectX-compatible plug-ins inside Cubase, you don't need to tell Cubase where to find them, since they are part of the DirectX database on your computer. However, you will need to tell Cubase which ones you want to activate or deactivate when choosing from the DirectX list of plug-ins (this would be the last option in the list shown in Figure 11.6). To choose which DirectX plug-in will appear in your pop-up menu, click on Panels > DirectX Plugins.

The DirectX Plugins dialog box will appear, as shown in Figure 11.35. Clicking in the column to the left of the plug-in's name to add a checkmark will make that plug-in visible in the DirectX plug-in list when you are choosing effects.

Figure 11.35
The DirectX Plugins dialog box.

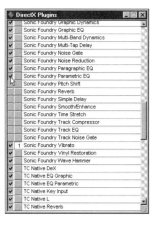

The second column in the DirectX Plugins dialog box will reveal any plug-in that is being used by your arrangement, as is the case in Figure 11.35, which shows the Sonic Foundry Vibrato plug-in. Right-clicking in that column will allow you to see exactly where it is used: the effect type, the track, and in which effect slot.

If you have more DirectX plug-ins that can fit in a pop-up panel, a menu at the bottom of the panel will indicate that there is another panel with the indication "More Plug-ins" and a little arrow pointing to the right.

TIP

If your computer is not equipped with DirectX plug-ins and you can't run more than one or two plug-ins at a time before your computer starts to skip audio here and there, there is a workaround for you. Start by assigning the effect to the track to which you wish to add an effect using send effects. Adjust the effect's parameters, making sure you only have a wet output. Assign the send effects to pre-fader and solo your track while bringing down the fader for this track completely. Make sure to disable the VST Channel Mixer's Write and Read automation buttons if you recorded any automation. Also, mute any MIDI recording, if you have any. At this point, when you press Play, you should hear only the output of the effect. Open the VST Master Mixer and click the Export button to export the audio. In the Export dialog box, select the appropriate options for your file and check the Import to Audio Pool and Import to Audio Track options. Click the Create File button to export the file. Cubase will create a file with the output of the effect and place it on a new track. You can now disable the effect, unsolo the other tracks, and raise your original track fader. You can use the new track fader to adjust the level of the wet signal in your mix. Since you recorded the effect, the computer doesn't need to calculate it anymore, and this will free up some resources for use with other effects when needed. The downside of this is that if you want to change the effect, you need to start the whole process once more, deleting the previously exported track.

Now You Try It

Here are the exercises you will find on the Web site for this chapter. Note that for this chapter, some audio files have been included with the song file, making the download a little bit longer. Efforts were made to keep these files to a minimal size, by using short samples and VSTi instruments included with Cubase VST.

- ▶ Record automation in the VST Channel Mixer.
- ▶ Record automation in the MIDI Channel Mixer.
- ▶ Edit VST Channel Mixer automation in the Controller editor.
- ▶ Edit MIDI Channel Mixer automation in the Controller editor.
- ▶ Add a VST Effect and automate its parameters.

You will find these exercises at the following Web address: **www.muskalipman.com/cubase**.

Simply follow the instructions on the Web site before starting the exercises.

You can refer to the passages in this chapter to find out how to do these exercises, but try doing them without peeking first, just to see how comfortable you are with these principles. If you don't remember how to do a task, refer to the appropriate header in this chapter.

As with exercises in previous chapters, you will need to have the Universal Sound Module installed on your computer to use the file provided for these exercises.

12
Working In Sync

Being able to synchronize Cubase to other devices is important, but synchronization is underused because often it is not well understood. It can lead to all kinds of problems, but when done properly, it can save you lots of time (and money) and allow you to accept new and interesting projects such as film and video soundtracks or sound design and editing.

This chapter will describe the differences between types of synchronization and establish ground rules. Also, it will explain different procedures you can use to synchronize Cubase with an external video player using timecode; an external MIDI device using MIDI Clock; an external tape recorder using MMC (MIDI Machine Control); and an internal video using the DS Video Monitor Module.

Once you understand how these various devices can lock together and play in sync, you will be happy to discover how to use the hitpoint features included in Cubase VST. These features can help you find the correct tempo for music or sound when synchronizing the time-related events typical of visual projects with the meter-related events characteristic of musical projects—all without having to use your calculator. This aspect alone can save you hours of work trying to figure out how to fit your music into a video scene that changes at times not regulated by bars and beats.

About Word Clock, SMPTE, and MIDI Clock

Before we start looking at how Cubase handles synchronization, it is important to understand the different types of synchronization, their terminology, and the basic concepts behind these terms. In synchronization, there will always be a master/slave relationship between the source of the synchronization (master) and the recipient of this source (slave). There can only be one master, but there can be many slaves to this master. There are three basic concepts here: timecode, MIDI Clock, and Word Clock.

Timecode

The concept behind timecode is simple: It is an electronic signal used to identify a precise location on time-based media such as audio and videotape or in digital systems that support them. This electronic signal accompanies the media that need to be in sync with others. Imagine that a postal worker delivering mail is the locking mechanism, the houses on the street are location addresses on the timecode, and the letter carries the matching address. The postal worker reads the letter and makes sure that it gets to the correct address the same way a synchronizing device will compare the timecode from a source and a destination, making sure they are all happening at the same time. This timecode is also known as SMPTE (Society of Motion Picture and Television Engineers) and it comes in three flavors. Each uses an hours:minutes:seconds:frames format:

- ▶ **MTC (MIDI Time Code)**—This is normally used to synchronize audio or video devices to MIDI devices such as sequencers. MTC messages are an alternative to using MIDI Clocks (a tempo-based synchronization system) and Song Position Pointer messages (telling a device where it is in relation to a song). MTC is essentially SMPTE (time based) mutated for transmission over MIDI. On the other hand, MIDI Clocks and Song Position Pointer are based upon musical beats from the start of a song, played at a specific tempo (meter based). For many nonmusical cues—think of sound elements that are not part of a musical arrangement but are found on movie soundtracks, such as Foley, dialog, ADR, room tones, and sound effects—it's easier for humans to reference time in some absolute way (time based) rather than musical beats at a certain tempo (music based). This is because these events are regulated by images that depict time passing, whereas music is regulated by bars and beats in most cases.

- ▶ **VITC (Vertical Interval Time Code)**—This is normally used by video machines to exchange synchronization information with any type of VITC-compatible device. This type of timecode is best when working with a Betacam or VTR device. You will rarely use this type of timecode when transferring audio-only data back and forth. VITC may be recorded as part of the video signal in an unused line, which is part of the vertical interval. It has the advantage of being readable when the playback video deck is paused.

- ▶ **LTC (Longitudinal Time Code)**—This is also used to synchronize video machines, but unlike VITC, it is also used to synchronize audio-only information such as a transfer between a tape recorder and Cubase, for example. LTC usually takes the form of an audio signal that is recorded on one of the tracks of the tape. Since LTC is an audio signal, it is silent if the tape is not moving.

Frame Rates

As the name implies, a frame rate is the number of frames a film or video signal would have within a second. The abbreviation for frame rate is "fps"—frames per second. There are different frame rates, depending on what you are working with:

▶ **24 fps**—This is used by motion picture film. In most cases, working with this medium will not apply to you, since chances are you do not have a film projector hooked up to your computer running Cubase to synchronize sound.

▶ **25 fps**—This refers to the PAL (Phase Alternate Line) video standard, used mostly in Asia, and the SECAM/EBU (Sequential Color And Memory/European Broadcast Union) video standard, used mostly in Europe. If you live in those areas, this is the format your VCR uses. A single frame in this format is made up of 625 horizontal lines.

▶ **29.97 fps**—This is also known as 29.97 Non-Drop and may be seen as 30 fps in some older two-digit timecode machines. (It should not be mistaken for the actual 30 fps timecode. If you can't see the 29.97 format, chances are the 30 format is its equivalent.) This refers to the NTSC (National Television Standards Committee) video standard, used mostly in North America. If you live in this area, this is the format your VCR uses. A single frame in this format is made up of 525 horizontal lines.

▶ **29.97 fps DF**—Also known as 29.97 Drop Frame (hence the DF at the end). This can also be referred to as 30 DF on older video timecode machines. This is probably the trickiest timecode to understand, since there is a lot of confusion about the drop frame. In order to accommodate the extra information needed for color when this format was first introduced, the black-and-white 30 fps was slowed to 29.97 fps. Though not an issue for most of you, in broadcasting the small difference between realtime (also known as the wall or house clock) and the time registered on the video can be problematic. Over a period of one SMPTE hour, the video will be 3.6 seconds, or 108 extra frames, longer in relation to the wall clock. To overcome this discrepancy, drop frames are used. This is calculated as follows: Every frame 00 and 01 is dropped for each minute change, except for minutes with 0s (00, 10, 20, 30, 40, and 50). Therefore, two frames skipped every minute is 120 frames per hour, except for the minutes ending with zero, so 120 – 12 = 108 frames. Setting your frame rate to 29.97 DF when it's not—in other words, if it's 29.97 (Non-Drop)—will cause your synchronization to be off by 3.6 seconds per hour.

▶ **30 fps**—This format was used with the first black-and-white NTSC standard. It is still used sometimes in music or sound applications where no video reference is required.

▶ **30 fps DF**—This is not a standard timecode protocol and usually refers to older timecode devices that were unable to display the decimal points when the 29.97 Drop Frame timecode was used. Try to avoid this timecode frame rate setting when synchronizing to video, because it might introduce errors in your synchronization. SMPTE does not support this timecode anyway.

http://www.muskalipman.com

MIDI Clock

MIDI Clock is a tempo-based synchronization signal used to synchronize two or more MIDI devices with beats per minute (bpm) for guide track. As you can see, this is different than a timecode, since it does not refer to a realtime address (hours:minutes:seconds:frames). In this case, it sends 24 evenly spaced MIDI Clocks per quarter note. So, at a speed of 60 bpm, it sends 1,440 MIDI Clocks per minute (one every 41.67 millisecond), whereas at a speed of 120 bpm, it will send double that amount (one every 20.83 millisecond). Because it is tempo based, the MIDI Clock rate changes to follow the tempo of the master tempo source.

When a master sends a MIDI Clock signal, it sends a MIDI Start message to tell its slave to start playing a sequence at the speed or tempo set in the master's sequence. When the master sends a MIDI End message, it tells the slave to stop playing a sequence. Up to this point, all the slave can do is start and stop playing MIDI when it receives these messages. If you want to tell the slave sequence where to start, the MIDI Clock has to send what is called a Song Position Pointer message telling the slave the location of the master's song position. It uses the MIDI data to count the position where the MIDI Start message is at in relation to the master.

MIDI Clock should be reserved for use between MIDI devices only, not for audio. As soon as you add digital audio or video, you should avoid using MIDI Clock, since it is not well suited for these purposes. While it will keep a good synchronization between similar MIDI devices, audio requires much greater precision. Video, on the other hand, works with time-based events, which do not translate well in bpm.

Another type of MIDI-related synchronization is the MIDI Machine Control (MMC). The MMC protocol uses System Exclusive messages over a MIDI cable to remotely control hard disk recording systems and other machines used for record or playback. Many MIDI-enabled devices support this protocol.

Digital Clock

Digital Clock synchronizes two or more devices by using the sampling frequency of the master device as a reference. This type of synchronization is often used with MTC in a music application such as Cubase to lock both audio sound card and MIDI devices with video devices, for example. The master device, in this case, would be the sound card. This is by far the most precise synchronization mechanism discussed here. Because it uses the sampling frequency of your sound card, it is precise to $1/44,100^{th}$ of a second when you are using a 44.1 kHz sampling frequency (or 0.02 millisecond). Compare this with the precision of SMPTE timecode (around 33 milliseconds at 30 fps) and MIDI Clock (41.67 milliseconds at 120 bpm) and you will quickly realize that this synchronization is very accurate.

Whenever you make a digital transfer between two digital devices, the digital or Word Clock of the master device is sent to the slave device, making sure that every bit of the digital audio from the master device fits with the slave device. Failure to do so would result in errors and degradation in the digital audio signal. When a slave device receives a Word Clock (a type of Digital Clock) from its master, it replaces its own clock with the one provided by this master.

A Digital Clock can be transmitted on one of these cables:

- ▶ **S/PDIF** (Sony/Phillips Digital InterFace)—This format is probably the most common way to connect two digital devices. Although this type of connection transmits Digital Clock information, it is usually referred to by its name rather than Word Clock. S/PDIF connectors have RCA connectors at each end and carry digital audio information with embedded digital audio clock information. You can transmit mono or stereo audio information on a single S/PDIF connection.

- ▶ **AES/EBU** (Audio Engineering Society/European Broadcast Union)—This is another common, yet not as popular, type of digital connector used to transfer digital information from one device to another. AES/EBU uses an XLR connector at each end of the cable, and like the S/PDIF format, it carries the digital audio clock embedded in its stream of data. You can also transmit mono or stereo audio information on this type of connection. Because it uses XLR connectors, it is less susceptible to creating clicks and pops when you connect them. However, since they are more expensive, you won't find them on low-cost equipment.

- ▶ **ADAT** (Alesis Digital Audio Technology)—This is a proprietary format developed by Alesis that carries up to eight separate digital audio signals and Word Clock information over a single wire fiber optic cable. Most sound cards do not provide ADAT connectors, but if yours does, use it to send and receive Digital Clock information to and from an ADAT-compatible device.

- ▶ **TDIF** (Tascam Digital InterFace)—This is a proprietary format developed by Tascam that provides eight channels of digital audio in both directions, with up to 24-bit resolution. It also carries clocking signals that are used for synchronizing the transmission and reception of the audio.

- ▶ **Word Clock**—A Digital Clock is called Word Clock when it is sent over its own cable. Since Word Clock signals contain high frequencies, they are usually transmitted on 75-ohm coaxial cables for reliability. Usually, a coaxial BNC connector is used for Word Clock transfers.

To be able to transfer digital audio information in sync from one digital device to another, all devices have to support the master's sampling rate. This is particularly important when using sampling frequencies other than 44.1 kHz or 48 kHz, because those are pretty standard on most digital audio devices.

When synchronizing two digital audio devices, the Digital Clock might not be the only synchronization clock needed. If you are working with another digital hard disk recorder or a multitrack analog tape recorder, you will need to send transport controls to and from these devices, along with the timing position generated by this Digital Clock. This is when you have to lock both the Digital Clock and timecode together. Avoid using MIDI Clock at all cost when synchronizing with digital audio. The next section will discuss different possibilities and how to set up Cubase to act as a master or a slave in the situations described above.

Resolving Differences

Synchronizing Cubase implies that you will be resolving the differences between machines to follow a single master clock, which will guide other clocks and tell them where they should be at all times. This section discusses how to resolve these differences and set your software and hardware preferences accordingly, depending on the situation.

Cubase VST offers a solution for most synchronization situations. If you have an ASIO 2.0-compatible driver for your sound card and an ASIO 2.0-compatible external device, you can have not only a sample-accurate synchronization but also a positioning protocol, which calculates the relation between the Word Clock and timecode positions to offer stable synchronicity. If your external hardware does not support ASIO 2.0, use MIDI Timecode options instead. You might want to consult your manufacturer's documentation in regard to ASIO 2.0 implementation to find out more about the possibilities it has to offer.

Cubase uses three different methods to synchronize to other devices: Resolving, Continuously Resynchronizing, and Referencing. These are not settings you can adjust in Cubase, but rather, ways that Cubase uses to stay in sync.

- ▶ **Resolving**—This implies that all devices are synchronized to a single digital and timecode reference, resolving their clock to the master's. This is the best synchronization method, but it is not practical in a small home studio, because it often requires an external module, called a house sync, which connects all devices and locks them together using a stable clock.

- ▶ **Continuous Resynchronization**—This implies that a timecode is sent to a digital audio device, which, in turn, uses this timecode as a reference to make sure its Digital Clock is always in sync, thus continually resynchronizing itself to this timecode.

- ▶ **Referencing**—If you don't have any timecode available but need to lock two devices together, you can create a SMPTE audio track by selecting the Generate SMPTE from the Options menu. This will create a timecode audio file that you can record later onto the audio track of the device that will act as a master, such as an analog multitrack recorder. Generating such a file will guarantee that the timing in this file coincides with the timing (clock) of your sound card, since it is this sound card's clock that is being used to generate the file in the first place. To record this timecode file on another device, import it and place it at the desired location in Cubase, then press Play after pressing Record on the destination device. Once your track has been recorded on your master device, you can reference this timecode in Cubase by assigning the audio output of the track containing the timecode to a timecode converter or directly into your computer if you have a SMPTE/MTC converter.

Internal and External References

First, you need to determine where your synchronizing reference is coming from. Since Cubase offers very stable synchronization, you might want to consider using this as your source, making it the master for other devices. But in the real world, this is not always possible.

Cubase can be slave, master, or both simultaneously: It can receive a sync signal from a master sync device and send it to another slave device, regenerating the sync information for a stable synchronization.

When Cubase is master, the synchronization should be set to Internal in the Synchronization dialog box, as shown in Figure 12.1. You can access the Synchronization dialog box by double-clicking on the Sync button in the Transport bar or by selecting Synchronization in the Options menu.

Figure 12.1
The Synchronization dialog box.

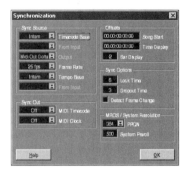

When you want Cubase to act as a slave to an external synchronization signal, it gets a little more complicated. In this case, you need to select the type of synchronization signal coming in. There are two dialog boxes where you can set which digital or timecode clock to use: the Audio System Setup and the Synchronization dialog box. In the Audio System Setup window found in Options > Audio Setup > System, you have options to set both the Audio Clock Source (as shown in Figure 12.2) and the MIDI Sync Reference. When Cubase is the master, the Audio Clock Source should always be set to Internal, as it usually is when you are working in Cubase and not working on sync-intensive projects. The options that you will see in this pop-up menu depend on your sound card. In this case, if you want to slave Cubase to an exterior Audio Clock Source, you would select either S/PDIF In or Word Clock.

By default, the MIDI Sync Reference will be set to Audio Clock. However, if you can't use the Resolve or Continuous Resync methods mentioned earlier, you can switch the reference for your MIDI sync to an external timecode by setting the MIDI Sync Reference field to Time Code. This will use an external timecode instead of the internal audio clock as a timing reference. You should avoid this if you have any audio in your arrangement, since the Audio Clock will probably be more stable than an external timecode anyway.

Figure 12.2
The Audio System Setup dialog box.

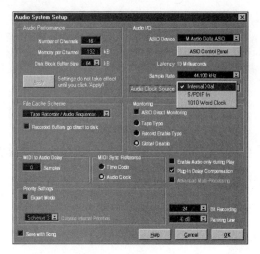

Setting Up Synchronizations

Let's take a closer look at the Synchronization dialog box (shown in Figure 12.1).

The first section is for Sync Source options.

▶ The **Timecode Base field** allows you to select the source of your timecode. Set this to Intern when you want Cubase to be the master or when you don't need synchronization to any other devices. If you are expecting Cubase to sync to an external timecode, you have four choices, which will be discussed in the next header.

▶ The **first From Input field** tells Cubase which MIDI input to expect the external timecode to come from. Note that this field is grayed out when the Timecode Base field is set to Internal, since it should not be expecting timecode information at that point.

▶ The **Output field** is used to tell Cubase to echo the MIDI Machine Control information to an external device using one of the MIDI ports available on your system. This is active whenever the Timecode Base field is set to something other than Intern. A typical use of this is when you are using an MMC Timecode Base and want to send the MMC to another MMC device.

▶ The **Frame Rate** determines the frames per second (fps) setting for the incoming or outgoing timecode. Once you have set this field, Cubase will be expecting a timecode with this frame rate before it begins. Changing this will also influence your time display in the Transport bar to reflect the proper frame rate. For example, if you set this value to 25 fps, you should not see frames 26 to 29 displayed when you play the arrangement.

- The **Tempo Base** allows you to tell Cubase to expect a MIDI Clock from a MIDI input. When Cubase's Timecode Base is set to Intern, this can still be set to MIDI Clock (or ASIO 2.0). This would mean that you are telling Cubase to not follow an external timecode, but rather to follow the tempo of a MIDI Clock from another sequencer or MIDI device such as MIDI Workstation, for example.
- The **second From Input field** tells Cubase which MIDI input port the MIDI Clock will arrive from. Again, setting the Tempo Base field to Intern will gray out this selection, since it will not be expecting any MIDI Clock.

The next section below the Sync Source is the Sync Out option. There are only two fields in this section: MIDI Timecode and MIDI Clock. Both fields will allow you to tell Cubase either to echo the synchronization information to a MIDI output port on your computer or to pass on MIDI Timecode or MIDI Clock information to another device. If Cubase is the master (Timecode Base set to Intern), you can set either the MIDI Timecode or the MIDI Clock to be sent to a MIDI output port of your choice. When a MIDI output is selected, the appropriate Sync Out field will display "On" instead of "Off." If you use this option while Cubase is set to receive timecode from an external source, it will act as the go between, following the master's timecode or MIDI Clock and sending it out to the slave device.

To the right of the Sync Source in the Synchronization dialog box, you will find the Offsets field: Song Start, Time Display, and Bar Display. When working with video, for example, chances are the timecode will not start at 00:00:00:00:00 (which represents hours:minutes:seconds:frames:sub-frames). It is a common practice to start the timecode at a different hour for each reel of film. For example, a ninety-minute movie might be divided on nine reels and then transferred on the same videotape or separate videotapes. To make sure that cues on reel 4 are not mistaken for cues on reel 7, the timecode for reel 4 will start at four hours (04:00:00:00), and reel 7 at seven hours (07:00:00:00). Furthermore, a lead-in time might be added before the reel to allow for video and audio calibration, setting the timecode to begin at least 30 seconds before the hour (in reel 4, this would be 03:59:30:00). If you want your song to begin at Bar 1, Beat 1, you will need to offset the timecode accordingly. In this example, you can set the offset for reel 4 to 04:00:00:00:00, which will tell Cubase that Bar 1, Beat 1 (1.1.000) corresponds to this value. The Time Display works in a similar way. The fact that your song starts at the timecode address of 04:00:00:00 doesn't mean that you want to calculate the time starting at four hours. Changing the time in this field will set your start position (1.1.000) at something other than a time equivalent of 00:00:00:00:00. The last field in this section allows you to precount and record bars before Bar 1, Beat 1 (1.1.000).

Let's say your timecode starts at 10:00:00:00, but you want to record a pickup bar (bars preceding bar 1.1.000) leading in to 1.1.000. You would set this field to the appropriate number of bars. So, when the timecode arrives at ten hours, it will play the precount or pickup bar(s) before hitting bar 1.1.000. Leaving this value at 0 will not allow you to record before 1.1.000; therefore, the timecode address of ten hours will correspond to this bar value.

The Sync Options below the Sync Source section in this dialog box will affect how fast it takes Cubase to lock to a timecode before it starts playback and how it handles drops in timecode. The first option represents the amount of frames Cubase needs to receive before it starts playing after it locks to that timecode. If you have many events to chase—program changes and mix automation parameters, for example—you might want to set this to a higher value so that all the data will load and play properly when Cubase starts playing. On the other hand, if you don't have that many events to chase, you can set this to a lower setting.

The Dropout Time is also a frame value. When you are receiving timecode from a tape recorder, degradation of the timecode signal might occur, leaving the timecode unreadable for a number of frames. If this were the case, Cubase would stop playing and then start playing again when it understood the timecode. To avoid this problem, you can raise the amount of Dropout Time tolerated by Cubase before it stops playing. If your timecode is really bad, you might want to consider rerecording the timecode track rather than setting this option high, because the shift in timecode between the estimated timecode (the one Cubase will estimate it's at when the signal is dropped) and the real timecode (the one on the Sync reference) might create undesired effects.

The Detect Frame Change option allows Cubase to update the frame rate automatically if it changes during playback. Not being common, it is disabled by default, but you can enable this option by checking this box.

The MROS/System Resolution refers to the MIDI playback resolution of Cubase. When you need high precision, select a high PPQN value (Pulse Per Quarter Note). If, on the other hand, you find that the quantity of MIDI information slows down your computer, use a value of 384 or lower. If you found that your computer ran very well without adjusting these values before synchronizing, chances are you won't need to adjust them when synchronizing either. As for the System Preroll, this is the startup time determined in milliseconds that your system takes when the Play button on the Transport bar is hit. It is set with reference to the sound card's latency. This should be left as is, unless you are having problems with timing. In that case, raising this value can help. But you will notice a greater delay before Cubase actually starts playing sounds after you press the Play button.

Now that you know what these fields do, let's look at how to use them in different scenarios. In all the following cases, the same basic rules apply and will be assumed:

- To open the Synchronization dialog box, double-click the Sync button in the Transport bar or select it from the Options menu.
- To close and accept the settings in the Synchronization dialog box, click the OK button.
- To activate synchronization, press the X key on your keyboard or click the Sync button.
- Adjust the Offset and Sync Option fields appropriately, independently of the synchronization options.
- If Cubase is the master, you should set the other device(s) to follow the master's synchronization signal. Inversely, if Cubase is the slave, you should set your other device(s) to send a synchronization signal to Cubase.

▶ When Cubase is master, the Transport bar will control the slave's transport. When Cubase is slave, the master's transport will control Cubase's transport when the master is transmitting a sync signal. When the master is not sending a sync signal, you can use the transport controls freely inside Cubase.

Cubase and SMPTE (MTC, LTC and VITC)

Tables 12.1 and 12.2 summarize how to synchronize Cubase using SMPTE timecodes.

Table 12.1
Setting Cubase as the master.

In the Synchronization dialog box	
Timecode Base	Intern
Frame Rate	Desired Frame Rate
Tempo Base	Intern
MIDI Timecode	Select the appropriate MIDI output port in the Audio System Setup dialog box
Audio Clock	Internal sync
MIDI Sync Reference	Audio Clock
Connections	
MIDI	Make sure your MIDI output carrying the MTC is hooked up to the MIDI input device slaved to the MTC from Cubase and set it to external sync from an MTC source. The same applies if you are hooking up the MIDI output to an external synchronization device that will convert MTC to VITC or, most likely, to LTC SMPTE. This will require an external device that can handle the conversion.
Word Clock	If your sound card has a Word Clock output, hook it up to the Word Clock input of the slaved device.

http://www.muskalipman.com

Table 12.2
Setting Cubase as the slave.

In the Synchronization dialog box	
Timecode Base	MIDI Timecode or ASIO 2.0 if your sound card and external device supports it (consult your sound card's and hardware's documentation to verify).
From Input	Select the MIDI input port that will contain the MTC format.
Frame Rate	Select the source frame rate coming from the master device.
Tempo Base	Intern
MIDI Timecode	Select the appropriate MIDI output port if you wish to transmit the timecode to another device.
In the Audio System Setup dialog box	
Audio Clock	Internal sync, unless you have a stable Digital Clock coming in and you wish to transfer digital audio as well as stay in sync with picture (if you are working with video).
MIDI Sync Reference	Audio Clock—unless you have only MIDI events and feel that the MIDI is not perfectly in time, in which case, select Time Code. If you have audio events, only the MIDI will follow the MTC's timing, but the audio will continue following its own timing. If you set the audio clock to follow an external clock, such as Word Clock, then the MIDI will follow the audio Word Clock as well, thus leaving this to Audio Clock
Connections	
MIDI	Make sure your MIDI output carrying the MTC is hooked up to the MIDI input device slaving Cubase to the MTC signal and set your master device to send an external sync to an MTC, LTC, or VITC connection. If you are using LTC or VITC, you will need to have the appropriate converter box that will understand and convert the signal in order for Cubase to handle it.
Word Clock	If your sound card has a Word Clock or S/PDIF input, hook it up to the Word Clock or S/PDIF output of the master device. Note that to be referenced to this signal, you will need both Digital Clock and timecode to correspond.

Slaving Cubase to an external timecode, as you can see, can create shifts between the MIDI events and the audio events, depending on the way the timecode reference is received and interpreted by Cubase. This is why it is recommended that you always use the same sync reference throughout your project. One way of avoiding drifts between MIDI and audio when synchronizing to an external sync signal is to use a single source for both. This comes in the form of a house sync device, which controls all devices and sends the same MTC, VITC, LTC, and Word Clock information to these devices. But if you don't have the need for this level of synchronizing precision, using the above settings will do fine.

http://www.muskalipman.com

Cubase and Another MIDI Device

Tables 12.3 and 12.4 summarize how to synchronize Cubase and another MIDI device.

Table 12.3
Setting Cubase as the master.

In the Synchronization dialog box	
Timecode Base	Intern
Frame Rate	Desired Frame Rate
Tempo Base	Intern
MIDI Clock	Select the appropriate MIDI output port.
In the Audio System Setup dialog box	
Audio Clock	Internal
MIDI Sync Reference	Audio Clock
Connections	
MIDI	Make sure your MIDI output carrying the MIDI Clock is hooked up to the MIDI input device slaved to this clock and set it to external sync.

Table 12.4
Setting Cubase as the slave.

In the Synchronization dialog box	
Timecode Base	Intern
Frame Rate	Select the source frame rate coming from the master device
Tempo Base	MIDI Clock (or ASIO 2.0, if the external device and your sound card supports it)
From Input	Select the appropriate MIDI Input port, which will receive the MIDI Clock information.
MIDI Clock	Select the appropriate MIDI output port if you wish to transmit the MIDI Clock to another device.
In the Audio System Setup dialog box	
Audio Clock	Internal
MIDI Sync Reference	Audio Clock
Connections	
MIDI	Make sure the MIDI output carrying the MIDI Clock is hooked up to the MIDI Input device slaving Cubase to this signal, and set your master device to send an external sync to this connection.

http://www.muskalipman.com

Cubase and MMC

MIDI Machine Control, or MMC, is a standard set of MIDI System Exclusive extensions that allow Cubase to follow analog tape recorders or other MMC-compatible devices. It allows you to send transport controls and record ready commands to a tape device from within Cubase. Then, once the tape machine receives these commands, it starts playing, sending the MTC timecode to Cubase and slaving Cubase to this timecode.

When using MMC-compatible devices, such as multitrack tape recorders, you will need to have a track containing SMPTE that can be converted into MTC and sent through its MIDI output when you want to slave Cubase or a MIDI In/Out connection to receive MIDI commands if Cubase is the master. In return, Cubase will send transport controls and record ready messages through the MIDI input port of this device when it is slaved to it.

Before you set up the Synchronization dialog box, you should make sure that the System Exclusive messages are not echoed back along the MIDI output port of your computer (going back to the MIDI input of the external devices). To do this, select Options > MIDI Setup > Filtering and uncheck the SysEx box in the Thru section, as shown in Figure 12.3.

Figure 12.3
The MIDI Filtering setup dialog box.

Table 12.5 summarizes how to set up Cubase when working with MIDI Machine Control.

Table 12.5
Setting up Cubase to work with MMC.

In the Synchronization dialog box	
Timecode Base	MMC (or ASIO 2.0/MMC if both your devices comply to this protocol)
From Input	Select the appropriate MIDI input port to receive the timecode information.
Output	Select the appropriate MIDI output port to send MMC commands to the external device.
Frame Rate	Select the source frame rate coming from the master device (in this case, an external device such as a tape recorder).
Tempo Base	Intern
From Input	Select the appropriate MIDI input port, which will receive the MIDI Clock information.
MIDI Clock and MIDI Timecode	Select the appropriate MIDI output port if you wish to transmit the MTC to another device.
In the Audio System Setup dialog box	
Audio Clock	Internal
MIDI Sync Reference	Audio Clock

Before proceeding, you should set the Song Start (as previously indicated) to match the location where the song on your tape begins, so that Cubase's start position (by default, 1.1.000) corresponds to the same location on the tape.

Once you have done the setup, press Play on your external device so that Cubase can read the timecode coming in and know this device's position in relation to timecode (basically reading the timecode to find out its value). Stop the external device once Cubase has read the timecode. Now, position your cursor in Cubase to the location where you want to start playback and press Play on Cubase's Transport bar. The device should relocate (rewind or fast-forward, depending on the location of the tape) and start playback. Once Cubase reads the timecode, it will start playing in sync.

If you plan to use this setup often, you can utilize a DEF.ALL or DEF.SET file to save your setting so that the next time you load Cubase, it will automatically be configured to work with this external device. Remember to always hit Play on the external device when you start a new session so that Cubase knows where this device is in reference to where Cubase wants it to be.

Now, that takes care of the transport controls. Let us look at how you can set up Cubase to tell this device which track it should enable for recording. To do this, you will have to create tape tracks in Cubase.

http://www.muskalipman.com

324 Working in Sync – Chapter 12

To enable recording on an external device using MMC:

1. In the Arrange window, create a new track.
2. Change the track's class for this new track to tape track by clicking in the "C" column in the Track List view of the Arrange window and selecting tape track from the pop-up menu.
3. Now that you have created one tape track, you can create as many as you wish. Typically, if you have a 16-track recorder, for example, you would create fifteen new tracks—keeping the track containing the timecode information free from harm's way. You don't want to be able to record over this one, since you need it for MMC. Once you have created one tape track, you can double-click below the last track you created to add a new track of the same track class.
4. Assign a different track channel number to each track. This is how Cubase will tell the external tape recorder to record enable Track 5, rather than Track 2, for example.
5. Select Options > Multirecord > Active to activate the multirecording for your external device. This will allow you to set more than one track at a time for recording. This will reveal an additional column with the header "R" for record-ready.
6. Click in the R column next to the tracks you wish to arm for recording (set as record ready).

   You can see in Figure 12.4 that tracks for channels one through three have been enabled. Note also that parts will appear in the Track View area to the right, indicating where recordings have been made. These parts do not contain any information, since when you are recording, you are not recording in Cubase but, in this case, on the external tape device. These parts simply serve as a visual reference to know when and where a recording started or ended.

Figure 12.4
Preparing tape tracks for recording when using MMC synchronization.

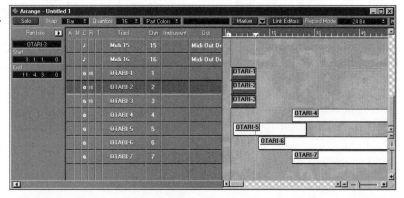

7. Press Record on Cubase's Transport bar when you are ready to record.

http://www.muskalipman.com

The rest is like recording any other track. You can create punch-ins and punch-outs using the Cycle Recording capabilities of Cubase, but unlike when you are using this in Cubase, you will have to wait until the physical tape rewinds and starts playing again so that Cubase locks to its time code.

Hitpoints

Hitpoints are markers that you can use to align time-related material with meter values in your arrangement. You can use hitpoints to find the right tempo for a score when working on a video project by defining key scene changes in the video, then aligning them with bars and beats in your arrangement. You can also use hitpoints to restore lost synchronizing tracks or match live music with the tempo of your arrangement, defining once again significant moments in the music and have them match up with a tempo track in the Graphic Master Track editor.

There are two types of hitpoints: Time hitpoints and Meter hitpoints. The Meter hitpoints can be found in the upper part of the Graphic Master Track editor just below the Meter Ruler bar, and the Time hitpoints in the lower part above the Time ruler (in timecode format) of the same editor, as shown in Figure 12.5. You would add Meter hitpoints to define specific locations in the Meter display, which are music or MIDI related, and you would add Time hitpoints to define specific locations in the Time display, which are video (image) related if you are working with video or audio related if you are using hitpoints to align MIDI events and audio events. An example of this would be to try to fit musical changes to happen at bar changes when a scene changes. So, in this example, a scene would change at the end of a bar, thus avoiding an awkward ending to a musical cue in a video. Another example of this would be to find a tempo from an audio file to match with the MIDI tempo inside Cubase so that they align and play in sync.

You can look at it this way: A musician can add markers to identify changes in musical sections such as chorus, verse, break, solo, and so on. In this case, these markers are referred to as Meter hitpoints. A video editor, on the other hand, would add markers to identify where a scene changes rooms, going from an inside shot of a hall to an outside shot and then to a car shot, for example. In this case, these would be referred to as Time hitpoints. Musicians therefore have a tool that will allow them to automatically find the right tempo so that the changes in scenes match the changes in music—this is what aligning hitpoints is all about.

Figure 12.5
The Graphic Master Track displaying the Meter and Time hitpoints.

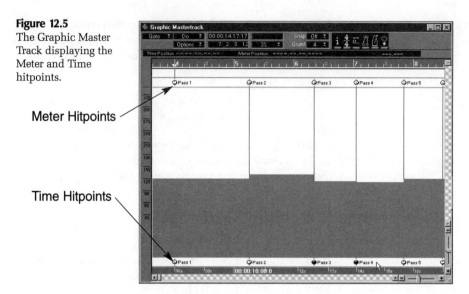

Before talking about hitpoints and how to use them, let me introduce Graphic Master Track's toolbar so that you will know where to click and what each button and menu does.

About the Master Track Editor

First, you can launch the Graphic Master Track Editing window in one of three ways: double-click the Master button in the Transport bar, select it from the Edit menu, or use the keyboard shortcut Ctrl+M. This will open the window, as shown in Figure 12.5.

This window is divided into eight rows of information. From top to bottom:

- The **toolbar** displays a list of menus and buttons as in any other editing window.
- The **Information Line** (starting with the Time Position information field) displays, when active, information on selected hitpoints.
- The **Meter Ruler**, which is always visible, shows time in bars and beats.
- The **Time Signature Strip** displays, when active, the time signature changes in your arrangement.
- The **Meter Hitpoint Strip** displays, when active, the Meter hitpoints and the names for the hitpoints you add to the arrangement.
- The **Tempo display**, which is always visible, shows the tempo changes or tempo setting for your active arrangement.

▶ The **Time Hitpoint Strip**, when active, shows the Time hitpoints and the names for the hitpoints you add to the arrangement.

▶ The **Time Ruler** displays, when active, the time in hours, minutes, seconds, and frames format.

The toolbar offers a couple of menus that you will recognize, such as the Goto, Do, Options, Time Display, Bar and Beat Display, Snap, and Quantize values. To the right of the time display, you will find a field that tells you the bpm value of the current location of your cursor. Below this is a tolerance field, which you will use when you are trying to match Meter and Time hitpoints.

Besides the Snap and Quantize values, you will find a set of six buttons. The first button on the left is the Information Line button that you can use to display or hide the Info Line mentioned above. The second button will display or hide the Time Signature Strip. The third displays or hides the Time Ruler at the bottom of your editor. The fourth shows or hides the Hitpoints Strips, for both Meter and Time. The fifth is a toggle button. When active, it displays the Meter Ruler using linear spacing between each value, making each bar equal, even if you add a tempo change. If the button is off (deactivated), it will display the Time Ruler in linear mode, making each second appear as equal length. You can see in Figure 12.6 that the top part is displayed in equal meter length and the bottom part is displayed in equal time length when you look at rulers above and below the tempo change slope. You can notice the changes in this figure by looking at the gray events, which represent tempo changes, and both Time and Meter Rulers as they display information differently, depending on the active meter display mode.

Figure 12.6
Changing the way rulers are displayed using the Ruler Display button.

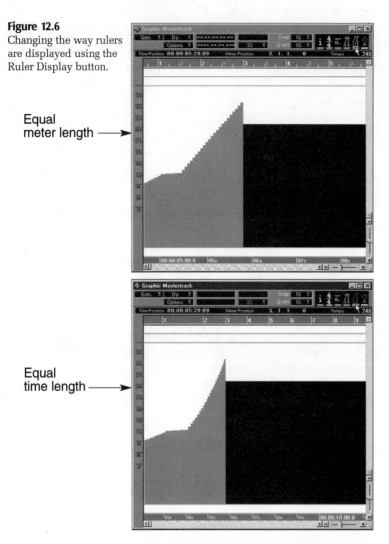

Equal meter length ⟶

Equal time length ⟶

The last button on the toolbar is the MIDI In button, which acts like the Step Record button in the Key and Drum editing windows. You can use this button to insert hitpoints at desired locations with your MIDI keyboard controller. When this button is active and the Graphic Master Track window is also active (on top), playing notes on your keyboard will add Time hitpoints at the location of that cursor (playback line). You don't need to be in Play or Record mode for this to work. Simply position your play cursor at the desired location—or start the external timecode if you are locked with a video—and press any key on your controller keyboard when you want to add a hitpoint. The MIDI keyboard in this case acts as a hitpoint input device.

Working with Hitpoints

The idea behind hitpoints is that you link both types of hitpoints together (Time and Meter). When a line linking them together is straight and full, they are aligned to a specific meter value change such as a beat or a bar. When the line is at an angle and it appears dashed, the moment in time the hitpoint occurs does not correspond to the appropriate meter position. Another concept when using hitpoints is the concept of matching hitpoints to meter points and aligning them by adjusting the tempo in the editing window. Here are some basic operations that you will need to know when working with hitpoints.

- **To add a hitpoint**—Use the Pencil tool and click in the Time Hitpoint Strip where you wish to add it. As discussed earlier, you can also use your MIDI keyboard to add hitpoints at your playback cursor's current location. If you were trying to align an audio file with MIDI events, you could use keys to tap in a drum beat found in this audio file, for example.

- **To rename a hitpoint**—Select it using your Pointer tool (right-click and select it from the toolbox), then double-click on its name in the Information Line. If you don't see the Info line, click the Info button to display it. When the name of the hitpoint is highlighted, type the new name for it.

- **To move or copy a hitpoint**—Click and drag it to its new location using the Pointer tool. To make a copy, keep the Alt key pressed as you move it. You can also select it and edit its position in the Info line.

- **To delete a hitpoint**—Select it with the Pointer tool and press Delete on your keyboard

- **To select multiple hitpoints**—With your Pointer tool, click before the first hitpoint you want to select in the Time Hitpoint ruler and drag your mouse to draw a box over all the desired hitpoints. A selected hitpoint appears black, and when not selected, it should be white.

- **To add a series of hitpoints between the left and right locators, evenly spaced to the Snap value**—Position your left and right locators and then select the Fill option from the Do menu.

- **To add a mirror image of your Time hitpoints on your Meter Hitpoint ruler**—Select the hitpoint and then the Mirror option from the Do menu. This will create a copy of a hitpoint in the opposing hitpoint ruler. For example, selecting a Time hitpoint and mirroring it will create a Meter hitpoint right above it with the same name. This will be used later when you want to align Meter and Time hitpoints.

- **To quantize Meter hitpoints**—Select them, change your Quantize field to the desired value, and press Q or select Quantize from the Functions menu. Note that you can quantize only Meter hitpoints, not Time hitpoints. Once your Meter hitpoints are quantized, the Time hitpoints will align to the correct significant meter values when they are matched together. If you are trying to align MIDI tempo to prerecorded audio, for example, a hitpoint at Beat 2 of Bar 17 in the audio must link to precisely that position on the meter scale.

▶ **To hear MIDI notes when Time and Meter hitpoints occur**—Select Hitpoint Click from the Do menu. A Hitpoint Click dialog box will appear (see Figure 12.7), displaying options for these click sounds. You can set a different note for the Meter and Time hitpoints. This can be useful to verify if the hitpoints are placed at the correct location and also to verify their correlation with one another.

Figure 12.7
The Hitpoint Click dialog box.

Linking Hitpoints

When you are working with music for film or video, you need to have musical elements change at specific locations. Sometimes, making these changes coincide with bars and beats can be challenging and involve hours of calculations. That's why you would use linked hitpoints: to see how they relate to one another. This is how it works.

Once your arrangement is synchronized with the video using the Synchronization dialog box and you have activated the Master Track button in the Transport bar, you can do as follows:

1. In the Master Track window, set an approximate tempo value for your arrangement. It doesn't have to be precise, but setting the value here will help later and make the matching process work better. So, let's say you have a slow romantic scene to score, and a 72 bpm tempo is what you had in mind. Using the Pencil tool, you can move the tempo line to this specific tempo, or double-click on the tempo area to select it and then double-click in the Tempo field found in the Info bar to enter the numeric value for the tempo (in this case, 72).

2. Double-click the Synchronization button on the Transport bar to open the Synchronization dialog box.

3. In the Synchronization dialog box, set the Offsets field so that the beginning of your musical cue begins at bar one, beat one (1.1.000).

4. Once your settings are done, close the Synchronization dialog box and go back to the Graphic Master Track window.

5. Enable the MIDI In button to record your Time hitpoints where important visual cues occur.

6. If you have slaved Cubase to an external video, start the playback of this video and hit a MIDI key on your keyboard to enter these Time hitpoints. When done, stop the video and go to the beginning of the sequence.

7. Enable the MIDI Hitpoint playback as described earlier and start playback once again from your video to see if the Time hitpoints coincide properly. Make the necessary adjustments to your hitpoints by moving them in time or deleting unwanted hits.
8. Rename your hitpoints if you wish to give them significant names. To rename a hitpoint, select it and double-click its name in the Information Line, and then type the new name.
9. Adjust the Snap setting in your Master Track toolbar. This will determine how the hitpoints should match with the Meter Ruler. For example, if you don't want to have cues (or Time hitpoints) arriving at eighth notes, set your Snap value to quarter notes, half notes, or bars.
10. Select the Time hitpoints in the Time Hitpoint Strip as described earlier.
11. From the Do menu, select the Mirror and Link Hitpoints option. This will create a mirror image of the hitpoints you have just created in the Meter Hitpoint Strip.
12. In the Options menu, make sure the Show Hitpoint Links option is selected to see the links.

There are two types of lines going from the Time to Meter hitpoints: Links and Match lines. Use links when you want the Time hitpoint to be linked with a specific Meter hitpoint. The Match lines show where the Time hitpoints occur in relation to the Meter hitpoints. They are not necessarily linked to any Meter hitpoints.

Your Time and Meter hitpoints are now linked and ready to be aligned. You can also link Time hitpoints to Meter hitpoints manually. To do this, you would start the same way that was just described, creating Time hitpoints. Then you would create Meter hitpoints where you wanted them to occur by clicking in the Meter Hitpoints Strip with the Pencil tool, renaming them if needed. Once both hitpoints are created, select the Arrow tool from the toolbox, click on your Time hitpoint, and drag your mouse over the Meter hitpoint where you want to link this hitpoint. When the Meter hitpoint becomes black, it means that it is selected. If you don't see the link line after this, select the Show Hitpoint Links from the Options menu in the toolbar. Figure 12.8 shows what happens when you drag a line from one hitpoint to another.

You can also use the Mirror and Link option found in the Do menu. Select the Time hitpoints you wish to mirror and select Mirror and Link Hitpoints from this menu (Do). Don't use this method if you have already placed Meter hitpoints in your Meter Hitpoint Strip. This would add more hitpoints to this strip. Once you have created mirror hitpoints and linked them, you can find a tempo match between them as described in the following header.

Figure 12.8
Manually linking hitpoints together.

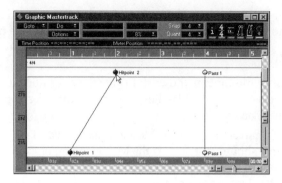

To remove a link between two hitpoints, select the Scissors tool and click and drag your mouse over the link. If you delete a hitpoint, any link that existed up to this hitpoint will be erased as well.

Tempo Matching

You have seen how to link Time and Meter hitpoints. Let's use this to find a tempo that will provide a match between them. Following the steps provided in the previous header, you would then proceed as follows:

1. Move the Meter hitpoints along the Meter Hitpoint Strip and place them where you think this cue should arrive in terms of musical event (which bar and beat). You can quantize Meter hitpoints to make sure that all Meter hitpoints arrive at appropriate Quantize values.

2. Select an appropriate Quantize value.

3. Select the Meter hitpoints you wish to quantize and press Q, or select Quantize from the Functions menu. Now that you have placed your Meter and Time hitpoints along their respective strips, we will proceed to find a matching tempo. If you haven't linked the Meter and Time hitpoints by now, you should do so before proceeding to the next step.

4. Adjust the Tolerance value below the Tempo field in the toolbar. By default, this value is set to 3 percent. This will determine the precision required for a match to be made. A lower value will be more precise but harder to match. Higher values will be easier to match but will be less precise. Start with a small value, increasing it gradually until you are satisfied that you can make matches later by adjusting the tempo.

5. Since this method works best when there are no tempo changes, make sure you don't have any such tempo changes by deleting them if you have inserted any. To delete a tempo change, use the Eraser tool from the toolbox and click on the tempo change.

6. In the Options menu, select Show Hitpoints Match. This will show a dotted line coming up from the Time hitpoint.

7. Switch back to the Pencil tool and click on your tempo line, raising it or lowering it. When a match occurs, the line will become solid, as shown in Figure 12.9. Zoom in vertically (bottom right corner) to have a higher tempo precision.

Working in Sync – Chapter 12   333

Figure 12.9
Adjusting the tempo to find a match between linked hitpoints.

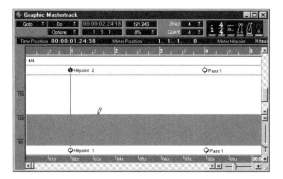

Remember that Match lines from Time hitpoints are not necessarily linked to Meter hitpoints. Figure 12.10 shows the Show Hitpoint Match option on top and the Show Hitpoint Links option on the bottom from the same set of hitpoints.

Figure 12.10
The Show Hitpoint Match (top) and Show Hitpoint Links (bottom).

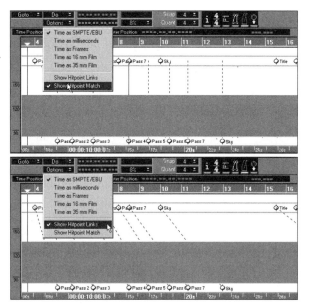

When a Match line becomes solid, you have found a match. Experiment with different Snap values and Tolerance values. If a match occurs but does not correspond to an appropriate Link line, it means that your tempo would be appropriate if the Meter hitpoint were at that Snap value in the Meter Ruler.

http://www.muskalipman.com

If you find this process to be too tedious, you can also use the Auto Tempo Scan option from the Do menu.

1. Lower the tempo using the Pencil tool to the lowest possible value you would be satisfied with.
2. With the Pointer tool, click on the first Time hitpoint you wish to use to determine the tempo.
3. Hold down the Shift key and select other Time hitpoints you would like to use to determine the tempo.
4. With the Shift key still down, click on the tempo value that you wish to adjust, as shown in Figure 12.11.
5. Select the Auto Tempo Scan option from the Do menu in the toolbar (see Figure 12.11).
6. Repeat Step 5 until Cubase finds a tempo with which you are satisfied. Each time you repeat this process, Cubase will raise the tempo to the next best match.

Figure 12.11
Using the Auto Tempo Scan option in the Graphic Mastertrack window.

When using this method, it might happen that not all hitpoints will match properly, depending on the Snap and Tolerance settings. You can then use the Straighten Up function to add tempo changes between hitpoints that don't match at this point. This is described next.

Straightening Up

Straightening Up tempo is a function that automatically calculates the tempo value needed between each linked Meter and Time hitpoint, adding tempo changes to "match" these hitpoints in time. Note that if you have crossed linked hitpoints, Cubase will be unable to straighten them.

To use Straighten Up Hitpoints:

1. Create Time and Meter hitpoints, positioning them to appropriate locations in both your Time and Meter Hitpoint Strips.
2. Link each Time hitpoint to its corresponding Meter hitpoint, as described previously, by dragging a line from the Time hitpoint to the Meter hitpoint.
3. From the Do menu, select Straighten Up Hitpoints.

Cubase will calculate the necessary tempo change needed to straighten up each hitpoint pair and add such a tempo change before the first set of linked hitpoints in the Graphic Master Track window. If Cubase can't find a perfect match, it will leave the link line dotted but will find the best match possible. Figure 12.12 shows the result of this operation.

Figure 12.12
Using the Straighten Up Hitpoints option in the Do menu.

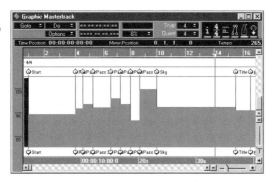

About Time-Locked Tracks

When working with video, you might want to place some sound effects, ambiances, or Foley where and when these events occur on screen. These are timing-sensitive events, not bar-and-beat-sensitive events. Changing the tempo of a song might not change only where a song starts in relation to the video but will also shift all these time-sensitive events with it as well. Locking these events in time will prevent this from happening. So the "big bang" that was supposed to happen at 10:00:03:22 will still occur at 10:00:03:22, even if this was at Bar 5:1:000 before and is now on Bar 3:3:096.

To timelock a track:

1. In the Arrange window, click in the "T" column to add a small lock icon in this track.
2. If you need to move a part in this track, set the Snap value to Off, because this value refers to meter values and timelocked tracks refer to timing values.

Tempo Mapping Locked Tracks

Sometimes you might feel the need to record something without the use of a metronome, freely recording your music on a MIDI track. This will give you freedom over your expression, because you aren't constrained to a static metronome click. The problem arises when you want to edit or add more events and need to make sure everything coincides with meter references. Just imagine trying to record any piano piece from the Romantic period while trying to keep up with the metronome—this would sound much too mechanical and would kill the intent. Recording the MIDI events as you interpret them without the metronome seems like a good idea at this point.

But what if you want to create an arrangement and add other instruments to accompany this piano? That's when adjusting the tempo to match your interpretation and aligning what you played with bars and beats become important. Using Cubase's hitpoints and timelocked tracks, you can extract important information from this freely recorded track and use hitpoints to determine which tempo or tempi should be used to reproduce the piece in sync with bars and beats. Here is how to tempo map freely recorded music on timelocked tracks using hitpoints:

Let us assume that you have already recorded your MIDI performance somewhere on a track.

1. Time-lock this track by clicking the "T" column in the Arrange window's Track List area. If you don't see this column, right-click in the column header section of the window and check the Time Lock option.
2. Double-click on the part to open the Key editor window.
3. Select all MIDI events in the editor and move the first event to the beginning of the sequence at Bar 1, Beat 1 (or as close as possible to have what should be at Bar 1, Beat 1 starting at that location).
4. Select significant events, such as MIDI events that occur on the first beat of each bar, for example. What is important here is that you have events that you know occur on specific meter positions. Use the Shift key simultaneously with the Pointer tool to select more than one event without losing previously selected events.
5. Select Copy from the Edit menu or hit Ctrl+C.
6. Close the Key editor and open the Graphic Master Track editor.
7. Set the Snap and Quantize values to off and position your cursor (playback position) at the beginning of your song (1.1.000).
8. Select Paste from the Edit menu or hit Ctrl+V. This will paste the MIDI events you had selected in the Key editor as Time hitpoints in the Master Track editor.
9. Use the Pencil tool to add a Meter hitpoint for each corresponding Time hitpoint, or select Mirror and Link Hitpoints in the Do menu. If you use this last technique, you will need to reposition all the hitpoints in the Meter Hitpoint Strip to correspond with appropriate references in the Meter Ruler, making sure that a Meter hitpoint placed at Bar 4, Beat 1 is linked to a Time hitpoint that would normally be played at that location had it been recorded using the metronome.
10. Select the Meter hitpoints and change the Quantize field to an appropriate value to quantize your hitpoints if needed, and apply a quantize to them.

11. Link all Time hitpoints to Meter hitpoints if you chose to add Meter hitpoints manually instead of using the Mirror and Link technique.
12. Select Straighten Up Hitpoints from the Do menu to insert tempo changes to your Master Track.

Once you have added these tempo changes, you can further quantize the freely recorded MIDI events so that they match meter values if you wish. But beware—this can destroy the feel of your music. And, having created a tempo map to your freely recorded music, note that applying a quantized rhythmic part against it will sound terrible if the tempo changes are not subtle (passing from 120 bpm to 126 and then back to 112, for example, would not sound good if you have a drum groove).

If you feel that the tempo changes are too abrupt, you can smooth the transition between two or more selected tempo changes by applying the Smooth Tempo option found in the Do menu. This will add transient tempo change values to make the tempo change smoother, but it will also change the link relation as well, because the events will not occur at the same moment in time anymore due to these additional tempo changes.

Working with Online Video Files

As you saw earlier in this chapter, you can synchronize Cubase to work with an external video, but you can also work with a digitized video file in one of two formats: AVI or PC-compatible QuickTime (*.MOV or *.QT) if you are using a PC version of Cubase. This allows you to open a video file on your computer and synchronize audio events to this video file. By default, the video file will always play with its first video frame starting at the first bar and beat (1.1.000) of your arrangement.

To activate the video display and import a video in your arrangement:

1. Select Modules > Setup. This will bring up the Modules Setup dialog box, as shown in Figure 12.13

Figure 12.13
The Modules Setup dialog box.

2. Click under the Active column next to the DS Video Monitor's name to activate the video display window, then click on Exit to accept this selection.
3. Hit select Modules > DS Video Monitor > Open Movie to select the location of a video file on your computer. This will show you the Open Movie dialog box.

4. Select the appropriate movie and click Open. This will open the video file inside Cubase, as displayed in Figure 12.14. This video will start at 1.1.000.

Figure 12.14
The DS Video Monitor displaying the video file at the location of the playback cursor.

If you need to change the offset time (video not starting at 1.1.000):

1. Select Modules > DS Video Monitor > Options. This will display the Options dialog box for the video monitor window.
2. Change the Offset time to the location where you want the video to begin. Note that you cannot set the video to start before 00:00:00:00. So, if your video has a long lead-in, you will not be able to set it up so that the video's actual content begins at Bar 1.1.000.
3. Use this window to set the size of the video display.

If you want this window to always appear when Cubase is opened, you can also click in the Preload column to switch from No to Yes. When you save a song or arrangement that contains a reference to a video file, it will activate the video monitor window anyway, so to avoid using unnecessary memory resources for an empty video display, you can leave the Preload column Off.

In the DS Video Monitor sub-menu, you will also find a few more options:

▶ **Close Movie**—Closes not only the window, but the movie as well. You will need to reopen it if you want to use it later.

▶ **Show/Hide Movie**—A practical alternative to Close Movie, it hides the video monitor window from your display but keeps the link active. Once a movie is hidden, use Show Movie in the same sub-menu to reactivate its display.

▶ **Show/Hide Title Bar**—Displays or hides the window box around the video monitor window's display.

▶ **Deactivate**—Closes the movie and deactivates the video monitor altogether. You will need to reactivate it by going into Modules > Setup.

13
Distributing Your Work

You have worked on your project long enough, and now it's time to mix everything down to two tracks. If you are new to this, first make a CD and have your friends listen to it. Once you have collected enough comments to feel comfortable with the quality of your work, you can start distributing the music you call your own. On the other hand, if you don't feel you need validation from others to know whether what you did sounds great, you can go straight from mixdown to mastering and then to distribution.

This chapter will describe various possibilities involved in mixing down your arrangements into a stereo master mix. Let's take a look at the last steps after you have finished working on the arrangements. For now, just remember these steps—you will read how to do them later in the chapter.

- ▶ Create an audio version of your external MIDI instrument.
- ▶ Touch up your mix to include the newly converted MIDI tracks into audio tracks.
- ▶ Once you are satisfied with the result of this mix, export a mixdown of it in a format that you can use to create a first-draft CD.
- ▶ Listen to this CD in different environments, collect comments, and go back to your project to make any necessary changes.
- ▶ Generate a new mixdown of your material, this time using the highest-quality rendering you can. Since the mastering process is a critical step, as you will see later in this chapter, using the best quality will allow you to get the most out of your sound. If you choose to have someone else do the mastering for you, you can ask the engineer which format and on which medium you should deliver your material.
- ▶ If, on the other hand, you decide to tackle the mastering of your CD yourself, export these files in a format compatible with your audio mastering tool. Again, compatibility is of the essence: If you export your files in a format your audio editing/mastering software does not support, it won't be of much help to you.

http://www.muskalipman.com

▶ Once you are satisfied with your mastering, create a second-draft CD and listen to it again in different environments. Just remember that the source material for an audio format CD (CD-DA) can only be 44.1 kHz, 16-bit, stereo file in either WAV or AIFF format. Once recorded, an audio CD will not display files in WAV or AIFF formats anymore.

▶ At this point, if you need to change something in the mastering, you need to make only slight modifications; otherwise, you are ready to burn copy zero of your CD. This should be done on a high-quality medium and at low speed to avoid the introduction of writing errors on the master copy. There are two acceptable media for master copies of your project: compact disc (CD) and digital audio tape (DAT), both of which contain uncompressed versions of your audio in a format that is accepted in most mastering studios. It is not advisable to use a minidisk or files that are compressed in any shape or form for audio distribution on a medium such as a CD; these formats are lossy-compression algorithms, which implies that you lose sound quality as a result of the compression. However, compressed formats are a must when it comes to Internet distribution.

▶ If you want to distribute your project commercially, you can look for pressing plants or distributors in your area. In the meantime, you can create your own Web site and add demonstration copies of your work in streaming format—or even send invitations to record label A&R people to visit your site and listen to your material.

Including Your MIDI in the Mixdown

MIDI is a great way to lay down ideas and record music using synthesizers (external or sound card based), samplers, and drum machines, among other things. However, distributing your work on a compact disc or through the Internet using MIDI is probably not the greatest solution, because, even with General MIDI standard, the sounds they produce are not necessarily what you had in mind. And for compact discs— well, they just don't support MIDI. VST Instruments and Rewire instruments are also MIDI based, so they, too, don't work well outside the VST environment. This is why you need to convert your MIDI events into audio events when you are satisfied that the tracks are what you want. In the next couple of sections, you will see how to do this. Note that if you are using sounds generated by a synthesizer, wave table, or any other sound-generating device found on your sound card, or if you are using any software-based samplers that are not VSTi or Rewire compatible, you will need to convert them into audio files to include them in your final audio mix.

Converting Your MIDI Tracks

There are a few ways you can approach the task of converting MIDI files to audio files: the simple way, the multitrack way, and the sample-based way.

The simple way involves mixing all your MIDI events using the MIDI Track Mixer and recording a stereo mix of all MIDI events as a stereo audio file that you then place on an audio track in Cubase.

The multitrack way involves recording each MIDI instrument as a separate audio file, mono or stereo, depending on the instrument itself. Later, you can treat these instruments the same way you would any other audio track in Cubase, using the VST Channel Mixer to adjust the effects and mixing levels. In both of these methods, the recording starts where the MIDI events start on a track, recording them as you would record any instrument.

In the sample-based method, you proceed in the same way, but to use space efficiently, you record only the parts that are different, then copy these parts on the tracks, as you would do for a drum. For example, if the bass line of a verse remains the same for the first eight bars, then changes for the second eight bars of each verse, you would record the first eight bars, copy it across the track, and then record the second eight bars for the remainder of the verses. Which method you use is entirely up to you and involves the same procedure with different levels of manipulations.

The following procedure describes how to convert MIDI tracks playing external MIDI devices—not VSTi or Rewire instruments. For VSTi or Rewire, skip to the next section.

1. Start by turning the MIDI metronome off, especially if the same device you are using to record generates this.

2. Mute all your audio tracks and create an empty stereo (or mono) audio track. If you have a multi-input sound card AND a mixer with multiple output buses, you can record more than one track at a time if you are recording your MIDI tracks on separate audio tracks. Just make sure to read Step 4 carefully to avoid having feedback loops.

3. Set up your MIDI tracks to play *only* the events (tracks) that send MIDI information to external events, muting all other tracks and unmuting the tracks you wish to record. You can use the Solo button to quickly isolate a specific track for recording.

4. Connect the outputs of your MIDI devices to the inputs of your sound card. If you have an external mixer, send the output of your mixer into the inputs of your sound card, making sure NOT to include the output of your sound card in the mix. This can be done in different ways, depending on your mixer capabilities. For example, if you have buses, assign all your MIDI devices to the bus or buses you are sending to the stereo input(s) of your sound card; make sure that the output of that sound card is sent only to your monitoring system, not to those same buses. If your mixer does not have a busing system, mute the inputs of your mixer corresponding to the outputs of your sound card. This way, you won't have a feedback loop. You may want to consult your sound card's manual to find out how to route the output of the sound card back into the input internally, using the sound card's mixer application if you are using the audio outputs as sound generators for your VSTi and Rewire instruments.

5. Activate the inputs for the audio channels on which you wish to record the MIDI events and start the playback to adjust the input level. If you are using the VST Score or VST/32 version, you may also activate the VST TrueTape module to add saturation to your MIDI devices once converted to audio material. It is important to keep the same resolution for all material in the arrangement.

6. Once you are satisfied with the input levels, position your playback line at the beginning of the MIDI event(s) you wish to record.

7. Start the recording of your MIDI events as audio events.

8. If you need to repeat the recording process, repeat steps 2 through 7 before every recording and mute the previously recorded MIDI and audio tracks, creating new tracks for every recording.

9. If you choose to use the sample-based technique, you will need to place the newly recorded parts at their proper location on each track.

At this point, you can mute all your MIDI tracks and listen to your newly created audio tracks. Because there might be volume changes between the original MIDI tracks and the audio tracks, you will probably want to adjust their levels using the automation in the VST Channel Mixer. You may also assign Insert or Send effects and adjust the EQ and dynamic processing for these tracks before moving on to the final mixdown of all these tracks.

About VSTi and Rewire Channels

Because VSTi and Rewire channels exist within the Cubase VST Channel Mixer, they will be included in the audio mixdown when the Export Audio function is used. Just remember to unmute these tracks if you want to include them in the mixdown file; otherwise, they will not be included in your exported audio file.

About Dithering

When you are recording material in Cubase VST, if your system allows it, you should be saving your audio data in 24-bit, or even 32-bit, resolution. This gives you the most dynamic range and the highest signal-to-noise ratio, which is the level of the noise with no signal applied, expressed in dB below a maximum level. As you saw in Chapter 1, this ratio is around 146 dB in a 24-bit recording, and 194 dB in a 32-bit recording. This suggests that when you record a sound using 32-bit resolution, your noise floor is at −194 dB. This is virtually inaudible and is negligible by any standards. Unfortunately, when you mixdown to transfer to a 16-bit DAT recorder, or want to record it on a CD for compact disc players, you need to bring this precision down to 16-bit.

There are two methods used to accomplish this: Truncating and Dithering. Truncating simply cuts the lower part of the digital word that exceeds the 16-bit word length. Here's an example: If you have a sample that would be stored in 24-bit, it would look like this:

1110 0111 1100 0111 0011 1100

Now, if this sample were truncated to 16-bit, it would look like this:

1110 0111 1100 0111

What happened is that the last eight digits were cut off. These last eight digits are often reverb trails dying in the noise or harmonics of instruments at low-level intensities. Cutting them off usually adds what is known as quantizing errors. This quantizing error sounds unnatural.

The solution is to add a special kind of random noise to the sound when you need to bring down the resolution. This random noise is dither noise. What it does, in reality, is to change the last bit in a 16-bit word randomly, creating a noise at −98 dB, which is pretty low. But this noise is low enough to perceive sounds at −115 dB. Dithering is not needed when you are working in a 24-bit or 32-bit environment. So keep this for the end. But when you do use it, this is how it works:

1. Launch your VST Master Mixer by selecting it from the Panels menu, or press Ctrl+Numeric Keypad + sign.
2. Activate the dither noise by clicking the On button, as shown in Figure 13.1.

Figure 13.1
Activating the Dither module from the VST Master Mixer window in Cubase VST/32. In Cubase VST and VST/Score, it simply says "Dither" rather than showing the UV22 icon.

Cubase VST/32 comes with an advanced dithering algorithm called UV-22, which was developed by Apogee. In Cubase VST and VST Score, you will have a standard dithering algorithm.

3. If you wish to edit the dithering settings, click the Edit button next to the On button.

   This will bring up one of two panels, depending on whether you are in VST, Score, or VST/32. In both panels, the dithering window appears as Master Effect 5, since it is inserted after all other processes.

   In VST and Score, you will have three options: Dithering type selection, Noise shaping, and Dither Bits. The Dithering Type 1 is the default setting for this parameter. Selecting Type 2 would simply emphasize the high frequencies more than the Type 2. The Noise Shape selection allows you to adjust the actual shape of the noise being added, and moving to higher settings would result in less noticeable noise added in the midrange frequencies where they are more apparent to the human ear. Try changing this setting and listen to the result that is most satisfying to you. Select the Dither Bit resolution for the final mix. If you intend to save the file as a CD-compatible digital audio format, choose 16 bits.

   In the VST/32 version (see Figure 13.2), you have only two choices. Selecting the Normal or Low buttons will toggle between a standard noise shape and a low-level noise shape. The second button, called AutoBlack, will automatically gate (mute) the dither noise when the audio is silent. You should leave this on for better results. This dither algorithm will always be at a 16-bit resolution.

Figure 13.2
The Apogee Dither editing window in Cubase VST/32.

4. Make the necessary adjustments in the Dither window if needed and close the window.

With this option selected, you are now ready to export your mix to an audio file.

Exporting Your Final Mix

Once you are satisfied with your mix and would like to render a final mixdown, or simply render a selection or a track containing effects or a VSTi or Rewire track or tracks, you can use the Export Audio Tracks function found in File > Export > Audio Tracks, or click the Export button found in the VST Master Mixer window. This function will not export MIDI tracks, but it will export VSTi and Rewire channels, so the following steps will assume that you have already converted your MIDI tracks into audio tracks.

To export your final mix as an audio file:

1. Mute the tracks you don't wish to include in your audio mix.

2. Position your left locator where you want to begin the audio mix and the right locator where you want to end the audio mix. If you wish to export only selected audio, Rewire, or VSTi parts as separate audio files, select these parts. If you want to export a range, use the Selection Range tool in the Arrange window to make the selection.

3. If you don't want to export the automation or effects when rendering either type of mixdown (between locators, selected parts, or selected range), turn the VST Channel Mixer's Read button off and set any other effect to Bypass or Off. If you do want to record these events, make sure they are on. Basically, set Cubase up so that you hear what you want to export. Note that if you decide to export selected parts, other nonselected parts will not be included in the audio export. It is important to make sure the master faders do not clip at any time during playback, since this clipping will cause distortion in your final mixdown. So, make sure that your levels stay below zero at all times.

4. Select File > Export > Audio Tracks or click the Export Audio button found in the VST Master Mixer window. This will bring up the Export Audio dialog box, as shown in Figure 13.3.

Figure 13.3
The Export Audio dialog box.

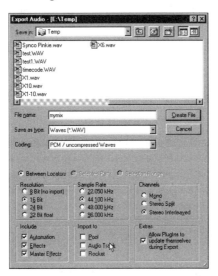

5. In the Export Audio dialog box, choose the proper folder to save the file. By default, this should be the same folder as your song file.
6. Under File Name, enter a name for the file you wish to export.
7. Select the Export mode by choosing one of the three following options: Between Locators, to export the audio between the locators as described above; Selected Parts, to export only the selected parts; or Selected Range, if you have made a selection with the Selection Range tool. Note that if you don't have a part or a range selected, you will have only one option.
8. Choose the resolution, sampling rate, and channel settings you wish to use for your exported file.

   Note that the Stereo Split will create a left and a right mono file rather than a single stereo interleaved file. This might be useful if you need to use this file in another audio application that does not support stereo interleave files, such as Pro Tools.
9. You can choose to include or ignore Automation, Effects, and Master Effects in your exported file. A check in the checkbox indicates that this option will be included when rendering the file. If you have added dithering to your mix, make sure to check the Master Effects option.
10. If you wish to import this file into your Audio Pool, Arrange window in a new track, or as a Rocket Network file (if Rocket Network is activated from the Modules menu), check the appropriate options.
11. If you have assigned program changes and automation for VSTi and VST effects and want to include them in your export, check the option under Extra.
12. Select the appropriate Save As Type and Coding settings (available with WAVE type) that you want to use for this file in the appropriate fields. For other formats, please consult the section "Exporting Formats" later in this chapter.
13. Make sure that all tracks that are supposed to be included in the mix are unmuted and routed to the Master output.
14. Click Create File when done.

If you have checked the Import to Audio Track option and had not previously selected an empty audio track, Cubase will simply create a new audio track and name it Mixdown. If you had selected a mono track, and the exported track is stereo, Cubase will also create a new track for you, since it can't put stereo content on a mono track, and vice versa.

Once the newly created track is in place, make sure to mute the source tracks for this new track (containing the audio mixdown). If you have chosen not to import the audio rendering of your mix back into your arrangement, you can proceed with your work as usual, continuing whatever work needs to be done, or save and close your song or arrangement and start working on the mastering of your album, as will be discussed later.

Exporting Formats

You can export your final mix in two different lossless formats: WAV and AIFF. These formats are standard and are compatible with both Mac and PC, not to mention that you must have your files in either of these formats to create an audio CD. But you will need to leave the WAV format at its default "PCM/uncompressed Waves" format if you want to import it back into your arrangement.

The Internet—more specifically, the World Wide Web—has been quite helpful to musicians in allowing them to publish their material online and use it as an effective distribution medium and a way to promote their skills. This is one of the reasons why other Web-related exporting formats are now available and are considered standards in the industry. Among those, Cubase supports Real Networks' RealMedia format and MP3 format (from MPEG Layer 3). A few other formats are available—QuickTime and Windows Media Format are just two other examples—but these formats were not supported at the time this book was written.

Since these formats were developed with the Web in mind, they make it easy to stream or distribute content over a low bandwidth system. As a result, a certain amount of data compression is applied to these file formats. The more you compress the files, the smaller they are, and this is also directly related to sound quality: The smaller the file, the worse the sound quality. All these compression algorithms are lossy, meaning that they will remove data from the original file when saving it into this new format, and by doing so, they will be reducing sound quality as well. It is important to understand at this point that there is a big difference between data compression, which is used to compress the size of a file, and dynamic compression, which is used to control the dynamics of the audio signal. Dynamic compression does not influence the size of the file. You will have to experiment with this and find a compromise that you are comfortable with. Keeping this in mind, remember the following: There are more people using 56K modems to download and listen to music than there are people with high-speed access. This is changing rapidly, but until that time arrives, make sure your potential customers will not be discouraged by the size of your files.

The following sections will describe particularities related to both RealMedia and MP3 format conversion when exporting your files for Web distribution.

Real Networks

Real Networks was one of the first companies to develop an algorithm to compress and deliver audio and video files over the Internet using a streaming technology. Today, Real Networks remains one of the leaders in this field, and its RealMedia formats have become one of the most popular streaming standards for distribution of audio and video content over the World Wide Web.

The principle behind streaming technology is the same, no matter which format you use. The idea is to have a file, which is compressed to a user specification, and have this compressed file available to others over the Net. What makes streaming "streaming" is that this file is associated with a compatible player on your computer. When you click on the link to this file, it loads the player into memory. This player then starts playing the content as it arrives, rather than waiting for it to be completely downloaded, thus reducing the waiting period before a user can listen to it.

For this to work properly, a go-between file is often created (see Figure 13.4). This is commonly known as a metafile. This metafile contains a simple piece of information: the location of the media file itself. Because a metafile is so small, it is downloaded quickly. Once it is downloaded, the player loads into memory and reads the address, telling the server to start sending packets of data, which it stores in a buffer memory. When the buffer memory is filled up, it starts playing. The time it takes to fill up this buffer memory depends on the connection speed a user has, the connection speed of the server, the amount of traffic over the Internet at that moment, and the size of the media file. For example, filling the buffer for a 100 KB file will be quicker than if the file is 100 MB. But once this buffer is loaded, the file begins to play while your Internet connection stays active, continuing the transfer of the rest of the information for this file.

Figure 13.4
How information flows as streaming media over the Internet.

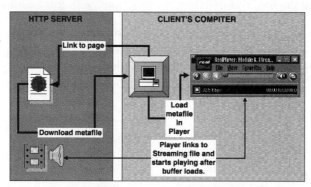

Now that you understand the basics about how streaming works, you'll understand how the settings in the Export audio window under the Real Networks (RealPlayer) format works and also what effect they would have from the end-user point of view.

To export a file for RealPlayer compatibility, you would proceed in the same way as for any other type of file (as described earlier in this chapter) until you reach the format of the file you wish to export. From there, you would proceed as follows.

1. Next to the Save As Type field, select RealAudio (*.RM) as your file type.
2. Next to the Coding field, select the appropriate format for your content.

    Remember that the compression you apply here will influence both the file size and the quality of the end result. If you were targeting the general public, then using a 32 Kbps (kilobits per second) format would be more suitable. On the other hand, if you are targeting people with access to a high bandwidth, such as businesses or other users who you know are using a faster connection, you can select a higher bit rate. Make sure to select the bit rate and the appropriate type of compression: If you have music, you should use the Mono or Stereo Music presets. However, if you have mostly voice content with no music, use the Voice presets. The Real Networks codec will treat those two types of audio information in a very different way, so making the right selection here is paramount.

    If your content is both musical and vocal, go for the music presets. Also, choosing mono music over stereo music will add definition, as it uses the additional space to allow a wider range of frequencies. The stereo music will be encoded in stereo and offer a stereo image, but with fewer high frequencies, because they are reduced to allow for the stereo information to fit into the same amount of bits per second.

    Finally, below the Coding field, you will see an information box telling you what this RealPlayer preset is most appropriate for, such as the example in Figure 13.5, where the 32 Kbps Music Stereo preset has been chosen.

Figure 13.5
The RealPlayer options in the Export Audio dialog box.

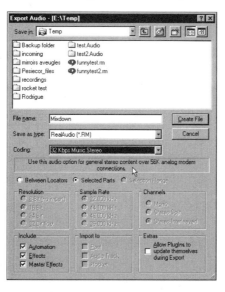

3. Click the Create File button when all of your settings are done in this window. This will bring up the RealAudio Settings dialog box.

4. Enter the appropriate title, author, and copyright information for your song. This information will appear in the user's Player window when a file is being played.

5. Check the Perfect Play option if you want to allow users to download the file for perfect playback instead of streaming it directly from the Internet. This would allow them to receive a better-sounding file.

6. The Selective Record option will give the user permission to record the file as it is being played. Again, if you allow this, users will be able to keep a copy of your music on their computers.

7. The Mobile Play options will allow users to download the file even if they don't have a RealPlayer installed on their system.

8. Click OK to start the compression process. This can take several minutes if your song is long.

MP3

MP3 files are similar to RealAudio files in that they are meant to be sent over the Internet and then played on a computer. This format has changed the face of audio distribution, allowing for high-compression algorithms that reduce file sizes without significantly compromising audio quality when you use higher bit rates.

This said, Cubase would allow you to save in MP3 format with a bit rate of up to 56 Kbps. You can purchase an MP3 plug-in on Steinberg's Web site to get more bit rates (up to 320 Kbps). As with RealAudio, the smaller the files, the lower the quality. Compare this as an example: The compact disc standard of 44.1 kHz, 16-bit, stereo in WAV format uses a bandwidth of 172.3 Kilobytes per second, whereas an MP3 file compressed at 320 Kbps (the highest quality available with the MP3 plug-in from Steinberg) uses only 39 Kbps of bandwidth. This is because a one-minute file in WAV or AIFF CD-compatible (44.1 kHz, 16-bit, stereo) format uses 10.09 MB of disc space, whereas the MP3 file at 320 Kbps uses only 2.29 MB, making it easier to transfer over the Internet. The MP3 standard relies heavily on algorithms to compress the information and on the computer processor to decompress this information as it plays back, as would any other file-compression algorithm (Zip, ARJ, StuffIt, and so on, which are not audio formats but compress the data nonetheless).

As with RealPlayer, you would proceed in the same way as with any other type of file, and as described earlier in this chapter, to compress in MP3. When you reach the format of the file you wish to export, you would proceed as follows:

1. Next to the Save As Type field, select MPEG Layer 3 (*.MP3) as your file type.
2. Next to the Bitrate field, select the appropriate format for your content, as shown in Figure 13.8.

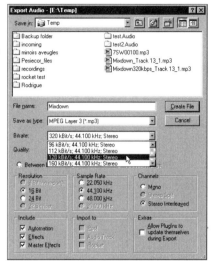

Figure 13.8
Selecting the bitrate for your MP3 files in the Export Audio dialog box.

3. Select from the Quality field the Best option, which will take more time to compress but will yield better results.
4. Click the Create File button when all of your settings are done in this window.
5. The MP3 additional options dialog box will appear. As with RealAudio additional options, this allows you to enter information about the creator of the file. Make the necessary changes and click OK to start generating the file. This can take several minutes if your song is long.

About Mastering

Mastering is the art of subtlety and involves adjusting your final mixes so that they all sound coherent and cohesive when played one after the other. This means that the first mix you did two months ago when you started working on your project will sound as good as the one you created today at 4 a.m. after consuming large amounts of caffeine.

When preparing an album, mastering is a must before pressing your master copy. The process is used to reduce the aforementioned differences between mixes by mastering every song one after another, in a one- to two-day span. This allows you to listen to the songs in the order they will appear on your album and correct the overall harmonic colors and dynamic range.

It is also a good idea to not master your album with the same listening reference you used for the recording and mixing process, since your ears have probably grown accustomed to this sound and might not be as critical to some aspects or coloring. Furthermore, if your monitoring system is adequate at best, you would benefit from a professional mastering facility rather than using a home studio mixing environment. The better equipment would allow you to truly isolate problems concerning consistency between your songs, not to mention provide a fresh pair of ears listening to your project. This can add an untapped dimension to your project, which is especially beneficial if you want to distribute the album commercially. Finally, there will always be a difference in quality between a home studio filled with inexpensive equipment with low-quality components and a quarter-million-dollar mastering facility where every piece of equipment in the room is meant to optimize your sound.

This said, if you don't have the financial resources, or don't feel the need for professional mastering because your project is for small and local distribution only, there are no recipes here and no settings that can apply to every situation. Rather, here are pointers that should help you get the most out of a mastering session. If you are unsure about how your mix sounds, try listening to music that you find is similar in style to what you have done and sounds like you would like your music to sound. Then, see if you can emulate these qualities. Another way of evaluating your mix is by listening to it in different environments—in a car, another room, or at a friend's place. Remember that the fresher your mind and ears are, the better for the mastering process. So, avoid starting a mastering session after a long day of work or after mixing the last song for your CD.

- ▶ Mastering is not where you mix your songs. If you are not satisfied with a mix, you should remix it rather than trying to fix it at the mastering stage.
- ▶ This might be very obvious to most people, but just in case: NEVER master using your headphones as a reference.
- ▶ When exporting your audio mixes in Cubase for the mastering process, use the highest quality available. If you have worked in 96 kHz, 32-bit stereo format and have a reliable system that can reproduce these specifications, go for it. You can always convert your final result after the mastering process to 44.1 kHz, 16-bit stereo format.

- Before you start your mastering session, sit down and listen to all the songs in order with your pencil and notepad at hand. Take notes on inconsistencies between songs.
- Generally, there are two important things that you want to adjust in a mastering session, and this should be kept in mind throughout the entire mastering process of a single album: EQ and dynamics.
- When tweaking the EQ, you are not trying to reinvent the mix, just tweak it. You want to give the bass more definition, add presence to the vocals and crispness to the high-end, and, most of all, make sure that all songs have the same equalization qualities.
- Dynamics give punch and life to a mix. Make sure all your tracks come into play at the same level. This doesn't mean they should all be loud or soft, but they should be consistent with the intensity of the song. If a song is mellow, it can come in softer, but the soft intensity in one song has to be consistent in relation to the soft intensity of another song. As with EQ, consistency is the key.
- There are more and more software packages out there that do a pretty good job at EQing and compressing audio. Steinberg's Clean and Mastering Edition and IK Multimedia's T-Racks are just a few tools you can use to help you get the most out of your home mastering session. You can use either the VST or DirectX effects in the Master Effects section of the VST Master Fader or, as with some of the above-mentioned software, use them as independent mastering tools.

Creating an Audio Compact Disc

Creating your CD is often one of the last things you do before having people outside of your studio environment hear your work. Once you have done an audio mixdown of your MIDI and audio tracks into a premastering file in whatever format you used, then mastered one or more tracks as discussed earlier, you are ready to create a compact disc. That's because your files have been saved and converted into a compact disc-compatible format. Cubase does not offer any tools to actually burn (record) a CD. But Steinberg offers two solutions through Wavelab and "Get It On CD." These are by no means the only tools available. If you purchased a CD recorder, it might have come with a CD recording application. One thing is certain: You will need software capable of creating a CDDA compatible disc (compact disc digital audio).

This brings us to formats. When creating CDs, the two most common types of CDs are CD-ROM and CDDA. CD-ROMs contain data suitable for your computer. CDDA contains audio that is suitable for both your computer and CD player. There are two variations of this: the Enhanced CD and the Mixed Mode CD, which are available in some software and some CD recorders. The Enhanced CD is a multisession CD, containing a series of CDDA-compatible tracks in the first session, making it compatible with your home CD Player, and a second session containing data, which is read by computers only. In Mixed Mode, it's the reverse: The data tracks are at the beginning and the audio tracks follow. This usually means that your CD player will not read it.

http://www.muskalipman.com

This type of CD is used for multimedia content such as games, educational material, or sales presentations. In light of this, understand that you need to select the proper type of CD for creating a CD within the software application. There are a few rules to follow if you want your CD to play back in any CD player.

When recording a CD, there are three aspects that come into play: the format of the CD (CD-ROM, CDDA, Enhanced CD, Mixed Mode, and so on), the session, and the disc. A session is an instance where you decide to write something on a CD. For example, today you decide to record a WAV file onto a CD. You would write a session, and to complete the process, you would close the session in order for the disc to be understood by the CD-ROM drive. A disc is considered closed when you can't record anything else on it and opened when you can add other sessions to it. In our previous example, if you close the session but leave the disc open, you can record another session on it, making it a multisession disc, each time closing the session but leaving the disc opened for another recording. When you wish to close the disc because it is full, you can do so after the last session you record, disabling it from being recorded anymore. This is called a multisession CD, which is common in CD-ROMs, Enhanced CDs, and Mixed Mode CDs, but this method of recording the CD is not compatible with audio CDs.

For an audio CD to play in a consumer CD player, you can have only one closed session and one closed disc in CDDA format unless using the Enhanced CD format; in Figure 13.9, you can see that the folder containing the audio content is at the beginning, making it compatible with consumer CD players. When creating this audio CD, you may use one of two methods of writing the information onto disc: TAO, short for Track-At-Once, or DAO, short for Disc-At-Once. You will probably want to consult your software and hardware documentation to see if these features are supported. However, for now, understand that TAO will record the audio CD one track at a time, leaving a two-second gap between each song that you added to the CD recording session. The DAO, on the other hand, will not record this two-second gap. In Figure 13.10, you can see the Music CD creation window in the back, where the source files appear on top and the destination or audio CD files appear at the bottom. In front of this window is the Recording options dialog box, where you can select whether you want to record the CD using TAO or DAO. Note that most mastering studios will require a DAO-mode CD master as a standard format.

Figure 13.9
Creating an Enhanced CD in the Get It On CD application from Steinberg.

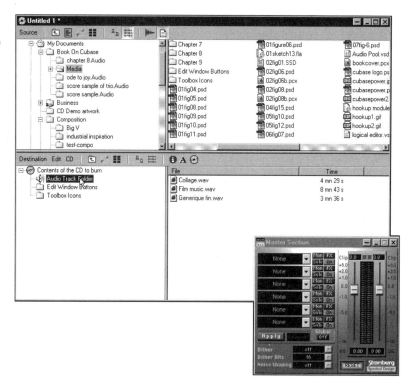

Figure 13.10
Creating a music CD in the Easy CD Creator application from Roxio (Adaptec).

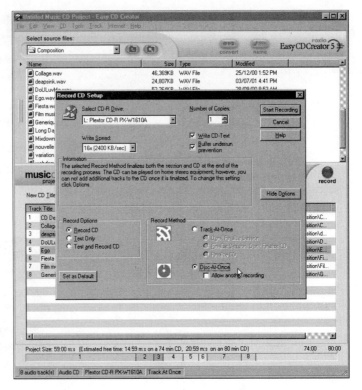

With these basic principles in hand, you can create audio CDs in your own home using the audio CD creation software of your choice. It is a good idea to create intermediate audio CDs to listen to your music on other sound systems, to see if you are pleased with what you hear before you produce the final master. Most newer domestic CD players will accept an audio disk on rewritable media (CD-RW). It is outside the specifications but can be, if your player is compatible, a good way to create test mixes on rewritable CDs. But remember that for your CD to play, it has to be in audio CD format (CDDA) and not in data CD format (CD-ROM).

Backing Up Your Work

Making backup copies of your work as you go is critical. Not only will it prevent you from having to start over if you make mistakes and erase files, but it is a good way to keep source material from being lost because of hard drive crashes. Another good reason to do backups is that you can always go back and change things in an arrangement or create a new arrangement altogether using the source material, rather than the master two-track recording. If these are not good enough reasons for you, consider this: When you are working on a project for someone else and charging studio time, I doubt that your client will be impressed by your work if you lose recordings this client paid to do in your studio.

There are many ways to do backups both in Cubase and outside of it:

▶ Create an archive folder containing all the audio present in the Audio Pool of your arrangement by using the Prepare Archive function in the File pop-up menu in the Audio Pool, as shown in Figure 13.11. This will prompt you to select a destination folder, where a copy of all the audio files used in the pool will be copied, making it easy to save this folder on backup media such as a CD-R (compact disc-recordable), CD-RW (compact disc rewritable), tape backup, or removable media drive. Once you've saved the audio files, you can also copy the .ARR and .ALL files as well to include them in the backup.

Figure 13.11
Using the Prepare Archive function in the Audio Pool to save all your audio files in a single folder for backup.

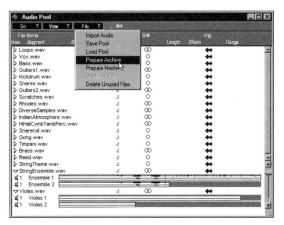

▶ As with the Prepare Archive function in the Audio Pool, you can also use the Prepare Master function in the same File pop-up menu in the Audio Pool. The Prepare Master function will look at all the referenced audio found in the song—all segments that are being used by the song—and save only those segments in a new designated folder. This will eliminate portions of your audio files in the Audio Pool that are not used anywhere in the song, reducing the quantity of audio needed to be archived.

- Use your CD creation software to create a data disc that will contain all the source material (audio, arrangements, song, preset, and setting files) used for this project, making sure to label your CD accordingly.
- Use a backup software or disk imaging software to create a backup image of your files.

Keeping in mind that computer crashes occur, unfortunately, quite often, and that disc failures are not as infrequent as we would wish, making backup copies of your work would make sense after each working session. This way, you will reduce the amount of time lost if something bad does happen.

Reading the documentation provided with your CD burning software to understand how it works and how you can retrieve information from a backup disk could prove useful, so take time to familiarize yourself with these options.

Distributing Your Work on the Web

Distributing your work on portable media such as cassettes, compact discs, or even vinyl was at one time the only way of promoting and selling it. Today, with the advances by software developers and the growing importance of the Internet, this new medium provides another way of distributing your work effectively and is also a low-cost solution to mass distribution of your work.

This section will discuss how to integrate a RealAudio file and an MP3 file inside a Web document (HTML or HyperText Markup Language). If you don't feel comfortable with this, or have no interest in knowing how to do it, you may stop reading now.

Remember that we have discussed how RealAudio and MP3 files use "go between" files called metafiles ("Exporting Formats," earlier in this chapter). In the case of RealAudio, they have the RAM or RPM extension, and in the case of MP3 files, they have the M3U file extension. In both cases, their content is quite simple: They contain a link to the actual media found on your Web page's server. When a user clicks on a link to listen to your audio file from a Web page, this link points to the metafile. Because this metafile is small (containing only a path to the actual media file), it is transferred quickly and loads the associated player into the client's memory. This player then reads the path and starts downloading the file, filling up its buffer memory before it starts playing the content.

To do this, you need to prepare the following documents:

- The HTML page that will contain the link to your metafile.
- The metafile containing the link to the streaming media file.
- The actual streaming media file containing the audio.

To create the HTML file, you can use any HTML editor or text editor, depending on the software you have on your computer. A link in an HTML document usually has three parts:

- ▶ The opening tag telling the browser that what follows is a link to another document. This tag tells the browser where to look for this file (its path). It would read something like this: `<a href= "http://www.yourserver.com/yourfolder/yoursubfolder/yourmetafile.ram">`, where "`a href=`" represents the HTML code for hyperlink references and what follows represents the complete path to the metafile in question. You would, of course, replace this path with the real location of your metafile's location.
- ▶ The text that appears in the Web page as being a link. This could be anything, and should immediately follow the opening tag.
- ▶ The closing tag telling the browser that what follows is not part of the link anymore. This always looks like this: `</a>`

Here is an example of a complete link as it would appear in an HTML document:

```
<a href=
"http://www.yourserver.com/yourfolder/yoursubfolder/yourmetafile.ram">Aud
io Demo</a>
```

To create the metafile, you can use an ASCII text editor and save the file with its appropriate extension. If you are creating a metafile for a RealAudio file, use the RAM extension, and if you are creating a metafile for an MP3 file, use the M3U extension. In both cases, all you have to enter is the path to your actual streaming media content. Here are examples of these paths:

For a metafile containing a link to RealAudio streaming content; this file should be saved with the *.RAM extension:

```
http://www.yourserver.com/yourfolder/yoursubfolder/yourmediafile.rm
```

For a metafile containing a link to MP3 streaming content; this file should be saved with the *.M3U extension:

```
http://www.yourserver.com/yourfolder/yoursubfolder/yourmediafile.mp3
```

Now that you have created the HTML document pointing to the metafile, the metafile pointing to the media file, and the media file from the Export Audio option in Cubase, you need to upload these files to the appropriate location on your Web site server using FTP (File Transfer Protocol) software or a Web browser if your Web site host allows it. Once your files have been uploaded, test your link in the HTML file and move the original files from your local computer. This is only a precaution. You see, if you have made a mistake in creating your link on the HTML page, trying to load the page from the server might look like it's working when, in reality, it's not. Your browser is loading the file from your local computer, giving you the impression that everything works although the HTML link is not correct. Moving the files temporarily when testing your links will give you an error if it can't find the file either on the server or on your local computer. On the other hand, if your link is correct, it will play the file once the player's buffer has been filled.

Remember that the time it takes to fill the player's buffer depends on the size of the streaming audio content and your Internet connection speed.

Appendix A
Optimizing Your Experience

In this appendix, you will find some tips on how to make changes to your working environment. Once you have made these changes to best suit your needs, you can save them so that every time you start a new project, Cubase loads them for you. This includes customizing the default environment by changing the default DEF.ALL song file, adding and saving keyboard shortcuts for Key Commands and Toolbar icons, saving the layout of your windows as you create a new project or the layout of different Window Sets, and turning the waveform creation process on and off.

Changing the Def.All File

The Def.all file is the default song file that loads when you launch Cubase, and it is the default file that opens when you select New Song from the File menu. This file is located in the Cubase program folder. You should avoid using this name to save personal project files that contain actual MIDI or audio data. However, if you really have to save a file with this name, make sure it isn't in the Cubase program folder. You can save your settings in this file, though, so that the next time you load Cubase, these settings will load by default without your having to change everything again each time you begin a Cubase session. Note that in the Macintosh version, this file is called Autoload rather than Def.All.

The Def.all file can recall the following settings. When you modify these settings and save them in this default song file, their values will be kept as the default values when a new song is created:

- ▶ Preferences found under the Edit > Preferences sub-menus.
- ▶ Custom key commands, remote MIDI setups, and toolbars (discussed later in this appendix).
- ▶ Window settings and sets, saving the size and position of the windows you would like to see when you create a new song or arrangement.

http://www.muskalipman.com

- ▶ Tracks—You can set up your song to open prenamed tracks, assign track classes to them, and assign specific output ports and channels to them. For example, if you always assign a particular keyboard to a particular MIDI port, you can set your default song as such and save it before you start working in it. Then, the next time you create a new file, whatever settings you saved will reappear as your new default.
- ▶ Parts—By storing System Exclusive messages on muted tracks in the Def.all song, you can store MIDI bulk dump messages to send messages to your MIDI instrument. Unmuting the track when necessary will automatically reset or send these messages to your external MIDI devices.
- ▶ Transport bar settings and position can be customized and saved. You can also save the Record and Cycle modes and set the Auto Quantize button active by default.
- ▶ Editors—You can load frequently used drum map settings in the Drum editor and window size options.
- ▶ Mixer windows—You can customize the MIDI Track Mixer and the VST Channel Mixer views.
- ▶ Audio Setup—Set up your audio system settings, initial mix settings, audio buses, and sends for specific operations. You can also set up how you want the pool to display information in the Audio Pool window. The same goes for MIDI To Audio Delay properties, audio performance settings, bit depth during recording, priority setting, audio I/O settings, and monitoring switch.
- ▶ Grooves and Quantize settings can load automatically in the default song.
- ▶ MIDI Setup—Your MIDI system setup, metronome preferences, and MIDI filter settings.
- ▶ Synchronization—If you are working mostly with one type of external sync, you can configure your sync options and have them also load as default parameters, such as the MIDI Sync Reference.

To save these changes and have them load by default, simply select Save As from the File menu and save this file as Def.all (if it's not already named that) and make sure that the folder in which you save this file is the Cubase program folder. You can also create a Def.all, which is the default Arrangement file that Cubase will create if you select the New Arrangement option in the File menu. This file should also be saved in the Cubase program menu.

If you wish, you can also create template songs. Look at templates as a default setting for a type of setup. For example, if you are in the business of recording live bands in your studio or anywhere else, you can create a default song that you call "LIVEBAND.ALL." You can set this up to reflect the type of work you will be doing in this situation, such as creating audio tracks, assigning them predefined channels and sound card ports, and naming these tracks accordingly. To access this template, simply double-click on it from the Explorer or Launcher window and it will load in the Cubase environment. Just use the Save As option rather than the Save option to avoid saving over this template when you want to keep your session for later use.

Key Commands

As you have seen in this book, many of the functions available in Cubase have keyboard shortcuts, also known as key commands. You can modify the standard set of key commands and create new ones to correspond to your working habits. However, these custom key commands are not saved in the song file but in a preference file in the system folder of your computer. You can also save the complete list of key commands in a separate file with the *.kbd extension. To modify key commands, select Edit > Preferences > Key Commands. The Key Commands dialog box will appear, as shown in Figure A.1. Click on the Tabs in the dialog box to select which set of key commands you would like to edit.

Figure A.1
The Key Commands dialog box.

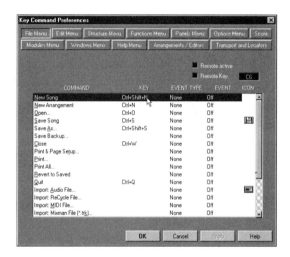

To assign a new keyboard shortcut for a command or to replace an existing one, click in the Key column next to the desired command. A dialog box will appear with four options:

- ▶ Press the desired keyboard keys you wish to use to activate this command.
- ▶ Click the OK button to confirm your selection.
- ▶ Click Remove to remove the current set of keys as a keyboard shortcut for this command.
- ▶ Click Cancel to forget the whole thing and start somewhere else.

Once you have made the changes to your key commands, you can select File > Save As and choose the Keyboard Layout option in the Save As Type field. This will create a new key command file. Make sure to save it in a folder that you will remember. To recall this file later, you can choose Open from the File menu and select Keyboard Layout as the file type. Once you have located the file in question, click on Open to replace the key commands with the new ones.

If you would like these new key commands to be part of your customized Def.all file, you need to open the option in your Def.all file, then save your song file once again. This will cause the default song file to load the *.kbd (Keyboard Layout) file every time you start a new song.

Creating a Toolbar

The toolbar in Cubase is a customizable set of buttons that you can organize in a floating toolbar through the Key Commands window. As you have just seen in the Key Commands header, you can also assign icons to specific commands. These icons (found in the Icon column, shown in Figure A.1) will be added to this toolbar. To view the toolbar, select Windows > Show Toolbar. To hide it, click the Close Window icon in the upper right corner of the toolbar or select Windows > Hide Toolbar.

Figure A.2 shows a list of icons that were added in the Key Commands dialog box. Some commands have default icons that can be associated with only that specific command, and they will appear automatically when you click in the Icon column next to their commands. However, if there are no default icons for this function, you can always select a list from the pop-up menu that will appear when you click in the Icon column. To remove an icon from the toolbar, select its associated command icon again or select the Off icon from the list of custom buttons that will appear.

The toolbar settings will be saved in your Cubase Preferences and will also be included in a Keyboard Layout file.

Figure A.2
The toolbar provides shortcut buttons for common commands.

If you wish to rearrange the position of the icons in the toolbar, you can Ctrl+click and drag it to a new position. Using Alt+click on a button is another way you can remove an icon from the toolbar.

Working with Window Sets

Window sets are snapshots of window settings that can recall in one step the size, location, and position of an associated toolbox and palette, as well as the magnification factor of that window. You can store these sets and recall them at will. The window sets works with the Arrange window and all the editor windows (Key, List, Drum, Score, Audio and Controller Edit) except the Master Track windows.

Since window sets are stored in your Preferences, all songs will share one common set of window sets.

To create a window set:

1. Set up the windows appearing on your screen as you want them to be recalled.
2. Select Windows > Window Sets > New Window Set. The Save Windows dialog box will appear.
3. Type in the name for your new window set.
4. Select one of the two options available: All Windows Including Settings or Top Window Only. If you select the latter, you may choose whether to include the settings for this window by checking the Include Settings checkbox.
5. Click the OK button to save the window set.

To recall window sets, go to Windows > Window Sets and select one of the saved window sets from this sub-menu. To remove a window set from this list, choose the Edit option in the Window Sets sub-menu. If you just want to rename it, follow the same path but double-click on the name of the window set you wish to rename and type in the new name.

To make this easy to use, you can also assign a keyboard shortcut to the first fifteen window sets in the Edit > Preferences > Key Commands option box under the Windows Menu tab. Once you have assigned a keyboard shortcut, you can recall any saved window set with a single keystroke (or combination, depending on the shortcut you created).

To save your window sets for later use, you can select the Save As option in the File menu and choose the Window Set file type from the drop-down menu. Name your window set and click the Save button. Again, to include these window sets in your Def.all file, open it in your empty default song file and save the Def.all file once again. The next time you create a new song, the Window Sets file will be loaded with it.

Turning off the Wave Image Creation

When you are in a recording session with a paying client, time is money. To accelerate this process, you can turn off the Use Waveforms option found in the Options > Audio Setup menu. This will stop the waveform image creation process. At that point, the parts containing audio events will appear to be empty, but the information will still be present. Once you are done recording, you can turn this option back on and Cubase will calculate the waveforms and create image files of the audio events on your hard disk. You can also manually update these waveforms by clicking on the image column's icon next to the file you wish to update in the Audio Pool.

Appendix B
Interactive Phrase Synthesizer

The Interactive Phrase Synthesizer (IPS) is a music generator that relies on the realtime input you provide. It does not work randomly but outputs interactive musical phrases generated from the keys you play—thus the name. The IPS doesn't generate sounds like a synthesizer does. It simply sends MIDI messages to a designated MIDI output port to have the MIDI device play the notes it generates. Once you are satisfied with the notes it generates from your input, you can save these notes onto another MIDI track to create a normal MIDI part out of it. You can also modify the parameters of the IPS in realtime and these parameters will be recorded as such.

To open the IPS, go to Panels > Interactive Phrase Synthesizer. The IPS dialog box will appear, as shown in Figure B.1.

Figure B.1
The IPS dialog box.

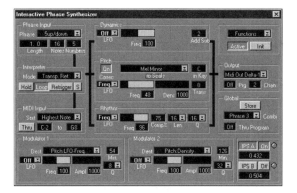

The IPS dialog box displays all the controls for one of two IPS modules—called A and B. To toggle between these two, you will use buttons on the lower right corner with the labels IPS A and IPS B. The active dialog selection is the pressed button. Next to these buttons are On/Off switches that will activate the IPS module. These buttons will determine which IPS will play when you activate the IPS module through the Active button, found in the upper right corner of the window, just below the Functions drop-down menu.

What the IPS module plays depends on what is loaded in the Phrase Input section of the window (found in the upper left corner). Phrases are your raw material, and you can either load preset phrases or create your own by selecting a MIDI part in the Arrange window and then selecting the Convert to IPS Phrase in the Functions menu. When you choose this option, the Copy Part to Phrase dialog box will appear, as shown in Figure B.2. Clicking on an empty slot from the drop-down menu, then clicking OK, will add your MIDI part as source material for the IPS.

Figure B.2
The Copy Part to Phrase dialog box allows you to select a place to store the Phrase Input you have created in a part.

You can have up to thirty-two phrases at a time, and these phrases can be chords, monophonic music lines, or drum beats of up to 1,000 notes. To rename a phrase in the IPS dialog box, double-click on it and type in the new name. Underneath the Phrase Input selected Phrase field, you can see three additional fields that give you information on the length of the phrase in bars and ticks, the number of notes in the phrase, and the number of numbers that are assigned to it. A number value is given to each different note in a phrase. This number will eventually be used by the Sort modes, as seen later. For now, remember that the only field you can edit here is the length of the phrase.

Phrases then go through an Interpreter. The interpreter has a Play Mode field from which you can choose how it will interpret the phrase. In the Play Mode popup menu, you will find four types of Play Mode interpretation: Sort, Transpose, Mute Play, and Repeat. These will determine how the IPS handles the phrase you selected. Here's a brief description of them:

> ▶ **Sort Normal, Replace, Skip**—This mode relies on giving a different number to each different note pitch in your phrase. For example, if you played the five notes C2, F2, G2, D2, and C2, the notes would be numbered as follows: C2 = 1, F2 = 2, G2 = 3, D2 = 4. Since the last note, C2, repeats the first note, it doesn't get a new number. Now, when you play a series of notes or chords, the Sort Normal function replaces the notes by numbers as well. As you can see in Figure B.3, the top staff displays the original phrase with its numbers underneath it. The second staff displays the chords that were played on the keyboard. Since the MIDI Input Sort option was set to Lowest Note, when it sorted the chord, it gave the lower number to the lower note, then played the corresponding notes as shown in the third staff. Since there are only three notes in the first bar, the note number 4 is skipped.

This is not the case for the second bar, where a four-note chord was played. What remains constant here is the order in which the notes appear and their rhythm. In Sort Replace mode, instead of skipping missing notes, it replaces the missing notes with the first numbered note. So, in our example in Figure B.3, the missing notes on the third staff would be replaced by a C3, since C3 is the first note in the chord played through the MIDI input. In Sort Skip mode, the missing note number is replaced by the next note number in the series to avoid holes. So, again in our example, the missing note would be replaced by note number 2 (F3).

Figure B.3
How the IPS interprets and gives numbers to the Phrase Input and assigns them to chords played through the MIDI input.

- **Transpose Retrig** and **Continuous**—This uses the note you play as a pitch value to transpose the phrase to that value. Which note it uses as the transpose value depends on the Sort Mode in the Input Module. The difference between Retrig and Continuous is that the latter option will stop and then continue the phrase from the point it was at when you change notes on the keyboard, whereas Retrig will start the phrase over again from the beginning.

- **Mute Play**—This mode works differently from the Transpose and Sort mode in that it will play back only the notes coming from the MIDI input corresponding to notes found in the phrase. In the example above, shown in Figure B.3, if you were to play these exact notes, nothing would play back, because the chord does not play any of the notes found in the phrase. If you were to play the same chord one octave lower, the C2 and F2 notes would play and the rest would be skipped. This mode can be useful in creating dubbing parts where only certain notes are doubled or to emphasize certain rhythmic patterns by holding down only the keys that correspond to the phrase notes you want to hear.

▶ **Repeat**—This mode will simply use the rhythm found in the phrase and assign the same rhythm to any chords or notes that are held down. Figure B.4 shows the result of this interpretation, using the same Phrase and chord inputs as before.

Figure B.4
Using the Repeat Mode in the IPS's Phrase Interpreter field.

The Hold button keeps playing the phrase until it reaches the end of the loaded phrase, even if you release the pressed key before the phrase reaches the end. The Loop button will repeat the phrase in a loop for as long as you press a key on the keyboard, but it will stop if you release the pressed key. The Retrigger button will always start over from the beginning of the phrase when a key is pressed, no matter where it is at the moment you press that key.

The MIDI input determines how what you play on the keyboard will be interpreted by the interpreter, as explained above. You use the MIDI input data that will trigger or influence how the IPS will interact with these notes. The Sort field lets you select which note should be considered as the source of your transposition, for example. It is quite straightforward, since it allows you to choose by note pitch (the highest or lowest), note velocity (again, the highest velocity or lowest), or by note order (the first note played or the last note played). Changing these options will influence how the phrase will be interpreted, as you can see in Figure B.5— the last staff displays the output, using the same phrase on Staff 1 and the same chord on Staff 2. In the first bar of Staff 3, the Transpose Retrig was chosen as the Play Mode and the MIDI Input Sort field was set to Lowest Note, using the C3 as your transposition value. In Bar 2, the MIDI Sort field was set to Highest Note, using the A3 this time as a transposition value.

Figure B.5
How the MIDI Input Sort field affects the Input Phrase as it is interpreted in Transpose Retrig mode.

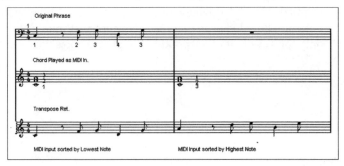

When the Thru button is pressed, the track you use to play the MIDI input values will also be heard. If it is turned off, what you play will not be heard, so it will only serve to trigger the IPS. Next to the Thru button, you can define a range of keys between which notes are interpreted by the IPS. Therefore, any note outside this range will be ignored. You can assign two different ranges, one for each IPS (A and B).

Next, the signal can pass through three additional modifiers: Dynamics, Pitch, and Rhythm, each with its own set of parameters. The output of the phrase after it passes into the interpreter is split three ways, with each module treated independently, and the modules affect only what is coming out of the interpreter. For a complete list of parameters and to see how they affect the output, you may consult the online documentation that came with Cubase called IPS.PDF. This document will give you the lowdown on how to adjust these parameters. For now, remember that the dynamics module affects the velocity of the notes found in the interpreter's output; the pitch affects how these notes are played (the order) and how they will follow pitch changes made in different scales; and the rhythm module affects the rhythm of the interpreter's output, the length of the notes, and their placement inside a quantize grid.

At the bottom of the IPS dialog box, you will find two Modulator modules that are identical. These modulators will add another variable to the treatment of the interpreter's output. In other words, these modules can send changes to other modules—such as the pitch, dynamics, rhythm, and scale—or even send changes to themselves or the other modulator, creating almost random effects. Again, understanding the different parameters might require a bit of reading from the IPS.PDF file provided with Cubase or simply some experimenting on your part.

The Output section controls which MIDI output port is used to produce the sounds coming out of the IPS. You can determine the MIDI output port and its channel, and you may also assign a program, if you like. Note that if you use one of the modulator's MIDI Out Channel destination modulations, the actual MIDI channel might vary, because you are applying a modulation on the channel itself.

The Global section allows you to save settings and select loaded settings. The Thru option allows you to turn the throughput of your MIDI input on and off. When turned on, the notes that you play can be recorded onto the selected MIDI track in the Arrange window.

The last setting section inside the IPS is called Functions. The Functions menu is a drop-down list of functions that can be applied to the whole IPS dialog box, such as load and save, copy, send, delete, sync, and others. Here is a brief description on how to use these functions:

> ▶ **Load and Save All Combis**—Combis are combinations or IPS settings that you can load into memory or save for later use. They include all the parameters and phrases you have used. You can have up to thirty-two combis at once. When you save a combi file, Cubase will give it a CMB extension. If you want a default set of combis to load automatically as you start Cubase, save your combi file as Def.Cmb in the Cubase program folder.

- **Load and Save Phrase Bank**—Since phrases are the source material for your combis, you can save them or load them separately from the combis themselves. Phrases are saved as two banks of sixteen, and they will be split between Bank A and B (sixteen in each). When you choose to save a set of phrases, a dialog box will appear, asking you in which bank you want to save them. Later, when you decide to load a bank, a similar dialog box will ask you which bank you want to replace with the content you are about to load, either the first sixteen phrases in Bank A or the last sixteen in Bank B.

- **Scale Info**—When working with the pitch and scale module active, you can view information on the actual notes that were used in this scale. This is useful when you want to use a scale that you are not familiar with and you wish to learn more about the tensions or notes that were used to create this scale.

- **Send Prg. Change**—You can set up the IPS to send a program change number each time a specific combi is selected from the Global menu. The Send Program Change is a toggle switch that will enable or disable this function. If it is not selected (disabled), there will be no program changes sent to the MIDI device.

- **Ext. Prg. Change**—After saving your current combi settings, you can set up the IPS to receive program changes from any incoming MIDI channel. When it receives such a program change, it switches to another combi. Like the Send Prg. Change function, this is an enable/disable (checked/unchecked). This program change may be triggered by an external device, but program changes added in a MIDI part will have no effect on the IPS. In other words, this is more of a realtime application than a programmed one.

- **Copy Combi to** and **Copy Phrase to**—You can select a combi from the Global module and then choose this function to copy a combi from one memory location to another. A dialog box will appear (see Figure B.6), asking you where you would like to copy the selected combi. Use this function to rearrange your combis for realtime performances when using it in combination with the Ext. Prg. Change. Just like the Copy Combi to, the Copy Phrase to function allows you to reorganize your phrases in one of the thirty-two memory locations.

Figure B.6
The Copy Combi to dialog box prompts you to select the destination location of the copied combi.

- **Delete Combi** and **Delete Phrase**—This allows you to delete the active combi or phrase (depending on the function you choose) from the current list of combis or phrases.
- **Sync A-B**—This allows you to synchronize the IPS A and IPS B so that they lock together rhythmically after the first note. You can set an offset time between them by setting a different trigger key range in the MIDI input section, thus using the lower part of the keyboard to start the IPS A, for example, and the upper part of the keyboard to start the IPS B.
- **Loop:LFO Reset**—Enable this function if you want the LFO parameters to restart their cycles whenever a new key is pressed, rather than continuing from their current locations when you change keys.
- **Wait for Play**—This function is intended for recording the output of the IPS into Cubase VST. Therefore, when you activate this, the IPS will wait until you press the Play button from the Transport bar before it locks up the IPS and starts interpreting the phrase. When using this function, press the desired note(s) on your keyboard; the IPS will know on which note(s) to begin and lock on so that as soon as you press Play, it will begin interpreting as well.
- **Erase All Data**—If you want to begin with a fresh start, erasing all the phrases and combis, this is the function for you.
- **M.ROS-IN: Tracks**—This works only if you have a track set to output MIDI on the MROS port (found in the Track List). This MROS track will then be sending MIDI information to the IPS, allowing you to automate some actions in the IPS. At this point, you can record the notes you were using through your MIDI input, save them as a part on a track, assign this track to the MROS MIDI output, and use it to trigger the IPS rather than play along with the sequence.

The Active button found under the Functions drop-down menu, as mentioned at the beginning of this appendix, toggles the IPS dialog window on or off. Next to the Active button is the Init button, which can be used to initialize all the parameters of the IPS dialog box, including the phrases and combi settings.

Now that you have doodled around with the IPS and have found some interesting things to try out, it would be nice at this point if you could record the output of the IPS to a MIDI track to use it as a creative and interactive musical instrument.

To record the output of the IPS:

1. Independently set the MIDI output of the IPS A and IPS B to the MROS output.

    If you want to record just the output of one IPS, set that IPS to the MROS output. You can also activate the Multirecord function found in the Options menu to record each IPS on a separate track.

2. Select Options > MIDI Setup > System.

3. Check the MROS input option in the MIDI System Setup dialog box, as shown in Figure B.7.

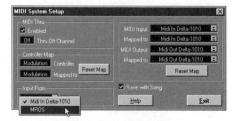

Figure B.7

Selecting the MROS Input in the MIDI System Setup dialog box will allow you to record the MIDI output of the IPS.

4. If you want to record both IPS synths on one track, go to the next step, but if you want to record them on separate tracks, select Multirecord from the Options menu and enable the Channel Split option from the Multirecord sub-menu.

5. Assign the MIDI outputs for your IPS to MROS and select the appropriate MIDI channel.

    If you are using one of the modulator modules in the IPS and have set it to affect the MIDI output channel, make sure your MIDI track is set to "any." In this case, you may want to record the output onto a single track rather than using the multirecord option. You can use the Explode by Channel option found in the Structure menu later if you want to create a separate track for all the MIDI channels used by the IPS.

6. If you have previously recorded the trigger notes on a MIDI track, make sure to set that track to MROS output and activate the M.ROS IN:Track option in the Functions menu of the IPS dialog box. On the other hand, if you will be triggering the notes live, make sure to set the appropriate Thru option in the MIDI input section of the IPS dialog box. Remember, if it is activated, the notes you play will be added to the recorded material coming out of the IPS.

7. You can now set aside the IPS dialog box or simply close it and start the recording process.

Once your IPS material is recorded onto a MIDI track, you can deactivate the IPS and close the dialog box, edit the MIDI parts as you would any other part, and even transform the output of the IPS in a new phrase and restart the process again to experiment with the IPS module.

In this appendix, we have discussed mostly melodic phrase material. However, you can also use drum patterns and harmonic content as phrase material to create interesting textures and rhythms, as well as harmonic and melodic content. You might look at the Interactive Phrase Synthesizer as a true synthesizer. However, rather than designing a sound by changing the parameters of an actual synthesizer, you are designing musical content in the same way, changing the output as you change a parameter. Experiment and have fun.

Appendix C
Making the Most of Modules

Modules are found in the Modules menu in Cubase. They are like sub-programs that can be loaded into memory—or not—depending on the resources available on your computer. So, if you don't use a module, you can unload it to free valuable RAM memory.

What you can do with a module depends on the module itself. There are nine modules included with Cubase VST. Two of them have been discussed in earlier chapters. This appendix will explain why you should use these modules and how you can use them effectively. Here, we will focus on the ones that are more useful to most people. These include the following:

- ▶ **DS Video Monitor**—DS stands for DirectShow, which is part of DirectX Media—an extension to Windows that allows you to play back movies on your screen. You can use this to synchronize a video playback with a Cubase arrangement. This module was described at the end of Chapter 12.

- ▶ **CD Player**—This is, as the name would suggest, a CD player utility that you can use within the Cubase environment. It offers nothing special that would warrant loading it over another, if you already have a good one installed. But, since it is included with Cubase, you can use it to monitor sampling CDs, for example, that are present in your CD-ROM drive.

- ▶ **Arpeggio**—The arpeggiator allows you to have up to a four-voice arpeggio generated from a held chord played on a MIDI instrument. You can use a recorded MIDI track as the arpeggio's input and record the MIDI output on another track or tracks, depending on the number of voices you are using in the arpeggiator.

- ▶ **Styletrax**—Style tracks are a combination of modules and Track Class. These track classes use predefined accompaniment patterns called styles. Styles are stored on your computer's hard disk and can be loaded on a styletrax when this module is activated. You can play with a styletrax in realtime and have an automatic accompaniment, or use a predefined chord track class to determine the harmonic structure of the styletrax, over which you can play a melody or solo, for example. You can also create your own styles and use them with styletrax.

http://www.muskalipman.com

- **SMPTE Display**—The SMPTE display module brings up a large counter display with customizable settings. If you are working with video or in sync with a SMPTE timecode, this window will help you to quickly see correspondances between the timecode format and the bars and beats format. Remember that you already have these two formats displayed in your Transport bar, but the SMPTE display module allows you to see the time in a bigger window.

- **MIDI Effect Processor**—This is a simple yet powerful MIDI processor similar to an audio effects processor, except that it processes MIDI events to produce echoes, choruses, and pitch-shifting over the selected MIDI channel.

- **Studio Module**—As you saw earlier in this book, you can assign instruments to tracks in order to save the names of your MIDI devices, VST Instruments, or Rewire instruments. The studio module simply allows you to set up your external MIDI devices so that you can import, save, load, or export instrument definitions through system exclusive messages. The studio module, once the instrument's device has been loaded, will know how to communicate with it. There are more than 150 devices included with Cubase. If your device is not included in this set, you can download an application called Dmaker from Steinberg's FTP site at this address: **ftp.steinberg.net.** This application will let you create your own instrument device driver so that you can use it with the studio module later. Once a MIDI device is loaded in the studio module, it will extract the names of your instrument's presets, banks, performances, or other set of sounds, depending on the make and model of this device. Use this module to automate your MIDI system settings by changing your sounds on your MIDI devices directly from the Cubase interface, rather than changing the settings on your machines. Think of it this way—you could put your MIDI devices in a completely different room and control them from Cubase without ever touching them again (unless you want to create new sounds, of course).

- **Rocket Network**—Rocket Network is a central server that you log on to. It coordinates a master "arrangement" of audio and MIDI parts that are shared by each user in a session. Users can post their audio or MIDI tracks to the session through their RocketPower audio software. Each time you send updates (post), the master arrangement and then the central server distribute the new parts to other session participants. Whenever users enter a session where there is a project in progress, the most up-to-date arrangement is downloaded directly into their audio application on their local computer. You do need to install Rocket Network software on your computer for this to work. This software is free for Cubase and Logic users and is cross-platform and cross-application. This will be discussed further in Appendix D.

To use any of these modules, you need to activate them first. If you know you will be using a module often, you can also select to preload it so that they will already be active the next time you load Cubase.

To activate or preload modules:

1. From the Modules menu, select Setup. The Module Setup dialog box will appear, as shown in Figure C.1.
2. Select a module by clicking on it, then click in the Active column next to the module's name to toggle between Yes or No.
3. If you want to preload a module, click in the Preload column next to the module's name (also to toggle between Yes or No). Remember that these modules will take up RAM, so if you find that your computer's performance suffers because of an overload of memory, you can deactivate unnecessary modules.
4. Click the Exit button to leave this dialog box.

Now, to access a module you have just activated, select it from the list in the Modules menu.

Figure C.1
The Module Setup dialog box allows you to activate or preload modules into memory.

MIDI Processor

Not unlike an effects processor, you can use this module to create interesting musical and rhythmical counterpoints without generating any audio data. However, the MIDI processor will generate additional MIDI events and, depending on your parameter settings, this may cause the MIDI data to choke your MIDI ports. So, to avoid this, let's first look at what the parameters involved are and how they will affect your sound.

▶ **Repeat**—Determines how many echoes (see next parameter) will be generated from the input note. This can be set anywhere between 1 and 64.

▶ **Echo**—Determines the time between the input note and its echo. The values on the slider bar are transformed into ticks, but to work effectively, follow this table to get an accurate Echo value/Quantize value correspondence. This will make more sense if the actual echo plays in time. However, you can use any in-between values to get the echo to sound off-beat.

Table C.1
The Echo values converted into Quantize values.

Echo Value	Quantize Value
3	64 (sixty-fourth note)
4	32T (thirty-second note triplet)
6	32 (thirty-second note)
8	16T (sixteenth note triplet)
12	16 (sixteenth note)
16	8T (eighth note triplet)
24	8 (eighth note)
48	4 (quarter note)
96	2 (half note)
192	1 (whole note or one bar)

▶ **Quantize**—Determines how close the echo will be to a Quantize value. The values here are identical to the Echo values (1 unit = 8 ticks, so a value of 3 would be the equivalent of 24 ticks, which is also one sixty-fourth note).

▶ **Vel Dec**—Implies that you can increase or decrease the velocity of repeat events by a certain velocity amount. For this to work properly, your destination sound has to be velocity sensitive. You can set this parameter to values between plus or minus 64.

▶ **Echo Dec**—Also implies an increase or decrease of a value, but this time you can add or remove time between each echo repetition. If you set this to a positive value, echoes will repeat with more and more time being added between each repetition; if you set this to a negative value, they will repeat with less and less time between repetitions.

▶ **Note Dec**—Allows you to change the pitch of each repeating echo by the amount of semitone you assign to this parameter, where each value corresponds to a semitone. So, a value of 7 would make each echo repeat a perfect fifth above the preceding echo. You can use this to create arpeggios by adding or subtracting notes to repeated notes.

To configure the MIDI processor to process the incoming realtime MIDI events and to record its output on a MIDI track:

1. From the Modules menu, select the MIDI Effect Processor > MIDI Processor option.

2. To turn the module on, click the Status checkbox to add a checkmark, as shown in Figure C.2.

Figure C.2
The MIDI Processor dialog box.

3. If you want to use this module with already recorded music as the source material for the module, skip to the next step. Next to the Input field, select an input from which to receive MIDI events to process. This is the input the MIDI processor will use as its source. Now, go to Step 5 unless you also want to process a MIDI part that is already recorded.

4. In the Arrange window, set the output or outputs of the desired track(s) to MROS, and set the input of the MIDI processor to MROS as well (for this to work, make sure your MROS is active in the MIDI System Setup dialog box). This will connect the output of the track to the input of the MIDI processor.

5. In the MIDI processor, select either an output port from the pop-up menu to send the output of the MIDI processor to an instrument or, if you wish to record the output of the MIDI processor back onto a track in Cubase, select the MROS output. You can also assign a MIDI channel and an instrument as well.

6. If you have chosen to record the output of the MIDI processor on a track, make sure it is set to the correct channel setting. To avoid confusion, you can put this track to "any." This way, the track will record anything coming out of the processor.

Now, you are ready to play with the sliders inside the MIDI processor window. You can record the changes you make if you have followed the steps as described above. You can change the values of the parameters in three ways: drag the slider's handle, click above or below the slider's handle, or double-click the numeric value under each slider to enter a new value.

7. Press Record on the Transport bar if you want to record this effect or simply play along with it.

To deactivate the MIDI processor, you need to either uncheck the Status checkbox or deactivate it from the Modules > MIDI Effect Processor > Deactivate menu.

Arpeggio to the Rescue

If you don't feel like entering a complex arpeggio style musical part one note at a time, if you can't play arpeggios correctly because the keyboard is not your thing, or even if you just want to experiment with the creative process, the arpeggiator module will serve you well.

There are two modes in this module, Easy and Expert (as shown in Figure C.3). Obviously, if this is your first time, stick with the Easy mode. Then, when you feel comfortable, switch to the Expert mode to experiment with the additional features. The following text will cover both modes.

Figure C.3
The arpeggiator's Expert mode dialog box offers additional controls over the arpeggios you can produce.

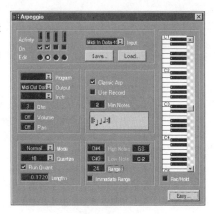

The arpeggiator offers a simple interface with a set of four different arpeggio engines. Which engine or module is apparent in the actual window depends on which radio button is selected in the Edit section. As you can see in Figure C.3, the current module selected is the second one. This means that the rest of the parameters in this window are those of this selected module. In other words, the arppegiator is really a four-page window with four times the parameters for more control over each arpeggio generator. To activate an arpeggio, simply check the On checkbox above the Edit radio buttons in the upper left corner. In Figure C.3, two arpeggios are active. The activity meter above the On checkbox allows you to see which arpeggio is currently generating notes. So, the settings you make for one arpeggio generator are valid only for that arpeggio. To get four different sets of parameters, you need to make the desired modifications to each arpeggio you activate.

The channel, program, output, instrument, and the additional pan and volume parameters in the Expert mode are identical to these parameters in the Track Info area. The only difference is that the program parameter is referred to as the patchname parameter in the Track Info area. Therefore, you can set these parameters to play a specific instrument, playing a specific program or patchname, on a specific MIDI channel, coming out of a specific MIDI output port. These settings can be different for each arpeggio in this module. The volume and pan parameters are only available in Expert mode.

The next set of parameters common to both modes are mode, quantize, octaves, and length.

- ▶ The **Mode** pop-up menu offers four options that affect the direction of the arpeggio notes: Normal, which will arpeggiate the notes up and down; Invert, which will invert the arpeggiated notes once they reach the top note; and Down and Up, which will arpeggiate notes in their respective directions only.
- ▶ The **Quantize** parameter determines the speed of the arpeggio. Therefore, if you set the Quantize value to 8, your arpeggio will play eighth notes, since the arpeggiator always follows the tempo set in Cubase.
- ▶ The **Octaves** parameter determines the range in octaves between the lowest note and the highest note it will play, based on the note you pressed, if you pressed only one, or the lowest note in the chord if you pressed more than one note. A setting of 2, for example, will cause the arppegiator to move up and down (depending on the mode) within a two-octave range.
- ▶ The **Length** parameter sets the output length of the notes in ticks. What number appears here depends also on the MROS resolution.

The next set of parameters appears only in the Expert mode of the arpeggiator. The Classic Arp checkbox in the Expert mode allows you, when it is checked, to use the arpeggio as you did in the Easy mode, creating arpeggios from the notes you play going up and down the range you set. When it is not checked, it will create arpeggios using the Sort Box area in concert with the Use Record and Rec/Hold checkbox options.

The Use Record checkbox works when the Classic Arp checkbox is unchecked. It basically uses a MIDI input from the Rec/Hold section to generate an arpeggio. So, the Rec/Hold allows you to input the actual notes, and the Sort Box area allows you to edit the arpeggio pattern. After this, you can use one or more notes to trigger this pattern based on the notes you previously entered to be part of the pattern structure. The range of the notes played is then determined by the range area through the High Notes, Low Note, Range, and Immediate Range options. Here's a simple example of how this works:

1. Click the Expert mode button to switch to this mode.
2. Uncheck the Classic Arp option.
3. Activate the first arpeggio by checking the first On box to the left and set the Edit radio button to this arpeggio to further edit these parameters.
4. Configure the input and output parameters to receive MIDI and send MIDI to the appropriate ports.
5. Check the Use Record option to enable this function. The Min Notes field displays the minimum number of notes you need to play to trigger the arpeggio, but this only works when Use Record is deactivated.
6. Check the Rec/Hold checkbox.
7. Play a chord on your keyboard to record these notes. The order in which you play them does not matter, nor does the timing. For this example, try a C major triad (C-E-G).

http://www.muskalipman.com

8. When satisfied with the input notes that will create your arpeggio, uncheck the Rec/Hold checkbox. If you wish, change these notes—the simplest way is to start the note input process again (repeating steps 6 through 8). Any note you press while the Rec/Hold is checked will be added to the pitch values used by the arpeggiator.

   The Sort Box is a graphical layout of the current active arpeggio page and is only active when the Classic Arp option is not active (or checked), since it is an alternative to using the Classic Arp. This graph represents notes between repeating bar lines or a relative pitch—relative pitch because they do not represent actual pitches, but rather, the direction the arpeggio will go when moving from one note to the other. So, if all your notes are at the same pitch in the graph, you will have a series of repeating notes. The actual pitch of the notes generated by your arpeggio will be determined by the Rec/Hold notes. Here's how you can manipulate this sequence:

   ▶ To insert a note, right-click on the end repeating bar.

   ▶ To raise a note, right-click on it; to lower it, left-click on it.

   ▶ To erase the last note entered, lower this note until it reaches its lowest position in the graph and then click once more. This will erase that note, and if it is not the last in the sequence, it will also erase all the following notes.

   ▶ To add semitones to your arpeggio pattern, hold the Alt key pressed as you left-click on a note. This will add an arrow pointing up to play the semitone above. Repeating this will toggle the arrow from pointing up to pointing down, which will lower that note by a semitone. Clicking a third time with the Alt key pressed will remove this semitone from the sequence.

   ▶ To remove all notes from the sequence, left-click on the first note to remove it. All following notes will be erased.

9. Create a four-note sequence, as shown in Figure C.4.

Figure C.4
Creating a custom arpeggio pattern in the Expert mode Arpeggio window.

10. Check the Immediate Range option. This will cause the arpeggio to switch immediately to the nearest note inside the set range when a chord or a note is pressed.

11. Set the range to 24 in order to have a two-octave (24 semitones) arpeggio.

12. In the Mode field, select Invert from the drop-down menu.

13. In the Quantize field, select 16 from the drop-down menu.

14. Check the Run Quant option to quantize the output of the arpeggio to the song's position when Cubase is in Play mode.

15. Set the length to 1.000 to record sixteenth notes without overlapping.
16. Now, play a note and listen to the result.

If you want to record this result, select a track, set it to play on Any channel, start your recording, and set the output of the active arpeggio to MROS, as described earlier in this section. If you want to use a pre-existing track as your input for the arpeggio, set this track to play on the MROS output port and set the arpeggio to receive a signal from the MROS input as well. When you start the playback in Cubase, the events found on the source track will feed the arpeggiator.

You can finally save your arpeggiator's setting to disk and load it later by clicking the Save button or the Load button.

As you will see when experimenting with this module, you can create interesting textures when combining more than one arpeggio at a time in this environment. The fact that you can create your own patterns and control the range, the spacing between notes, and the length of these notes separately for each arpeggio leaves you with a rich creative tool.

Style Tracks

Style tracks are like using auto accompaniment software for you to play with either in realtime or when using prerecorded harmonic structures. It makes it easy for you to play along with other instruments without having to record each instrument individually, and you can use a wide range of musical styles as templates. In reality, the style tracks function could be its own little software application, because the implications when using this module run pretty deep.

Style tracks uses a set of parameters to determine how it reacts and what it will be outputting:

- **Style**—As the parameter suggests, a specific musical style. Use this to determine the type of accompaniment you wish to use.

    Each style plays over a certain number of MIDI channels and MIDI ports. This means that a style can play and, in most cases, will play more than one instrument at a time. When you use an existing style, the MIDI channel, MIDI output, mute, program change, bank, transposition, velocity, volume, mode, and range settings are saved with this style so that the style track plays over the appropriate channels and instruments.

- **Variation**—This is a section within a style to create variations within the accompaniment of a specific style. Typical variations are Intro, Main, Fill, Break, Ending, and so on. You can create a whole song structure using different variations of a style.

- **Mode**—How the style track reacts to your input or to a chord track depends on the mode you select; for example, you don't want to transpose the drums in a style track when you are playing different chords to control the harmonic progression of a style. You can also let a chord track decide which chords are used when playing with the style tracks. There are six different modes to choose from (with the Off mode deactivating the style track).

http://www.muskalipman.com

▶ **Chord track**—If you have set your mode to have the style track follow a chord track, you will need to have a chord track present or create one. This will not necessarily control the pitch of these chords, but rather the chord's structure and coloring and its progression in time.

▶ **Switch**—You can choose when and how the variations occur through the Switch drop-down menu. This will let you select a variation trigger. For example, you could set some notes on your keyboard to act as variation triggers in the style track.

Now that you know what comes into play, let's look at how it's laid out in the Track Info area of the style track (see Figure C.5) from top to bottom.

Figure C.5
The Track Info area of a style track.

▶ The **top three fields** display, respectively, the name of the selected part on a chord track and its start and end times.

▶ The **style field** allows you to select which style will be active. You can have up to fifteen different styles loaded at once. The set of fifteen boxes underneath the style field displays the available style slots. A blue square means that there is a style in this memory; a red square means that this is the current selected style. Click on a gray square to prompt Cubase to load a new style for you into memory. To remove a style from memory, you can hold down the Alt key as you right-click on a square where a style is loaded. To make a style active, select it from its drop-down menu or click on its corresponding blue square.

▶ Each style can hold up to eight different variations. Like the Style buttons described above, the **Variation buttons** appear blue when there is a variation, red when a variation is active, and gray when the variation memory for this style is not available. You will see later how to record variation changes in time, or how to automate these changes.

▶ The **Mute section** allows you to mute or play a specific MIDI part within the style. Since each style uses different MIDI instruments to play back its accompaniment, you can isolate a part or parts. Blue buttons will play through MIDI, red ones are muted, and gray ones mean that there are no parts loaded for these instruments.

▶ The **mode** you choose will determine how the style track works and how it will handle your input when playing notes and chords on a keyboard to trigger proper chord progressions, for example. The following list describes these modes.

Off—Turns the style track off.

Slave—Will use a chord track to play chords. When this mode is selected, your keyboard will have no effect on the chord structure or direction. See how to create an appropriate chord track later on in this appendix.

Listening—Cubase will interpret the chords you play and use this information to create an accompaniment that will follow the loaded style. Here are the rules:

1. You need at least three notes to properly use chords.

2. Doubled octaves will be interpreted the same way as if the octave wasn't played.

3. If you play the chords in their simplest form and move upward, for example, the accompaniment will also go upward if possible. However, if you play different chord inversions, this will influence the direction of the transposition.

4. If you are only using chords to control the style track, use the simplest accompaniment as possible to avoid misinterpreted information. Again, if you are recording your chords as an integral part of the music, you can play the chords as you would normally do. Cubase should be able to understand and interpret the values correctly.

Easy—In this mode, what you play determines where Cubase will go in terms of pitch. However, instead of playing full chords, you only need to press one note on your keyboard and Cubase determines which chord would be best suited for the accompanying parts. Which scale it will use depends on the Easy Mode Key setting found in the Style Track Edit window found under Modules > Styletrax > Styletrax. In this window, shown in Figure C.6, select the Settings option in the Edit button or click on the center button showing three knobs. This will allow you to see the scale parameters, where you can change the scales used by the style track when interpreting the notes you play in Easy mode

Roland, Yamaha, and Casio—This is the same as the Easy mode but with an addition control over the tensions you can add to the chords. For a complete list of options you can use when using these modes, please consult your online documentation called Modules.pdf in the "Style Tracks — Using Style Tracks" > Chord Mode Details section.

Figure C.6
The Style Tracks Editor window.

- The **Switch pop-up menu** offers you different ways to change your variations using MIDI. The Rem./Man. is the default setting. This will allow you to use the first left-hand keys of your keyboard to switch between these variations. If your switch parameter is set to Ext. Cntrl, you can use MIDI Control Change messages to trigger variation changes. An example of this could be the modulation wheel used as a trigger. The Vel. Switch option, like both preceding methods, will rely, in this case, on Note On Velocity coming from the note or chords you are playing to trigger variation changes. In this case, the MIDI input plays two roles: It determines the pitch and the variations. If you are using a chord track as a guide for the style track, there's not much use for this option. The Random and Random-Mix options will allow the computer to select which variation to play. What is particular about the Random-Mix is that it can allow one instrument to play one variation, and another to play another variation. For example, the piano could be playing a section called "Main 1" and the bass could be playing a section called "Fill 2."

- The **Snap field** allows you to determine when exactly the chords will change when they are triggered in realtime. When this option is set to Off, the transposition to a new chord is done immediately. When Bar is selected, the change will occur at the beginning of the next bar. Finally, when Part is selected, the change will occur when one of the variations' parts reaches the end of its part (as they normally appear in the Arrange window) and repeats itself. If your variations in a style are of different length, you should consider leaving this setting to Bar.

- **Record On/Off** allows you to record the output of a style track onto other MIDI track as regular MIDI events when this option is set to On. You can record the output of a style track the same way as you would record the output of a normal track.

- The **Global Output field** determines on which MIDI port the recorded style track material will be exported to, as well as determining the main MIDI output port for playback.

To create chord tracks for use with style tracks as harmonic progressions, please refer to "Working With Chords" in Chapter 7. Once your chord track is created, you can use it with the style track in slave mode to have the style track follow these predefined chords.

There are many more options available to the style track through its Style Track Editor window, as shown in Figure C.6. For further information on how to use the Style Track Editor, please refer to the online document called Modules.pdf in the "Style Tracks—Using Style Tracks." This editor will let you customize Track List information used by the loaded styles, review and remap sounds in your General MIDI module, change the different trigger parameters and scale parameter, configure your remote keyboard to send variation changes, start and stop messages, and so on. Finally, the styles panel in this editor will allow you to see the different styles that are loaded with their respective variations.

Although this is not an in-depth coverage of the style track module, I hope it gave you an insight into what it has to offer. You can create your own styles, create styles out of entire songs to have them triggered in a live performance by a single press of a key, or create random variations of drum tracks when using the style tracks in Random Mix mode with drum instrument patterns set on different tracks. The tool is yours to use.

Studio Modules

As mentioned at the beginning of this appendix, studio modules are very useful in automating your MIDI device setup by allowing you to make patch changes directly from the Cubase environment through the use of System Exclusive messages. Because the information for using this module is extensive and already well documented in the online help file provided with your Cubase VST CD-ROM (go to the Documentation folder under Modules.pdf), consult this to better understand how to use this function.

The studio modules can be activated in the Modules menu. Once activated, a series of options will allow you to import and export instrument settings and patchnames, as well as group names such as combis, performances, and other sets of multichannel layouts your MIDI device might support.

Appendix D
Interacting with Others over the Web

RocketPower, Rocket Network, RocketControl, and Cubase VST—If you thought a four-way relationship could not work, you're in for a surprise. In this appendix, we will explore the possibilities of collaborating with other professionals and music (even sound) enthusiasts like you all over the world. The Internet has redefined how people communicate with each other. Now, with this combination of applications, all available in Cubase VST, RocketPower will transform the way studios produce music. Does this seem a little overly enthusiastic to you? Well, perhaps. Obviously, if you like working alone and aren't excited about the prospect of sharing ideas with other people, or about cutting transportation costs, or delays caused by transportation of sound material on a production, then I guess you would feel this is not such a big deal.

It's Not Just for Rocket Scientists

Cubase VST allows you to create, mix, record, and distribute music. RocketPower, as an integrated module in Cubase VST, allows you to communicate the audio and MIDI material in your arrangement to a host on one of the Rocket Network's servers. This server hosts other projects as well, so you can join in an existing project or create your own project by posting your files to this server. Through RocketControl, a simple chat utility, you can talk to people who contribute to your project or to people who have already started working on a project you just joined. This is how it works, step by step:

1. You install Rocket Network's RocketPower software on your computer.
2. You create a song in Cubase or you simply launch Cubase.

http://www.muskalipman.com

3. You click on the RocketPower button in the Arrange window. This will prompt a Connect To Rocket Network dialog box. (see Figure D.1).

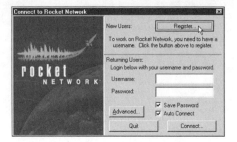

Figure D.1
The Connect To Rocket Network dialog box allows you to create a new profile or connect directly to the Rocket Network server if you already have a registered profile.

4. Create a new registration that will allow you to access the Rocket Network servers or log on as a preregistered user if you have already registered once. The software will recognize you if you already have a username and a password.

5. If you are a new user, you will need to fill out some information. This is a free subscription that gives you access to the Rocket Network servers; however, if you want to have your own private project session, using this service for professional use, you will need to pay a user fee.

6. Next, you need to download the RocketControl application, which will allow you to chat with people who will be sharing a project with you. RocketControl (see Figure D.2), once installed, will launch automatically when you log onto the Rocket Network servers and join a room or create a new session.

Figure D.2
The RocketControl chat interface.

7. As you are being connected to the server, your Web browser will launch and try to establish a contact with the Rocket Network server. Once a contact is established, you will be logged onto this network and a list of available "Project Sessions" will appear. By default, you will be joining the lobby area, which is a standard welcoming session.

8. At this point, RocketControl will also launch and connect you with users participating in that room (or session).

9. Rocket Network will ask you if you want to receive the current files belonging to the lobby area. If you don't wish to start at the lobby, you can skip the reception and look at other public sessions. Public sessions are there for you to join in. As Figure D.3 suggests, you can click one of the existing sessions or create your own public or private session for a fee.

Figure D.3
The lobby area of Steinberg's Inwire Studios. This is a standard Web page hosted on one of Rocket Network's servers (in this case, Steinberg). From here, you can join or create a studio session.

10. Once you have chosen to enter a studio session, the media files will begin to download onto your computer. Once downloaded, you can add your own material to the arrangement, but you cannot edit material that is not yours.

11. To post your own updates, simply click the Post button next to the active RocketPower button in the Arrange window.

12. When done, you can save the work for later use. Add material and save again. The next time you open the song or arrangement file, Cubase will ask you if you want to validate the files, which means that you can continue working with the version you have or check on the Rocket Network's server to see if someone else posted a newer version of the arrangement. If so, all new files will be downloaded to your copy of the arrangement and you can later upload your upgrades as well.

That's it for the 12-step introduction to Rocket Network.

If you are not familiar with Web technology such as chat rooms, you might need a little bit of experimenting before you feel comfortable, but most of the steps are done automatically. The longest it takes is when you create your identity on the server for the first time, adding information to the database. After this, it is a much quicker process.

How Rocket Network Integrates into Cubase

Now that you understand how a Rocket session flows from start to finish, let us look at how it is integrated into Cubase VST. The first place you will notice Rocket is through the RocketPower button found on your Arrange window toolbar. This button will allow you to connect to the Rocket Network.

The second place to look is in the Modules > Rocket Network sub-menu, where you will find a list of options relating to the transfer of files to the Rocket Network server. Until you log onto one of the Rocket Network servers, most options in this sub-menu will be disabled. However, the Preferences option, which will bring up the Rocket Preferences dialog box, as shown in Figure D.4, and the RocketPower option will be available at all times.

Figure D.4
The Rocket Preferences dialog box.

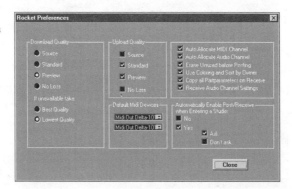

To the left of this dialog box, you will find the Download Quality radio button options. This determines the quality, as well as the file size, of material you download from an existing remote studio session on the Rocket Network. You can choose between Source (which uses no compression) and Preview (which uses maximum compression). The No Loss uses compression with a lossless algorithm. Under these four choices, you can select an alternative option in regard to file quality.

The Upload Quality section allows you to decide which formats will be available when uploading (posting) files to the servers. These options won't do anything to the original files you record, but rather save off a compressed copy of the audio into a special folder. You can check more than one option. This will have an impact on the size of your project's upload/download time, and its quality as well. It will also determine what type of file quality you can choose from in the Audio Pool under the Quality column.

Below Upload Quality, you will find the Default MIDI Devices selection for Rocket sessions. Since the files you post using Rocket are used by others or come from others, using non-GM or third-party VSTi and Rewire-compatible software is not a great idea, unless you are working on a private session and you know the other user also has the same software on his/her computer. Therefore, most of the material posted with Rocket will be audio files, so setting the Default MIDI device to a MIDI port that points to a GM-compatible device would be advisable.

The Switches section in the upper right corner offers different options for how Rocket will handle the allocation of MIDI and audio channels when transferring, as well as offering optimal settings for posting, organizing events by contributors, and parameter configurations. You should leave these options checked for now, since they will provide you with standard options as you begin working with Rocket.

The last options in this dialog box ask you whether or not you want Rocket to start uploading or downloading files automatically as you log onto a Rocket server.

The next stop to look for Rocket presence is the Audio Pool. As you saw in Chapter 9, the Audio Pool has two specific columns dedicated to RocketPower, as shown in Figure D.5. The Quality Column shows you which quality of audio file you are currently using. If you created a Rocket session, this would probably set to Source (Src). On the other hand, if you joined an existing session, what will be available to you will depend on your preference settings in the Rocket Preferences dialog box, as we just saw. This brings us to the Post As column, which lets you choose which qualities you would like to include in your posting. Checked options will be transferred and will become available to other users.

Figure D.5
The Rocket Network options available in the Audio Pool.

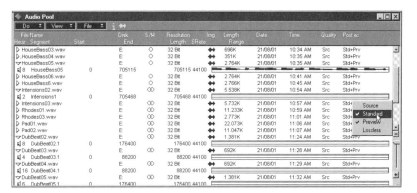

Connecting with Rocket Control

Connection to the Rocket Network servers is done though RocketControl. You will need to download this software from the Rocket Network site (**http://www.rocketnetwork.com/**). Once installed, the interface will load automatically when you click the RocketPower button inside Cubase VST. As you saw in Figure D.2, you will be presented with four major functions:

- ▶ **Sessions**—This allows you to browse through existing sessions and join one.
- ▶ **Details**—This offers additional information on the current studio session you are in. Figure D.2 showed the "Steinberg–Welcome Lobby" session; clicking the Sessions button will bring up details on who is in the session and what the session is about. This is shown in Figure D.6. Notice that you can see who created the session and how big the transfer of files will be in Source, Standard, and Preview format. In this case, the files haven't been provided in Source format, so it is not active.

http://www.muskalipman.com

Figure D.6
The details of a session as they appear on the Rocket Network's Web site.

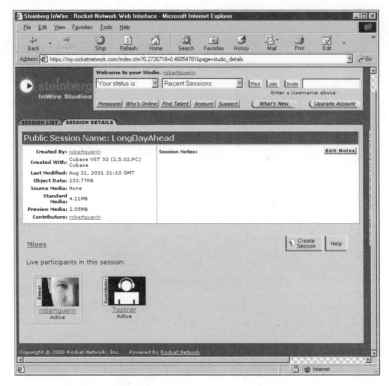

- **Messages**—Since this is a communications application, after all, you can see the people in the current session in the RocketControl interface. You can also send messages to people who are not in the same session as you or receive messages from people in other sessions as well.

- **Support**—This will bring you directly to an online support Web site.

When you wish to post new recorded files to a session you have joined, you can click the Post button in the Arrange window, next to the RocketPower button. The process can be monitored through the RocketControl application, as seen in Figures D.7 and D.8. In Figure D.7, notice that the information starts by being compressed on your computer, allowing for a quicker transfer later. How it compresses the files depends on two settings: your Rocket Network preference settings and your post settings in the Audio Pool. This might take some time, depending on the size of your files. Then, in Figure D.8, you can see the process as the compressed files are being posted to the server. This is what will appear later when the whole posting will be completed on the session's site (as shown in Figure D.6).

If you wish to talk to someone individually, rather than to everyone all at once in a studio session, you can click on the little icon with a face in the lower right corner of the window. This is a pop-up menu showing you who is online. Select a name and a new private window will appear.

http://www.muskalipman.com

Figure D.7
Rocket Control compresses the audio files for transfer to the Rocket Network server.

Figure D.8
Rocket Control posts (uploads) the audio files to the Rockst Network server after compressing them.

Additional Tips

At the time of this writing, Rocket did not support 24- or 32-bit files. So, it is advisable to use 16-bit resolution when you are considering working on Rocket, especially with version 2.3 of the RocketControl application.

If you have worked in 24- or 32-bit prior to connecting to Rocket, you can always save a copy of your work in a new location, then use the Prepare Archive found in the Audio Pool, and select the same folder as your work copy. Using an external editor like Wavelab or Sound Forge, change the resolution of your copied files to 16-bit, but don't change anything else. Then, open the copy of your arrangement. If Cubase doesn't change the links to the original files automatically, click on the drive letter in the Audio Pool to reload the files, which have been converted. If you have not modified the length of your audio content, all the files can be replaced to use only 16-bit audio files for your Rocket session.

Although participating in public studio sessions is free, you will have to pay a one-time fee for registering your information to create or participate in private studio sessions. You can try out this tool for as long as you wish, however. If you feel it could be an interesting creative tool for you, it'll be worth spending the money to create your own sessions. If you need help once on the site, look for online support from people whose log-on names begin with "onlinesupp". They are there to help you out and solve basic problems you might have with your Rocket application.

As mentioned previously, working with audio files is probably the best way to work with Rocket, since MIDI, although much smaller in size, does not include the instrument used to create the sound. Therefore, you will have no control over how the MIDI parts will sound on the other end. This is not necessarily a bad thing, but you need to be aware of it. Along the same lines, the use of third-party plug-ins such as DirectX or commercial VST effects will not be heard properly unless the other users or contributors have the same effects.

http://www.muskalipman.com

Appendix E
Cubase Resources on the Web

This appendix will give you some of the best-known resources for information on the World Wide Web. These links have been separated into two sections for your convenience: "Finding Help" and "Plug-In Resources and VST Instruments."

Finding Help

Cubase is pretty well documented, so now that you have a book that simplifies the most common functions and operations, you might want to learn about a specific issue or problem. These resources offer some relief and insight by sharing their knowledge base with you. They can also provide updates on available upgrades, fixes and patches, and the most valuable of all—discussion forums where thousands of users like you join to discuss many topics.

Cubase.net
http://www.cubase.net/
If you are looking for news, interviews, tips and tricks, or even a group forum discussing Cubase and other Steinberg products, Cubase.net is the place to go. This site provides the information you can't find on Steinberg's site, but it has close ties with the company. You can also subscribe to Club Cubase, a support group for registered Cubase users online, at this site.

Steinberg's Info Center
http://www.steinberg.net/infocenter/
This is ground zero for Cubase users. Steinberg provides additional tutorials, information on newly released software, plug-ins, and VST Instruments. It is also a good place to look for special events, such as trade shows or master classes.

Cubase FAQ
http://www.cubasefaq.com/
This site was created in March 1998 because Cubase users needed an FAQ site. The owner of the site compiles the information, so it's not always up to date, but you will find a lot of information and resources. You can also subscribe to a Cubase mailing list to receive news about Cubase-related events through your e-mail.

K-v-R VST
http://www.kvr-vst.com/
This site is dedicated to VST Instruments resources. It provides up-to-the-minute news, resources, beta testing results of software applications, ASIO and latency issues related to sound cards, VST Instrument patches, and much more. This is a very nice and well-thought-out site—a must if you want to get quick information.

Rocket Network
http://www.rocketnetwork.com/
If you would like to know more about Rocket Network's services and how they integrate into Cubase, this is the place to get your information.

Steinberg Newsgroups
alt.steinberg
alt.steinberg.cubase
There are two newgroups available through the Internet that address Steinberg-specific topics. You will need a news reader to access these newsgroups.

Plug-in Resources and VST Instruments
Cubase as a stand-alone software is quite nice, but adding VST or DirectX-compatible plug-ins or VST Instruments transforms it into an unusually versatile creative instrument. Here you will find some of the manufacturers that develop third-party software that can be integrated into Cubase. For a complete list of all VST plug-ins and Instrument manufacturers, visit Steinberg's site at: **http://www.steinberg.net/infocenter/discoveries/pluginzone/**

Antares
http://www.antares-systems.com
Antares develops high-end audio plug-ins. The Autotune and Microphone Modeler software allow you to shape your input by adding a virtual model of a high-quality microphone response curve, then use Autotune to correct any pitch problems you might have had when recording the session. These two tools combined will transform an average performance into a pretty good one.

Arboretum
http://www.arboretum.com
This is another top-notch plug-in maker. Arboretum has developed tools that will transform your sound in many different ways. Countless recording artists, including Nine Inch Nails, White Zombie, and Public Enemy, have used its Hyperprism plug-in series. The effect the plug-ins produce is amazing. Some of the plug-ins available include HyperVerb, New Granulator, Hyperphaser, Formant Pitch Shifter, Harmonic Exciter, and Bass Maximizer.

Native Instruments
http://www.native-instruments.net/
You can't talk about VST Instruments without talking about Native Instruments. This company has created some of the best "virtual synthesizers" that musicians have seen on the market. The legendary B3 organ has been perfectly reproduced (sometimes surpassing the original) by the company's B4 software version, for example.

Prosoniq
http://www.prosoniq.com
Have you ever wondered what an Orange Vocoder is? To find out, you can head out to Prosoniq's Web site. This is another company that has turned out some very cool VST-compatible plug-ins. With Orange Vocoder, Prosoniq offers you an all-digital simulation of a realistic analog vocoder effect that can be fully customized and comes with an eight-voice virtual analog synthesizer unit, Freeform EQ, and Filterbank Reverb, all in one plug-in.

Spectral Design
http://www.spectral-design.com
This company develops software that is distributed by Steinberg. So, it's safe to say that the products integrate very well into Steinberg's suite of products. The deNoiser, deClicker, Clean, and Freefilter applications are probably their best-known products. The deNoiser plug-in works especially well on constant noises in your recording, such as hums and tape hiss.

TC Works
http://www.tcworks.de/home/content/en/Welcome/render_top
TC Works has been at the forefront of the high-end plug-in industry with its TC Native Bundle. All tools are heavily performance optimized, so they really work in your multitrack environment without bringing the computer to its knees. The intuitive user interfaces make these plug-ins invaluable tools you'll be able to use instantly. The company also produces a very nice VST Instrument called Mercury-1, which nicely emulates old analog monophonic synthesis.

Waves
http://www.waves.com
Waves began developing plug-ins originally for Pro Tools as TDM software. With the arrival of VST and the potential power this format provided, however, Waves developed a VST version of its popular plug-in packages. The Native Power Pack is the package that started it all for Native users. This package includes a De-Esser, and a special 2-tap version of SuperTap rounds out the essential collection for everyday music and production work. Waves also provides support for 88.2/96 kHz for many Native components.

Index

NUMBERS

( ) button, 183
? button, 183
* key, *59*
+ key, *59*
- key, *59*
/ key, *59*
(+) sign, 90, 93
0 key, *58*
16-bit resolution, 21
1 key, *59*
24-bit resolution, 21
2 key, *59*
32-bit recording, 20–22, 52
3 to 9 keys, *59*

A

accidental notes, 174, 183
Accidentals page, 174
Activate Recording function, *59*
activating modules, 379
Active button, 373
Active column, 203
Adaptec's Easy CD Creator (software application), 356
ADAT (Alesis Digital Audio Technology), 313
Add cycle record mode, 54
Additional Settings page, 175
Add Out option, 90
AES/EBU (Audio Engineering Society/European Broadcast Union), 313
After filter Play Parameter, *88*
Aftertouch, reducing, 100
AIFF file format, 347
Alesis Digital Audio Technology (ADAT), 313
ambiance, 295
amplitude
　See also sampling frequency; volume
　explanation of, 9–10, 11
　measuring, 12
　reducing dynamic range between, 211
analog sound, 9–10
Analytic Quantize function, 150
Antares (Web site), 400
Any Channel setting, 18–19
"Any" setting, for MIDI tracks, 17
Appearance column, 77
Arboretum (Web site), 400
archiving files, 244
arpeggios, 377, 382–385

Arrange Window, 43–71
　configuring options for, 45–52
　　Link Editors, 51
　　Markers, 49–51
　　Part Colors option, 48–49
　　Quantizing, 47–48
　　Record Mode, 52
　　Snap function, 46
　exercises, 71
　MIDI tracks in, *16*
　parts of, 43–45
　toolboxes, 64–71
　　See also Arrange Window Toolbox
　　Audio Editor Window Toolbox, 66
　　Controller Edit Window Toolbox, 71
　　Drum Edit Window Toolbox, 68
　　Graphical Master Track Window Toolbox, 69
　　Key Edit And List Edit Window Toolbox, 67
　　Score Edit Window Toolbox, 70
　Transport bar, 53–63
　　controls, 58–59
　　Cycle Recording option, 53–56
　　Left and Right locators, 57–58
　　MIDI activity display, 63
　　Recording mode, 56–57
　　signature settings, 61–63
　　tempo setting, 59–61
Arrange Window Toolbox, 161–167
　Eraser tool, 162–163
　Glue or Glue Tube tool, 163
　Groove tool, 166
　Logical editor tool, 166
　Match Quantize tool, 164
　Mute tool, 164
　overview, 64–65
　Pan tool, 165
　Pencil tool, 161–162
　Pointer tool, 161
　Selection Range tool, 164–165
　Speaker tool, 163
　Stretch tool, 166–167
　Transpose tool, 165
　Volume tool, 165
　Zoom tool, 164
ASIO 2 VST Plug-ins, *298*
ASIO Control Panel button, 29
ASIO drivers, 28–32
ASIO Multimedia Advanced Setup window, 31
ASIO Multimedia Driver Setup application, 30–32
ASIO Multimedia Setup Advanced Options dialog box, 32

asterisk key, *59*
ATA drives, 36
atonal music, 175
Attack parameter, 210
audio CDs, creating, 353–356
audio channels, 17, 200, 201
audio editing. *See* Audio editor; Audio Pool; Wave editors
Audio editor, 250–275
    audio envelope controls, 269–272
    audio functions, 272–275
    auditioning audio, 256
    customizing view, 254
    editing audio events, 257–259
    events, lanes, and segments, 251–253
    importing audio, 255
    M-points, 261–265
    overview, 250–251
    Q-points, 260
    quantizing audio, 265–268
    uses of, 249
Audio Editor Window Toolbox, 66
Audio Engineering Society/European Broadcast Union (AES/EBU), 313
audio envelope controls, 269–272
audio events
    in Audio editor, 251–253
    copying, 259
    creating crossfades between adjacent or overlapping, 270–271
    defined, 235
    deleting, 259
    muting, 259
    splitting, 259
audio files
    converting from MIDI to, 341–342
    exercises, 247
Audio functions, 272–275
Audio I/O section, 28
Audio Mix track, controller events in, 131
Audio Pool, 234–245
    archiving files, 244
    audio file operations, 240
    customizing view, 238
    dragging segments into other windows, 243
    file usage, 235, 239
    headings and columns, 236–237
    importing and exporting audio from, 243
    loading content, 245
    overview, 234
    saving, 245
    segments, 235, 239, 241–242
audio recording, 228–234
    See also Audio Pool
    controlling input levels, 234
    importing audio files, 245–247
    setting up, 199–226

    See also VST Channel Mixer; VST Master Mixer
    selecting recording resolution, 233
    using more than two inputs, 231–232
    using only two inputs/outputs, 228–231
Audio Stream Input/Output. *See* ASIO
audio system settings, 26–27
Audio System Setup dialog box accessing, 30
    Audio I/O section, 28, 29
audio track class, 79
audio tracks, 18–19, *104*
auditioning audio, 256
AutoBlack button, 344
Auto Gain dynamic control, 211
AutoGate function, 210, 213
Auto Grouping option, 180
Auto Layout button, 183
AutoLevel processor, 211, 214
automation, MIDI, 289–291
Autopan effect, 295
Auto Quantize button, 47

B

backing up, 42, 357–358
Banks column, 77
bars
    numbering and layout, 175
    showing location of elements in relation to, 184
bass instrument group, *85*
bass notes, 187
Bass parameter, 299
baud rate, 7
beams, 175, 180
Beams and Bars page, 175
Beige channels, 200
bit rate, 349
bit resolution, 20–21
Blue channels, 200
braces, 196
brackets, 196
Breath Controllers, 100
Build Trill option, 181
Build Tuplet dialog box, 178
Built-In Wave editor, 276–277
buses, 218
By Output option, 254
Bypass button, 209, 215

C

C7 button, 184
Calibrate button, 213
Casio mode, 387
CDDA (compact disc digital audio) compatible disc, 353
CD Player module, 377
CDs, creating, 353–356

Channel column, 76
Channel Mixer window, 19, 95
channels
 audio, 17, 200, *201*
 Group, 200
 MIDI, 16
 Rewire, 200
 setting inputs of, 19
 setting properties to ANY, 87
 settings in VST Channel Mixer, 282
 specifying for audio recordings, 229
 specifying in Drum Edit window, 122
 VST Instrument (VSTi), 200
Chn column, 122
Chopper2 effect, 298
Chord Font page, 174
chords, 185–188
 generating in scores, 177
 inserting into scores, 179, 184
chord track class, 82
Chord track parameter, 386
chord tracks, *104*
Chord Types page, 174
Chorus and Chorus 2 effects, 294
Chorus effect, *298*
chromatic percussion instrument group, *85*
Classic Arp checkbox, 383
Clean Lengths option, 194
Click button, 99
clipping, 205
Close Movie option, 338
Close Program dialog box, 32
Color menu, 114
colors
 assigning to events, 114
 of channels, 200
 display, reducing, 37
 for parts, displaying, 238
 specifying for Arrange window's Track View section, 48–49
combis, 371, 372, 373
commands, assigning keyboard shortcuts to, 363
comments, adding to music sheets, 176
Common controllers, 130
compact discs. *See* CDs
Compression column, 77
compression, data, 347
Compression dynamic control, 211
Compression Play Parameter, *88*
Compress Play Parameter, *88*
Compute Scale option, 113, 177
Confirm Record dialog box, 231
Connect Dynamics function, 178–179
connecting
 equipment, 33–36
 notes with beams, 180
 to Rocket Network, 392

connectors, MIDI, 8–9
continuous controller events
 editing, 126–130
 general information, 118, 119
Continuous mode, 369
Continuous Resynchronization setting, 314
Contour parameter, 299
Controller editing window, 81
Controller editor, 130–134
 for audio mixing, 286
 editing MIDI automation with, 290
 seeing more than one controller at time in, *291*
Controller Edit window, 93, *105*
Controller Edit Window Toolbox, 71
controller events, MIDI
 adding new, 133
 deleting, 133
 editing, 118–119
  in Controller Edit window, 132–134
  non-note events, 126–130
 erasing, 133
 smoothening transition between, 133
Controller Map setting, 26
controller messages, mapping, 100
controllers, drawing, 93
Controller window, 104
Convert to IPS Phrase in the Functions menu, 368
Copy Combi to function, 372
copying
 for backups, 357–358
 combis, 372
 events, 259, 291
 hitpoints, 329
 locator ranges, 158
 lyrics, and pasting into scores, *192*
 M-point quantizing, 267
 note properties to other notes, 181
 parts, 162
 tracks, 259
Copy Locator Range function, 158
Copy Part to Phrase dialog box, 368
Copy Phrase to function, 372
copyright information, adding to music sheets, 176
Copyright page, 174
crescendo, 178
crossfades, 270–271
Cubase FAQ (Web site), 399
Cubase.net (Web site), 399
cursor, graphical position of, 184
Custom palette, 185
Cut Flag tool, *70*
Cut function, 155
cutting tracks, 259
Cycle mode, 56
Cycle Playback/Record mode button, *58*
Cycle Recording option, 53–56

D

Damp parameter, 299
data compression, 347
Date item, 237
Deactivate option, 338
Decrease Tempo function, *59*
dedicated ASIO drivers, 29–30
DEF.ALL file, 323, 361–363
default file, 323, 361–363
DEF.SET file, 323
delay
    drum, 122
    and VST Instruments (VSTi), 97
Delay column, 77, 122
DelayMod parameter, 300
Delay parameter, 299
Delay Play Parameter, *88, 90*
Delete Combi function, 373
Delete Last Version option, 56
Delete Note option, 111
Delete Phrase function, 373
Delete Sub Track option, 56
deleting
    combis, 373
    controller events, MIDI, 133
    events, 259
    files, 239
    hitpoints, 329
    notes, 111
    parts, 162
    phrases, 373
    region markers, 51
    segments, 238, 242
    shadow tracks, 90
Delta X and Y coordinates, 184
Depth parameter, 300
desktop mixers, connecting, 39–40
desktop, removing wallpaper images, 38
Details function, 395
Detect Frame Change option, 318
devices, hooking up, 33–36
digital audio
    analog sound, 9–10
    digital sound, 11–12
    sampling, 13–14
Digital Clock, 312–313
digital distortion. *See* distortion
digital sound, 11–12
diminuendo, 178
Direct ASIO monitoring, 29–30
Direct Show (DS) Video Monitor module, 377
DirectX effects, 281, *282*, 307–308
Disc-At-Once (DAO), 354
Disk block buffer size field, *201*
disk fragmentation, 34

Disk item, 236
Disk tools, 34–35
Display Quantize tool, *70*
distortion
    adding, 297, *298*
    cause of, 12
distributing music, 339–359
    audio CDs, 353–356
    backup copies, 357–358
    converting MIDI tracks, 341–342
    dithering, 343–344
    exporting, 345–347
    HTML page, 358–359
    mastering, 352–353
    metafile, 359
    MP3 files, 350–351
    Real Networks, 348–350
    streaming media file, 359
    VSTi and Rewire channels, 342
dithering, 14, 343–344
Dmaker (software application), 378
DMA setting, 36
Do Fixed Note option, 110–111
Do menu, 110, 177
dotted notes, 48
DoubleDelay effect, *298*
Download Quality radio buttons, 394
dragging segments into other windows, 243
drawing
    controller lines, *66*
    controllers, 93
    events, *64*
    parts, 161
    ramps, 93
    selections across different tracks, 164
Draw tool, *69*
Drive parameter, 300
drivers
    ASIO, 28–32
    MIDI, 23–26
    multi-client, 32
    troubleshooting, 27
drop frames, 311
Dropout Time, 318
Drum Edit window, 120–125
Drum Edit Window Toolbox, 68
drums
    mapping, 123–125
    score editing, 192–195
Drum Stick, 105–107
drum track class, 80
drum tracks
    editing window for, *104*
    step recording, 97–98
Drum window, 104
Dry/Wet parameter, 300
DS Video Monitor module, 377

http://www.muskalipman.com

Index

duplets, 178
duplicating
    files, 239
    segments, 241
Duration slider, 152
Dynamic button, 204
dynamic compression, 347
Dynamic Events option, 254
dynamics, adding to scores, 178
dynamics control, 210–215
Dynamics effect, *298*

E

Earlier Effects submenu, 294–297
Easy CD Creator (software application), 356
Easy mode, 387
Echo Dec parameter, 380
Echo parameter, 379–380
Edit Behavior page, 173
Edit button, 95
Edit mode, 171, 175–176
editors, MIDI, 103–126
    Controller editor, 130–134
    Drum Edit window, 120–125
    editing MIDI controller events, 118–119
    editing multiple tracks, 117
    Info line, 115–116
    List Edit window, 126–130
    toolbar options, 110–114
    toolbox options, 105–109
Edit window, 104
effects
    in Cubase 5.0, 298–306
    DirectX, 307–308
    Earlier Effects submenu, 294–297
    parameters of, 293
    realtime, *293*
    saving, 295
    VST, 215–219
    VST Master Mixer, 219–221
    why to use, 291
effects button, 204
E-IDE drives, 36
Electro Fuzz effect, 296
End item, 237
Enhanced CDs, 353, 354
enharmonic chords, 187
enharmonic notes, 183
ensemble instrument group, *85*
Enter key, *58*
EQing, 207–209
equalization button, 204
equalizing, 207–209
equipment, hooking up, 33–36
Erase All Data function, 373
Eraser tool
    in Arrange Window Toolbox, *64*, 162–163
    in Audio Editor Window Toolbox, *66*
    in Controller Edit Window Toolbox, *71*
    in Drum Edit Window Toolbox, *68*
    in Graphical Master Track Window Toolbox, *69*
    in Key Edit And List Edit Window Toolbox, *67*
    in Score Edit Window Toolbox, *70*
Erase Unused function, 242
erasing
    combis, 373
    controller events, MIDI, 133
    events, 109
    keys, 56
    phrases, 373
    region markers, 51
    segments, 242
Espacial effect, 295
events
    adding
        with Paint tool, 108–109
        with Pencil tool, 105
    assigning colors to, 114
    in Audio editor, 251–253
    copying, 259
    creating crossfades between adjacent or overlapping, 270–271
    deleting, 259
    determining start position or velocity value, 115
    editing
        with Line tool, 107–108
        more than one at a time, 134
        non-note, 126–130
    erasing, 109
    fitting to loop areas, 268
    monitoring, *114*, 256
    moving, 109, 258
    muting/unmuting, 109, 259
    resizing, 106
    reversing order of, 113
    splitting, 157, 259
    stretching, 166–167
    types, 130–131
    unmuting, 109, 113
Exact Length option, 274
exercises
    Arrange window, 71
    audio editing, 279
    audio files, 247
    MIDI Editing windows, 135
    mixing, 308
    score editing, 198
    setting up audio recording, 226
    setting up MIDI recording, 101
    track editing, 167
Explode by Channel option, 374
Explode function, 159

http://www.muskalipman.com

exporting
    from Audio Pool, 243
    formats for, 347
    mixes as audio files, 345
External Wave editor, 278–279
    launching, 273
    specifying default, 273
    uses of, 249
External Wave editor option, 273
Ext. Prg. Change function, 372
extracting parts, 159

F

Factory Presets parameter, 300
Fade Dialog option, 275
fade in/fade out, 272, 273
fader area, of VST Channel Mixer, 205
faders, 200
Fast button, 206
Fast Forward function, *58*
Fast Rewind function, *58*
F button, 173, 182
Feedback parameter, 301
File Name item, 236
files
    archiving, 244
    compression, 347
    defined, 235
    deleting, 239
    duplicating, 239
    finding, 239
    importing/exporting, 243, 245–247
    Mixman, 246–247
    paths to, 238
    recycling, 245–246
    renaming, 239
    replacing, 239
    saving, 42
Filter Hi/Lo Cut parameter, 301
filtering MIDI, 100
finding files, 239
Find Parts option, 242
FireWire drives, 36
Fixed Note option, 110–111
fixed text, 188
F key, *116*
Flanger effect, 294, *298*
flat setting, 174
Flip Direction option, 185
flipping waveform, 273
Flip Stems option, 180, 183
floating point resolution, 21
folders
    assigning tracks to, 80
    creating structure before audio recording, 230
    Library folder, 124
    saving, 42
folder track class, 80
folder tracks, 138
Follow Song option, *116*
Force Update option, 184
(fps) frames per second, 311
fragmentation, disk, 34
frame rate, 311, 316
frames per second (fps), 311
Freeze Play Parameters option, *88*, *91*
Freeze Quantize function, 46
Freq or Rate parameter, 301
frequency
    adjusting, 209
    defined, 9
    sampling, 11, 12
Frequency control, 207
From Input field, 316, 317
FuzzBox effect, 296
FX button, 204

G

Gain control, 207
Gain Reduction meter, 214
Gating dynamic control, 210
General MIDI instruments, 85–88
Get Form Only button, 197
Get Layout button, 197
Global Cut edit, *58*
Global Disable option, 29
Global Output field, 388
Global settings, 282
Global text, 191
Glue tool, 163
Glue Tube tool
    in Arrange Window Toolbox, *65*
    in Score Edit Window Toolbox, *70*
Go To Left Locator function, *59*
Goto menu, 110
Go To Right Locator function, *59*
gramophone record, 10
graphic acceleration, reducing, 37
Graphical Master Track window, 104
Graphical Master Track Window Toolbox, 69
Gray channels, 200
grid, creating in Track view, 46, 74
Groove Control, 151–154
Groove Quantizing, 150
Groove template, 264–265
Groove tool, *65*, 166
Group channels, 200
grouping
    notes, 180
    tracks, 80
Group option, 180
Group Selection tool, *65*

group track class, 82
group tracks, 139–141
Grungelizer effect, 297
guitar instrument group, *85*
guitar symbols, 179

H

Handles option, 254, 257–258
hard drive
    configuring, 33–36
    types and performances, 35–36
hardware
    requirements, 22
    setting up
        hard drive configuration, 33–36
        hooking up equipment, 38–41
        video display adapters, 37–38
H button, 183
headphone amplifiers, 232
Hear item, 237
help, Cubase, 399–400
Hertz, defined, 9, 11
Hertz, Heinrich, 11
Hide option, 180
hiding elements from scores, 180, 183
High Pass Filter (HPF) option, 209
High Pass Filter option, 209
Hi parameter, 299
hitpoints, 263, 325–335
    basic operations, 329–330
    linking, 330–332
    Master Track Editor, 326–328
    Straightening Up tempo, 334–335
    tempo matching, 332–334
Hold button, 206, 370
hooking up equipment, 38–41
HPF (High Pass Filter) option, 209
HTML files, 359
hums, 297
hyperlinks, 359

I

I button, 183
Img item, 236
Immediate Range option, 384
importing
    audio files, 245–247
    to Audio Pool, 243
    files, 245–247
    mono tracks, 255
    stereo tracks, 255
Increase Tempo function, *59*
Info line, MIDI editor, *114*, 115–116
Information button, 183
Information Line, 326

Init button, 373
I-Note column, 121
In port
    configuring, 24–26
    MIDI, 8–9
        activating/deactivating, 26
        data flow, 14–15
Input and Output parameter, 301
Input channel, 203
Input From field, 26
Input meter level button, 230
Input Note value, 121
Insert button, *114*, 204
Insert Effect, 293
Insert function, 156
inserting
    braces, 196
    brackets, 196
    chords, 179, 184
    crescendo, 178
    diminuendo, 178
    guitar symbols, 179
    between locators, *155*
    mono segments, 18
    notes, *70*
    rests, 197
    slurs, 177
    symbols, 180–181
    trills into scores, 181
    tuplets, 178
Insert Quantize option, 178
Insert Slur option, 178
Insert Tuplet option, 178
insets, of events, 257–258
Inspector panel, 44–45
Instrument column, 76, 121
instruments
    modifying names of, 121
    muting, 121
    selecting, 121
    setting up, 85–88
intensity, 178
interacting with others. *See* Rocket Network
Interactive Phrase Synthesizer (IPS), 367–375
    IPS dialog box, 367
        Functions section, 371–373
        Global section, 371
        Output section, 371
        Phrase Input section, 368–371
    overview, 367
    recording output of, 374–375
Internal Wave editor, 249, 273
Internet, interacting with others over.
    See Rocket Network
Interpretation Flags section, 194
invisible items, 173
IRQ settings, *27*

Iterative Quantize function, 149

K

Karlette effect, *298*
kbd (Keyboard Layout) file extension, 363
Keep Note option, 111
keyboard, connecting, 39
keyboard shortcuts
    for control panel, 58–59
    modifying, 363
    for velocity levels, 122
    for Zoom tool (in Track View), 74
Key Edit And List Edit Window Toolbox, 67
Key Edit window, 115–116
Key Erase option, 56
keys
    erasing, 56
    reassigning to play other keys, 123–125
K-v-R VST (Web site), 400

L

Lane Info option, 254
lanes, 243, 251–252
laps, 53
latency, 28, 97
layers, in scores, 175, 177
layout
    bar, 175
    refreshing, 184
    scores, 195–197
Layout tool, *70*
L button, 183
Left locators, 57–58
Len column, 121
Length column, 77
lengthening notes, 106, 194
Length item, 237
Length parameter, 383
Length Play Parameter, *88*
Lev1, Lev2, Lev3, and Lev4 columns, 122
level meters, of VST Channel Mixer, 206
Library folder, 124
Limiting dynamic control, 211, 215
Line Draw tool
    in Audio Editor Window Toolbox, *66*
    in Controller Edit Window Toolbox, *71*
    in Drum Edit Window Toolbox, *68*
    in Graphical Master Track Window Toolbox, *69*
    in Key Edit And List Edit Window Toolbox, *67*
Line tool, 107–108
Link Editors function, 51
links, in HTML files, 359
List Editor, 91
List Edit window, 126–130
Listening mode, 387

List Master Track editing window, 61–62
List Master Track window, 104
List window, 104
LM-9 (VST Instrument), 96
Load and Save All Combis function, 371
Load and Save Phrase Bank function, 372
loading
    Audio Pool content, 245
    layouts, 197
Local Off setting, 25
locator functions, 154–160
    Copy Locator Range function, 158
    Cut function, 155
    Explode function, 159
    Insert function, 156
    Merge function, 160
    Split function, 157
locators, 57–58
Lock Events page, 175
Lock Event tab, 177
Lock Layer numbers, 177
logical editing, 141–148
    Easy vs. Expert mode, 146
    parameters, 143–146
    setting values, 147–148
Logical editor tool, 166
Logical tool, *65*
Log tool, 166
Longitudinal Time Code (LTC), 310
Loop button, *114*, 276, 370
Loop:LFO Reset function, 373
Loop Playback function, 50
loops
    enabling in edit window, *114*
    fitting events to, 268
    MIDI, 9, 111–112
lossy compression, 347
Low Cut button, 209
lower root checkbox, 187
Low Shelf button, 209
LTC (Longitudinal Time Code), 310
lyrics, 188–189, *192*

M

M3U file extension, 359
Macintosh computers
    disk defragmentation, 34
    keystrokes for, 6
magnifying. *See* zooming
magnifying areas, *64*
Main Volume control, *118*
Make Chords option, 179
Make Guitar Symbols option, 179
MakeUpGain knob, 214
mapping, MIDI, 100
margin settings, 197

markers, 49–51, 261–265. *See also* hitpoints
Master button, 206
master effect routing, 224–225
mastering, 352–353
Master Output, 20
Match Quantize tool, 64, 164
match quantizing, 267
M column, 121
Measure in value, 184
Memory per channel field, *201*
Merge function, 160
merging tracks, 160
Messages function, 395
metafiles, 348, 359
Metalizer2 effect, *298*
Meter hitpoints, 325, 326
    finding tempo providing match between, 332–334
    hearing MIDI notes when occurring, 330
Meter Hitpoint Strip, 326
Meter Ruler, 326
Meter section, 206
Meter time display, 254
metronome, 99
microphones, sound card inputs, 38
MIDI automation, 289–291
MIDI Clock, 312
MIDI connector button, *114*
MIDI controller events, 118–119
MIDI drivers, 23–26
MIDI editing, 103–135. *See also* editors
MIDI Effect Processor module, 378
MIDI events
    adding
        with Paint tool, 108–109
        with Pencil tool, 105
    assigning colors to, 114
    determining start position or velocity value, 115
    editing
        with Line tool, 107–108
        more than one at a time, 134
        non-note, 126–130
    erasing, 109
    muting/unmuting, 109
    resizing, 106
    reversing order of, 113
    unmuting, 109, 113
MIDI filtering, 100
MIDI In button, 328
MIDI Machine Control (MMC), 322–325
MIDI mapping, 100
MIDI (Musical Instrument Digital Interface)
    See also score editing
    activity display, 63
    channels, 16
    converting to audio, 341–342
    Cubase recording of MIDI information, 14–16
    history of, 5

    overview, 6–9
    ports, 8–9
        changing sort order, 25
        configuring, 24–26
        data flow, 14–15
        renaming, 24
        verifying appearance in system configuration, 23
        virtual, 15
    quantizing events, 46
MIDI part, 388
MIDI patch bays, connecting, 40–41
MIDI Processor, 379–381
MIDI recording, setting up
    See also Track Info; Track List; Track View
    exercises, 101
    MIDI filtering, 100
    realtime recording, 99
    step recording, 97–98
    VST Instruments (VSTi), 94–97
MIDI System Setup dialog box, 24, 25
MIDI Thru option, 25–26
MIDI track class, 79
MIDI Track Mixer, 92–93, 287–291
MIDI tracks, *16*, 17, 90, *104*
MIDI volumes and panning, 92–93
Mid parameter, 299
Mirror Active option, 134
Mirror and Link Hitpoints option, 331
Mixed Mode CDs, 353–354
mixers, desktop, 39–40
mixing, 281–308
    See also effects
    editing mixes, 285–286
    exercises, 308
    MIDI Track Mixer, 287–291
    overview, 281–282
    VST Channel Mixer automation, 282–286
Mixman files, 246–247
Mix mode cycle recording, 54
Mix parameter, 301
mix track class, 81
mix tracks, *104*
MMC (MIDI Machine Control), 322–325
MME audio drivers, 278
Mobile Play options, 350
ModDelay effect, 298
Mode parameter, 383, 385
Modern Style page, 175
Modulation Wheel controller messages, 100
Modulator modules, 371
modules, 377–389
    activating, 379
    arpeggios, 382–385
    MIDI Processor, 379–381
    studio, 389

style tracks, 385–389
types of, 377–388
Modules Setup dialog box, 337
Monitor button, *114*
Monitor function, 256
mono segments, inserting or recording, 18
mono tracks, importing, 255
moving
    events, *66*, 258
    hitpoints, 329
    lyrics, 189
    parts, 161
MP3 files, 350–351, 359
M-points, 265–266
M.ROS-IN: Tracks function, 373
MROS/System Resolution, 318
MTC (MIDI Time Code), 310
multichannel recording, 18–19
multi-client drivers, 32
Multi Insert option, 180–181
Multimedia Drivers, ASIO, 30–32
Multimedia Properties window, *24*
Multi Out feature, 90
multiple channels, 206
multiple tracks, editing, 117
Multi Rests option, 197
multisession CDs, 354
multitrack window, 117
Musical Instrument Digital Interface. *See* MIDI
music sheets. *See* scores
Mute button, 205
Mute Enable column, 75
Mute Play mode, 369
mutes, programming and recording, 83
Mute tool, 109
    in Arrange Window Toolbox, *64*, 164
    in Audio Editor Window Toolbox, *66*
    in Drum Edit Window Toolbox, *68*
Mute/Unmute Selected option, 181
muting
    channels from playback, 205
    events, 109, 259
    instruments, 121
    parts, 164
    tracks, 90, 288

N

Names option, 254
National Television Standards Committee (NTSC)
    video standard, 311
Native Instruments (Web site), 400
Neon (VST Instrument), 96
noise, adding, 297, 343–344
Noise Shape selection, 344
noncontinuous controller events, 118, 119

non-note events, 126–130
No Overlaps option, 194
Normalize option, 273
Normal record mode, 54
Norton Utilities' Speed Disk (software application), 34
Note Dec parameter, 380
Note Off/Velocity button, *114*
Note On Quantize function, 149
Note On/Velocity button, *114*
notes
    See also score editing
    accidental, 174, 183
    adding
        with Paint tool, 108–109
        with Pencil tool, 105
    bass, 187
    beaming together, 180
    copying properties of to other notes, 181
    deleting, 111
    drum
        assigning outputs to, 122
        assigning velocity value to, 122
        and drum mapping, 192–195
    enharmonic, 183
    filling part, cycle, or loop areas with, 113
    flat, settings for, 174
    inserting into score, *70*
    joining, *65*
    lengthening, 194
    modifying
        how tied together, *70*
        length of, 106
        with Line tool, 107–108
    muting/unmuting, 181
    number and name table, *125*
    quantizing, 47–48
    repeating, 111–112
    selecting with controller keyboard, *114*
    sharps, settings for, 174
    spacing of, 197
    specifying voice for, 182
    stems of, flipping, 180
Note tool, *70*
NTSC (National Television Standards Committee)
    video standard, 311
Nudge tool, 109
    in Audio Editor Window Toolbox, *66*
    in Drum Edit Window Toolbox, *68*
    in Graphical Master Track Window Toolbox, *69*
    in Key Edit And List Edit Window Toolbox, *67*
    in Score Edit Window Toolbox, *70*
numbering bars, 175
Number of Channels field, 17
numeric keypad, keyboard shortcuts using, 58–59
Nyquist, Harry, 11–12

O

Octaves parameter, 383
On button parameter, 302
online video files, 337–338
O-Note column, 121
Optimize Arrangement function, 160
Order Segments option, 238
organ instrument group, *85*
Out port, configuring, 24–26
Output column, 76, 122
Output field, 316
Output Note Value, 121
Overdrive effect, *298*
Overdub mode, 56, 57
Over Quantize function, 148

P

PageDown key, *58*
Page mode, 171, 175–176, 184
Page Numbering page, 174
page numbers, for sheet music, 174
page setup, 197
Page text, 189
Paint tool, *67*, *68*, 108–109
PAL (Phase Alternate Line) video standard, 311
panning
    controls, 205, 269
    MIDI, 92–93
Pan parameter, 302
Pan Play Parameter, 88
Pan tool, *65*, 165
Parenthesis button, 183
Part Colors option, 48–49
parts
    copying, 162
    deleting, 162
    drawing, 161
    joining, 163
    listening to contents of, 163
    moving, 161
    muting, 164
    quantizing, 164
    splitting, 162–163
Part View. *See* Track view
Paste Note Attributes option, 181
pasting tracks, 259
patch bays, 9, 40–41
patches, 16, 86
Patchname column, 76
patchnames, 91
patchname scripts, 87
paths to files, finding, 238
PCI video card, reducing graphic acceleration, 37
Pencil tool
    in Arrange Window Toolbox, *64*, 161–162

    in Audio Editor Window Toolbox, *66*
    in Controller Edit Window Toolbox, *71*
    in Graphical Master Track Window Toolbox, *69*
    in Key Edit And List Edit Window Toolbox, *67*
    in Key Edit window, 105–107
    modifying regions with, 51
Perfect Play option, 350
peripherals, hooking up, 33–36
Phase Alternate Line (PAL) video standard, 311
Phaser effect, *298*
phrases, 368, 373
phrases, musical, 177
piano instrument group, *85*
pitch, 183, 274
Pitch Bends, reducing, 100
Pitch button, *114*
Pitch parameter, 302
Pitch Shift option, 274
playback, of mixes, 283–284
Play button, in Built-In Wave editor, 276
Play function, 58
Play Mode popup menu, 368–370
Play Parameter Delay setting, 91
Play Parameters, 88–90
plug-ins, 400–401
plugs, MIDI, 8–9
Pointer tool
    in Arrange Window Toolbox, *64*, 161
    in Audio Editor Window Toolbox, *66*
    in Controller Edit Window Toolbox, *71*
    in Drum Edit Window Toolbox, *68*
    in Graphical Master Track Window Toolbox, *69*
    in Key Edit And List Edit Window Toolbox, *67*
    in Score Edit Window Toolbox, *70*
Polyphony mode, 182
ports
    MIDI, 8–9
        changing sort order, 25
        configuring, 24–26
        data flow, 14–15
        renaming, 24
        verifying appearance in system configuration, 23
        virtual, 15
    sound card, 31
Post As item, 237
Post-Fader mode, 205
practice. *See* exercises
PreDelay parameter, 302
Predict mode, 213
Pre-Fader mode, 205
preloading modules, 379
Prepare Archive function, 244, 357
Prepare Master function, 244, 357
preset, and MIDI channels, 16
printing scores, 197
program changes, 91

Program column, 76
Prosoniq (Web site), 400
Punch record mode, 54–55
Purge Segments option, 241

Q

Q column, 121
Q control, 207
Quality item, 237
Quantize Last Version option, 56
Quantize parameter, 380, 383
quantize values, adding/displaying, *70*
quantizing, 148–154
    audio events, 265–268
    editor window options, 113
    and Groove Control, 151–154
    match, 267
    Meter hitpoints, 329
    overview, 47–48
    parts, 164
    and Q points, 260
    Quantize values, 178, 188
    and realtime recording, 99
    before scoring, 170
    and step recording, 97–98
Question Mark button, 183
Quieten option, 273
quintuplets, 178

R

RAM file extension, 359
ramps, 93
Range item, 237
Ratio parameter, 210
Read button, 92, 206
RealAudio, metafiles for, 359
Really Fast Forward function, *58*
Real Networks, 348–350
realtime effects, 293
realtime recording, 97–98, 99
Recall Locator Points function, *59*
re-channelizing, 17
Record Enable Type setting, 29
Record Info button, 19
recording
    See also audio recording
    32-bit, 20–22
    audio. *See* VST Channel Mixer; VST Master Mixer
    MIDI automation, 289
    mixes, 283–284
    mono segments, 18
    multichannel, 18–19
    output of IPS, 374–375
    realtime, 99

    step, 97–98, 117
    stereo instruments, 18
Recording mode, 56–57
Record Mode, 52
Record On/Off mode, 388
recycling files, 245–246
Red channels, 200
reducing
    Aftertouch, 100
    color display, 37
    graphic acceleration, 37
    Pitch Bends, 100
    volume, 273
Referencing setting, 314
Refind option, 279
refreshing layout, 184
regions, creating, 50
Release parameter, 210
remapping port information, 26
Remove Unused option, 124
removing
    segments, 238, 242
    ties, 194
    wallpaper images, 38
renaming
    files, 239
    hitpoints, 329
    layouts, 196
    phrases, 368
    ports, 24
    segments, 241
repeating notes, 111–112
Repeat mode, 370
Repeat parameter, 379
Replace mode, 56, 57
replacing files, 239
Reset button, 206
resetting VST Channel Mixer's parameters, 206
resizing
    events, 106
    notes, 106
    parts, *65*
    segments, 241
resolution
    bit, 20–21
    recording, 233
Resolving setting, 314
resources, Cubase, 399–401
rests, inserting into scores, 197
Rest tool, *70*
Retrigger button, 370
Reverb effect, *298*
Reverb Length parameter, 303
Reverse option, 273
reversing order of events, 113
Rewind function, *58*
Rewire channels, 200, 342

Rewire technology, 224–225
Right locator, 57–58
Rocket Local column, 78
Rocket Network, 391–397
    connecting with Rocket Control, 395–397
    integrating into Cubase, 394–395
    using, 391–393
    Web site, 400
Roland mode, 387
Roomsize parameter, 303
room tone, 295
Routing parameter, 303
Roxio's Easy CD Creator (software application), 356
Ruler bar, 173
Ruler bar, in Built-In Wave editor, 276
Ruler Display button, *328*
Run Simulation button, 31
Rythme preset, 194

S

Sample and Hold process, 14
sampling, 13–14
sampling frequency, 11, 12
saving
    Audio Pool, 245
    default file, 362
    drum maps, 124
    effect programs/banks, 294
    effects, 295
    EQ settings, 209
    files and folders, 42
    segments, 243
    window sets, 365
Scale Info function, 372
Scale pop-up menu, 182
Scandisk (utility), 34–35
Scissors tool
    in Arrange Window Toolbox, *64*
    in Audio Editor Window Toolbox, *66*
    in Graphical Master Track Window Toolbox, *69*
    in Score Edit Window Toolbox, *70*
Score Drum Map option, 194
score editing, 169–198
    See also Score Edit window
    adding text, 188–192
    chords, 185–188
    drum and percussion tracks, 192–195
    exercises, 198
    layouts, 195–197
    overview, 169–171
    page setup, 197
    printing, 197
    Symbol palettes, 184–185
Score Edit window, 171–184
    Edit mode, 175–176
    overview, 171–173

Page mode, 175–176
Score Preferences window, 173–175
Score toolbar, 182–184
Status bar, 177–182
Score Edit Window Toolbox, 70
Score Palettes option, 184
Score Preferences window, 173–175, 177
Score toolbar, 172, 182–184
Score window, 104
Scorpion effect, 295
scratches, adding, 297
screen savers, 36
Scriptmaker (patchname scripts), *87*
Scrub function, 256
SCSI drives, 36
SECAM/EBU (Sequential Color And Memory/European Broadcast Union) video standard, 311
seek time, 35
Segment item, 237
Segment Range Selection box, 275
segments
    in Audio editor, 251–252
    defined, 235
    deleting, 242
    dragging into other windows, 243
    duplicating, 241
    listening to, 241
    modifying, 241
    removing, 238, 242
    renaming, 241
    resizing, 241
    saving, 243
    sorting, 238
    using, 238
Selection Range tool, 164–165
Selective Record option, 350
send effects, 217–218
    assigning and setting up, 218–219
    sending signal to headphone amplifiers with, 232
Send Effects signal path, *217*
Send Prg. Change function, 372
sessions, 354
Sessions function, 395
Set Position To Left Locator function, *59*
Set Position To Right Locator function, *59*
setting up
    See also backing up; folder management
    audio recording, 199–226
        See also VST Channel Mixer; VST Master Mixer
        selecting a recording resolution, 233
        using more than two inputs, 231–232
        using only two inputs/outputs, 228–231
    hardware
        hard drive configuration, 33–36
        hooking up equipment, 38–41
        video display adapters, 37–38

instruments, 85–88
MIDI recording, 73–101
    See also Track Info; Track List;
        Track View exercises, 101
    MIDI filtering, 100
    MIDI mapping, 100
    realtime recording, 99
    step recording, 97–98
    VST Instruments (VSTi), 94–97
send effects, 218–219
software
    ASIO drivers, 28–32
    audio system settings, 26–27
    MIDI drivers, 23–26
Setup MME application, 24–25
shadow MIDI tracks, 90
Shapes parameter, 304
Shape Sync knob parameter, 304
Sharpness parameter, 304
sharp setting, 174
sheets, music. *See* scores
shortening notes, 106
Show Controllers button, 118
Show Headings option, 236
Show/Hide Movie option, 338
Show/Hide Title Bar option, 338
Show Hitpoint Matches option, 263
Show Invisible Filter bar, 172
Show option, 180
Show Part Colors option, 238
Shuffle option, 194
signature settings, 61–63
Silence option, 273
Single Line Drum Staff option, 194–195
Skip mode, 370
Slave mode, 387
slurs, inserting into scores, 177
S/M item, 236
smoothening transition between events, 133
SMPTE Display module, 378
SMPTE (Society of Motion Picture and Television Engineers), 310
SMPTE timecodes, 319–320
SMPTE time format, *46*
Snap field, 388
Snap function, 46
    in editor windows, 113
    and step recording, 97–98
sockets, MIDI, 8–9
SoftClip limiting, 211, 215
software
    running other applications simultaneously with audio programs, 32–33
    setting up
        ASIO drivers, 28–32
        audio system settings, 26–27
        MIDI drivers, 23–26

Solo button, 205, 288
solos, programming and recording, 83
Song Position Pointer message, 311
Sony/Phillips Digital InterFace (S/PDIF), 313
Sort Box, 384
sorting segments, 238
Sort Normal mode, 368
Sort Replace mode, 369
sound cards
    for 24 or 32-bit recording, 21
    ASIO (Audio Stream Input/Output) drivers, 28–32
    checking installation and operation, 26–27
    connecting outputs of MIDI devices to, 342
    inputs, 221–222
    microphone inputs, 38
    multi-client drivers for, 32
    troubleshooting, 26–27
    using with External Wave editor, 278
Sound column, 121
sound effects. *See* effects
space
    between elements, 175
    between notes, 197
    between staffs, 184
space (as dimension of sound), 11
Spacebar, 58
Spacing page, 175
S/PDIF (Sony/Phillips Digital InterFace), 313
Speaker Simulation parameter, 305
Speaker tool
    in Arrange Window Toolbox, *64*, 163
    in Audio editor, 256
    in Audio Editor Window Toolbox, *66*
    in Drum Edit Window Toolbox, *68*
    in Key Edit And List Edit Window Toolbox, *67*
    in Score Edit Window Toolbox, *70*
Spectral Design (Web site), 400
Speed Disk software application, 34
Speed parameter, 305
Split function, 157
splitting
    events, 259
        at locators, 157
        with M-points, 265–266
    notes and audio segments, *64*
    parts, *64*, 162–163
SRate item, 237
staccato symbols, 180–181
Staff Option dialog box, 194
Staff Setting dialog box, *193*
staffs, space between, 184
Stages parameter, 305
Start item, 237
start position of events, determining, 115
Status bar, 172, 177–182
staves, size of, 197

Steinberg Newsgroups (Web site), 400
Steinberg's Info Center (Web site), 399
stems, note, 180
step recording, 97–98, 117
Step Recording button, *114*
Stereo Basis parameter, 305
Stereoecho effect, 296
stereo files, for streaming media, 349
Stereo in the Track Info section, 18
Stereo/Mono button, 305
stereo tracks, importing, 255
Stereowizard effect, 296
Stick tool, *68*
Stop Follow Song After Scrolling option, *116*
Stop function, *58*
Store button, 31
Store Locator Points function, *59*
streaming technology, 348–351
stretching events, 166–167
Stretch tool, 65, 166–167
strings instrument group, *85*
studio modules, 378, 389
style field, 386
Style parameter, 385
style track class, 83
style tracks, 385–389
Styletrax module, 377
support, for Cubase, 399–400
Support function, 395
Switch parameter, 386
Switch pop-up menu, 388
Symbol palettes, 184–185
symbols, inserting into scores, 180–181
Symphonic effect, *298*
Sync A-B function, 373
Synchronization dialog box, 316–320
synchronizing Cubase, 309–338
    with another MIDI device, 321
    and another MIDI device, 321
    Digital Clock, 312–313
    hitpoints, 325–326, 325–335
        basic operations, 329–330
        linking, 330–332
        Master Track Editor, 326–328
        Straightening Up tempo, 334–335
        tempo matching, 332–334
    internal and external references, 315–316
    MIDI Clock, 312
    online video files, 337–338
    Synchronization dialog box, 316–319
    timecode, 310–311
    time-locked tracks, 335–337
    using MIDI Machine Control, 322–325
    using SMPTE timecodes, 319–320
synchronizing, IPS A and IPS B, 373
Syncopation option, 194
Sync Out option, 317

System Exclusive messages, filtering out, 100
System Preroll, 318
System Properties dialog box, 26–27
System text, 189

T

TAO (Track-At-Once), 354
tape track class, 82
TC Works (Web site), 400
TDIF (Tascam Digital InterFace), 313
templates, 362
tempo, 263–264
Tempo Base, 317
Tempo display, 326
tempo setting, 59–61
Tempo Sync Popup menu, 305
tension, adding to chords, 187
text
    adding, 188–192
    creating templates for styles, 174
Text Attribute Sets page, 174
Threshold parameter, 210
Thru Off Channel option, 26
Thru option, 371
Thru socket, 9, 25–26
ties, removing, 194
timecode, 310–311
Timecode Base field, 316
Time hitpoints, 325, 326
    finding tempo providing match between, 332–334
    hearing MIDI notes when occurring, 330
Time Hitpoint Strip, 327
Time item, 237
Time Lock column, 75
time-locked tracks, 335–337
Time/Meter button, 254
Time parameter, 305
Time Ruler, 46, 327
time signatures, 62–63
Time Signature Strip, 326
Time Stretch option, 274
Timing slider, 152
TIP boxes, 3
title, adding to music sheets, 176
TmpSync parameter, 306
Toggle Cycle mode, *59*
To Looped Selected Ev. option, 110
To menu, 110
Tone parameter, 306
To Next Staff value, 184
toolbar options, MIDI editor, 110–114
toolbars, creating, 364
toolboxes, 64–71
    Arrange Window Toolbox, 64–65
    Audio Editor Window Toolbox, 66
    Controller Edit Window Toolbox, 71

418   Index

Drum Edit Window Toolbox, 68
Graphical Master Track Window Toolbox, 69
Key Edit And List Edit Window Toolbox, 67
Score Edit Window Toolbox, 70
toolbox options, MIDI editor, 105–109
tools, Cubase, 5–6
To Prev Staff value, 184
top three fields display, 386
Track Activity column, 75
Track-At-Once (TAO), 354
Track Class column, 75
track classes, 79–83, 103
Track Info, 19, 84–93
    adding shadow MIDI track, 90
    MIDI volumes and panning, 92–93
    overview, 44–45
    Play Parameters, 88–90
    program changes, 91
    setting up instruments, 85–88
Track Info view, 19
Track List, 45, 75–83
    columns in, 75–83
    creating views, 78
    mutes and solos, programming and recording, 83
    Track Classes, 79–83
Track Name column, 75
tracks
    audio, 18–19
        converting from MIDI to, 341–342
        editing window for, *104*
    chord, 82, *104*
    copying, 259
    cutting, 259
    drawing selections across different, 164
    drum
        editing window for, *104*
        score editing, 192–195
        step recording, 97–98
    editing, 141–148
        See also locator functions; logical editing; quantizing
        exercises, 167
        folder tracks, 138
        group tracks, 139–141
    grouping, 80
    information about, 44–45
    merging, 160
    MIDI, *16*, 17
        converting to audio, 341–342
        editing window for, *104*
        shadow, 90
    mix, *81*
    mix, editing window for, *104*
    mixing, 287–289
    multiple, editing, 117, 259
    muting, 288
    pasting, 259

specifying colors of, 48–49
style, 377
summary list of, 45
switching between, 117
time-locking, 335–337
Track View, 45, 46, 74, 75–78
Tranceformer2 effect, 298
transfer rate, 7, 35
Transport bar, 53–63
    controls, 58–59
    Cycle Recording option, 53–56
    Left and Right locators, 57–58
    MIDI activity display, 63
    Recording mode, 56–57
    signature settings, 61–63
    tempo setting, 59–61
Transpose column, 76
Transpose Play Parameter, *88*
Transpose Retrig mode, 369
Transpose tool, *65*, 165
trills, 181
Trim Events To Part option, *155*
triplets, 178
troubleshooting
    conflicting IRQ settings, 26–27
    drivers, 27
    not seeing MIDI activity when playing back messages, 63
    sound cards, 26–27
TrueTape 32-bit recording technology, 21
TrueTape emulator, 234
truncating, 343
tuplets, 47, 175
    in drum tracks, 193
    inserting into scores, 178

U

Ultra DMA 33 drives, 36
Ultra DMA (UDMA) technology, 36
Ultra Wide 3 drives, 36
Undo Quantize keyboard shortcut, 47
Universal Sound Module (USM) (VST Instrument), 96
unmuting events, 109, 113
UPD button, 184
Upload Quality section (of Rocket Network), 394
Use Drum Map option, 193
Use Record checkbox, 383
Use Waveforms option, 240, 365
using SMPTE timecodes, 319–320
USM (Universal Sound Module) (VST Instrument), 96
UV-22 dithering algorithm, 344

V

valleys, in crossfades, 271
Variation buttons, 386

http://www.muskalipman.com

Variation parameter, 385
VB-1 (VST Instrument), 96
Vel Dec parameter, 380
Velocity column, 77
Velocity Play Parameter, *88*
velocity value, 115, 122
Velocity Value Play Parameter, *88*
Vel slider, 152
video display adapters, 37–38
video files, online, 337–338
View menu, 254
vinyl recordings, simulating, 297
virtual effects, 215
virtual MIDI ports, 15
VITC (Vertical Interval Time Code), 310
Voice Selector Insert button, 182
voice, specifying for notes, 182
voltage values, 12
volume
    adding controls, 269
    increase/decrease in, 178
    MIDI, 92–93
    reducing, 273
Volume and Pan column, 76
Volume parameter, 306
Volume Play Parameter, *88*
Volume tool, 65, 165
VST Audio Bus System, 221–223
VST Channel Mixer, 199–219, 206
    adding effects to signals, 204–205
    audio channel dynamics control, 210–215
    channel effect routing, 215–219
    channel EQ, 207–209
    customizing, 202–203
    fader area, 205
    level meters, 206
    list of channels, 200
    modifying channel input, 202–203
    option menu, 206
    overview, 199
    panning control, 205
    selecting multiple channels, 206
    specifying which channels displayed, 201–202
VST Channel Mixer 1 window, 19
VST Channel Mixer automation, 282–286
VST Channel Mixer window, 95
VSTi channels, 342
VST Input window, 18
VST Instruments (VSTi)
    general information, 94–97
    resources, 400–401
VST Instrument (VSTi) channels, 200
VST Master Mixer, 219–225
    effects, 219–221
    master effect routing, 224–225
    VST Audio Bus System, 221–223

VST plug-in parameter descriptions, 299–306
VST Plug-ins, *298*
VST TrueTape emulator, 234

W

Wait for Play function, 373
wallpaper images, removing, 38
Wave editors, 249, 275–279
waveform
    displaying in Audio Pool, 238
    explanation of, 10
    flipping, 273
    periods of, 11
    refreshing, 240
    reproducing, 11
    of stereo signal, displaying, 295
Waveform buttons, 306
wave image creation, 365
Waves (Web site), 400
WAV file format, 347
Web, interacting with others over. *See* Rocket Network
Web sites, Cubase resources, 399–401
wet/dry signal ratio, 215
window sets, 364–365
Word Clock, 312, 313
Write button, 92, 93, 206
Wunderverb 3 effect, 297

X

X/Y Position button, 184

Y

Yamaha mode, 387

Z

zooming
    in Arrange Window Toolbox, *64*, 164
    in Audio Pool window, 238
    in Built-In Wave editor, 276
    in Score Edit Window Toolbox, *70*
    into scores, 182
    in Track View, 74

MUSKA & LIPMAN Publishing

We want to hear from you.

We are interested in your ideas and comments. When you provide us the feedback, we'll add you to our monthly announcement list if you wish so you can hear about new books. We won't sell or share your personal information with anyone.

Tell us what you think of this book—what you like and what you don't like or what you would like to see changed.

Let us know what other books you would like to see from Muska & Lipman. You are a valuable resource for us.

Visit our Web site to submit your feedback:

http://www.muskalipman.com/feedback.html

Or send us a letter with your feedback at:
Muska & Lipman Publishing
P.O. Box 8225
Cincinnati, Ohio 45208-8225